ENGLISH PALEOGRAPHY AND
MANUSCRIPT CULTURE, 1500–1800

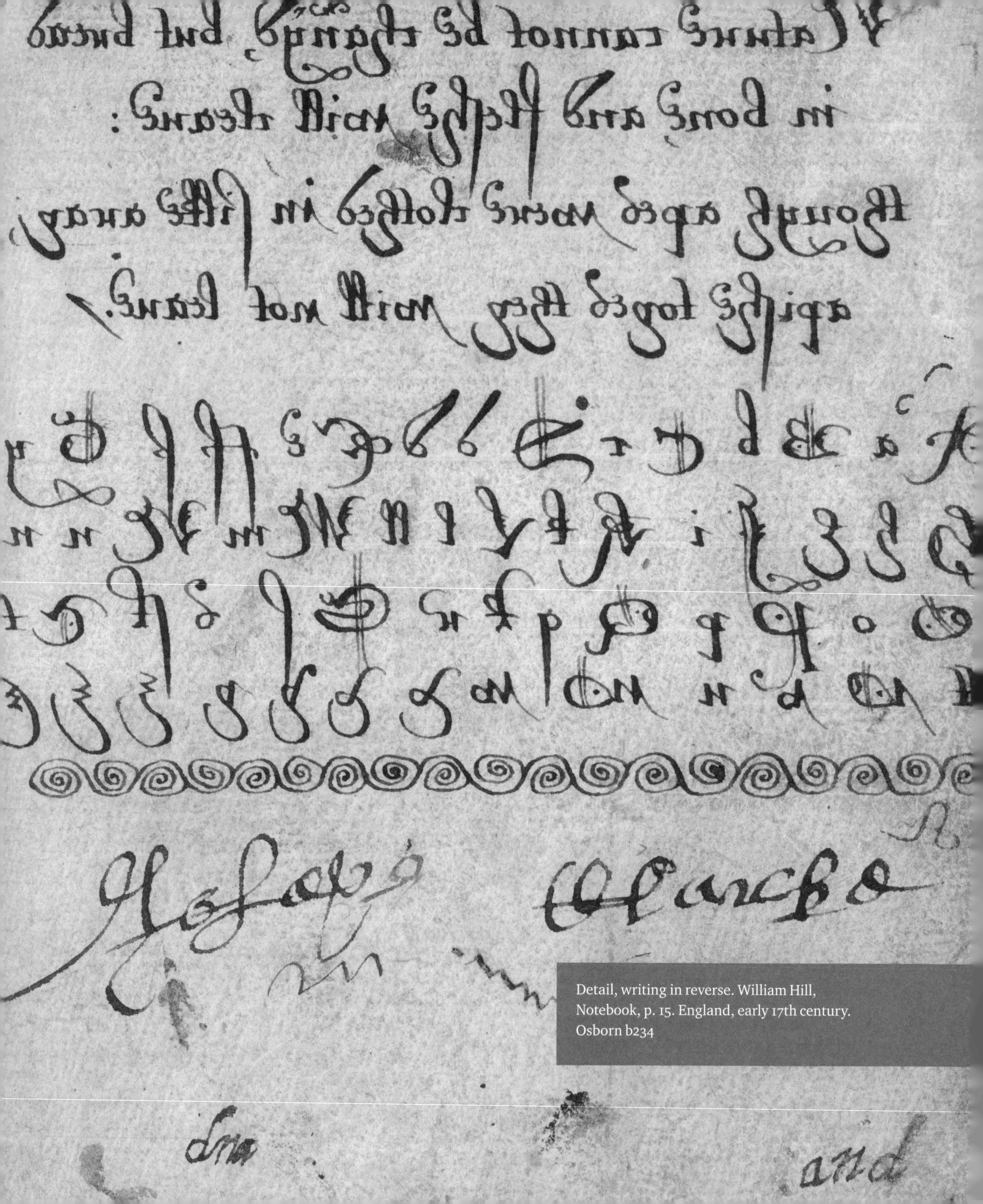

Detail, writing in reverse. William Hill, Notebook, p. 15. England, early 17th century. Osborn b234

ENGLISH PALEOGRAPHY AND MANUSCRIPT CULTURE, 1500–1800

Kathryn James

Beinecke Rare Book & Manuscript Library, Yale University

Distributed by Yale University Press, New Haven and London

Copyedited by Lesley K. Baier
Designed and set in Brandon Grotesque
and Charter ITC typefaces by Rebecca Martz
Office of the Yale University Printer

Photography by the Beinecke Digital Services Unit and Imaging4Art; additional photographs courtesy of the British Museum, Lewis Walpole Library, Yale Center for British Art, and Yale University Art Gallery

Indexed by Brian Hotchkiss, Wordesign Services

Printed by GHP in West Haven, Connecticut

Published by Beinecke Rare Book & Manuscript Library, Yale University

Distributed by Yale University Press, P.O. Box 209040, New Haven, Connecticut 06520-9040
www.yalebooks.com/art

Library of Congress Control Number: 2019956780
ISBN 978-0-300-25435-8

Yale

CONTENTS

Canzonetts.

how J shall stay, though she purloyne me thus
And how posteritie shall know itt too
how thine may out dure
Sibillijs glory e obscure
Her who from Pinder could indure.

Studie thes manuscripts, thos Meriades
of letters wch have past twixt her e me,
then write our Annales e in them will be
To all whom loves sublyming fier inbades
Rule e example found
there ye faith of any ground
No Sphymaticke will dare to wound
That sees how love to vs of this grace affords
To make, to keepe, to vse, to be thes his records.
This

ACKNOWLEDGMENTS

This book is rooted in the Beinecke Rare Book and Manuscript Library and the collections, colleagues, and researchers who together sustain that scholarly institution. The project has from the outset benefited from the generosity of E.C. Schroeder, Director, and I wish particularly to thank E.C. and my new colleague, Lucy Mulroney, for their encouragement and support.

This book reflects the learning of many friends and colleagues, and our often whispered conversations in the reading rooms, staff lounges, classrooms, conservation labs, and hallways of rare book and manuscript libraries. For their generosity and insight, I must thank Rebekah Ahrendt, Cathy Baker, Nicolas Bell, Ann Blair, Ray Clemens, Dean Cooke, Jana Dambrogio, Margreta de Grazia, Diane Ducharme, Juliet Fleming, Alex Franklin, Elizabeth Frengel, John Gambell, Karen Jutzi, Elisabeth Leedham-Green, Marie-France Lemay, Richard Linenthal, Ivan Lupić, Jesse Meyer, Melina Moe, Mike Morand, Cathy Nicholson, Susanne Paul, Cathy Shrank, Kathryn Slanski, Adam Smyth, Tiffany Stern, Toshi Takamiya, Katie Trumpener, John Wells, Heather Wolfe, and Paula Zyats. The Yale Program in the History of the Book has been a continual education, and I am particularly grateful to my co-organizers, past and present: Andrew Brown, Eve Houghton, Trina Hyun, David Kastan, and Aaron Pratt. The Elizabethan Club, the Lewis Walpole Library, the Yale Center for British Art, and the Yale University Art Gallery have generously allowed me to include images from their collections, and I must thank Molly Dotson, Elisabeth Fairman, Francis Lapka, Cindy Roman, Sue Walker, and Anders Winroth for their assistance.

Fig. 1. Scribal copy of 33 poems by John Donne, entitled Poems, with a few prose problems, p. 256. England, ca. 1620. Osborn b114

A draft manuscript on English paleography is the test of any relationship, and I am indebted to the many colleagues and friends who so patiently read all or part of this manuscript. My thanks go to Keith Wrightson, whose kindness and generosity informed this project from its first proposal through its final draft. David Kastan helped me, as always, to recognize the questions I was trying to ask, and then read the manuscript through, not once but twice. I am deeply grateful to Maria Del Mar Galindo, Eve Houghton, Dana Key, Lucy Mulroney, Gill Partington, Aaron Pratt, Peter Stallybrass, and Phil Withington, whose help and comments have been invaluable.

The formidable expertise and grace of my colleagues in the Office of the Yale University Printer are everywhere visible in this book. I am very grateful for the opportunity to work with such talented colleagues, and particularly with Lesley Baier and Rebecca Martz.

To Arthur and Rosie, who have lived with this project so patiently, I give my profound thanks and love (and sympathy). To my mother and father, and Matthew and Ali, I offer my thanks for the sustaining gift of their love and friendship. And to Julian, whose love made this book possible, I say:

> Studie thos manuscripts, thos Meriades
> of letters wch have past twixt thee & me
> then writte our Annales & in them will be
> To all whom loues sublyming fier invades
> Rule & example found

Fig. 2. John Nixon, "The Oaken Chest or the Gold
Mines of Ireland a Farce," 1796. BM Satires 8884.
British Museum K,64.72. Reproduced with permission
from the collections of the British Museum

INTRODUCTION:
THINKING ABOUT HANDS
IN EARLY MODERN ENGLAND

In December 1794 a remarkable literary event occurred. Manuscripts written by William Shakespeare were revealed by the nineteen-year-old son of a London publisher. Before this, little had been known to survive in Shakespeare's hand: a few signatures on a few legal documents, but nothing to show England's national poet at work as writer or reader. The discovery unearthed a trove of Shakespearean relics: love letters, unknown play texts, financial papers, a profession of faith, a lock of his hair, and books owned by the Bard, with his thoughts penned in the margin, where over and over again he signed his name (figs. 2–4).

The boy, William Henry Ireland, claimed he had found them. The papers were said to have been kept, unknown and undiscovered, in an oak chest in the house of a country gentleman: one "Mr. H.," who wished to remain anonymous. In February 1795 Ireland's father opened their London house to visitors wishing to see the manuscripts. Week by week, Ireland presented these riches to an electrified audience of the London literati. Many believed—or wished to believe. Some were also skeptical.

Fig. 3. Detail of fig. 2. John Nixon's satirical portrayal of documents in the "oaken chest," including the "Deed of gift to Ireland Will Shakespeare," "Verses to Anna Hatherrewaye," and, beside the chest, "Ould Deeds ready Drawn to Fill up as Occasion may require," among other papers

Fig. 4. Detail of fig. 2. William Henry with forged volumes, including "Fifteen Plays by Shakespeare which will be brought forward" and "Leaves from old Books to Write Plays upon with Various Water Marks"

The Spirit of Shakspere appearing to his Detracters

Tremble, thou wretch.
That hast within thee Undivulged crimes.
Unwhipp'd of justice.

Shakspere.

Ah me. Ah me. O dear, O dear,
What Spectre's this, approaching here.

Surely tis Shakspeare's injured shade.
It fills my soul with so much dread
It is, it is thus on our knees.
Let's strive his anger to appease.
O Father of the British Stage.
Whose wit has charm'd from age to age.

Pardon the base unworthy flame.
That Burnt to rob thee of thy fame.
But now this Solemn mockry's o'er
Thy gracious mercy wee implore
Weil never more disgrace thy page.
Our Brains were gone a pilgrimage.

1796

For the skeptics, the abundance, the absurd materiality of Shakespeare's writings, became the object of satire (fig. 5). There was also the problem of their mediocrity. After so much reverence and longing, Shakespeare was raised from the dead with terrible penmanship, writing a series of often drearily mundane documents, with at best unorthodox spelling. Detractors mocked the archival mustiness of the find. "Ah Sammy! Sammy! Why call forth a ghost?" asked the *Familiar Verses, from the Ghost of Willy Shakspeare to Sammy Ireland* (1796). Shakespeare's "genius unconfin'd with fancy plays," the satirist wrote,

Fig. 5. Sylvester Harding, "The Spirit of Shakspere appearing to his Detracters," 1796. BM Satires 8883. British Museum J,4.100. Reproduced with permission from the collections of the British Museum. Shakespeare's ghost appearing to William Henry Ireland and his family, with some of the Shakespeare manuscripts below

Not lock'd in trunks,—in *auncient dirtie* scrolls,
Long shreds of parchment, deeds, and *mustie* rolls;
Receipts for candles, bills, and notes of hand,
Some that you may—but more not understand.
Samples of hair, love songs, and sonnets *meete,*
Together met by *chaunce* in *Norfolk-street;*
Where, fruitful as the vine, the tiny elves
Produce *young manuscripts* for Sammy's shelves.[1]

"The Oaken Chest" (1796; see figs. 2–4) adeptly satirizes Shakespeare's over-presence in the Ireland documents. The print critiques the excesses of the Shakespeare manuscripts: the "Leaves from old Books to Write Plays upon with Various Water Marks"; the books, published after Shakespeare's death in 1616, yet conspicuously annotated in Shakespeare's hand: "Bacons History of Henry VII. 1622 notes by Shakspeare," "Haywards life of Edw[d]. 6 1630. With notes by Shakespeare."

The Ireland forgeries reveal the essential strangeness of earlier manuscript culture to an eighteenth-century audience. For many readers in the 1790s, William Henry Ireland's illegible inventions seemed plausible—that is, as indecipherable as other early manuscripts (fig. 6). Many of the readers who visited the Irelands' house to view the manuscripts would have struggled to read Elizabethan or Jacobean handwriting, nor would they necessarily have known how to identify the characteristics of an authentic sixteenth-century document or hand. Others, like the

Fig. 6. William Henry Ireland's forgery of Shakespeare's annotations in a copy of Edmund Spenser's *The faerie qveene* (1590). 2014 160. Ireland's pseudo-Shakespearean hand was so difficult to read that transcriptions were later bound into this and the other forged volumes.

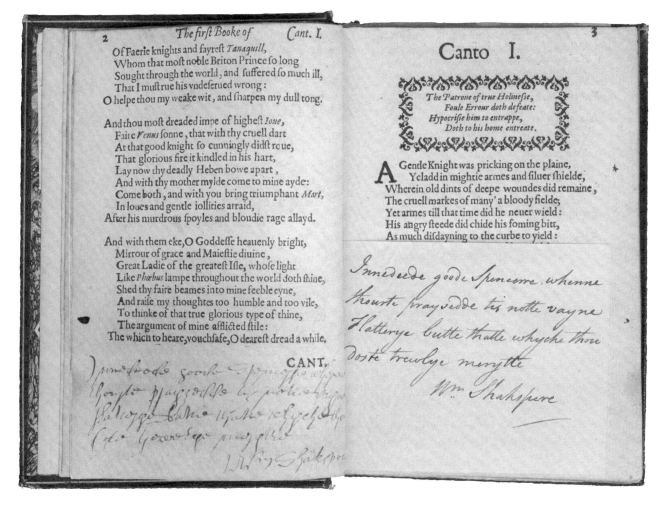

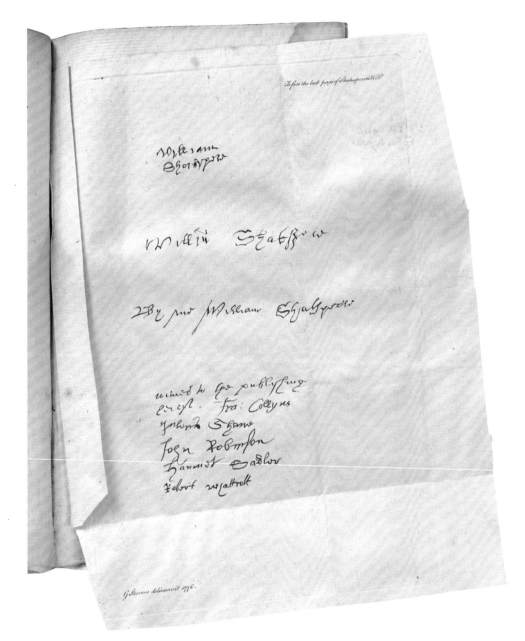

Fig. 7. Engravings of Shakespeare's signatures. From George Steevens, ed., *The plays of William Shakspeare* (London, 1778). 2000 3141

journeyman bookbinder who made the ink Ireland used in his forgeries, would have been all too familiar with earlier hands and documentary forms—familiar to the point that forgery and amendment might be practicable possibilities.[2]

The forgeries also highlight the intersections of manuscript culture with that of printed and visual materials. Ireland's forgeries had been made possible by the publication of George Steevens's 1778 edition of Shakespeare's plays, with its engraved facsimile representations of Shakespeare's signature (cf. figs. 7–8).[3] These were the first images to be published of

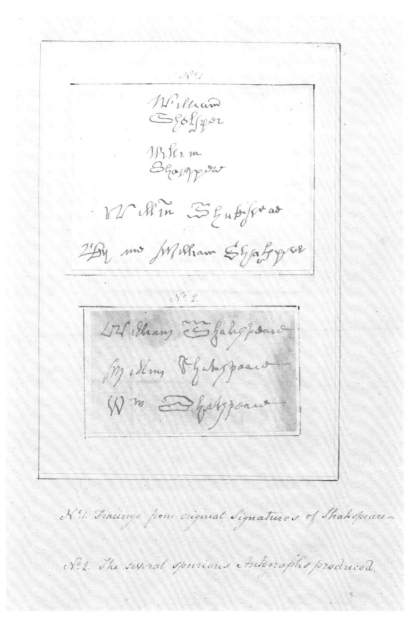

Fig. 8. Tracings and forgeries of Shakespeare's signature. From William Henry Ireland, An album of "The Shakespearian productions," 1805. Osborn fd83

Shakespeare's handwriting, and they had a transformative influence on their audience. Edmond Malone, Steevens's colleague and fellow Shakespeare obsessive, recounted that, "in the year 1776 Mr. Steevens, in my presence, traced with the utmost accuracy the three signatures affixed by the poet to his Will."[4] Steevens and Malone presented the signatures as a form of empirical evidence of Shakespeare's spelling of his name, eyewitness testimony to Shakespeare's writing of himself. The facsimile engraving, seemingly so immediate a rendering of an original document, also borrowed some of the original's evidentiary authority.

Then, as now, manuscript seemed to offer the promise of a more potent, a more direct connection with the past. To touch Shakespeare's signature—or to see it in a facsimile engraving—was to come as close as possible to Shakespeare's hand itself. There was an affective significance to manuscript; it seemed to bear witness to the presence of its author. Malone had himself searched ceaselessly for Shakespeare's manuscript remains; his exasperation with the forgeries was both scholarly and personal. He savagely debunked Ireland's manuscripts—which included not just renderings of the signature of Shakespeare, but also those of other canonical Elizabethan figures, including Elizabeth I herself (cf. figs. 9–10)—in a rebuttal of some four hundred pages that he began on January 10, 1796, and finished at the press some twelve weeks later, on March 28.[5] In the process, he articulated one of the first descriptions of the history of English handwriting and the characteristics of early modern English manuscript culture.

Malone's intervention in the controversy surrounding the Ireland Shakespeare manuscripts presents us with several of the overarching themes traced by this book. First, Malone could not call on an existing tradition of English paleography: he had to invent a method of analysis, drawing on the tradition of documentary analysis known as diplomatics. His understanding of English manuscript culture was, like ours, a recent invention, superimposed on the textual survivals from the past. Second, Malone (like Ireland) looked to manuscript culture for the figure of the author, Shakespeare. As Malone had

Fig. 9. Document signed by Elizabeth I, on April 7, 1593, directing Sir Thomas Heneage to pay 133 6 s 8d to Richard Fletcher, Bishop of Worcester. Osborn fa64

already discovered, few manuscript traces survived of Shakespeare's life—or, for that matter, of any early modern English author. As Roger Chartier has observed, the "author's hand" was the concern of a later age, one in which the manuscript might be taken as distilling some aspect of an author's essence, the individual manuscript as trace of the individual's soul. Third, when he sought to annihilate his opponent, Malone turned to print: it was his printed rendition of documentary evidence, alongside the social weight of his scholarly polemic, that turned public and learned opinion against the Irelands. In Malone's response, as we will see throughout this book, early modern manuscript culture was not only inseparable from that of print, but also a vital energy circulating in an overall economy of textual production and reception.[6]

When forging Shakespeare in the late eighteenth century, William Henry Ireland could still persuade many readers simply by writing something illegible.

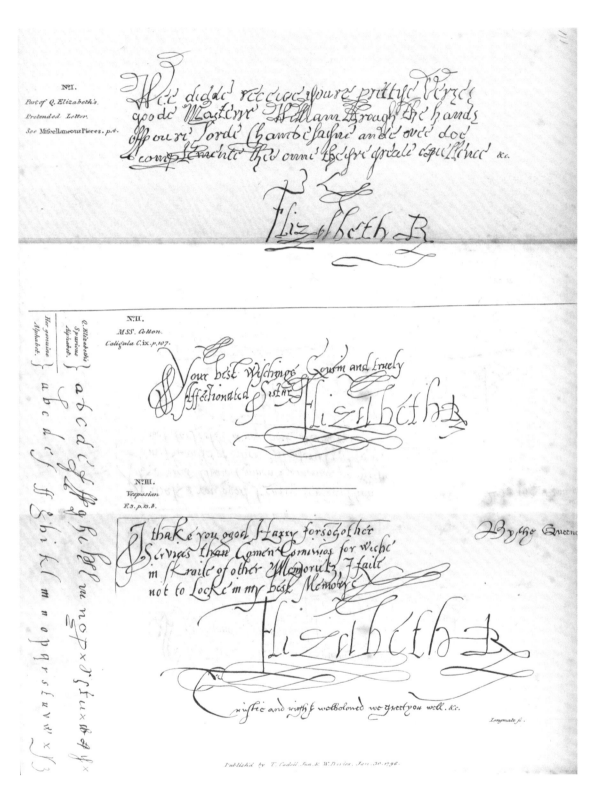

Fig. 10. Engraving of Elizabeth's signatures and a
comparison of her "spurious" and "genuine" Alphabet.
From Edmond Malone, *An inquiry into the authenticity
of certain miscellaneous papers and legal instruments*
(London, 1796), facing p. 111. Tinker 1520

English Paleography and Manuscript Culture, 1500–1800 asks how the manuscript text was understood by English readers and writers in the early modern period, examining the ways in which writing and the written text were learned, created, described, preserved, and encountered. The book looks particularly at the relationship of manuscript culture to that of print, drawing on the discussion of manuscript found in early modern printed texts and the representations of writing in engraved plates-books, illustrations, or broadsides. English handwriting was shaped by printed and visual media, just as manuscript culture continued to inform the ways in which text was categorized and understood. In print, authors took pen to hand, just as they did in manuscript.

The book asks the extent to which English manuscript culture should be understood as European in the early modern period. England's hands and documentary formats were closely connected to those in use on the Continent. English penmanship followed the fashions of Italian and French humanist and court cultures. When the French Huguenot émigré Thomas Vautrollier published the first English penmanship manual in 1570, he did so because works in the French style were guaranteed to sell, helping to fund his mission of publishing Protestant works for an English audience.[7] Until the middle of the seventeenth century, England imported penmanship. One shift traced by this book is the emergence of British round hand as a cultural export from the mid-seventeenth century.

There was also a particularly English history to early modern English manuscript culture. The creation of the Church of England by Henry VIII

Fig. 11. "The mape off Ynglonnd." Astronomical and astrological treatises, f. 47v–48r. England, mid-16th century. Beinecke MS 558

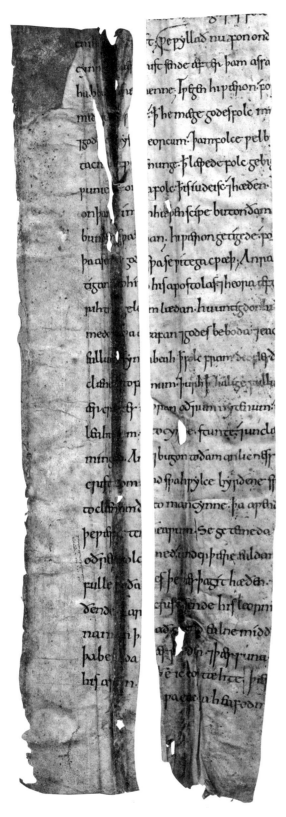

Fig. 12. Two binding fragments of Aelfric, Catholic homilies. England, 11th century. Osborn fa26

Fig. 13. Detail, annotations in red crayon, probably by Matthew Parker (1504–1575). Chronicles of England, f. 13r. England, ca. 1420–50. Takamiya MS 29

and the dissolution of the monastic libraries set the course for manuscript studies over the early modern period. Scholars like Matthew Parker, Archbishop of Canterbury under Elizabeth I, consciously collected and studied earlier English manuscripts in order to establish the political precedents of an English Church. To read or understand early English texts was, then as now, to assemble them from surviving fragments, to compare examples, and to acknowledge that much had not survived. Loss, incompleteness, unfamiliarity: these features of English manuscript culture informed the engagement of scholars in the seventeenth and eighteenth centuries, and their efforts to create a linear and satisfying explanation of the history of an English Church, an English language, or an English literature (figs. 11–13).

Between 1500 and 1800, Britain was politically and economically transformed. In 1500 Britain could quite reasonably have been described as an island nation

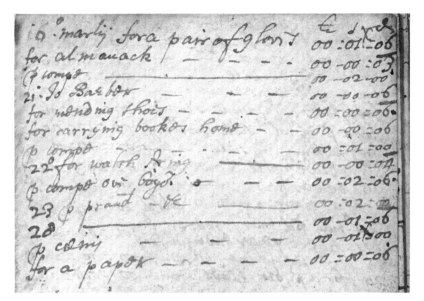

Fig. 14. Detail, a reader's account of expenses. Annotations in a copy of *Riders (1699.) British Merlin* (London, 1699), front free endpaper. OSB MSS 184, Box 23, Folder 175. Included are prices for a pair of gloves, an almanac, mending shoes, carrying books home, and a paper, among others.

at the western margins of a civilized Europe. By 1800 Britain had become an aggressive imperial power whose economic and cultural interests extended westward across the Atlantic and east into the Indies trade. The three centuries spanned by this book brought periods of shocking upheaval and uncertainty: the break with the Catholic Church, national civil war, continued anxieties over the political succession, vehement and unhappy disagreement over the nation's political and religious state, and the uneasy brokering of political stability. The nation's capital was rebuilt after the fire of 1666; by 1800 London had more than quadrupled in population and urban sprawl, to become the largest city in Europe.[8] In its politics, its religion, its economic and cultural norms, the England of 1500 was in nearly every way remote from the nation it had become by 1800.

Textually, however, English culture remained remarkably consistent. The materials and practices of reading, writing, producing, and consuming text in 1800 were recognizably related to those of 1500. From birth to death, parish record to probate inventory, the arc of an individual's life was still charted by hand. Other aspects of textual culture also remained the same: in the print shop, type was still set in forms; paper was still made from rags; books were still bound in calf and morocco. Writers still wrote with pens made from the flight feathers of geese and other birds.

Professional writers still worked as clerks, scriveners, and secretaries. Wealthy children were still taught their letters and penmanship by poor scholars, working for a living.

By 1850 this familiarity had been effaced entirely—and forever—as had the pre-industrial, largely pre-imperial nation to which it belonged. A study of early modern English handwriting and documentary culture offers a glimpse into a moment by which England's identity was and is still defined, in a world that is otherwise lost to us almost entirely.

English Paleography and Manuscript Culture draws on the Yale University collections—and in particular, those of the Beinecke Rare Book and Manuscript Library—to offer an introduction to early modern English handwriting and manuscript culture. It is indebted to the work of Elisabeth Leedham-Green, Heather Wolfe, and Laetitia Yeandle, whose scholarship has defined the field of English paleography and manuscript studies; it also draws on a history of instruction in early modern English paleography, and particularly on the work in the mid-twentieth century by Leonard Hector, Hilary Jenkinson, and Anthony Petti.[9]

The work of Raymond Clemens, Albert Derolez, Timothy Graham, Malcolm Parkes, and Barbara Shailor in medieval and fifteenth-century paleography has offered many of the organizing categories by which this study has been framed.[10] As with other vernacular paleographies, however, the study of early modern English manuscripts turns in a different direction from that of earlier Latin paleography: the same conditions that led to the rise of the vernacular book, charted by Parkes, and the influence of cursive, followed by both Derolez and Parkes, resulted in a breakdown in the categories by which English hands could be characterized, taught, and understood by sixteenth-century writers. Early modern English hands, like those of other vernaculars, are far less normative than their medieval and Renaissance precursors.

This instability is the focus, even fascination, of this book. Early modern English manuscript culture allows us to think about the implications of textual instantiation: that manuscript text can exist at once in the particular and in the abstract, as a text and the text, and that this relationship is neither exact nor chronologically finite. This book asks its reader to take seriously the question of what text is, and how its relationship to the textual object should be defined. Our manuscript examples give us readers and writers who keep account of their books and papers, alongside the cost of mending shoes and buying gloves (fig. 14), as they do the writer who so exactly renders a charter in a professional hand, and the later writer who, with so much more uncertainty, copies "God saue the kynge" (fig. 15), for reasons that we, as later recipients and readers, might never understand.

This book follows in a tradition that seeks to examine and understand the materials and practices by which manuscript texts were created in early modern England, and the mechanisms by which they were commissioned, circulated, and consumed.[11] It extends this tradition to include the examination of the relational economy of the manuscript: the aspects such as temporality and affect that have shaped understandings of the manuscript object from the early modern period into our own. These aspects, alongside awareness of political and social influences, have characterized scholarship in fields relating to media studies and book history since the 1990s.[12] This approach to an idea of manuscript culture draws on the responses in recent decades to D.F. McKenzie's call for a sociology

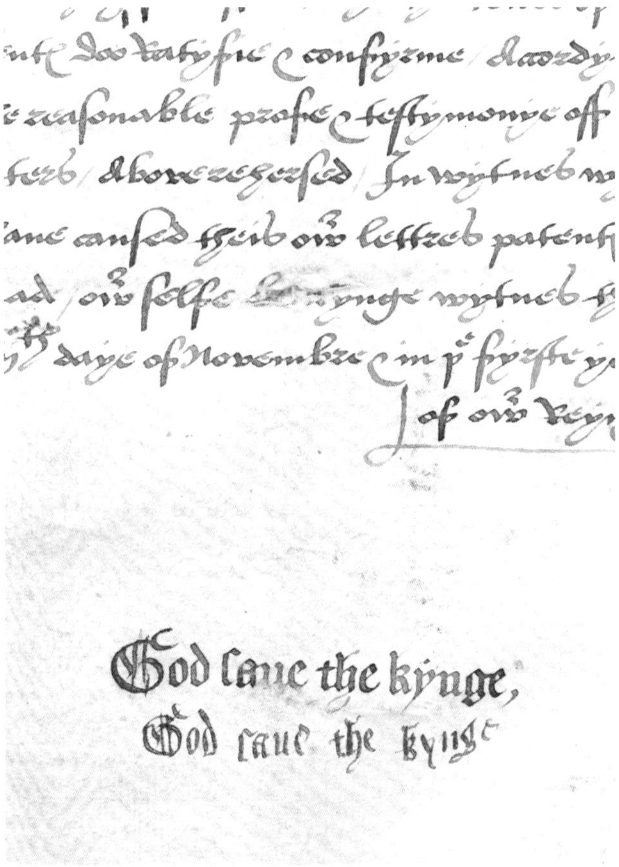

Fig. 15. Detail, "God saue the kynge," by a professional writer, and copied by a student. Contemporary copy of a charter granted by Edward VI to the burgesses of Devizes. England, [Nov. 27, 1547]. Osborn a64

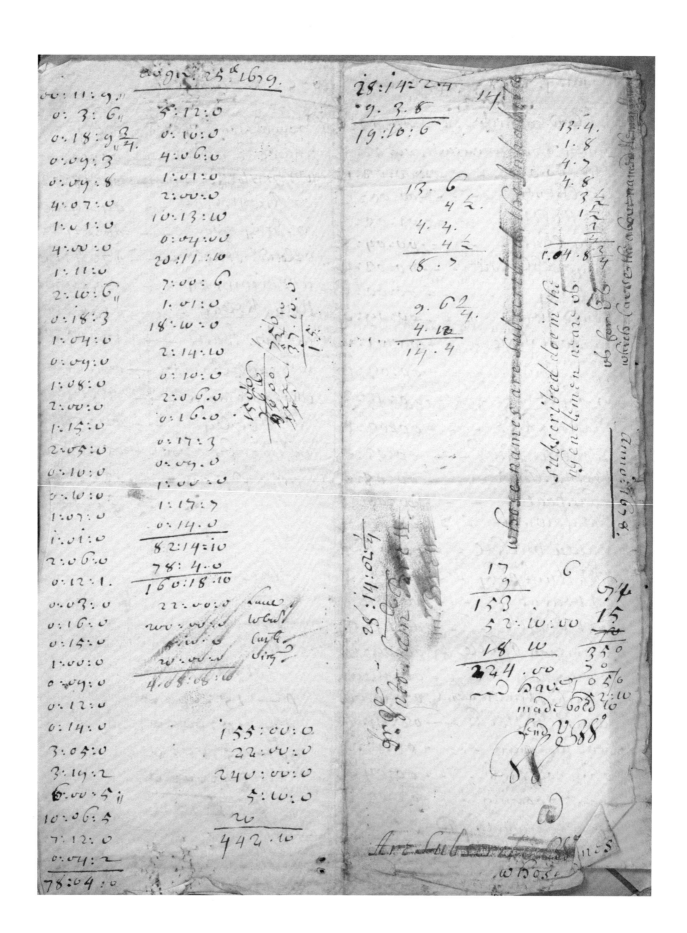

Aug: 25ᵈ 1679.

00:11:9	
0: 3: 6	5:12:0
0:18:9 ¾	0:10:0
0:09:3	4:06:0
0:09:8	1:01:0
4:07:0	2:00:0
1:01:0	10:13:10
4:00:0	0:04:00
1:11:0	20:11:10
2:10:6	7:00:6
0:18:3	1:01:0
1:04:0	18:10:0
0:09:0	2:14:10
1:08:0	0:10:0
2:00:0	2:06:0
1:15:0	0:16:0
2:05:0	0:17:3
0:10:0	0:09:0
0:10:0	1:00:0
1:07:0	1:17:7
1:01:0	0:14:0
2:06:0	82:14:10
0:12:1	78: 4:0
0:03:0	160:18:10
0:16:0	22:00:0
0:15:0	
1:00:0	
0:04:0	4:08:08:10
0:12:0	
0:14:0	155:00:0
3:05:0	22:00:0
3:19:2	240:00:0
6:00:5	5:10:0
10:06:4	
7:12:0	442:10
0:04:2	
78:04:0	

28:14:24
9: 3: 8
19:10: 6

13. 6
4 ½
4. 4.
4 ½
18. 3

9. 6 ¾
4. 12
14. 4

13.4.
1. 8
4. 3
4. 8
3
1

17
9
158
52:10:00
18 10
224. 00

6
64
15
350

78:04:0

of texts, and a study of the textual object that is closer to an epistemology of the text, concerned with the intersecting relationships—technological, emotional, philosophical—of the self and the textual object.[13] In this, the work of Roger Chartier, Margreta de Grazia, and Peter Stallybrass has been incisive; their influence can be seen throughout this book.[14]

English Paleography and Manuscript Culture is an introductory text, with the quite straightforward aim of teaching students to read early modern English manuscripts and to understand some of their characteristics as critical and historical sources. The book is organized in four parts. Part One, Writing Materials and Writers, offers an introduction to the practices of writing by early modern writers. It begins with a detailed examination of the characteristics of the manuscript as material object, before introducing writing as a form of work, undertaken by many types of writers, and situated always in particular spaces and within often highly regulated contexts.

Part Two, Hands, examines the categories by which hands and letterforms are described before introducing the main forms of handwriting encountered by early modern English readers and writers: Anglicana, secretary hand, bastard or mixed hands, italic hand, chancery hand, and round hand. The defining characteristics of these are introduced and situated within a broader historical context and alongside an introduction to the main forms of abbreviation, punctuation, dates, and numbers.

Part Three turns to case studies of particular categories and types of manuscript, drawn from examples in the Yale collections. From student penmanship books to account books to pen trials to manuscript waste or scrap (fig. 16), these case studies examine the intersections of manuscript format—the material structure of a document—and genre, the meaning it might have or purpose it might serve for its readers and creators.

Fig. 16. Accounts, pen trials, and writing practice. Collection of accounts, receipts, memoranda, letters, and other documents, nearly all relating to Devonshire. England, ca. 1679–1716. Osborn b124

Part Four offers a practical introduction to reading and transcribing manuscript documents. It situates transcription within a broader epistemological framework, in which the always imperfect empirical project of transcription is made to serve as the basis for a reader's interpretation. A series of transcription exercises provide examples of the hands and documentary forms discussed in the book. A partial transcription is provided in these exercises as throughout the book to assist the student with an initial reading while leaving the remainder of the document for practice.

The book concludes with a glossary of technical terms that the reader is likely to encounter in the course of research in early modern English manuscript collections.

A note on transcription

Partial transcriptions are offered throughout the book to guide readers as they begin to read. These transcriptions follow the diplomatic format in order to articulate the writing and letterforms as closely as possible for the reader. In the gallery of exercises in Part Four, transcriptions are offered in a combination of standards to allow the reader to compare iterations and become familiar with the strengths and uses of each. Abbreviations are represented throughout by the tilde, e.g., ab̃viations. The virgule, or slash, is used both to demarcate its usage within the text and to mark a line break for long lines. Both these examples highlight the often incomplete or conflicted editorial decisions that must be made when rendering manuscript text in typographical format. The inherent inconclusiveness of any practice of transcription is one of the governing principles outlined in this book. In my approach to transcription, I am guided particularly by the example of Anthony G. Petti and his introduction to English literary manuscripts, *English Literary Hands from Chaucer to Dryden* (1977).

To make inke .

Take foure or fyve ounces of galls, three
ounces of bitriall copprisse two ounces of
gumme arrabeck and a quart of
... beat the galls grosse and put
them altogether into an earthen
pott stirr them altogether ...
... glasse ...

Lett noe man know t
thy friende haue a
whilest friendship la
he once may bee

for fam & a

PART ONE: WRITING MATERIALS AND WRITERS

Fig. 17. "To make inke" and an excerpt of the decorative "Cloven hande." Detail, William Hill, Notebook, pp. 12–13. England, early 17th century. Osborn b234

"These verses she wrot w[t] her diamond in a glas window," records the Protestant historian John Foxe of Elizabeth I, in his *Actes and monuments* (1563; fig. 18):

> Much suspected by mee,
> Nothing proued can be.
> Quod Elisabeth the prisoner.[15]

In 1558, four years after her half-sister, Mary, held her under house arrest in Woodstock Palace, Elisabeth, prisoner, became Elizabeth, queen. The poem she wrote on the window does not survive: Woodstock Palace was destroyed, years later, in the English Civil War. Elizabeth's graffiti is known today because it was published by Foxe in his history of the English Reformation, a work that came overwhelmingly to define the heroes and villains of an English Protestant culture. Written by Elizabeth in her own hand on the window of her prison, the verses were remediated in print by Foxe as an episode in the destiny of England's queen and her Protestant realm.

Manuscript, as a term, derives from Latin: it means "written by hand." Lives and thoughts were, overwhelmingly, recorded by hand in early modern England: all drafts and corrections for publication; all correspondence; all legal and administrative paperwork, such as receipts, contracts, wills, inventories, depositions, or parish records. Part One introduces the material culture of writing: the ink and quills, parchment and paper with which most early modern English writers would expect to write—when not writing on their prison window with a diamond. These materials were so familiar to English writers as to be the vehicle of satire: Ben Jonson, in his *The diuell is an asse* (1616, 1631), has his Mistress Fitz-dottrell, herself a prisoner not unlike Elizabeth, asked why her husband should

> Forbid you paper, pen and inke, like Rats-bane.
> Searche your halfe pint of *muscatel,* lest a letter
> Be suncke i' the pot: and hold your new-laid egge
> Against the fire, lest any charme be writ there?[16]

For Jonson's audience, the paper, pen, and ink were both the accoutrements of the familiar and the instruments by which a writer's agency was expressed. Part One examines the traces left by writers, the materials

Fig. 18. Detail, John Foxe, *Actes and monuments of these latter and perillous dayes, touching matters of the Church* (London, 1563), p. 1714. Mey34 F83 +1563

they used, and the spaces in which manuscript writing was produced and consumed. Writing was a commodity circulating in a broader economic and social context in early modern England. In the types of evidence left us—the glimpses of often quotidian and anonymous writers—we can begin to see the daily work done by writers and writing in the early modern period.

Writing Materials

In June 1657, Oliver Cromwell made his procession through the City of London to Westminster Hall to be installed as Lord Protector. Here he was met with the Chair of Scotland, brought from Westminster Abbey and set on a platform under a "prince-like canopy of state." Before Cromwell was laid a table, "covered with pink-coloured velvet of Genoa, fringed with fringe of gold." On this, alongside the Bible, sword, and scepter of the Commonwealth, were "pens, ink, paper, sand, wax, &c." In the pageantry of this moment, Cromwell was to be seen to write, the accoutrements of writing arrayed alongside the other equipment of the English state.[17]

Pen, ink, paper, pounce, and wax: these would have been immediately recognizable to Cromwell's observers in 1657, as they would have been to those reading about the ceremony in 1800. Writing materials and equipment remained remarkably consistent over the early modern period. A writer in late-fifteenth-century London could expect to buy ink, parchment, and "pennes of swannes, pennes of geese" from George the bookseller (or his equivalent) in Caxton's London of 1480.[18] In 1740 an advertisement for the Southwark premises of Thomas Crosby and John Robinson shows that a reader and writer could buy "all Sorts of Writing-Paper, and Paper Books neatly bound and ruled for Shops or Compting-Houses," along with "Cards, Leather Cases, Pocket-Books, Slates, Quills, Pens, the best Ink and Ink-Powder, Leaden and other Standishes, Blacklead-Pencils, Wax, Wafers, and all other Stationary Wares."[19]

SUBSTRATUM OR SUPPORT

I may call my Text *Nehemiah's* profession; and a profession, by our Saviours warrant, is like to an house, *Matth.* 7. 25. as therefore an house may bee resolved into two parts; *superstructum,* the building that is apparant to the view of the world; and *substratum,* the foundation which lyes hid in the ground;... The wise builder takes care that his house bee right set, and therefore workes by line and levell, but especially hee lookes to the ground-worke, for if this bee not well laid, the frame is weake.

Thomas Wetherel, *Five sermons, preached upon several texts* (London, 1635), 48–49

In 1635 the sermons of the Suffolk parson Thomas Wetherel were published by his successor, to whom he had bequeathed his manuscripts. In his Assizes sermon, Wetherel referred to the text of Matthew 7.25, the house that is built on a foundation of rock. Like a profession of faith, Wetherel preached, the house was built of two parts: the superstructum, "apparant to the view of the world," and the substratum, "the foundation which lyes hid in the ground."[20]

In writing, as in Wetherel's description of faith, the text requires the foundation of the substratum in order to be made visible. It is a curious characteristic of writing that it must always be on something: whether dyed, stained, painted, impressed, or otherwise affixed, text must be carried on a support. This relationship between text and support is hierarchical: following the *Oxford English Dictionary* definition, the textual substratum also acts as the underlying principle on which something is based.[21] Writing or printing is always a relationship of subordination, in which one

> S. Difpatch, what dooft thou? come hether quickly, out of hand.
> L. Here I am, what would you? what lack you? what feeke you for?
> S. Giue me my defke, and fom pen and ynke, and paper.
> L. I haue no paper: neither is there any in the houfe.
> S. Goe buie fome, here is monie.
> L. How much fhall I buye?
> S. A quire: but let it be good, and that it doo not finke.
> L. It is verie deare of late.
> S. Let it coft what it will, I muft needes haue fome.
> L. Who fhall deliuer your letters?
> S. The pofte, the corrier, the cariour.
> N. Take heede you fend them not by Tom long the cariour.
> S. Giue me my penknife, to make a pen.
> D. It is in your penner. you doe nothing but write.
> S. Yet I am as loath to goe to it, as a beare is to goe to the ftake.
> M. Haue you done alreadie? that you beginn to fould?
> S. When I once goe to it, I haue done in leffe than a trice.
> D. You would make a good fecretarie.
> S. Giue me fome wax, fome fealing thrid, my duft box, & my feale,

Fig. 19. John Florio, *Florios second frutes* (London, 1591), p. 89. Hb50 3. "Yet I am as loath to goe to it, as a beare is to goe to the stake," is the writer's verdict on writing, having called for a desk, pen, ink, and a quire of good paper.

meaning is foregrounded over another: for a reader, text is by definition more legible than its support. Text is also always situated in circumstance: a manuscript or printed work is always a specific instance; it is written or printed at a particular moment, on a particular piece of parchment or paper, by a writer who might be more—or less—engaged with the act of writing (fig. 19). In the life of the textual object, text and substratum are always bound together, vulnerable to damp, decay, or accidents of circumstance, interacting chemically and materially, aging together, inseparable from each other as aspects of a unified whole.

Paper and parchment were the two main forms of textual support in early modern England. In the *Glossographia* (fig. 20), Thomas Blount could define "Chart (*charta*)" as "paper, parchment or any thing to write on."[22] Other writing surfaces included wax

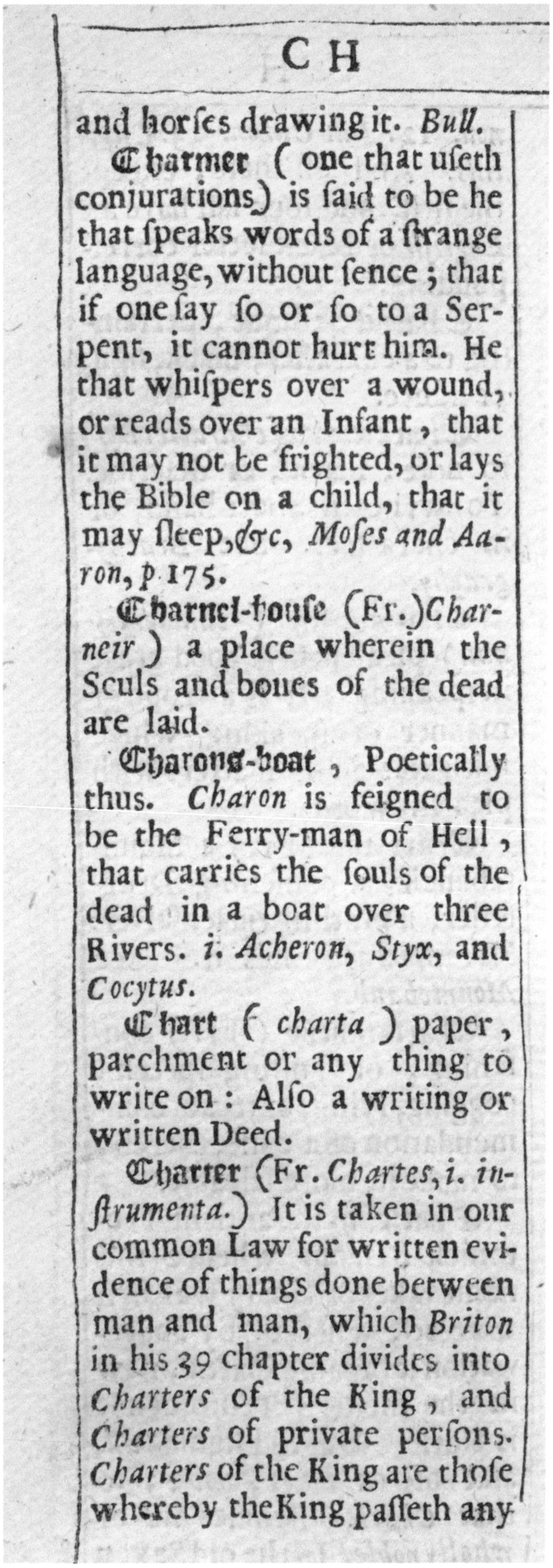

C H

and horſes drawing it. *Bull.*

Charmer (one that uſeth conjurations) is ſaid to be he that ſpeaks words of a ſtrange language, without ſence; that if one ſay ſo or ſo to a Serpent, it cannot hurt him. He that whiſpers over a wound, or reads over an Infant, that it may not be frighted, or lays the Bible on a child, that it may ſleep, *&c*, *Moſes and Aaron*, p. 175.

Charnel-houſe (Fr.) *Charneir*) a place wherein the Sculs and bones of the dead are laid.

Charons-boat, Poetically thus. *Charon* is feigned to be the Ferry-man of Hell, that carries the ſouls of the dead in a boat over three Rivers. *i. Acheron*, *Styx*, and *Cocytus.*

Chart (*charta*) paper, parchment or any thing to write on: Alſo a writing or written Deed.

Charter (Fr. *Chartes*, *i. inſtrumenta.*) It is taken in our common Law for written evidence of things done between man and man, which *Briton* in his 39 chapter divides into *Charters* of the King, and *Charters* of private perſons. *Charters* of the King are thoſe whereby the King paſſeth any

Fig. 20. Detail, Thomas Blount, *Glossographia: or, A dictionary, interpreting all such hard words of whatsoever language, now used in our refined English tongue,* 2nd ed. (London, 1661), f. 12v. Ia742 656B

writing tablets, slates, boards, and surfaces such as walls or beams. Just as John Locke compared human consciousness to the blank paper book, a seventeenth-century almanac publisher compared the soul to the wax writing table:

> Borne voide of knowledge, rude and ignorant,
> The meanest character of good we want,
> Like to a smooth and waxed writing table,
> Its voide, but write you, to receive its able.[23]

Parchment

"Is not parchment made of sheepskin," Hamlet asks, watching as a grave was dug, and wondering for whom it was intended. "Ay, my Lord," answers Horatio, "and of calfskin too."[24] This same question was still asked and answered in the eighteenth century, when Ephraim Chambers introduced parchment in the *Cyclopædia: or, an universal dictionary of arts and sciences* (London, 1728) as "Sheep's or Goat's Skin prepared after a peculiar Manner, which renders it proper for several Uses; particularly for writing on and covering of Books, &c." As Chambers explained, the term parchment derived from the Latin *pergamena* and the Greek city of Pergamon.[25]

Parchment (figs. 21–23) is made from animal hide, typically from the skins of calf, goat, or sheep. Just as leather is made by tanning, parchment results from a particular method of treating the hide. As Chambers described, "Parchment is begun by the Skinner, and ended by the *Parchment*-Maker." The initial stages of treatment are the same for leather and parchment: once removed, the hide is rotted, using lime or salt, to loosen the hair from the follicles; the hide is then scraped to remove the flesh and hair. At this point, tanning and parchment production diverge. To make leather, the tanner treats the skin with a solution of alum. To make parchment, the parchment-maker dries the skin while stretching it on a rack. Once the

It would not out at windowes, nor at doores, | As it on earth hath bene thy fe
There is fo hot a fummer in my bofome, | Now, now you Starres, that r
That all my bowels crumble vp to duft : | Where be your powres? Shev
I am a fcribled forme drawne with a pen | And inftantly returne with me
Vpon a Parchment, and againft this fire | To pufh deftruction, and perp
Do I fhrinke vp. | Out of the weake doore of ou

Fig. 21. "I am a scribled forme drawne with a pen Vpon a Parchment." Detail, William Shakespeare, "King John." From *Mr. William Shakespeares comedies, histories, & tragedies* (London, 1623), b5v. 1978 +83

skin has dried, it is scraped and polished with coarse and fine grit: this process of scraping renders the parchment opaque. Parchment is finished by being rubbed smooth, using pumice or other granular objects (glass baked into bread loaves is a method said to have been used by the English), and smoothed with ground chalk.[26] The overall process realigns the molecular formation of the skin: what was once loose, even gelatinous, is transformed into a stiff, opaque surface.[27] The result, in well-made parchment, is a thin, white, velvety writing surface.

Because of the way parchment is made, it is extremely sensitive to changes in humidity, which can cause it to stiffen and change in shape, or buckle. Exposure to liquid or humidity changes the molecular structure, returning it to its original state. In the words of Jesse Meyer, parchment-maker, parchment always wants to return to the animal.[28]

Technically, parchment can be made from any type of animal (or bird or fish) hide that can be dried and stretched under tension, before being scraped smooth. In practice, calf, sheep, and goat were the most common early modern sources for parchment. Some hides, like pig (and, to a lesser extent, sheep), contain more fat or oil and are more difficult to use. Other hides, such as deer, might be too damaged from life in the wild or difficult to source consistently; hides from smaller animals like squirrels might be too small to be useful for textual objects.

Any type of parchment will share two characteristics: it will have been formed at a molecular level through being dried under tension and scraped; it will have two sides, reflecting its origins as the skin of an animal. The hair side will often have visible follicles remaining; the skin side will be smoother. Parchment will also retain marks from the animal's life (e.g., insect bites), or the process of production (e.g., cuts and nicks from the removal of the hide), or the shape of the animal's body (e.g., the mark of the hip bones, the curve of the neck). It is one of the most beautiful writing materials, often exquisitely white, velvety, and supple, and is in every way the product of the most visceral transformation of the skin of a once living animal.

Parchment is the bearer of its animal's DNA. The biologists Sarah Fiddyment and Matthew Collins have explored the nondestructive extraction of DNA samples from parchment to determine the species of origin, the sex, and the genetic relationship to other parchment specimens.[29] One result of their work has been to challenge the description of the very thin, white parchment in thirteenth-century Paris Bibles as uterine vellum, indicating that the fineness of the parchment was the result of production practices, rather than the originating animal.[30]

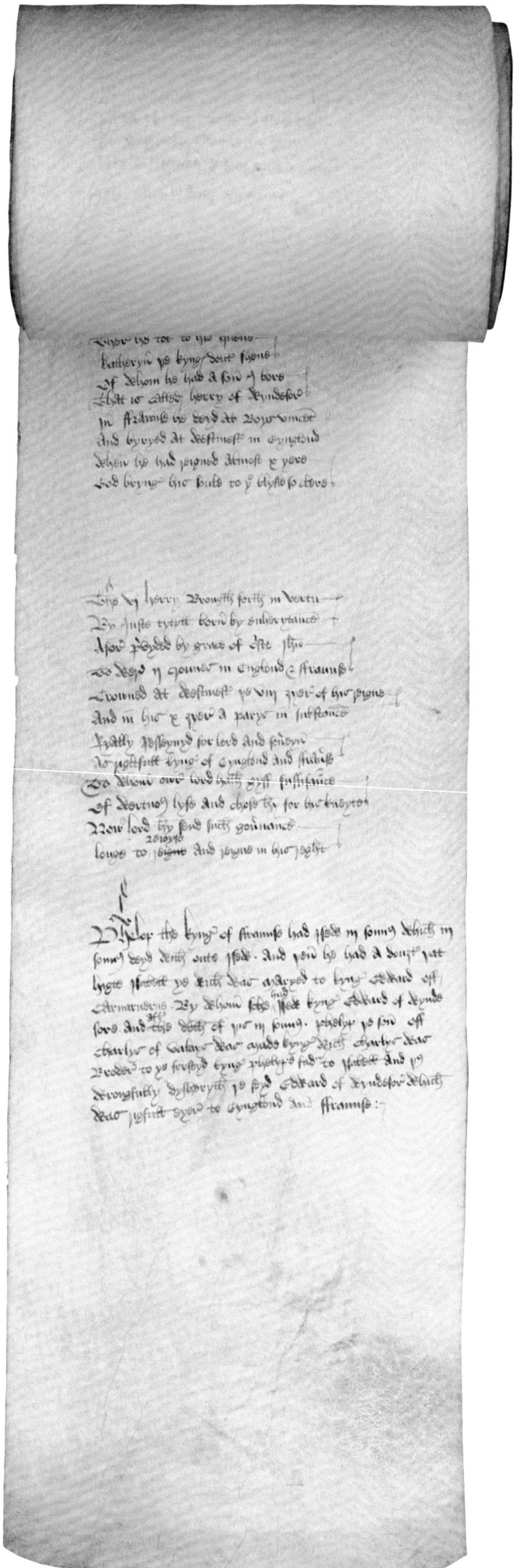

Fig. 22. The end of a parchment roll, containing a copy of John Lydgate, The kings of England sithen William the Conqueror. England, 1475–99. Osborn a14

Fig. 23. Detail of fig. 22

Paper

Until the fourteenth century, parchment was the primary substratum used in the production of European texts. By the sixteenth century, paper had overtaken parchment in all but particular uses, such as for legal documents. The British Parliament only recently voted to print new laws on archival paper, rather than recording on parchment.[31]

Paper fell into two main categories in early modern England: that used for textual production, and that used for other material purposes. All types of paper were made from rags, primarily of linen. Paper's quality derived from the fineness and color of the rags used to make it: whiter, finer rags made whiter, finer paper. Fine white paper (fig. 24) was the most expensive and highest quality, and the category primarily associated with textual production, either as writing or printing paper. Coarse paper (figs. 25–27), usually blue or brown, was also used for wrapping, lining, and other daily household or commercial purposes. Blue paper was often associated with sugar production, as coarse paper was used to wrap cones of sugar for export from the West Indies. Writing and printing paper were also finished in slightly different ways because of the different consistencies of ink used in the two processes: printer's ink was oil-based and more viscous than the ink used for handwriting.

Paper was a necessary staple in early modern England. Quite aside from its uses for writing and printing, paper was used as wadding, wrapping, packaging, and, as papier-mâché, for construction. It was used to wrap sugar, carry pills, line pans, house pins, make fans (fig. 28). It was an essential for the many occupations concerned with sewing, from tailoring to hat-making. Paper goods, such as playing cards (figs. 29–30), were an enormously popular commodity, as can be seen in the regular customs duties paid on shipments of playing cards imported into England.[32]

Paper was so familiar to early modern audiences as to be recognizable within a hierarchy of use and social status. One author could mock the weakness of another's argument by comparing it to a "browne paper building."[33] In *A pleasant commodie, called looke about you* (1600), the concealed prince asks that the sugar for his sack be brought in white paper:

…heere ye boy?
Bring Suger in white paper, not in browne;
For in white paper I haue heere a tricke,
Shall make the purseuant first swound, then sicke.[34]

White paper was a literary trope of expense, quality, and purity: white paper as man's soul, inked with God's blood; white paper as the potential relationship between writer and reader; white paper as the expensive marker of mismanagement or corruption. In his *Newes from Graues-end: sent to nobody* (1604), Thomas Dekker mocked the "white paper-gallery of a large Chronicle" as a familiar site of contradictory and meaningless displays.[35]

Paper as metaphor bore little relation to the complicated, arduous process of its material production. Early modern papermaking was a specialized industry: it required a location with access to a good, clean source of water as well as a reliable supply of rags. It was also labor-intensive, requiring workers for distinct and sometimes highly specialized tasks. Paper was produced in two overarching phases: first, the production of the materials used to make paper; second, the preparation of the paper sheets themselves. In the first stage, linen rags were taken by the paper mill and sorted into groups based on the quality and lightness of color of the fibers. The rags were retted, or fermented, to begin to break down the fibers; they were also cut into small pieces. These already decomposing materials were then repeatedly washed with water and beaten, using mechanical beaters powered by water. This process of cutting, fermentation, washing, and beating combined to break the textile down into its constituent fibers, sometimes still visible in the final sheet (fig. 31).

In the second stage, this "stuff," the cleaned and decomposed textile fiber, was processed to make individual sheets of paper. This procedure depended on specialized labor and a particular set of tools, the mold and deckle. A papermaking mold was essentially a metal mesh, consisting primarily of tightly spaced "laid" wires. These were held in place by relatively widely spaced "chain" wires. The deckle, a shallow wooden frame, was placed over the mold to create a reservoir. Together, the mold and deckle acted like

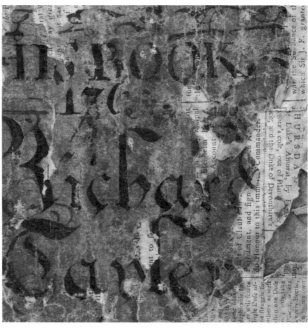

Fig. 24. Detail, white paper, showing chain lines and watermark. England, ca. 1571. Beinecke MS 610

Fig. 25. Detail, blue paper, used as the wrapper binding of Richard Tayler, Notebook, with printed waste visible beneath. England, ca. 1766–67. Osborn c438

Fig. 26. Detail, brown paper wrapper for James Byrd Cox, Penmanship exercise book. England, 1844. Osborn d510

Fig. 27. Detail, brown and blue sugar paper wrappers, used as the cover for a diary kept by Thomas Thistlewood. Jamaica, 1767. OSB MSS 176, Box 4, Folder 18

Fig. 28. Efficacious Grace the 11th. Notes by Jonathan Edwards on the paper scraps used to make fans. Northampton, Massachusetts, ca. 1746. Gen MSS 151, Box 15, Folder 1206. I am grateful to Ken Minkema for his suggestion that Edwards started this manuscript in Northampton in 1746.

a sieve: working with a vat of diluted stuff, a vatman would scoop the mold and deckle in the mixture, lifting and quickly shifting it back and forth as the water drained. This process caused the fibers to interlock, shaken into position within the mold. The pressure of the water draining through the perpendicular wires also left an impression on the sheet of paper: laid lines from the primary parallel wires in the mold and chain lines from the perpendicular chains (fig. 32). Some papermakers also wove a wire ornament into the paper mold, which would leave the ornament's impression, known as a watermark (fig. 33).[36]

At this point, the vatman removed the deckle and handed the mold with its sheet to the second person: the coucher. The coucher turned the sheet out onto a felt, handing the mold back to the vatman. This process continued: the coucher covering the new sheet with a layer of damp felt, upending another

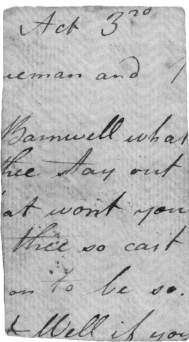

Figs. 29–30. "Wapping &c. is ours," one of a set
of playing cards illustrating the Rye House Plot,
a political conspiracy. The reverse (fig. 30) shows
its origins as manuscript waste. England, 1684.
Cary Playing Cards Collection, 1917

sheet onto it, to create a post, or stack of damp sheets of paper. The layer, the third position in the team, separated the damp sheets from a previous post. The sheets were then pressed, to squeeze out the remaining moisture; they might be shuffled within the stack and pressed again, to create a softer finish. The paper sheets were then dried—hung in a spur, or gathering, of seven to eight sheets, on a horsehair or other line coated in beeswax.

Once dried, paper was treated with size, a mixture made from gelatin. Size acted as a membrane between the paper surface and the liquid of the ink: untreated paper, like blotting paper, is naturally porous, absorbing rather than resisting liquid. Different types of paper might be treated with slightly different recipes of sizing, depending on their intended use. Because the ink for writing in manuscript is more liquid than printer's ink, for instance, paper for printing might

be treated with a different size than paper for writing by hand—or for painting with watercolor. The sizing might also affect the way in which paper changed color or aged over time: Cathleen Baker has pointed out the "Tuesday–Saturday" sizing characteristic, identifying color changes in sheets sized earlier and later in the course of a particular week, as the sizing mixture changed in consistency. Finally, depending on its intended use, paper might be finished after sizing, pressed with a smooth stone to even out the surface, and sometimes trimmed to remove the deckled edge (fig. 34).[37]

Early modern paper was organized by the sheet, quire, ream, and bundle. A sheet of paper was as large as the paper mold that had been used to make it (fig. 35). Sheets were the base unit of paper. A quire consisted of twenty-four sheets; a ream, twenty quires; a bundle, forty quires (fig. 36). Paper was produced

Fig. 31. Detail of the textures and materials still visible in one example of white paper. England, 1586. Osborn a40

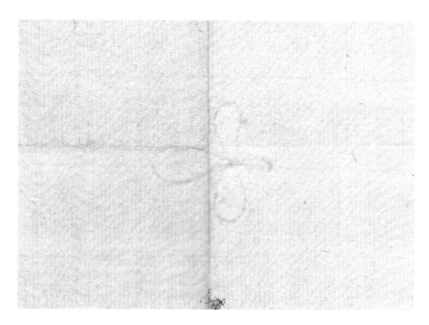

Fig. 32. Detail of chain lines, laid lines, and watermark. England, 1659. OSB MSS 40, Box 2, Folder 55

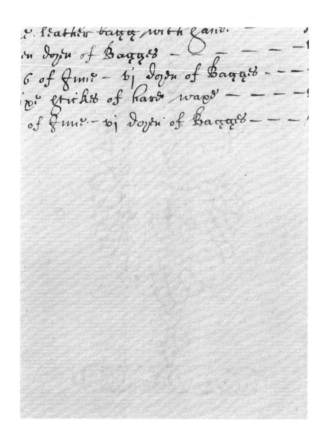

Fig. 33. Detail of watermark. England, 1567–1717. Osborn fb131

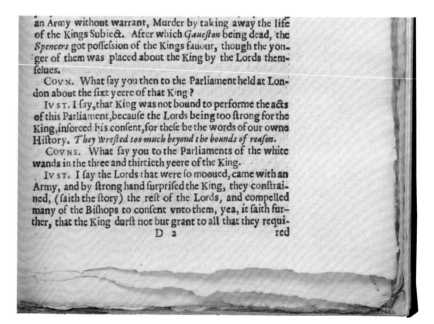

an Army without warrant, Murder by taking away the life of the Kings Subiect. After which *Gaueston* being dead, the *Spencers* got posseſsion of the Kings fauour, though the yonger of them was placed about the King by the Lords themſelues.

COVN. What ſay you then to the Parliament held at London about the ſixt yeere of that King?

IVST. I ſay, that King was not bound to performe the acts of this Parliament, becauſe the Lords being too ſtrong for the King, inforced his conſent, for theſe be the words of our owne Hiſtory. *They wreſted too much beyond the bounds of reaſon.*

COVNS. What ſay you to the Parliaments of the white wands in the three and thirtieth yeere of the King.

IVST. I ſay the Lords that were ſo mooued, came with an Army, and by ſtrong hand ſurpriſed the King, they conſtrained, (ſaith the ſtory) the reſt of the Lords, and compelled many of the Biſhops to conſent vnto them, yea, it ſaith further, that the King durſt not but grant to all that they required

D 2   red

Fig. 34. Untrimmed page showing deckled edge. Walter Raleigh, *The prerogatiue of parliaments in England* (London, 1628), D2r. Omd40 628rb

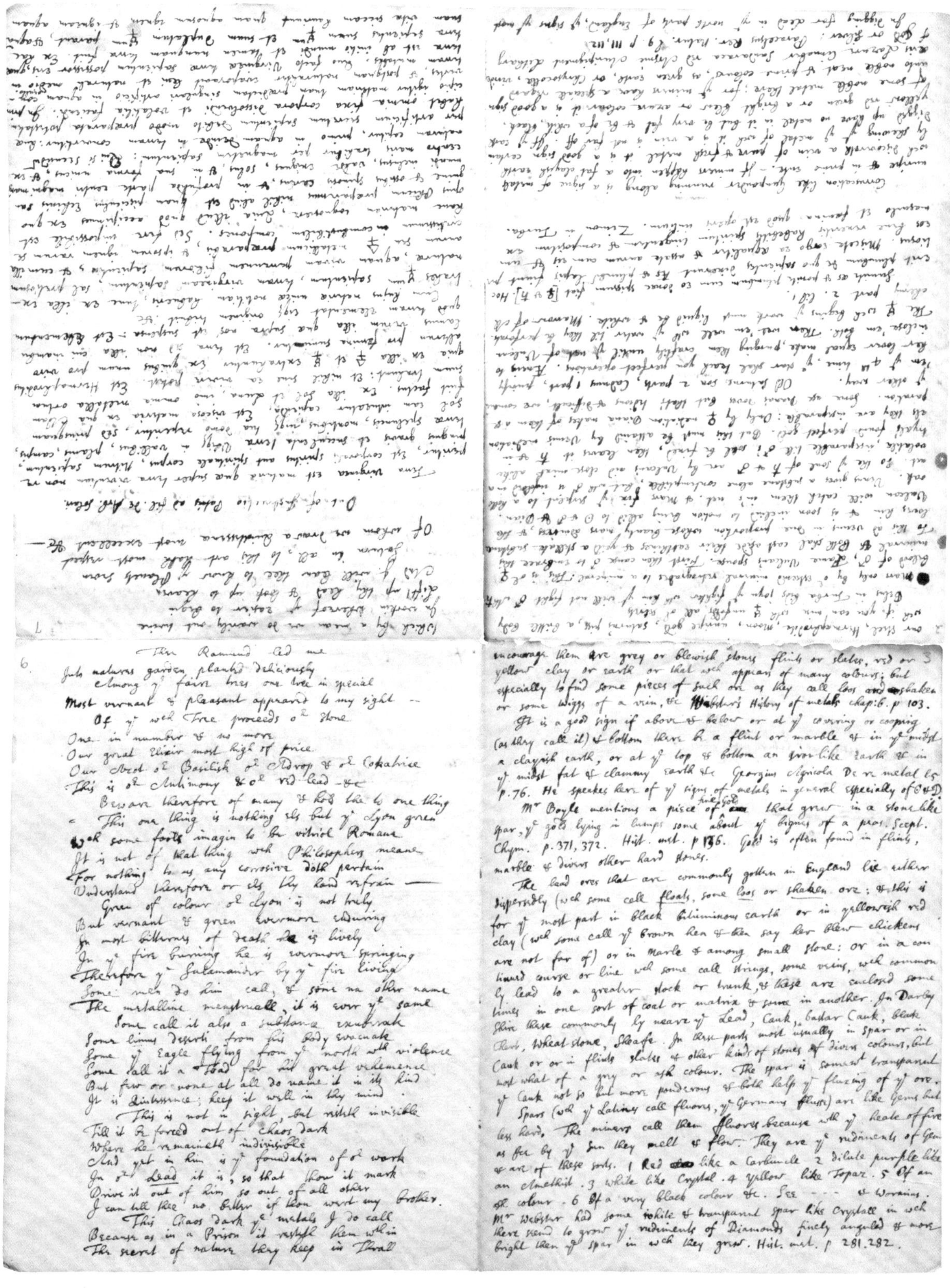

Fig. 35. A single sheet of paper, folded twice, and used by Isaac Newton for his reading notes on alchemy. England, ca. 1700. Mellon MS 79

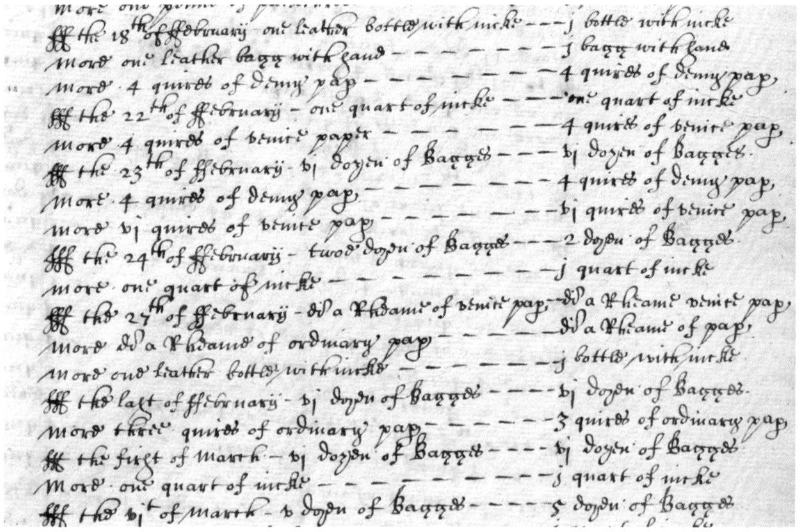

Fig. 36. Detail, listing the purchase of "demy" and Venice paper by the quire and ream, as well as ink and document bags. Accounts of materials used by the clerks of the Exchequer. England, 1567–1717. Osborn fb131

in certain distinct categories of size. These were not rigorously standardized: different paper mills made sheets of slightly different dimensions. The *Dictionary of Arts and Sciences* (1765) listed the following dimensions, from the largest to the smallest:

Atlas
Elephant
Imperial
Super-royal
Royal
Medium
Demy
Crown
Fool's cap
Pot-paper[38]

Names derived from the watermark came to be associated with size: as one example, "pot," the smallest size of paper, had the watermark of a jug.[39]

Paper was also taxed. Over the early modern period, British industry came increasingly under the control of a centralizing administration. In 1711, under Queen Anne, a stamp act imposed a duty on imported paper and paper made in Britain; the rate per ream of paper depended on the paper size.[40] Over the course of the eighteenth century, the paper industry was brought under the regulatory oversight of the Excise, and paper had to receive an Excise stamp in order to be sold legally.[41]

England for the most part imported paper in the early modern period rather than producing it. Through the sixteenth and seventeenth centuries, high-quality writing and printing paper was imported into England from France, Italy, and elsewhere. While there were several dozen paper mills in England by the mid-seventeenth century, these largely produced the coarser white or brown paper used by the local commercial or industrial markets.[42] By contrast, the London port books, recording the customs duties paid on imports into the harbor of London, show a steady weekly traffic into London of paper imports from France and the Netherlands. A few examples from the single month of July 1568 include:

July 3, *Mychell* of Antwerp: John Jackson imported 200 bundles of brown paper, for £6 13s 4d

July 6: *Sampson* of Antwerp: Jackson imported 100 bundles of brown paper, for £3 6s 8d

July 14: Hugh Offley imported 100 reams of paper and 10 gross of playing cards for £23 6s 8d

July 27: *Christopher* of London: Richard Renolds imported 150 reams of printing paper for £20.[43]

These are just a sampling of the dozens of paper imports into London over the course of the month, in a trade that included all grades and types of paper, from the "cap-paper" to make hats to the higher-end commodities of loose paper, printing paper, and

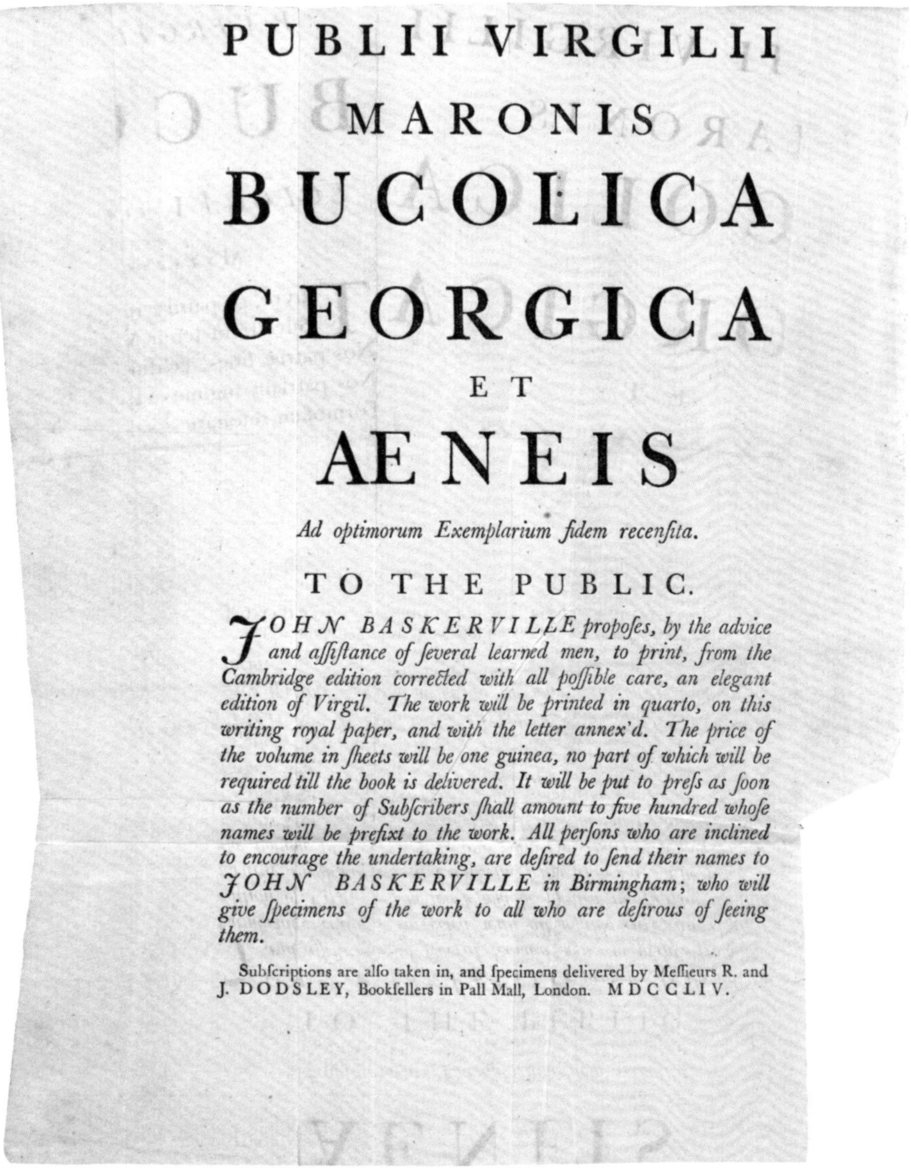

PUBLII VIRGILII

MARONIS

BUCOLICA

GEORGICA

ET

AENEIS

Ad optimorum Exemplarium fidem recenfita.

TO THE PUBLIC.

*JOHN BASKERVILLE propofes, by the advice
and affiftance of feveral learned men, to print, from the
Cambridge edition corrected with all poffible care, an elegant
edition of Virgil. The work will be printed in quarto, on this
writing royal paper, and with the letter annex'd. The price of
the volume in fheets will be one guinea, no part of which will be
required till the book is delivered. It will be put to prefs as foon
as the number of Subfcribers fhall amount to five hundred whofe
names will be prefixt to the work. All perfons who are inclined
to encourage the undertaking, are defired to fend their names to
JOHN BASKERVILLE in Birmingham; who will
give fpecimens of the work to all who are defirous of feeing
them.*

Subfcriptions are alfo taken in, and fpecimens delivered by Meffieurs R. and
J. DODSLEY, Bookfellers in Pall Mall, London. MDCCLIV.

playing cards. London, and England, consumed paper by the shipload.

By the mid-eighteenth century, the English paper industry had become competitive in the production of writing and printing papers. At Turkey Mill, his paper mill near Maidstone in Kent, James Whatman produced high-end writing and printing paper, first used in a publication in 1740.[44] Whatman invented a new type of paper mold in which the wires were finely woven together into a mesh, allowing the production of sheets without visible chain or laid lines. This new wove paper was first introduced in John Baskerville's 1757 edition of Virgil, believed to be one of the most beautiful works ever published in England.[45] The promotional advertisement shown here (fig. 37) emphasizes that it is printed on the same "writing royal paper" to be used for the book, although the work was in fact printed on both laid and the new wove paper.

Fig. 37. "The work will be printed in quarto, on this writing royal paper, and with the letter annex'd." Advertisement (1754) for subscriptions to John Baskerville's edition of Virgil's *Aeneid*. Baskerville +1754B

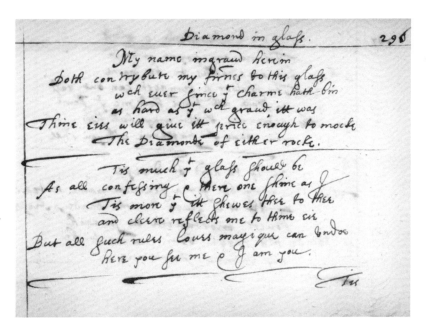

Fig. 38. John Donne, "Diamond in glass" [Valediction of my name, in the window]. From a scribal copy of 33 poems by Donne, entitled Poems, with a few prose problems, p. 296 [i.e., 196]. England, ca. 1620. Osborn b114. Note the use of superscripted abbreviations: y^t (that) and w^{ch} (which).

Diamond in glass.

My name ingraud herein
Doth contrybute my firñes to this glass
wch euer since y^t charme hath bin
as hard as y^t wch graud, itt was
Thine eiss will giue itt price enough to mocke
The Diamonds of either rocke.

Tis much y^t glass should be
As all confessing & there one shine as I
Tis more y^t itt shewes thee to thee
And cleere reflects me to thine eie
But all such rules loues magique can undoe
here you see me & I am you.

Tis

PENS AND WRITING IMPLEMENTS

"My name ingraud herein / Doth contrybute my firñes [or, firmness] to this glass," wrote John Donne, on writing his name with a diamond on his lover's window (fig. 38). Early modern writers wrote with a range of implements: pens, crayons or pencils, styluses on wax tablets, chalk on writing slates—and diamonds on glass. By far the most common implement was the quill pen, made from the flight feather of a goose. The quill was so pervasive in early modern English culture that it could be used as a measure of thickness or length ("as thick as a small Goose quill"[46]), as a metaphor ("he then singles out some *Scrivener (alias, Goose-quill),*[47]), or as a joke ("*God deliver me from a Goose quill, viz.* from Lawyers Bills"[48]).

Much of what we know about the quill pen derives from penmanship manuals, written by writing masters to advertise their services. Advertisements inform us that pens could be purchased: a printer's advertisement of 1700 lists pens, along with "all sorts of Stationary Wares," including paper, ink, wax, bonds, bills, and funeral tickets.[49] They could also be made. The writing master Edward Cocker taught his readers how to prepare a pen, cited here from the second edition of his popular *The pen's triumph* (1659). Cocker directs his reader to "procure the first, second, or third Quill in the wing of a Goose or Raven." The quill first had to be softened, either soaked in water or heated in "warme Embers"; it then had to be cleaned, usually scraped with a well-sharpened penknife or "small thin French Blade"; next the quill was cut, trimmed about a quarter-inch from the end. Last, and most important, the nib was cut, a slit at the end of the quill.[50] Different types of feather could be used: goose or swan quills were the most common choice. But quills were also made from the feathers of turkeys, crows, ravens, and other birds.[51] Crow feathers are said to have been used for particularly small or delicate writing.[52] There was a market trade in feathers for quills: flight feathers, which were preferred, were harvested seasonally at molting time. Quills were imported into England from Holland, Norway, Iceland, Greenland, and elsewhere, as colder climates were said to create particularly strong quills; there was also an economy within

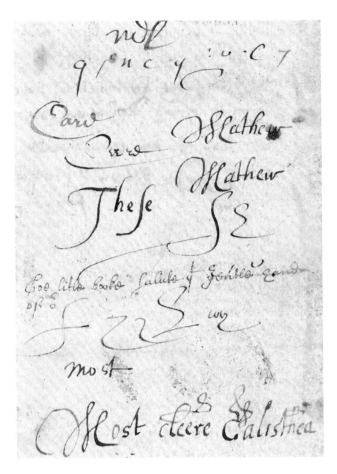

Fig. 39. Detail, pen trials in front endpaper of a manuscript miscellany. England, mid-17th century. Osborn b205

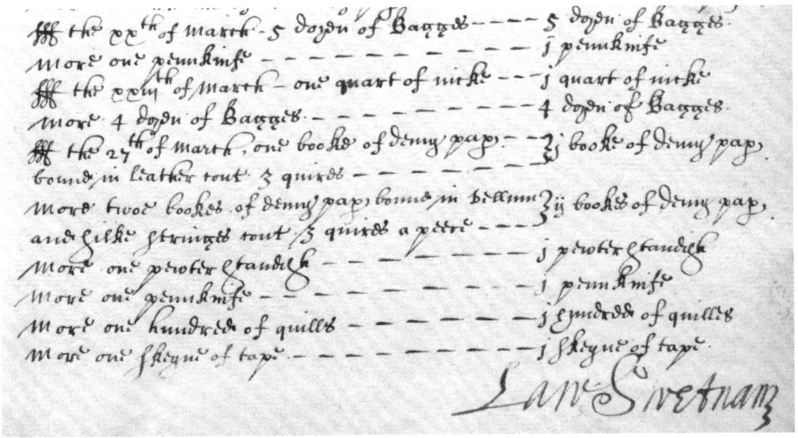

Fig. 40. Detail, listing the purchase of one hundred of quills, alongside two books of demy paper, bound in vellum; one pewter standish; one penknife; one skein of tape. Accounts of materials used by the clerks of the Exchequer. England, 1567–1717. Osborn fb131

England, as quills were produced by farmers in the goose trade in Lincolnshire and elsewhere.[53]

Care and attention had to be given in cutting the nib, as it affected the use of the pen for particular hands. For italic, Cocker emphasizes that the nib should be "small, and almost round, with a long slit." For secretary hand, it should be broader; for large italic, even broader.[54] "The very end of the Nib will shine if it be truly cut, being held betwixt your eye and the light," Cocker writes in *Multum in parvo. Or the pen's gallantrie* (1660).[55] It is generally stated that right-handed writers found feathers from the left wing fit their hands more easily, and vice versa, but Cocker does not specify which wing—left or right—should be used for a quill.

Once cut or sharpened, the pen was tested. The endpapers of early modern English books are filled with pen trials, or the practice text used when a writer tested his or her quill. "Goe litle booke salute y[t] gentle hande," someone has written on the endpaper of this seventeenth-century pocket notebook (fig. 39).

The quill seems to have been by far the most common writing instrument through the early nineteenth century (fig. 40), although references to other types of pen can be found. "Send the silver pen which is broken, and it shall be mended quickly," wrote Roger Ascham to the warden of his new charge, the Lady Elizabeth.[56] In January 1567 Anthony Scoloker imported five gross of wooden writing pens (along with four and a half dozen needles and two gross of lute strings) on the *Ellen* of London.[57] In 1780 a steel pen is said to have been created for Joseph Priestley by the Birmingham manufacturer Samuel Harrison; by 1830 the steel pen was commercially produced and widely available.[58]

INK

English notebooks and copybooks, in manuscript and print, are filled with recipes for ink, which had to be produced from its component parts or purchased. Cocker's *Pen's triumph* advertises "a choice Receipt [or recipe] for Ink" on its title page. The instructions offer the reader a recipe for making iron gall ink, created with iron sulfate and tannins. The name, iron gall, refers to the combination of the two primary ingredients: iron sulfate and oak galls, the most common form of tannin. Oak galls are a byproduct of the oak tree, a small round growth produced by the tree in response to a wasp bite. They acted as tannins within the mixture, reacting with the other agents to create the ink's color. Oak gall is the most commonly mentioned in recipes, but other forms of tannin could be substituted. The acid from the oak gall tannin combined with iron sulfate, or coppresse. Gum arabic was added to control the ink's texture, smoothing and thickening it. The mixture was left to age in a solution of wine or "the best drink." Cocker also recommends that sugar or pomegranate bark be added and the whole simmered over a gentle fire, "to make your Ink shine and lustrous."[59]

Ink was a familiar trope for early modern writers. "That in black inck my loue may still shine bright," wrote Shakespeare in his sixty-fifth sonnet (fig. 41). And: "All gall, and coppresse, from his inke, he drayneth," laughed Ben Jonson in *Volpone* (1607; fig. 42). Ink recipes were also the object of considerable interest for early modern readers (figs. 43–45). "Inke to make itt verie good," reads the index to the recipe book of Robert Paston, first Earl of Yarmouth. "A direction to make good inke," reads one of several ink recipes in William Hill's notebook from the early seventeenth century (fig. 45): "Take six ounces of galls, three ounces of gumme Arabeck three ounces of green coppresse. Crack the galls grosly and put all these to two quartes of the best drink ready to be put up, as followeth."[60] Hill's recipe corresponds almost exactly with Cocker's printed version.

Iron gall ink was intended specifically for writing. It acts as a dye on the substratum, physically staining the text into the paper or parchment. The ink continues to interact over the course of the manuscript's lifetime with the elements it encounters: air, light, or the book or document itself.

Unlike iron gall ink and other inks intended for writing, printer's ink was oil-based (fig. 46). Because the oil was sticky, it remained in place during the printing process. Printer's ink was also made with carbon, either soot or lamp-black, mixed with oil into a solution.

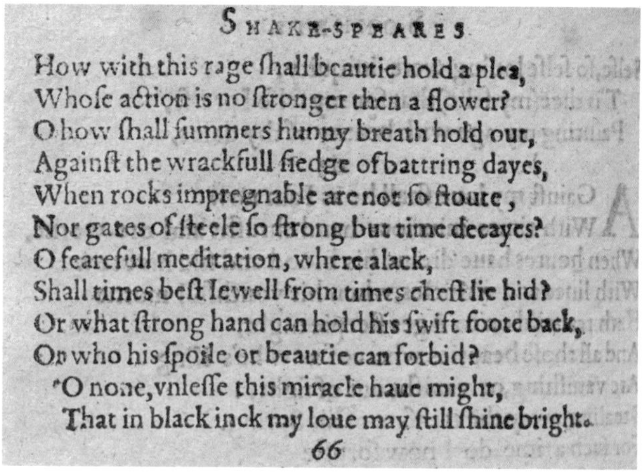
SHAKE-SPEARES
How with this rage ſhall beautie hold a plea,
Whoſe action is no ſtronger then a flower?
O how ſhall ſummers hunny breath hold out,
Againſt the wrackfull ſiedge of batt'ring dayes,
When rocks impregnable are not ſo ſtoute,
Nor gates of ſteele ſo ſtrong but time decayes?
O fearefull meditation, where alack,
Shall times beſt Iewell from times cheſt lie hid?
Or what ſtrong hand can hold his ſwift foote back,
Or who his ſpoile or beautie can forbid?
O none, vnleſſe this miracle haue might,
That in black inck my loue may ſtill ſhine bright.
66

Fig. 41. Detail, William Shakespeare, *Shake-Speares sonnets. Neuer before imprinted* (1609), E2v. Elizabethan Club, Yale University. Eliz 194

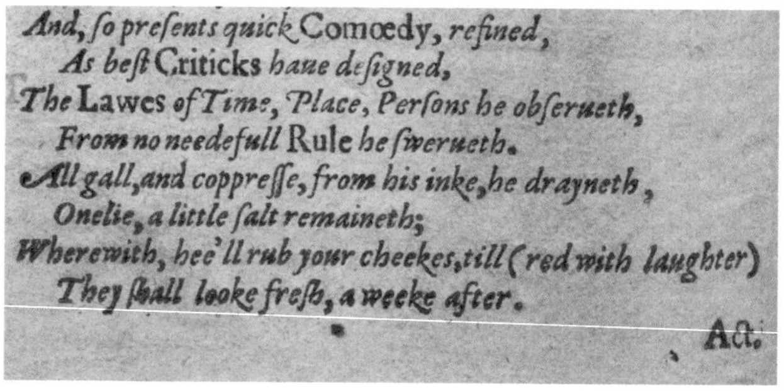
And, ſo preſents quick Comœdy, *refined,*
As beſt Criticks *haue deſigned,*
The Lawes *of Time, Place, Perſons he obſerueth,*
From no needefull Rule *he ſwerueth.*
All gall, and coppreſſe, from his inke, he drayneth,
Onelie, a little ſalt remaineth;
Wherewith, hee'll rub your cheekes, till (red with laughter)
They ſhall looke freſh, a weeke after.
Act.

Fig. 42. Detail, *Ben Jonson, Ben: Ionson his Volpone or the foxe* (1607), A4v. Elizabethan Club, Yale University. Eliz 108

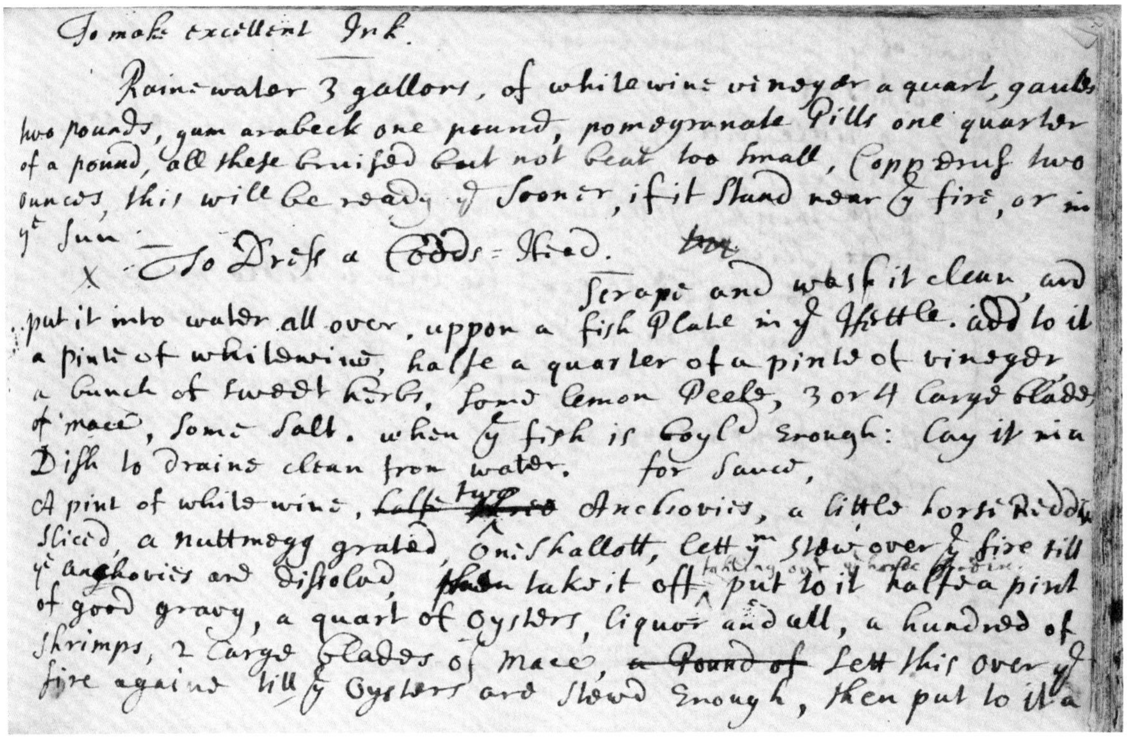

Fig. 43. "To make excellent Ink." Notebook of recipes and poems, f. 59r. England, late 17th century. Osborn b115

To make excellent Ink.

   Raine water 3 gallons, of white wine vinegar a quart, gauls two pounds, gum arabeck one pound, pomegranate Pills one quarter of a pound, all these bruised but not beat too small, Copperus two ounces, this will be ready y^e sooner, if it stand near y^e fire, or in y^e sun.

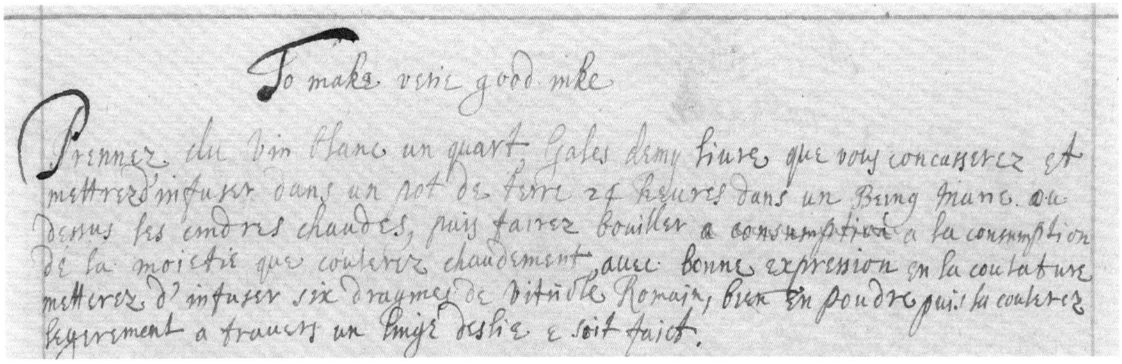

Fig. 44. Robert Paston, "To make verie good inke." Recipe book containing medical, chemical, and household recipes and formulas. England, ca. 1670–83. Osborn fb255. Paston's recipe called for a quart of white wine and oak galls, broken and infused in an iron pot over hot embers for twenty-four hours.

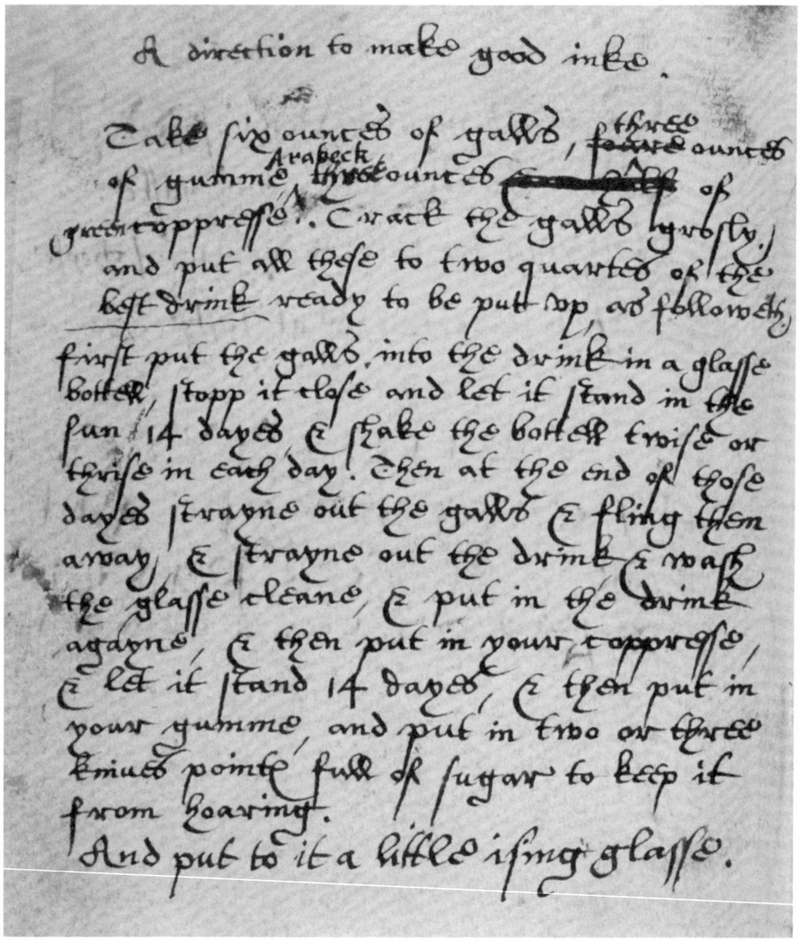

Fig. 45. Hill, Notebook, p. 22. Osborn b234. See also fig. 17 for another ink recipe in Hill's notebook.

A direction to make good inke.
Take six ounces of galls, ~~foure~~ ^three ounces
of gumme ^Arabeck three ounces ~~coppresse~~ of
green coppresse. Crack the galls grosly
and put all these to two quartes of the
best drink ready to be put up, as followeth.
First put the galls into the drink in a glasse
bottell, stopp it close and let it stand in the
sun 14 dayes & shake the bottell twise or
thrise in each day. Then at the end of those
dayes strayne out the galls & fling them
away, & strayne out the drink & wash
the glasse cleane, & put in the drink
agayne, & then put in your coppresse,
& let it stand 14 dayes, & then put in
your gumme, and put in two or three
kniues points full of sugar to keep it
from hoaring.
And put to it a little ising glasse.

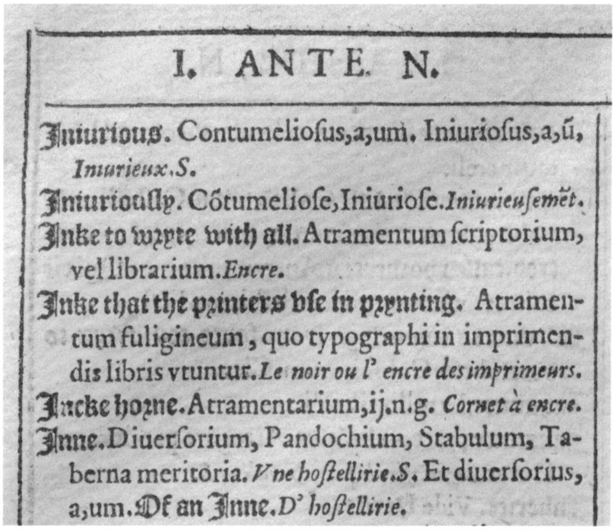

I. ANTE N.

Iniurious. Contumelioſus,a,um. Iniurioſus,a,ũ, *Iniurieux.S.*
Iniuriouſly. Cõtumelioſe, Iniurioſe. *Iniurieuſemẽt.*
Inke to wryte with all. Atramentum ſcriptorium, vel librarium. *Encre.*
Inke that the printers vſe in pryntyng. Atramentum fuligineum, quo typographi in imprimendis libris vtuntur. *Le noir ou l' encre des imprimeurs.*
Incke horne. Atramentarium,ij.n.g. *Cornet à encre.*
Inne. Diuerſorium, Pandochium, Stabulum, Taberna meritoria. *Vne hoſtellirie.S.* Et diuerſorius, a,um. **Of an Inne.** *D' hoſtellirie.*

Fig. 46. Detail, *Huloets dictionarie, newelye corrected, amended, set in order and enlarged* (London, 1572). Ha49 +572h. Huloet's Latin-English dictionary defines ink for manuscript, "to wryte with all," and "Inke that the printers use in prynting."

INKWELLS, INKHORNS, PENNERS, PENKNIVES

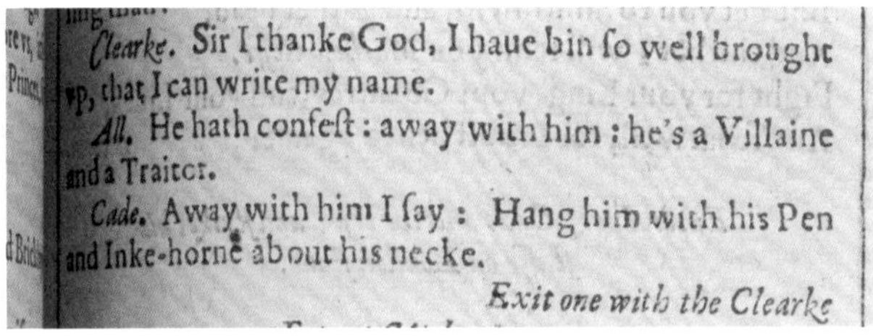

Fig. 47. "Hang him with his Pen and Inke-horne about his necke." Detail, William Shakespeare, "The second part of King Hen. The Sixt." From *Mr. William Shakespeares comedies, histories, & tragedies* (London, 1623), 139. 1978 +83

Quill pens needed to be maintained: trimmed, sharpened, shaped. Writing manuals recommended that writers carry a penknife for this purpose. Surviving examples in the Victoria and Albert Museum show short knives with thin, angled blades; these sometimes have a pointed end, to hold paper or parchment in place. "E.B.," in Jehan de Beau-Chesne's 1570 writing manual, recommended to the writer that "Your Peneknife as staye in leaft hand lett rest, / The mettell to softe nor to hard is best."[61] Pen and penknife could also be carried in a penner, or pen case. Surviving examples are often carved or decorated, made from ivory, leather, or other materials. They sometimes had a compartment to carry ink. Ink could also be carried in an inkhorn (figs. 47–48), named for its fabrication from an animal horn; it might be mixed and stored in an inkwell or standish (fig. 49).

The inkhorn, and other material aspects of manuscript culture, could also signify the archaic. In the late sixteenth century, the inkhorn was taken as a synonym for the antiquarian or pedantic, and was used as metaphor to critique the use of Latin or Greek terms instead of a native English tongue. The soldier and poet George Gascoigne mocked the use of "wordes of many sillables," enjoining his compatriots that "the more monasyllables that you vse, the truer Englishman you shall séeme, and the lesse you

Fig. 48. Detail, showing quill, inkwell, and letter. The writer hands a letter to the carrier, who wears an inkhorn or posthorn around his neck. From Jean-Puget de la Serre, *The secretary in fashion: or, an elegant and compendious way of writing all manner of letters,* 6th ed. (London, 1683), frontispiece. 1992 227. See also fig. 88.

Fig. 49. R. Higs, Eight studies for inkwells. England,
18th century. Yale University Art Gallery. 1988.107.2.1-4

shall smell of the Inkehorne."[62] Roger Ascham dismissed Hall's *Chronicles* for its "Indenture English," recommending that writers "first change, strange and inkhorne tearmes into proper, and commonlie used wordes."[63]

FINISHING: WAX, SEALS, WAFERS, FOLDS, WRAPPERS

Text forms only one aspect of the textual object. Volumes, documents, letters, and other forms of printed and manuscript culture moved through the world as objects needing to be closed and opened, authenticated, delivered, and stored. The three documents shown here—a late-sixteenth-century lease on parchment (fig. 50), a late-eighteenth-century personal letter on paper (fig. 51), and a late-seventeenth-century authentication seal (figs. 52–53)—reveal some of the ways in which documents were finished and presented to their recipients and audiences.

Seals were one of the most common ways of closing, authenticating, and personalizing documents, ranging from everyday letters to royal patents and proclamations. A document was sealed by pressing a seal matrix (also simply called a seal) into hot wax. The wax was usually red; black wax was also used to denote mourning or misfortune. Seals were often decorated: a device, carved in relief, might relate to an individual's personal, family, or institutional connections. A wafer was also used to close documents, sometimes in conjunction with a seal. Wafers were small round adhesive tabs made of starch and a binding agent. These were dampened with hot water, before being pressed between the sections of a document to hold it together, after which a seal might also be applied.[64] Richard Grenville signed this lease below the text, signing over the parchment tag used to affix the seal (fig. 50); the letter to James Boswell was folded and closed by a seal (fig. 51).

These three very different documents share the traces of their life as documents in motion. Grenville's lease was a chirograph: two copies of the lease were made, then separated; the jagged top edge of the lease

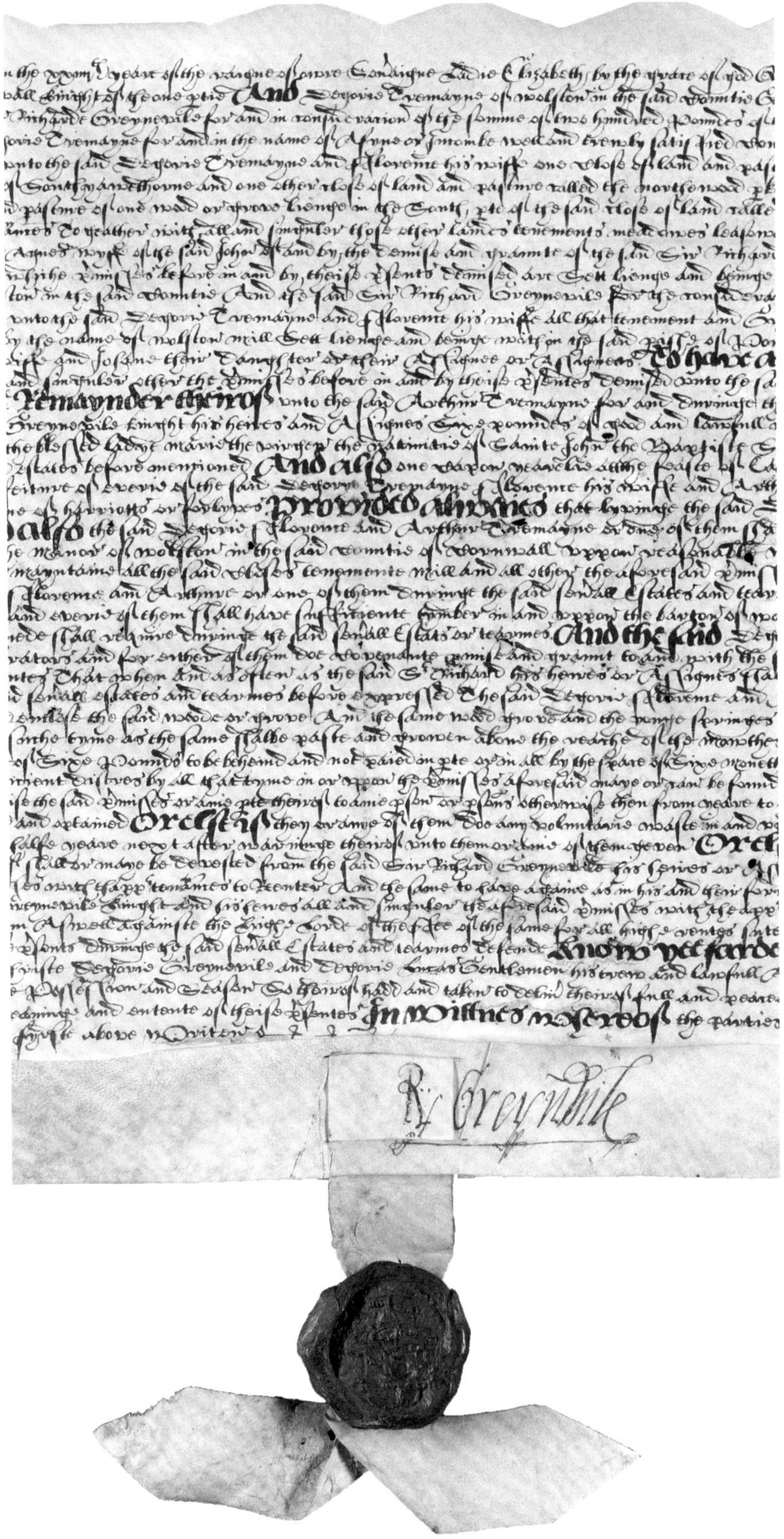

Fig. 51. Detail of wrapper, with seal and postmarks, of an unidentified letter to James Boswell. England, May 15 [late 18th century]. Gen MSS 89, Box 36, Folder 916

Fig. 50. Detail, showing Richard Grenville's signature and seal on a lease. England, January 1, 1582. Beinecke MS 680 would match that of its pair. The lease has also been folded and docketed (labeled) on the other side: its keepers have added further information to it over the document's four-hundred-year life span. The letter to Boswell was folded and closed with a seal, and the two round stamps (15 | Ma and 16 | Ma, for May 15 and 16) indicate that it was sent through the post to Edinburgh, likely from London. What survives is the paper wrapper to the letter, rather than the letter itself.

In our third example, taken from the papers of the Court of Quarter Session, the seal is used as a reinforcement of testimony (figs. 52–53). In this character defense of a fellow Anabaptist, or religious dissenter, the subscribers—literally, those who have written under the testimony—have attached their seals to their signatures as a statement of authentication.

Fig. 52–53. Papers of the Court of Quarter Sessions. Middlesex, ca. 1690. Osborn fb30

Wee whose names are hereunto subscribed & seals affixed being members of a Congregation of Christian protestant dissenters called Anabaptists meeting near Barbican in the parish of St. Giles without Cripplegate London Doe hereby certifie That Christopher Inch of the parish of St. Paul Shadwell in the County of Mid͠dx Baker is a — member of our s^d Congregation and that wee believe him to be an honest man a good protestant & well affected to the p^{r}sent governm^t though under Scruple of Conscience of Swearing in any Case whatsoever.
The 4th of May 1690./

To the right Worshipfull the justices of
for the County of Middle-sex

Wee whose names are hereunto subscribed & seals affixed being
members of a Congregation of Christian protestant dissenters called
Anabaptists meeting near Barbican in the parish of St Giles without
Cripplegate London Doe hereby certifie that Christopher Jucks of the
parish of St Paul Shadwell in the County of Midd: Baker is a
member of our sd Congregation and that wee beleive him to
be an honest man a good protestant & well affected to the present
governmt though under Scruple of Conscience of Swearing
in any Case whatsoever
this 4th of May 1690./

WM Smith

John Jarvis

William Elliott

Thomas Gason
Daniell Jowster
Henry Copley

Willm Woodland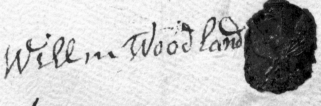

Rich: Drew

John Shotwell

John Skeate

John Redding

Robert all

Textual Structures

ROLL, CODEX, DOCUMENT

In his entry for "roll" in *A dictionary of the English language* (1755), Samuel Johnson cites a passage from Edmund Spenser's *The faerie qveene* (1590; fig. 54). Here, the "man of infinite remembrance"—an "old, old man, half blind"—sits in his library.

> His chamber all was hangd about with rolls,
> And old records from auncient times deriud,
> Some made in books, some in lõg parchment
>   scrolls,
> That were all worm-eaten, and full of canker
>   holes.

Spenser's "chamber of memory" highlights the intersections between format, or the material structure of a text, and genre, the type or category of textual content. For Spenser, the act of memory could be associated with the particular formats in which historical documents were most often found: parchment rolls and records, some in books. By 1755 the mustiness of this association could even underpin Johnson's second use of the passage as the example of the worm-eaten and its associations with the ruins of the archive.

There are three main formats, or material structures, for early modern English manuscripts: the roll or scroll; the codex; and the single-sheet document. Though potentially made from the same materials, the three formats have distinct structures. These also carried associations: as Johnson and Spenser indicate, a format might bear a set of connotations for its readers.

The roll (figs. 55–56; see also figs. 22–23) consists of a single linear strip of paper or parchment, usually made from multiple sections, or membranes, stitched or glued together. As texts, rolls can be oriented either vertically or horizontally. They are also frequently

> The yeares of *Neſtor* nothing were ſo his,
>   Ne yet *Mathuſalem* though longeſt liu'd;
>   For he remembred both their infancis:
>   Ne wonder then, if that he were depriu'd
>   Of natiue ſtrength now, that he them ſuruiu'd.
>   His chamber all was hangd about with rolls,
>   And old records from auncient times deriud,
>   Some made in books, ſome in lõg parchment ſcrolls,
> That were all worm-eaten, and full of canker holes.

Fig. 54. Edmund Spenser, *The faerie qveene. Disposed into twelue books* (London, 1590), Book II, 323. 2014 160

docketed on the exterior, with a title or summary of the contents (fig. 57). Rolls are not bound: they can be found loose, often housed in a box; they are also sometimes wrapped, tied, or mounted on rods or cords. By virtue of their format, rolls were often used for texts involving a linear narrative, such as heraldic or genealogical texts, or lists, such as inventories.

The codex is structured around the unit of the page. This is a deceptively simple statement: the page is to the codex as, say, sight is to the human body, a complicated intersection of material substratum and anatomical format. There are several technical terms that help to define and visualize the units of the codex: the sheet, or entire piece of paper or membrane of parchment, is folded one or more times to form a gathering. Each gathering consists of a set of openings, or the two pages facing each other across a fold, e.g., the right and left pages before you now. Each page represents one side of a leaf, or the front page and back page, also called the recto and verso. Leaves are foliated, i.e., counted as one unit, with a front (recto) and back (verso); pages are paginated,

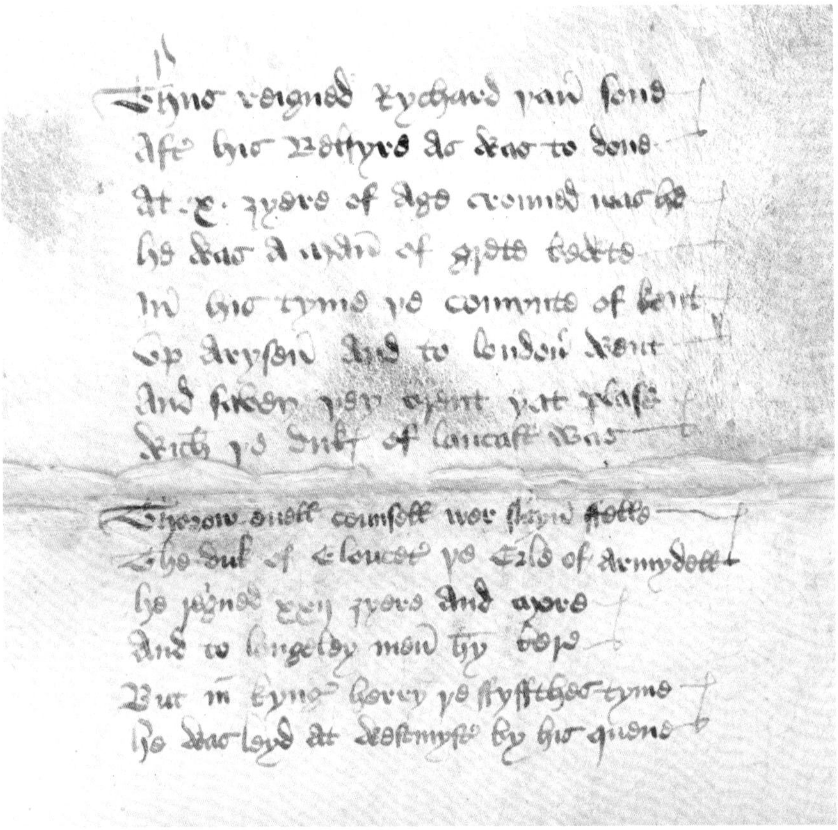

Fig. 55. Detail of the joining of two membranes, in a copy of John Lydgate, The kings of England sithen William the Conqueror. England, 1475–99. Osborn a14

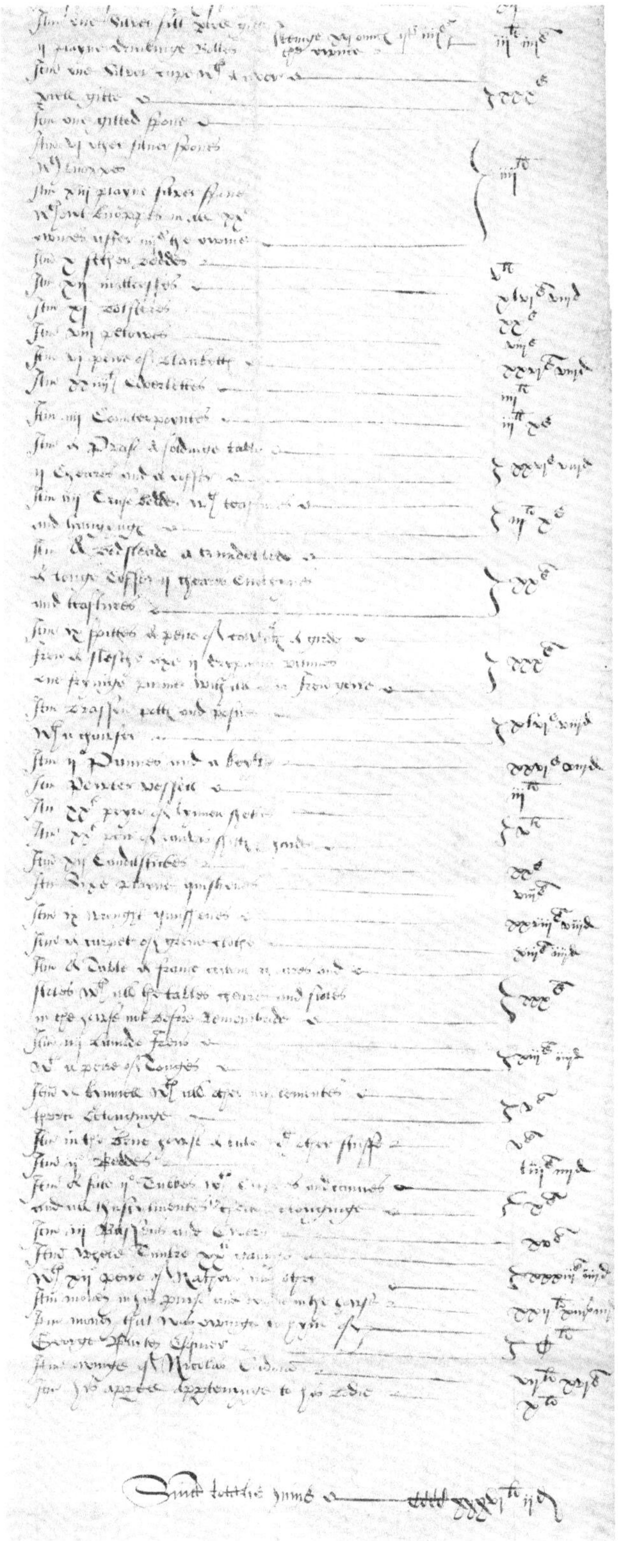

Fig. 56. Detail, inventory on parchment of the goods of Sir Peter Frescheville. Stavley, England, November 25, 1559. Osborn a33

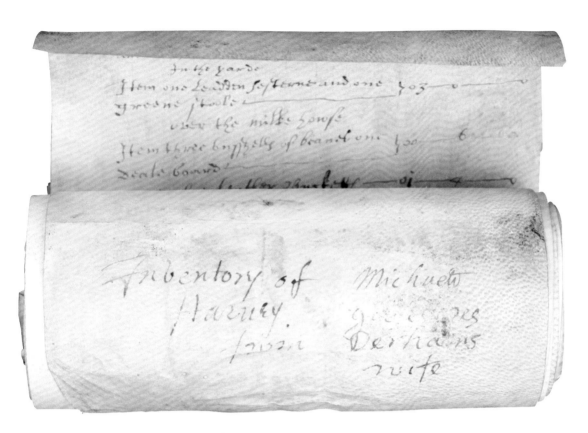

Fig. 57. Detail of the docket to the exterior of an
inventory roll on parchment. England, April–May 1634.
Osborn b375

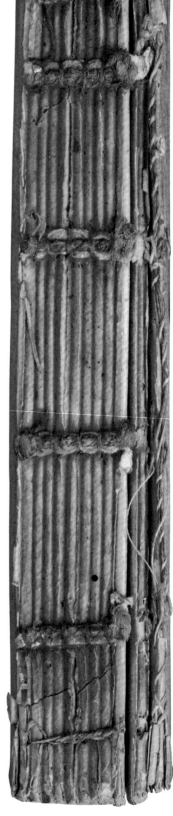

Fig. 58. Exposed text block. Notebook kept by
William Camden. England, ca. 1600. Beinecke
MS 370

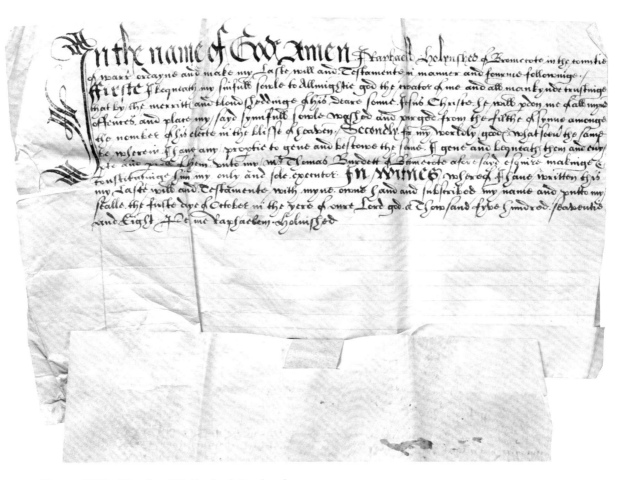

Fig. 59. Will of Raphael Holinshed. England,
October 1, 1578. Osborn a61

or counted individually. The codex is formed when these gatherings—that is, the individual units of the substratum, usually paper or parchment, folded one or more times—are quite literally gathered together and stitched to form a text block (fig. 58).

The textual structure, or format, informs the process by which text is produced. For a printed book, text would be printed on the sheets of the substratum before these were folded, gathered, and stitched into the codex format. For a manuscript codex (and, in fact, for a manuscript roll or document), text would be added to the codex after it was created. The textual structure also shaped creators' and readers' expectations of how a text was meant to operate. By contrast with the roll or document, the movement of the codex is horizontal and organized around the page. Pages are seen together, as an opening. They move

dimensionally in space as they are turned: up, toward the reader, and down. Where the roll's primary axis is two-dimensional, the codex works in multiple dimensions and directions.

The document (fig. 59) is created by a single piece of substratum, whether parchment, paper, silk, or other material. Documents can be large or small: a letter might be folded to fit into the palm of a hand, while a charter might use an entire parchment skin. Documents can also be produced in print, manuscript, or hybrid form, e.g., a printed form completed by hand. As a format, documents come in many guises, including letters; notes; individual or institutional forms, such as wills; contracts; receipts; and other types of legal, administrative, financial, or personal records.

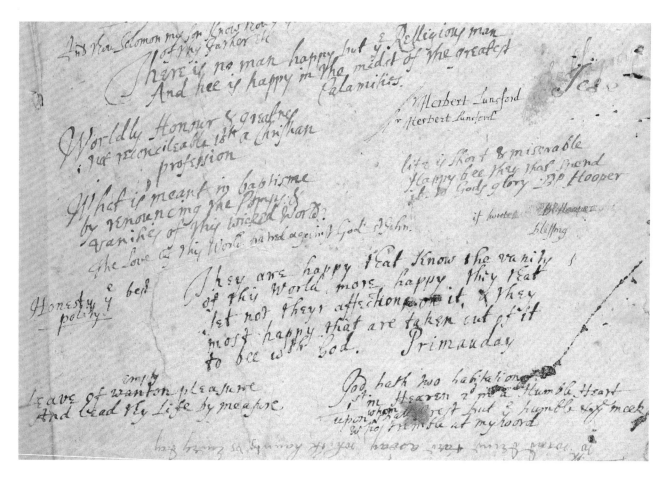

Fig. 60. Detail, Notes on happiness. From Richard
Fitzherbert, Commonplace book, front fixed endpaper.
England, ca. 1630–70. Osborn fb252

MARGINS AND ENDPAPERS

Both the structure of the page and the bound codex are
designed to preserve the text from harm, whether from
injury, loss, dirt, weather, or simple accidents of for-
tune. The purpose of the margin is to protect the text,
providing a barrier between the edge of the text column and that of the substratum. The margin also plays
an important aesthetic and literary role in shaping
the space of the text column on the page. In marking
the edge of the text, the margin also provides a place
for the reader's hands to hold or turn the page—and
to add handwritten notes. In his instructions on
note-taking, or commonplacing, John Locke tells his
readers to structure their blank books from the index
and the margin, working backward from the apparatus
of the notebook to the space allocated for content:

The Index being thus made, I mark out, in the
other Pages of the Book, the Margin with Black
Lead; I make it about the bigness of an Inch, or a
little bigger, if the Volume be in *Folio,* but in a less
Volume the Margin is proportionably less also.[65]

The endpaper is another protective device within
the bound codex. It acts as a kind of wrapper, protecting the text from the binding, and offering a cover
around which the binding can be sewn. In performing
this function, the endpaper also provides a textual
space often inhabited by readers and writers, like
Richard Fitzherbert, making notes on happiness
and other subjects for his commonplace book in the
mid-seventeenth century (fig. 60).

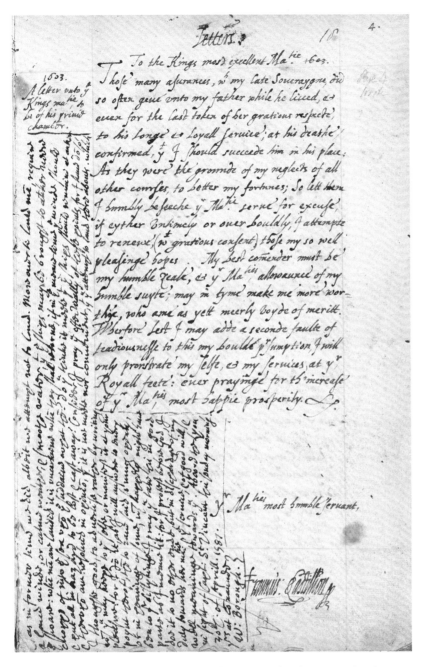

Fig. 61. Francis Castillion, Notebook, 4r. England,
ca. 1590–1638. Osborn fb69

OPENINGS AND PAGES

The opening is the unit of text presented to the reader by a particular format. An opening in a roll acts and moves differently than an opening in a codex. The reader can control the opening of the roll (see fig. 22), or the unit of visible text, in a way that isn't possible with the codex. A roll might be divided by its constituent membranes, the sections of parchment or paper that are joined together to form the overall roll; these membranes bear no necessary relationship to the text (see fig. 55).

By contrast, the structure of the codex is framed around the opening, with its two constituent pages. When overlaid with text, the codex can create the expectation of meaning simply by joining two discrete pages into a single opening, reinforcing an impression of contiguity or interconnection. As Francis Castillion shows in his notebook from the early seventeenth century, the writer could also simply ignore the conventions of the codex, organizing text over an opening or page (fig. 61).

A writer or reader also forms a relationship, over time, with textual structures. A particular document, codex, or roll will carry the reader's weight of expectation that it will act like any document, or any codex, or any roll, a specific instantiation of a generic type. In this space of convention, between the iteration and the rule, one sometimes finds moments of playfulness or surprise: a letter-writer might ignore the social conventions of spacing on the page, or might fold his letter to send in a size that its recipient might find transgressively small and personal.[66] In copying one letter, Francis Castillion might turn his book to the side, secure in the knowledge that his codex would work just as well at a ninety-degree angle.

RULING AND LINES

Text acts in space: its negative spaces define its boundaries and edges, the structures that inform both the writer's and the reader's engagement. Often in medieval and early modern manuscripts, the page is ruled: lines are drawn to mark the planned shape of the text on the blank space of the paper or parchment of the substratum. Ruling, or the marking of the text block and (often but not always) the lines within it, was most often done in dry point, lead, or ink. One technique was to take the folded pages, pierce or prick them in a stack, and then draw or rule the lines from the holes on each page (figs. 62–63). Because the holes were in the same place on each page, the lines and shape of the text would also line up on each page.

Fig. 62. Detail, showing pricking marks.
England, mid-16th century. Beinecke MS 558

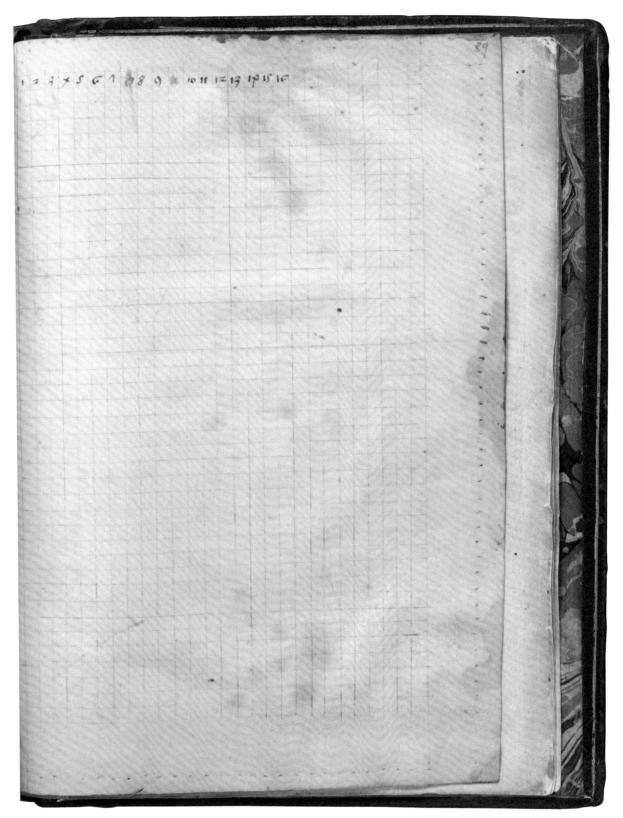

Fig. 63. Page pricked and ruled for a mathematical table. England, mid-16th century. Beinecke MS 558

The first page of text in Osborn fa50 shows the spaces created by ruling (fig. 64). Vertical and horizontal lines demarcate the space of the text, framing a margin on all four sides. This margin has a distinct proportion, following a Renaissance standard: thin at the inner margin, closest to the gutter or binding of the book; thin at the top edge; slightly deeper on the front edge, by the opening of the book; widest at the bottom. The overall effect of ruling is to organize and regulate the textual space, both for the text's copyist and for its audiences.

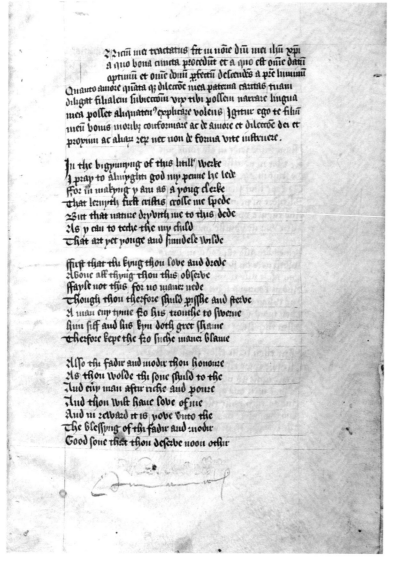

Fig. 64. Peter Idle, Instructions to his Son. England, late 15th century. Osborn fa50. Space was left for an initial that was never added.

BINDING STRUCTURES

Binding structures serve one overarching function: to organize a set of sheets or leaves into a working codex. In protecting a text and allowing a volume to be stored or housed, bindings also shape the lives of the objects they enclose. To scholars of early modern manuscript culture, the binding can help to reveal a text's intended use, or uses. It can also offer some indication, although often unclear, of a volume's perceived meaning or value to an owner at some point in its history.

Early modern binding structures show the many different expectations of text, and the situations in which readers expected to use and store them. Letters, receipts, or legal and administrative documents might be filed or housed in boxes or chests. A reader might use a printed almanac as a diary or to keep notes, and house it in a wallet binding, to be carried (figs. 65–66).

Text might begin in one form and later assume another. Texts might be copied into a bound blank notebook (fig. 67). They might also be bound later: first written on a quire of paper, and then perhaps later stab-stitched into a paper or parchment wrapper or gathered with other quires into a more elaborate binding structure (fig. 68). A writer might also use a tacket binding, in which a simple external sewing structure allowed quires to be added or removed from a collection (fig. 69).

Texts were also produced from the outset with an understanding of how (or whether) they would be preserved. A letter might be produced with no intention, on its writer's part, that its recipient would bind the letter into a volume. An administrative document might be written under the assumption that it would be housed in a chest or box, alongside other records. Later owners might reverse or alter these decisions: a letter might later be bound into a collector's album; a text might later have been disbound, perhaps if it was removed from a volume. A collector might decide to rebind a work, perhaps to highlight the changed understanding or value of a particular text, or simply to protect a text from a no longer adequate binding structure.

Fig. 65. Wallet binding in which Edward Benet kept
his manuscript notebook and *British Merlin* (1706).
England, ca. 1706–10. OSB MSS 184, Box 48, Folder 367

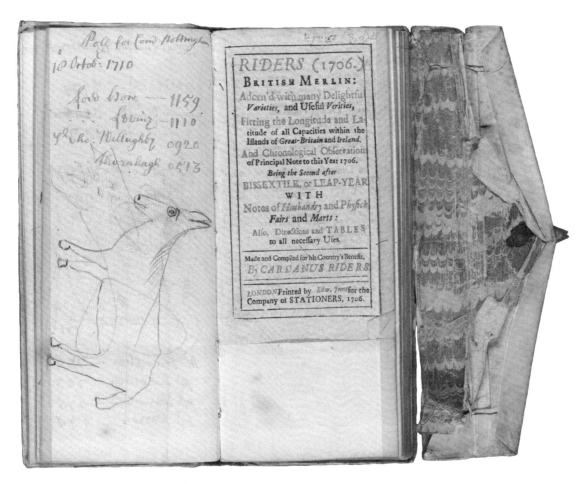

Fig. 66. Inside cover of the wallet binding (fig. 65),
showing the inlaid almanac, Benet's notes on a 1710
poll for the county of Nottingham, and an anonymous
writer's drawing of a horse.

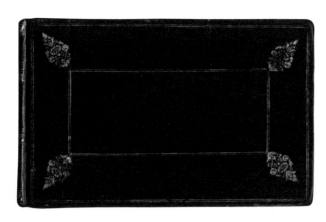

Fig. 67. Pocket-sized oblong white paper notebook,
filled with recipes, bound in gilt-stamped calf.
England, late 17th century. Osborn b115

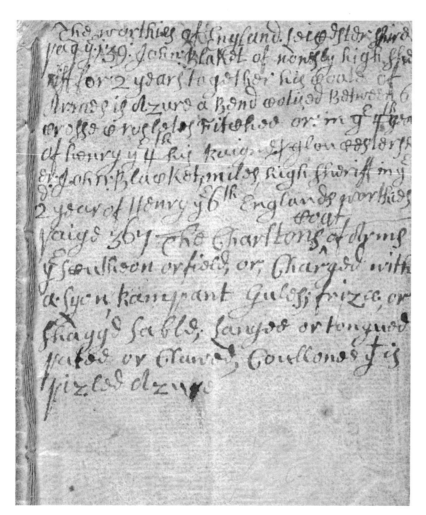

Fig. 68. Detail of cover annotated with notes
on a paper wrapper, stitched with packthread.
England, ca. 1690. Osborn Manuscript File 19745

Fig. 69. Tacket-style binding. Richard Tayler,
Notebook. England, ca. 1766–67. Osborn c438

For scholars of early modern English manuscripts, the bound codex represents something of a paradox: while a far less prevalent format for manuscripts in the early modern period, by comparison with epistolary or administrative documents, the bound codex remains the form in which certain genres of manuscript are most often encountered. Miscellanies, recipe or household books, account books, and literary texts are more likely to have been transmitted in bound codices, while correspondence or other documentary collections often remained unbound, or were bound into albums during or after the nineteenth century.

Fig. 70. Parchment binding. England, ca. 1571. Beinecke MS 610. Note the laced binding supports on the left, which attach the parchment wrapper to the text block.

As bound codices, early modern English manuscripts generally resembled their printed counterparts. Whether for a printed or manuscript work, the codex binding takes a deceptively simple form. The quires of paper or parchment that comprise the entire text are stitched together to form a text block (see fig. 58). The text block, in turn, is then attached to its enclosure by a sewing structure. At its simplest, the enclosure might be a vellum or paper wrapper (figs. 70–71). For a more elaborate binding, the text block was attached to boards, either of wood (typically oak) or, later, paste- or pulpboard. In the volume's interior, the boards were often covered in waste, or scrap paper; these pastedowns and endpapers (front and rear) act to protect the text block from damage, including damage from the binding's own covering material. The spine might also be padded with waste paper. This structure was then wrapped in an external cladding of leather, textile, or other material (figs. 72–73).

Common early modern binding materials include parchment (often called vellum), calf, and morocco (goat) leather. Decorative features were also common: the edges of the text block might be stained or gilded; stamped or colored papers were also used as external wrappers or interior pastedowns. In later volumes, marbled paper was often used as a decorative endpaper. Last, the binding might be decorated: with a panel, stamped and tooled with gilt on the spine or covers (figs. 74–75); initialed; or, for parchment or paper bindings, given a title in ink on the front or spine (see fig. 202).[67]

The binding can also indicate expense, or a book's presence in a particular owner's library. Yet bindings can often be ambiguous or misleading, as a representation of the value placed on a book by an early owner. An otherwise generic calf-bound notebook might have been consumed as writing space by its owner, every inch covered in text (see fig. 67). Equally, a manuscript might have been presented as a New Year's gift to the court, to be bound sumptuously in a royal binding— whether or not it had ever actually been read (fig. 75).

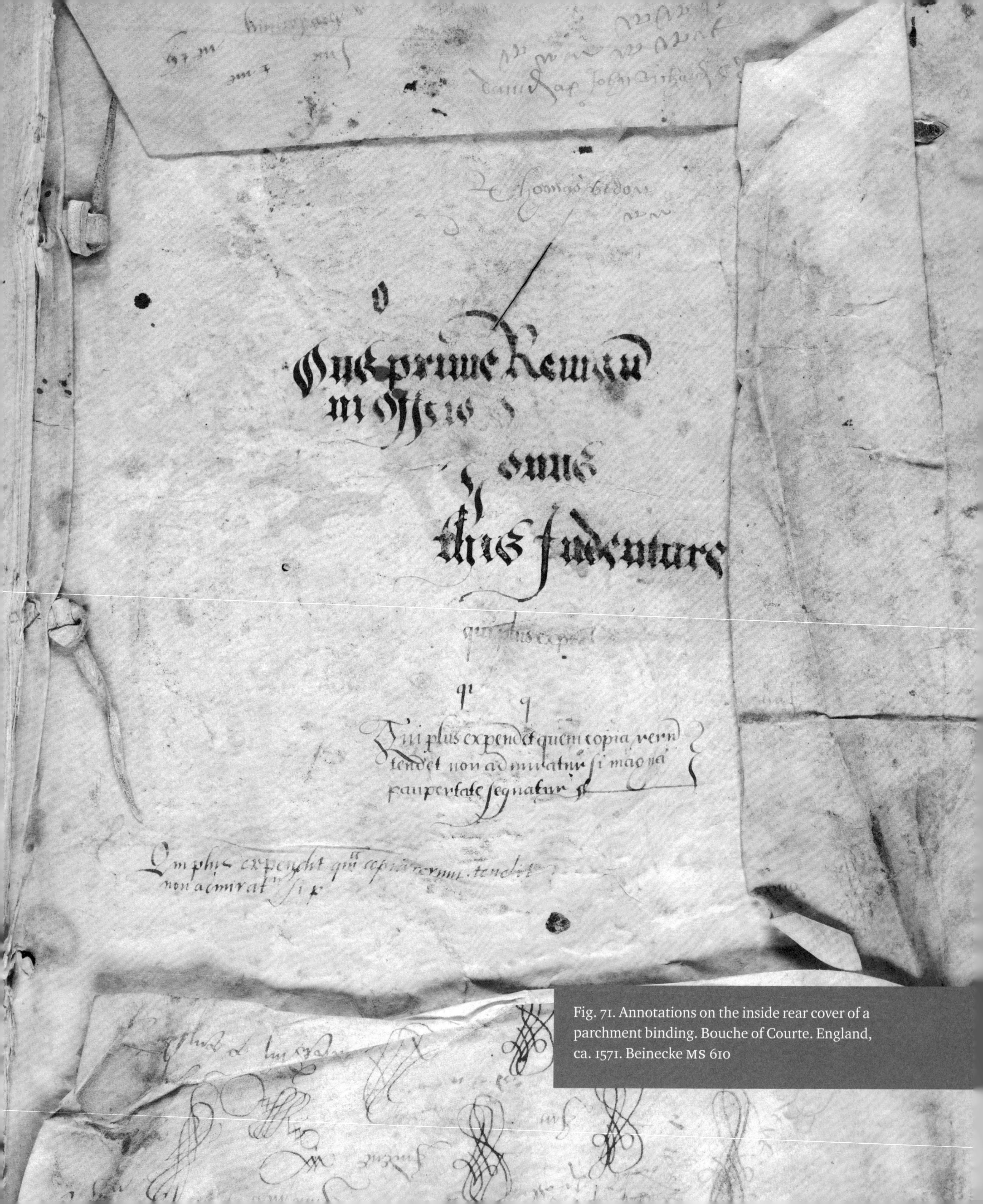

Fig. 71. Annotations on the inside rear cover of a parchment binding. Bouche of Courte. England, ca. 1571. Beinecke MS 610

Fig. 73. Verso of embroidered binding, in silver thread, for a manuscript notebook of recipes and poems. England, ca. 1684. Osborn b226

Fig. 72. Front interior binding of a volume holding copies of cases from the Court of Arches. Papers from the Court of Arches. London, ca. 1620–35. Osborn fb24. Note the front board, of pasteboard; the marks of the sewing structure attaching the text block and the front board; and the calfskin binding, with one (of two) green silk ties still attached.

Fig. 74. Detail of a stamped binding, bound between 1521 and 1546 by the Cambridge bookbinder Nicholas Spierinck. Me35 +J764 1521

Fig. 75. Gilt-stamped royal binding on a manuscript presented to James VI & I. George Waymouth, Jewell of Artes. England, 1603. Beinecke MS 565

STORAGE, FURNITURE, SPACES

"In the highest Boxe," begins this page of an Elizabethan inventory of the royal papers and documents held in Whitehall Palace (fig. 76). The papers on this page move across time: an early entry relates to Henry VIII's reign; later entries concern records from the cataloger's near present, in the thirty-first year of Elizabeth I's reign. An earlier page is entitled simply "Old thinges," reinforcing the papers' temporal identity as understood by their cataloger.

The inventory offers insight into the conditions in which books, manuscripts, and documents were often housed in the early modern period. The writer of this inventory is clearly situated in a particular space, working through the contents of the "highest Boxe" in a room almost certainly also containing lower boxes. This "highest Boxe" also holds a tremendous documentary variety, offering us a glimpse of the forms and genres through which political bureaucracy was administratively enacted: a bundle of letters, a manuscript account book, a declaration, a grant, a copy of a treaty, a financial estimate.

Inventories like this hint at early modern archival and housing practices. Documents are often described as held within book chests, book boxes, and other containers; inventories also directed their readers to look in a particular size of chest, held in a particular location, to find certain manuscripts. The "highest Boxe" at Whitehall, with its surprising jumble of documents, calls to mind William Henry Ireland's "oaken chest," with its archival abundance. The inventory reinforces the recognizable quality of Ireland's wooden chest as a literary device, one likely to have been just familiar enough to his readers to seem plausible.

The Whitehall inventory also invites us to consider that documents were often housed separately from books—and were likely perceived as quite different textual objects by their producers and owners. Just as a public library and a government record office might serve entirely different functions in our period, so early modern records, archives, documents, literary manuscripts, printed ephemera, and printed codices might share the common category of text, while serving entirely different ends and occupying entirely separate spaces (fig. 77).

The textual object might seem more text-like (or more object-like), in varying contexts. As Jeff Knight reminds us, books acted both as subject and object within spaces:

Fig. 76. Inventory of the Archives at Whitehall, 1347–1589, f. 3r. England, ca. 1589. Beinecke MS 927

[Left margin: In the highest Boxe.] Tempus Regis Henrici Octavi

A Bundell of l~res of Mr Robert Wyngfeild the kinges Amb^d in France towchinge the entreveiwe betwene the kings Matie and the French kinge

A l~re of the Quene of Hungary sister to the Queene Katherine queene of England advertizinge of her marriadge and coronacon dated 1522 A° Regis 14°

A Booke of the Army sent into France und^r the charge of the duke of Suffolk Anno 1522 Reges 15°

A l~re of Mr Style the kinges Amb^r wth the kinge of Arragon toutchinge the kings marriadge to the Lady Katherine his brothers wyddow

In the highest Boxe.   Tempus Regis Henrici Octavi

A Bundell of lres of Mr Robert wyngfeild the kinges Amb in
France towchinge the entrevewe betwene the kinge Matie and the
frensh kinge

A lre of the Quene of Hungary sister to the Quene Katherine
quene of England advertisinge of her marriadge and coronacon
dated 1522 Ao Regis 11°

A Booke of the Army sent into France under the charge of the
Duke of Suffolk Anno 1522 Regis 15°

A lre of Mr Style the kinges Amb wth the kinge of Arragon
towchinge the kinge marriadge to the lady Katherine his brothers
wyddow

A declaration delivered to kinge Henry the 8 by the under Threr
of the Exchequ of all fees and wages paid out of the recept
of the Exchequ the 13th yeare of kinge Henry the 7th

A lre of Sr Thomas Spinelli to the kinge beinge the Agent
of the late kinge in the lowe Countries Dated 15 Junij 1509

A lour of Mr Richard Jernyngham to the kinge Ao 1510
advertisinge of hire of Armors bought for his matie at Milan
c of the state of the frensh in Italie at that tyme

A graunte made by the kinge to the Quene his wife of certaine
royalties and freedomes in landes of her Joynture

A coppie of a treaty betwene Comissions of the kinge of
England & of Charles prince of Spaine after the dorease
of the Arch duke Phillypp

An estimate of the charge of an Army of 20000 men
for the land and fiftye shipps for the Sea for the space of
three yeares for a voyage to be made by the kinge to the Holy
land.

Like the walls, pots, tables, bed pillars, and other domestic objects whose significance was at once material and semiotic, books formed part of the physical environment that conditioned the intellectual environment of their users.[68]

Books were a type of furniture, a possession to be itemized as property in an inventory. As objects, they also need to be put away, to be stored somewhere when not in use. The ways in which books and documents are housed can reveal the expectations of their use, and the roles of the textual object within the domestic or institutional space.

Both probate inventories and sale catalogs indicate that early modern libraries were often arranged by size. Folios, quartos, and octavos were housed on shelves or in presses accommodating the size of the bound volumes. As Leedham-Green observes in her study of probate inventories, this could also by default lead to some arrangement by subject:

> It is neither a coincidence nor, probably, any manifestation of reverence, that so many of the more substantial lists open with the multi-volume folio compilations of works of the Fathers. Similarly, medical lists are inclined to start with Galen and Hippocrates, and legal ones with the civil and/or canon course. By the same token, monographs, tracts, individual sermons and books of more nugatory import often appear towards the end of the lists.[69]

Other material aspects of books reveal their life, as objects, being stored or read. In the early modern period, books often had their title (or an abridged version) written on the fore-edge of the pages, as the volumes were shelved with the pages facing outward. Bindings can also hint at a book's early owners and audiences. As Burnett Streeter has remarked, the use of chains to attach library books to their shelves within early modern English institutions had significant consequences for the design of libraries as architectural and reading spaces (fig. 78). "A chained book cannot be read unless there is some kind of desk or table on which to rest it *within the length of the chain,*" he observes; "Again, since a chained book cannot be moved to the window, the window must be near the book; that determined the plan of the building."[70] Although it might seem restrictive to us (and, one can only imagine, also to early modern readers), the chained binding is actually an indication of use. In Streeter's analysis, English cathedral and college libraries moved from housing their books in chests or cupboards in the medieval period to systems in which they were organized around presses, or bookcases, designed for use by readers.[71]

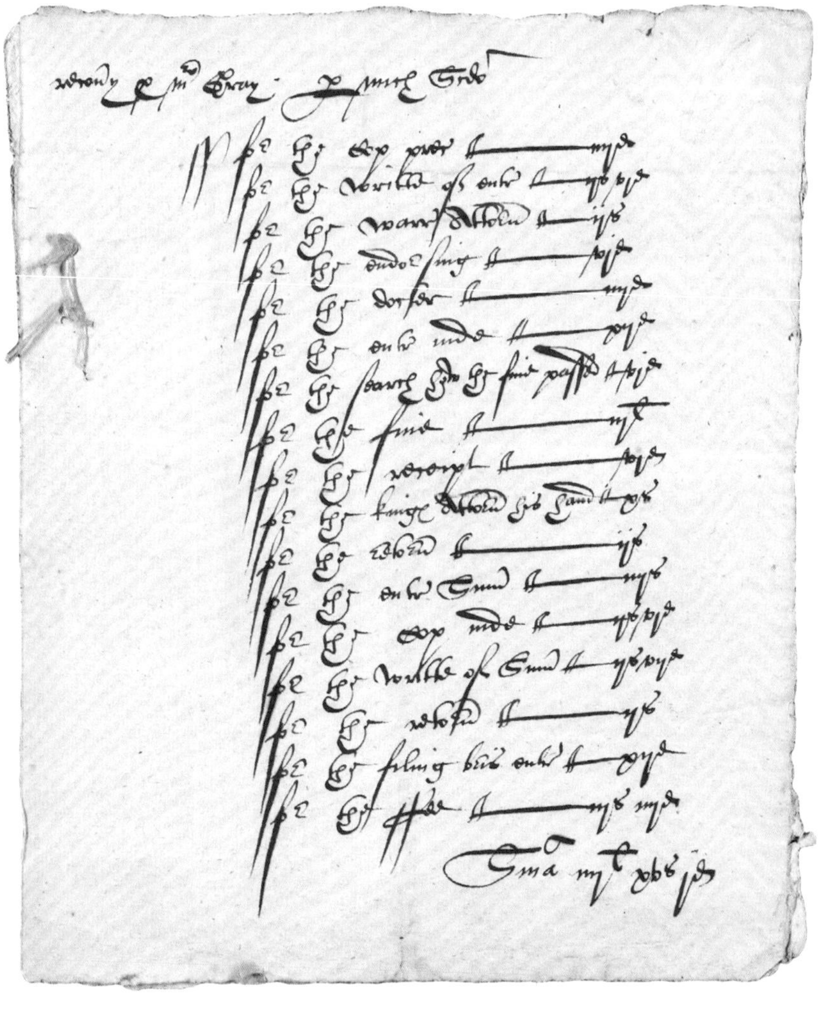

Fig. 77. This legal bill was strung with thread to be filed. England, ca. 1600. OSB MSS 184, Box 48, Folder 367

Fig. 78. Chained binding, for a book bound between 1521 and 1546 by the Cambridge bookbinder Nicholas Spierinck. Me35 +J764 1521. Note the title, written on the fore-edge, as the volume would have been housed with its fore-edge facing out.

Writing and Writers

Writing was work, undertaken by individuals across occupations and professions and in the course of daily life. As work, writing often required specialized training, drawing on a writer's knowledge of varying hands or different legal or financial forms. Writing was a set of practices that had to be taught: children learned to write the alphabet; students learned to copy notes; clerks and other professional writers learned the hands and forms of the writing trades.

Manuscript informed the structures of daily life for literate men and women. Doodles in the margins of copybooks, sums, letters, sermon notes, poems, family trees, excerpts from their reading, and other forms of evidence show us writers at work (figs. 79–80). Early modern English writers were authors and recipients of many kinds of text, including those for publication or circulation in manuscript or print.

Last, writing was the means by which the state controlled its resources, including the records of its citizens. Parish records record the births and deaths of their inhabitants; wills and probate inventories mark the passing of individuals. These and other records document the accounts, in lives or sums, of the spheres of local, parish, church, and state governance in early modern England (fig. 81).

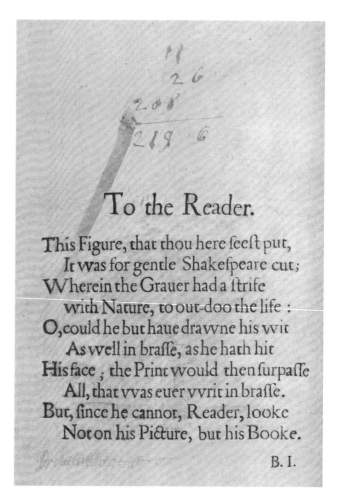

Fig. 79. Detail, a writer's sum, perhaps calculating a debt, on the frontispiece of this copy of the first folio edition of Shakespeare's plays. *Mr. William Shakespeares comedies, histories, & tragedies* (London, 1623). 1978 +83

Fig. 80. Detail, notes by Francis Castillion in his notebook, p. 192. England, ca. 1590–1638. Osborn fb69

Fig. 81. Detail, indenture of receipt by John Williams, Master of the Jewels, for ceremonial plate and jewels collected from religious houses. England, February 27, 1540. Osborn fa37. See also fig. 280.

PROFESSIONAL WRITERS

"A kinde of Officer (as I may so tearme him) betwixt a Clerke and a Scriuener that is conuersant in Paper-businesses," wrote Mateo Alemán in *The rogve: or the second part of the life of Guzman de Alfarache* (1623).[72] These "Paper-businesses"—satirized by Thomas Rowlandson in "A Merchant's Office" (fig. 82)—were the profession of many writers in early modern England, employed in composing or copying manuscripts for a living. This chapter introduces several of the main categories of professional writers, both those who wrote and those who taught others to write. These figures populate English literature, just as they inhabited the offices, household, and public or domestic spaces in which paper business was conducted each day in early modern England.

Clerks and Scriveners

When William Henry Ireland confessed to forgery, he described how he had used seventeenth-century legal documents (and the parchment on which they were written) found in the law office in which he was articled, in order to craft Shakespeare's "legal instruments."[73] At every level, from the copying of documents to the recording of Parliamentary proceedings, the profession of law produced a significant amount of writing (fig. 83). The English judicial system hinged on the services of clerks and scriveners, professional writers who recorded depositions, copied evidence

Fig. 82. Thomas Rowlandson, "A Merchant's Office." England, 1789. Watercolor with pen, ink, and graphite on paper. Yale Center for British Art. B1977.14.150

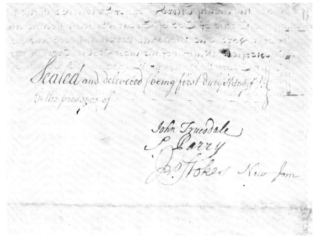

and documents, and produced contracts and other legal documents in the required legal form, or template (fig. 84). Early modern documentary evidence has for the most part been created through the mediation of clerks and scriveners, who copied, transcribed, or recorded the words of other people. In witnessing or authorizing documents, these figures often leave traces of their own lives: in *Ralph Tailor's Summer* (2011), Keith Wrightson traced the wills and inventories notarized by a scrivener in Newcastle during an outbreak of the plague.

Different spheres of the English legal world produced varying types of manuscripts. The Inns of Court regulated the profession of barrister, or lawyer called "to the bar" and admitted into practice in the courtroom. These comprised several independent institutions: Gray's Inn, Lincoln's Inn, the Middle Temple, and the Inner Temple. All were located near the boundary of the City of London and Westminster, where the courts were then sited. The Inns of Court were an important educational institution, drawing young students from wealthy and less wealthy families to study law.[74] They were also a crucial site for the circulation of popular culture, like manuscript copies of satirical or otherwise unpublished poetry, which flourished within the confined circle of the Inns of

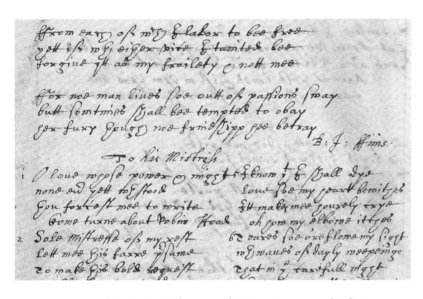

Fig. 85. Detail, poems by Ben Jonson and John Donne. Professional scribal copy. England, early 17th century. Osborn b148

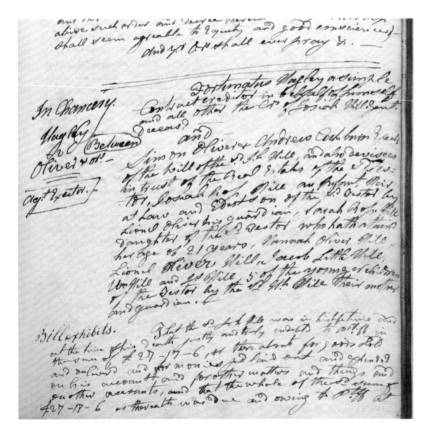

Fig. 86. Detail, a copy of a bill in the Court of Chancery, relating to a dispute over the estate of Josiah Hill, deceased in infancy. England, ca. 1810. OSB MSS 184, Box 12, Folder 71

Court in the early decades of the seventeenth century (fig. 85). As Harold Love observed, for the many poets and authors who studied at the Inns of Court, collecting and exchanging scribally published poetry "would be the counterpart of a student today becoming involved in the University literary magazine."[75]

The Court of Chancery was another key institution for the training and employment of legal clerks. The court addressed pleas outside the common law, directed to the monarch and, subsequently, the Lord Chancellor. These cases involved civil disputes on issues relating to property, contracts, estate management, and other areas. The Court of Chancery was a significant records body; it was overseen by the Master of Rolls, who supervised the clerks and clerk apprentices who wrote and kept these records (fig. 86). As we will see, the Court of Chancery also exerted a significant influence on English handwriting in the late medieval and early modern period.

Other branches of English Crown and legal administration included the common law courts in the judicial districts of the realm. These were overseen by local Justices of the Peace, with regular meetings of the circuit court and, at the highest judicial level, the assize court. Matthew Hale (1609–1676), a judge, political servant, and legal scholar on the common law, kept a diary when on circuit, in 1668 (fig. 87).[76] Ecclesiastical courts oversaw the jurisdiction of the Church of England, as in an example from the Court of Arches (see fig. 266), which oversaw those cases on morality or other matters of church jurisdiction referred from the parish church or bishop to the attention of the archbishop. The Exchequer was another significant branch of Crown administration, overseeing the accounts, debts, transactions, and arrangements of all financial matters relating to the Crown. In all cases, these branches of the English judicial system employed clerks, trained to produce documents according to particular legal requirements and forms.

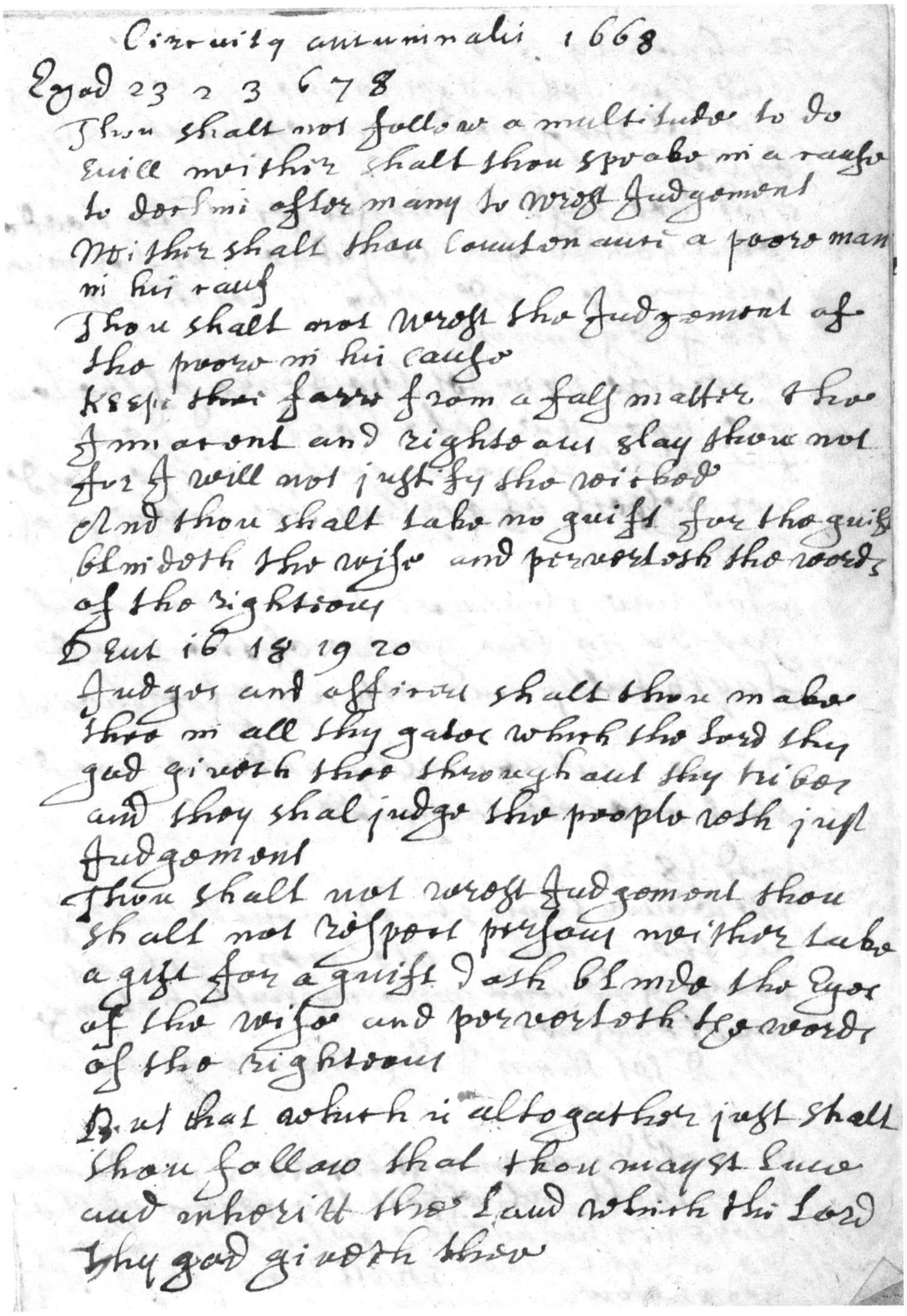

Fig. 87. Matthew Hale, Holograph diary, kept on tour of the circuit court, p. 3. England, 1668. Osborn Manuscript File 6450

Circuitij autumnalis 1668

Exod 23 2 3 6 7 8 [Exodus 23:2, 3, 6, 7, 8]
Thou shalt not follow a multitude to do
Euill neither shalt thou speake in a cause
to decline after many to wrest Judgement
Neither shalt thou countenance a poore man
in his caus
Thou shalt not wrest the Judgement of
the poore in his cause
Keepe thee farre from a fals matter the
Innocent and righteous slay thou not
for I will not justify the wicked
And thou shalt take no guift for the guift
blindeth the wise and perverteth the words
of the rightious

Fig. 88. Jean-Puget de la Serre, *The secretary in fashion: or, an elegant and compendious way of writing all manner of letters,* 6th ed. (London, 1683), frontispiece and title page. 1992 227

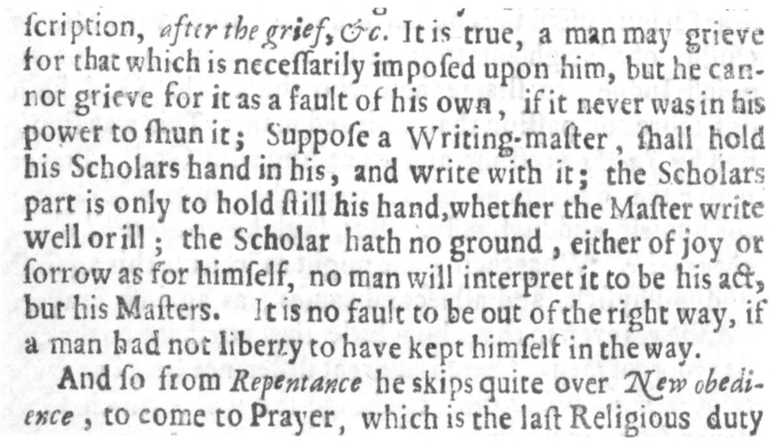

fcription, *after the grief, &c.* It is true, a man may grieve for that which is neceffarily impofed upon him, but he cannot grieve for it as a fault of his own, if it never was in his power to fhun it; Suppofe a Writing-mafter, fhall hold his Scholars hand in his, and write with it; the Scholars part is only to hold ftill his hand, whether the Mafter write well or ill; the Scholar hath no ground, either of joy or sorrow as for himfelf, no man will interpret it to be his act, but his Mafters. It is no fault to be out of the right way, if a man had not liberty to have kept himfelf in the way.

And fo from *Repentance* he skips quite over *New obedience*, to come to Prayer, which is the laft Religious duty

Fig. 89. Detail, Thomas Hobbes, *The questions concerning liberty, necessity, and chance* (London, 1656), 145 (i.e., 155). K8 H65 k656. Hobbes adopts the writing master as metaphor in his discussion of free will.

Secretaries and Amanuenses

The secretary or amanuensis was another category of professional writer (fig. 88).[77] Employed within a household or office, they become visible as proxies: writers of letters, editors, researchers, and in other guises as the hand of their employer. Secretaries and amanuenses are often difficult to identify, discernible only as a different hand in a series of letters or other writing. As Ann Blair has observed, "while few early modern scholars collaborated directly with peers, almost all relied on the help of others who were considered intellectual and social inferiors and were typically omitted from explicit mention."[78]

Writing Masters

From the late sixteenth century, ideas of the public weal encompassed a powerful political vision of the importance of writing in the English language (fig. 89). In his *Positions…for the training up of children* (London, 1581), the schoolteacher Richard Mulcaster presented his view of the formative role of writing in relation to language and a child's moral character:

> The same reasons which moued me to haue the child read English before Latin, do moue me also, to wishe him to write English before Latin, as a thing of more hardnesse, and redier in use to aunswere all occasions. Thus farre I do thinke that all my countreymen will ioyne with me, and allow their children the use, of their letter and penne.[79]

In his *Elementarie…of the right writing of our English tung* (1582), Mulcaster went further, writing that:

> I handle speciallie in it the right writing of our English tung, a verie necessarie point, and of force to be handled, ear the child be taught to read, which reading is the first principle of the hole Elementarie. For can reading be right before writing be righted, seing we read nothing else, but what we se writen?[80]

Mulcaster emphasizes the moral force of "the right writing of our English tung." The moment of writing instruction was also one in which students absorbed, and learned to understand, the moral precepts they copied in their exercises.[81]

In 1616 the writing master Richard Gething published his *A coppie-booke of the usuall hands,* with its title page engraved in elaborate flourishes like a pattern of lace (fig. 90). The title page advertises the book for sale at Gething's house, on Fetter Lane, and at the "signe of the hande and golden Penne," located in St. Paul's churchyard. Writing masters like Gething had offered their services in London at least since the late sixteenth century, and the profession began particularly to flourish after the Restoration. In the seventeenth century, writing masters can be found advertising their services in broadsides and penmanship manuals, inviting students in the arts of writing and, often, arithmetic. These advertisements often list the premises at which students, male and female, would be taught during "grammar school hours," or offered private tuition in the home.[82]

Fig. 90. Richard Gething, *A coppie-booke of the usuall hands* (1616). Elizabethan Club, Yale University. Eliz +10. Gething held a writing school at his house on Fetter Lane, "at the signe of the hande and golden Penne."

Spaces for Writing

Writing is always situated in place. Mulcaster's students imbibed their penmanship in the English schoolroom; the scriveners and writers of the "mistery of the court letter" practiced within a strictly bounded perimeter of the City of London. Then as now, the constraints governing writing are always also those informing the movement of individuals in the world: gender, class, occupation, education, political or religious affiliation.

In his "Allegory of Trade" (fig. 91), the English painter John Theodore Heins situates his actors outside, on a Venetian promontory, winged Mercury overlooking from his plinth. In the foreground, two merchants are consulting on a document: the one kneels to write with his quill; the other stands over him to intervene, perhaps dictating or offering a correction. Behind the writer and his colleague, the scrum of daily commerce continues with hardly a glance in their direction. Writing is here the incidental relational outcome of commerce: a note, a receipt, a contract. Heins's object is to comment on trade and its relations: yet the painting highlights the often comical difficulties presented by writing in the wrong space, whether simply in an exterior rather than interior space, or within the more figurative spaces of profession, education, gender, race, and class.

Fig. 91. John Theodore Heins, "Allegory of Trade," 1743. Oil on canvas. Yale Center for British Art, Paul Mellon Collection. B1981.25.330

Writing was framed within the relational spaces of early modern England, organized by and organizing the architecture of daily life (fig. 92). In this mid-eighteenth-century portrait, or conversation piece, of the Buckley-Boar family (fig. 93), writing also marks the structures of power within the family circle. From left to right, the portrait shows the father, holding a quill in one hand and a letter in the other, looking toward the mother, who is seated next to the children. Seated at a table, pencil and paper in hand, the son stops to look at the viewer; on one side, the first sister holds her toy bird; on the other, the second winds her embroidery thread. Standing incongruously with his pen and letter in the sitting room, far from an ink stand or other accoutrements of writing, the father acts to delineate the figurative power of writing within the social structure of the family.[83]

We find a similar table and domestic space in an engraving by Louis Truchy (fig. 94).[84] In this image, modeled on an influential series of twelve paintings by Joseph Highmore from 1744, we find the heroine of Samuel Richardson's bestselling novel *Pamela; or, virtue rewarded* (1740–41). The caption reads: "Pamela is represented in this first Piece, writing in her late Lady's dressing room, her History being known only by her letters. She is here surprised by M[r]. B. who improves this occasion to further his designs."

Here, writing marks the relational discord at the core of the novel. Pamela is surprised in the dressing room of her employer's deceased mother. The table before her is littered with the equipment to write those letters to her own mother that drive the epistolary motion of the novel: two sizes of paper, her quill, a writing box. In this, the first letter, Pamela tells her mother the results of the scene we observe:

I have been scared out of my Senses; for just now, as I was folding this Letter, in my late Lady's Dressing-room, in comes my young Master! Good Sirs! how was I frightned! I went to hide the Letter in my Bosom, and he seeing me frighted, said, smiling, Who have you been writing to, *Pamela?*—I said, in my Fright, Pray your Honour forgive me!—Only to my Father and Mother. He said, Well then, Let me see how you are come on in your Writing! O how I was sham'd!—He, in my Fright, took it, without saying more, and read it quite thro', and then gave it me again;—and I said, Pray your Honour forgive me;—yet I know not for what.[85]

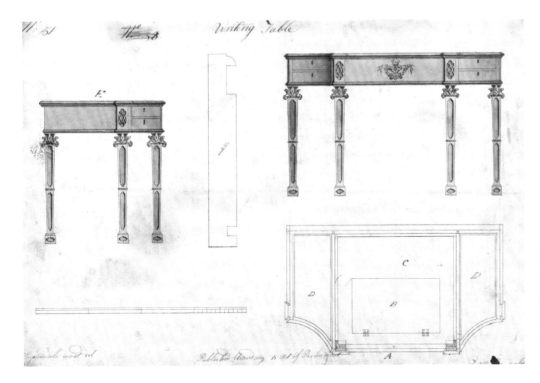

Fig. 92. Thomas Chippendale, Design for a Writing Table, 1754. Graphite, gray wash, and pen and ink on paper. Yale Center for British Art, Paul Mellon Collection. B1975.4.1630

Fig. 93. Artist unknown, "The Buckley-Boar Family," ca. 1758–60. Oil on canvas. Yale Center for British Art, Paul Mellon Collection. B1981.25.227

Fig. 94. Louis Truchy after Joseph Highmore, "Pamela...writing in her late Lady's dressing room," 1762. Engraving. Yale Center for British Art, Paul Mellon Collection. B1977.24.48

Museum & Complete Mag. Feb.ʳ 1765

Mʳ Woodhouse the Poetical Cobler

Fig. 95. Joseph Wright, "Philosopher Giving a Lecture on the Orrery," ca. 1768. Oil on canvas. Yale Center for British Art, Paul Mellon Collection. B1981.25.719

Fig. 96. "Mʳ. Woodhouse the Poetical Cobler," 1765. Etching with engraving. From *The universal museum and complete magazine of knowledge and pleasure* (London, Feb. 1765). The Lewis Walpole Library, Yale University. 765.02.00.01

In both the Buckley-Boar portrait and the engraving of *Pamela,* writing (and specifically letter-writing) also acts as a connection between the writer and an unseen space beyond the edge of the image. The father in the Buckley-Boar family is deliberately situated as one end of a correspondence ranging beyond the domestic sphere, just as Pamela is shown writing the letter that connects her to her mother, in the familial correspondence of the first part of the novel.

In "Philosopher Giving a Lecture on the Orrery" (ca. 1768; fig. 95), Joseph Wright offers a romanticized rendition of the scientific demonstration. A group of children and adults, men and women, gather in this domestic setting to witness the action of the orrery, a model of the solar system and the model in miniature of a deistic power.[86] Behind them, at the end of the orrery's circle of light, an observer makes his notes with a pencil on a loose quire of paper.

The illustration "Mʳ. Woodhouse the Poetical Cobler" (1765; fig. 96) takes its force, by contrast, from the absurdity of juxtaposition. Seen here in his cobbler's workshop, seated on a workman's bench, the poet writes with a quill pen, quire of paper precariously balanced on his knee. The two roles of poet and cobbler coincide only as the object of satire. The engraving was published after James Woodhouse, poet and shoemaker, had achieved an initial literary success following the publication of his *Poems on sundry occasions* (1764) by Robert Dodsley. In this engraving for a popular magazine, the awkward combination of Woodhouse's two identities is shown as a form of physical comedy, one in which writing is made incommensurate with the space occupied by an individual of his profession and social class.[87]

PART TWO: HANDS

George Bickham's "An Emblematic Representation of the Usefulness of Penmanship" (fig. 97) makes its own argument on the political and economic power of handwriting. Recumbent in this exuberant harbor scene, Wisdom whispering in his ear, bound volumes on accounts and mathematics at his feet, the figure of "an ancient celebrated Penman" takes quill to hand. At his feet, a young student learns to write. Meanwhile, the bare-bosomed figure of "History, Law, and Poetry" leans her book on Time's head as she records her thoughts. Engraved in copperplate, the caption argues that "Penmanship will be Valued and Practis'd, as long as the World endures." By 1731, when Bickham engraved this scene, the copperplate hand it portrays had become the face of British commercial and political ambition.

Hands formed part of early modern England's history of itself. Part Two begins with a general introduction to the categories by which early modern English handwriting can be understood, before focusing on the dominant hands of the early modern period: Anglicana, secretary hand, italic, chancery, mixed hand, and copperplate or round hand. This survey of English hands highlights some of the questions that might be asked of early modern English manuscript: Why and how do hands become dominant? How much of the individual is situated in his or her hand or writing? To what extent can handwriting be seen to reflect a national culture?

Fig. 97. Detail, George Bickham, "An Emblematic Representation of the Usefulness of Penmanship." From George Bickham, *Penmanship in its utmost beauty and extent* (London, 1731). Yale Center for British Art. Folio A Z1

Scripts and Hands

Fig. 98. Hill, Notebook, p. 1. England,
early 17th century. Osborn b234

This book follows the early modern usage of the term "hand," using it interchangeably with the modern term "script."[88] When William Hill practiced his penmanship in the early seventeenth century, he copied a passage written in the dominant English cursive script, or "Secretarye hande" (fig. 98). In this context, the terms script or hand denote the template for a particular style of handwriting: a recognizable, consistent, and learned approach to writing the shapes of the letters of the alphabet. As Hill's example indicates, a script might be understood by a community of readers and writers to designate a specific type of writing: in the Italian, or italic style, for example.

Script, or hand, refers to this shared understanding of a category of penmanship. As a term, hand is also used to refer to individual style, or the often idiosyncratic manner in which an individual scribe might write. Although students in early modern England might have been taught to normalize their hand, any individual's writing might possess distinguishing characteristics. One can write secretary hand, the script, with a cramped or narrow or nearly illegible hand, or style.

CALLIGRAPHIC AND CURSIVE

The calligraphic and the cursive are two of the primary categories by which to characterize early modern English hands (fig. 99). In a calligraphic hand, the writer lifts the pen after each individual line, or stroke, of the letter. The scribe or writer builds the letter through these consecutive strokes. A scribe or writer might be familiar with several different scripts, which could be used for different purposes or in separate contexts. To know or learn a hand, a writer needed to

Fig. 99. The Fawkners' Glasse, IV and 2r. England, ca. 1590–1620. Beinecke MS 100. The red glossing hand on both sides of this opening offers an example of a calligraphic hand, in which each stroke of the letterform is made separately. This contrasts with the cursive secretary hand of the body of the text.

understand the ductus, or number and order of strokes in forming the letters, their angle and orientation on the page, and other aspects of penmanship, such as how to cut the pen nib for a particular style of writing. Ductus, as a term, can also refer to the characteristics of an individual's hand. Calligraphic hands, in their various forms, are also known as text hands or textura (see fig. 115); their typographical equivalent, in print, is known as black letter (see fig. 114).

In a cursive hand, the writer keeps the pen for the most part on the page, connecting letters together. Cursive script has its origins in the Roman Empire (fig. 100): it is as old as the pressures of administrative work and the need to write more quickly. Daily and administrative life under the Romans was conducted in a cursive script throughout the Roman Empire and continued in its varying forms after the fall of Rome in the former colonies, including the Britannia, or Britain.[89]

Fig. 100. Roman writing tablet. London, ca. 100–125. Osborn fa62

Cursive—or, following the Latin, running or *currens* script—is by definition a more rapid and, by extension, less formal script. A cursive script can be defined by its "simplified ductus," or the deliberate minimization of the number of strokes required to make a letter. Many of the characteristics of cursive hands follow from their emphasis on speed: the use of the ligature, or connection between letters; the presence of curved or looping ascenders and descenders at the tops and bottoms of letters.[90] The two categories might also intersect: some scripts represent the cursive adaptation of a more formal calligraphic hand.

COURT HAND AND TEXT HAND

Writing was both occupation and practice in the early modern period. It was a service, a commodity required by institutions across English society. Paperwork originated from every body of English government and society, from the courts to the Church to the Exchequer and the military. This paperwork was, for the most part, produced by professional writers, who were often required to understand and create specific types of document, in specific styles of handwriting. Clerks, scriveners, scribes, and secretaries populate the pages of early modern English legal and administrative documents, as they do its poetry, drama, and prose.[91]

While calligraphic and cursive are useful categories by which to analyze early modern text, they were not necessarily terms used by early modern writers and readers. Many of the overarching categorizations defining early modern English paleography derive instead from the organization of the writing professions in medieval London. Two main categories of hands were used by writers: court hand (with the associated category of the set hands, used by several English courts and administrative departments) and text hand (or book hand).

Court Hand

Court hand (fig. 101) refers to a set of scripts used by writers affiliated with the "misteries of the Court Letter," the association concerned with the drafting and copying of legal documents. By the early modern period, these writers were known as scriveners.[92] Equivalent to contemporary notaries public, scriveners were regulated in London by the Worshipful Company of Scriveners. The 1616/17 letters patent for the Company outline the legal corporation surrounding the "science art or mistery of Writers of the Court Letter." As with most of the companies, scriveners were apprenticed before being admitted as freemen of the Company. The 1616/17 letters patent stipulates that scriveners were allowed to practice professionally within a radius of three miles of the City of London.[93]

Several courts or administrative departments of the English government produced documents in

Fig. 101. "Courte hande." Hill, Notebook, p. 7. Osborn b234

specific hands, described as set hands. In his *Booke containing divers sortes of hands,* the publisher Thomas Vautrollier included several plates of set hands, including "The sett chauncery hande." Some examples of set hands include the pipe roll hand, used to record the accounts of the sovereign's debtors; the chancery hand, used in the Court of Chancery; and the two hands of the Exchequer (the King's remembrancer and the Lord Treasurer's remembrancer).[94]

Scriveners drafted legal documents, such as contracts, indentures, wills, and other legal forms.[95] These were formally copied, or engrossed. In this example from 1666–67, a scrivener has submitted "A Bill of writings" to an employer, with expenses itemized for "drawing and ingrossing" pairs of indentures and contracts, or "condicionalls" (fig. 102). For this work, the scrivener charged £1 10s, per pair; or £3 for longer works requiring three "larg Skinns of parchment."[96]

Text Hand

Text, as a term, derives from the Latin, *texere,* to weave; it refers to the woven appearance of writing.[97] Text hand, or book hand, designates a formal hand used for copying primarily nonlegal texts, whether religious, historical, literary, or works of other genres. A professional writer—a term used here to encompass writers whose primary employment was as a clerk or

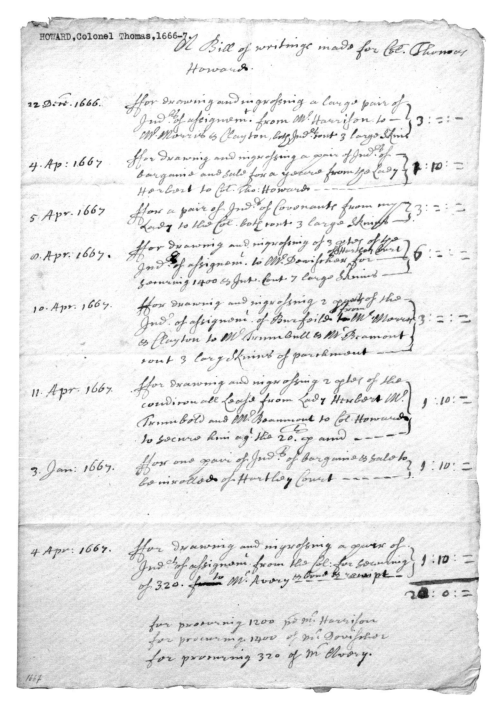

Fig. 102. "A Bill of writings made for Col. Thomas Howard," 1666–67. Clayton Papers. England, 1589–1824. OSB MSS 40, Folder 13

22 Dec[r]. 1666. For drawing and ingrossing a large pair of Ind[rs]. of assigment. from M[r]. Harrison to Mr. Morris & Clayton, both Ind[es] sent 3 large Skins } 3: = : -

4. Ap: 1667   For drawing and ingrossing a pair of Ind[es]. of bargains and sale for a yeare from the Lady Herbert to Col. Tho: Howard } 1:10: =

5 Apr. 1667   For a pair of Ind[s] of Covenants from my Lady to the Col. both sent 3 large skins } 3: = : =

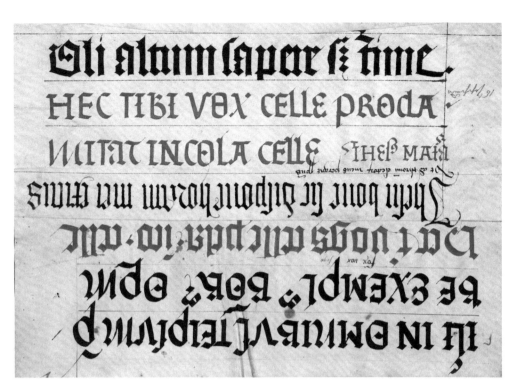

Fig. 103. A selection of different formal hands, probably used as a scribal sample sheet. Germany, 1475–1500. Takamiya MS 117

scribe and those who were paid for occasional writing work—might employ a text hand in rendering one of these types of document. Facility with a range of formal hands was also a professional qualification, to be advertised to potential patrons in examples like the late-fifteenth-century German sample sheet shown here (fig. 103).[98]

The Guild of Stationers, founded in 1403, and incorporated in 1557 as the Worshipful Company of Stationers, was established by professional writers, limners (or illuminators), and bookbinders.[99] Although the focus of the Stationers' Company shifted after the advent of publication by print, the Company had from the outset overseen the copying or publication of text in manuscript, as well as the decoration and binding of books.[100] In his 1603 *Survey of London,* John Stow described the changes in the location of the proto-stationers within the City: the "*Pater noster* makers of olde time, or Beade makers, and Text Writers, are gone out of *Pater noster* Rowe, and are called Stationers of *Paules Church* yarde."[101]

Text hand was familiar enough to act as the object of satire. In his *Nashes Lenten stuffe* (1599), Thomas Nashe described the history of Great Yarmouth, as found in a "Chronographycall Latine table, which they haue hanging up in their Guild hall." Here, a visitor might read "in a text hand texting us, how in the Scepterdome of *Edward* the Confessor, the sands first began to grow into sight at a low water." With "text hand texting us," Nashe referred to a formal book hand, one sufficiently known to his readers to evoke the stuffiness of its context: the guild hall in the provincial town, the records cited by the historian William Camden, the chronological table hanging in Latin on the wall, "texting" its reader in the calligraphic hand that denoted a particular mode of textual formality.[102]

As Nashe's example shows us, court hand and text hand were terms already available to early modern readers; they are used in penmanship manuals of the period, although their meanings can often seem diffuse to us. Early modern writers also had recourse to other categories and terms (often outrageous and witty) by which to understand and describe handwriting. "Let them glory in Pen-scolding, and Paper-brabling, that list," wrote Gabriel Harvey to a rival in 1592, "I must not, I cannot, I will not."[103]

LETTERS AND LETTERFORMS

Penmanship is the art of managing the techniques of hand, pen, ink, and writing surface to write in a particular style. A letterform is created through strokes, whether through the formal architecture of textura or the more idiosyncratic connections of cursive. As noted earlier, the overarching style of an individual's handwriting (and, sometimes, of a particular hand itself) is known as the ductus. This term encompasses characteristics such as the angle at which the pen is held, the way in which the pen nib is cut, the thickness or thinness of the letterforms and their overall angle (slanted right or left, or upright) on the page. The stroke refers to the movement of the pen on the writing surface, from the moment the pen touches the writing surface to the moment it is lifted. Some strokes might be straight; others might be angled, or "broken."

The letterform is the basic unit of handwriting. In his 1616 penmanship guide, Richard Gething illustrated the letters of the alphabet, showing his reader how to recognize the letterforms written in secretary hand, from *A* to *Z* (fig. 104; see also fig. 109). A scribe writing in textura builds letters through the individual strokes of the pen. Equally, a scribe writing in cursive will connect an individual letterform with its neighbors.

Letterforms have structures. They have heads, bodies, and feet. They sometimes have tails, the part of a letterform that might hang below the baseline, or the line at the foot of the letters. Supralinear letters rise above the line (*d, k, h*); infralinear letters drop below the line (*p, y*). Rounded letters, like *a,* have a lobe (the rounded part) and a stem (the linear part). The lobe can also be called a compartment. Some letters, like the Anglicana *a,* are double-lobed or have two compartments. Letterforms also have strokes heading in different directions: ascenders, the stem of *h;* descenders, the stem of *p;* a cross-stroke in a modern *t* or a head-stroke in an italic *t.* The ends of letters have particular terms: a hook, a curl or finial, a thick end or club. Just as in typefaces, manuscript letterforms often end in serifs, or the trailing finish to letters, known as incised, curved, horizontal, slabbed, and situated at the head or foot. Letters also take their particular position within a word: initial, at the start; medial, in the middle; finial, at the end. For instance, the letter *s* might be an initial *s,* "start"; a medial *s,* "biscuit"; or a finial *s,* "limits."[104]

Writing also took forms, beyond those of the letterform itself. One example can be found in the flourish, an ornamental stroke of the pen (fig. 105). Writing (and perhaps particularly penmanship exercises by students) is often decorated with elaborate flourishes, sometimes drawn with a single stroke of the pen. The visual medium of engraving was particularly well suited to representing the flourish. Plate-books advertising the mastery (and services) of writing masters are often extensively decorated with flourishes (as in fig. 104; see also fig. 90), often followed diligently by students in their penmanship copybooks (figs. 106–107).

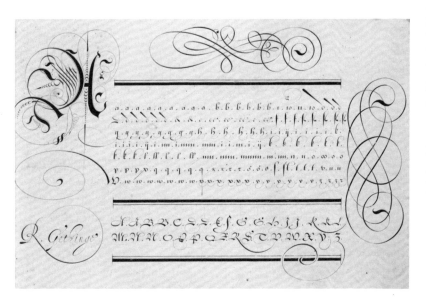

Fig. 104. Richard Gething, *A coppie-booke of the usuall hands* (1616). Elizabethan Club, Yale University. Eliz +10

Fig. 105. A presentation inscription, with flourishes, by the later owner of this volume. William Lytlestone, Intelligence of Spain and Portugal arranged in tabular fashion. England, 1582. Osborn fa52

Fig. 106. "Judge not that field because 'tis Stubble! Nor him that's poore and full of trouble!" Henry Phillipps of Wanborough, Copybook. England, 1655. Osborn b156. Phillipps can be seen here, hard at work on his capital letters and flourishes.

Fig. 107. An ornament of a swan. Mary Serjant, Arithmetic and penmanship notebook. England, 1688. Osborn fb98

THE ALPHABET

In this late-fifteenth-century English herbal, the letters of the alphabet are presented to the book's readers alongside the names and illustrations of "Affadille," or daffodil, and other flowering plants (fig. 108). The alphabet—its forms and order—was a textual landscape learned by early modern readers, its features familiar to children or students learning to write. It circulated in the primers, hornbooks, and writing manuals by which students might learn to write, and it can be found copied laboriously in notebooks and the endpapers of books (figs. 109–110). In learning to write the alphabet, students also learned the unit of the letter, or letterform, the organizing unit of handwriting.

The early modern alphabet had twenty-four rather than twenty-six letters. Then, as now, it began with *A* and finished with *Z,* but contained two fewer letters: *I* and *J* were interchangeable, as were *U* and *V.*

Fig. 108. An ornamental alphabet, facing an illustration of flowering plants. Helmingham herbal and bestiary. England, ca. 1500. Yale Center for British Art. Folio C 2014 4

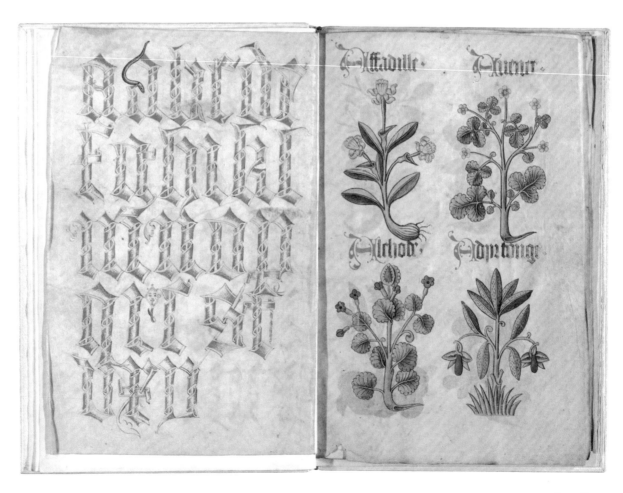

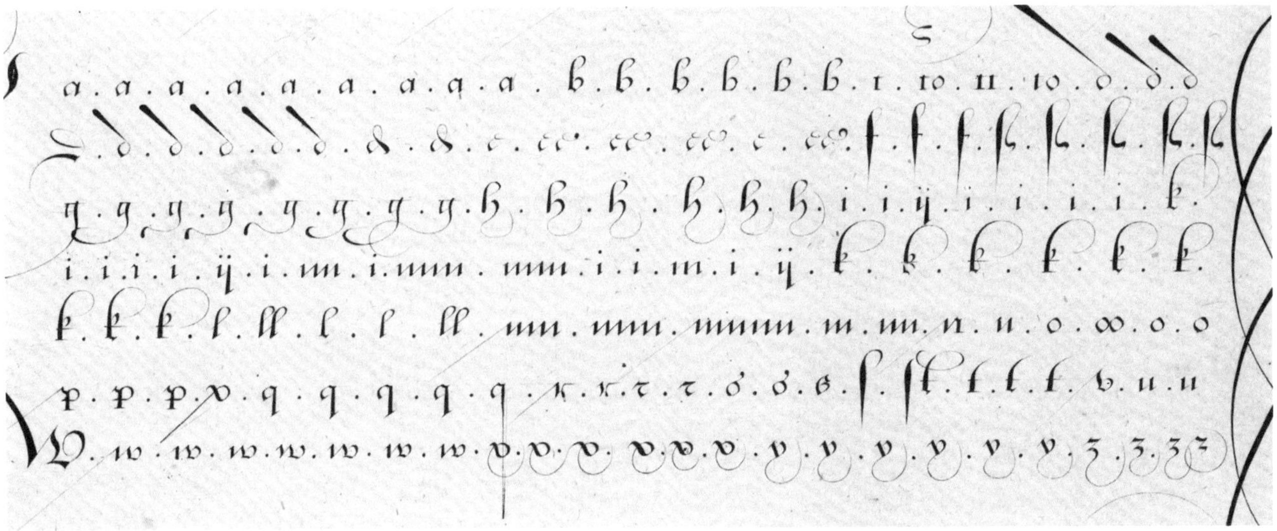

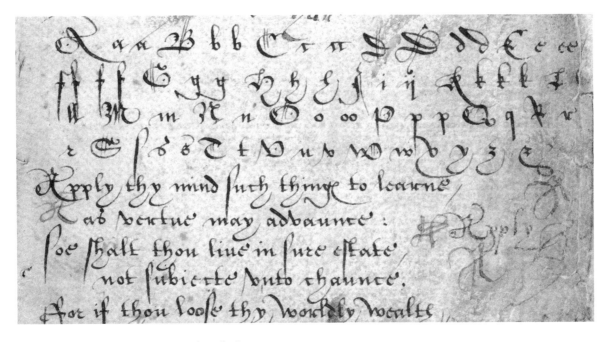

Fig. 109. Detail of fig. 104

Fig. 110. Alphabet in "Secretary hande."
Detail of fig. 98

A a a B b b C c c D D d d E e e
F f f f G g g H h h I i i j K k k k L
ll M m N n O o oo P p p Q q R
r S s s s T t U u u W w X y z z
Apply thy mind such things to learne,
as vertue may advaunce:
soe shalt thou liue in sure estate
not subiecte unto chaunce.

OLD HANDS

The English alphabet could act as a historic monument, the face of an ancient English language. In 1566 Matthew Parker published *A testimonie of antiquitie,* the first book to represent the Old English, or Anglo-Saxon, language in print (fig. 111; cf. fig. 12). Parker was the Archbishop of Canterbury, the primary religious leader for Elizabeth I, and the book was a conscious political act, defending the historical antiquity of the Church of England. By implication, it also defended the decision made by Elizabeth's father, Henry VIII, to break with the Catholic Church, found the Church of England, and establish himself as his nation's spiritual leader. In printing an Old English sermon by the venerated priest Aelfric, Parker asserted the claims of an ancient English language and religious precedent as the basis of the Church of England and the English monarch's spiritual authority.[105]

Parker's publication of Old English also reveals the intersections of manuscript and print culture in early modern England, and the political situations these could present. Aelfric's sermon, as Parker's introduction proclaimed, had been "written in the olde Saxon tounge before *the Conquest.*"[106] Parker made the decision to print Aelfric's sermon in Old English, laying claim to the visual heritage of a native English language. To do this, he first had to create an Old English

Fig. 111. Old English and English in Matthew Parker, *A testimonie of antiquitie, shewing the auncient fayth in the Church of England* [London, 1566], 19v–20r. Ic Ae4 n567

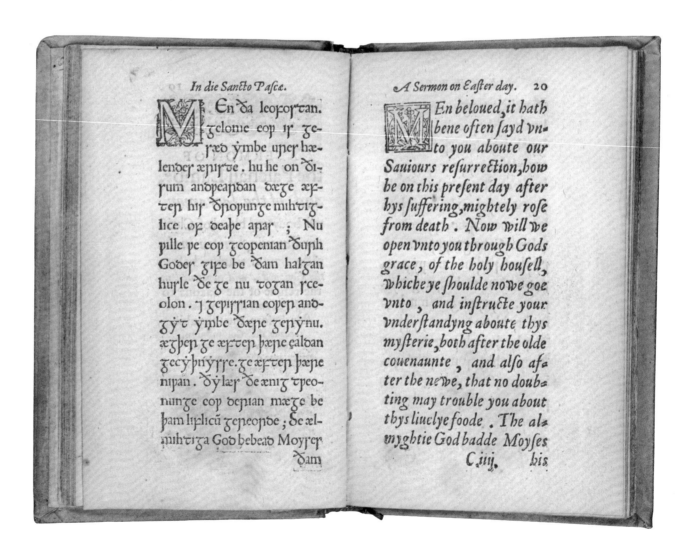

typeface (fig. 112), basing this on the appearance of the manuscripts in his private collection, texts he had gathered after the destruction of the English monastic houses and the dispersal of their libraries (see fig. 13).

Parker's *Testimonie of antiquitie* was a radical work: it laid claim to an Old English language and religious authority, situating this within an English vernacular. Most of his readers might never have had occasion to see a manuscript written in Old English. However, Old English manuscript studies would be one of the driving forces for English scholarship in history and manuscript culture through the early eighteenth century.

British manuscript culture was also situated within a broader European tradition. Just as early modern English readers sought out Continental styles of fashion, manners, and music, so they absorbed and responded to Continental styles of handwriting (fig. 113). Like fashion or manners, handwriting was a form of costume, a presentation of the self to the world. Anglicana, secretary, and italic hands are all examples of the English adoption and adaptation of European hands. As fashions could come to seem archaic, so too could hands.

For the early modern English reader, the archaic could take any of several possible forms: Roman, medieval, or even humanist. By the sixteenth century, early modern Britain had already undergone a transformation in its textual culture. Situated as it is within the early modern period, this book begins in the aftermath of several significant changes in book production that had occurred in fifteenth-century Europe. As Malcolm Parkes and others have observed, the fifteenth century saw an efflorescence of vernacular

The Saxon Caracters or letters, that be most straunge, are here knowen by other common Caracters set ouer them.

d. f. g. i. r. s. t. w. y. z. and. th. th. that.

Æ. Æ. E. H. M. S. W. X. Th. Th.

One pricke signifieth an vnperfect point: this figure ; (which is like the Greke interrogatiue) a full point, which in some other olde Saxon bookes, is expressed with three prickes, set in triangle wise thus :.

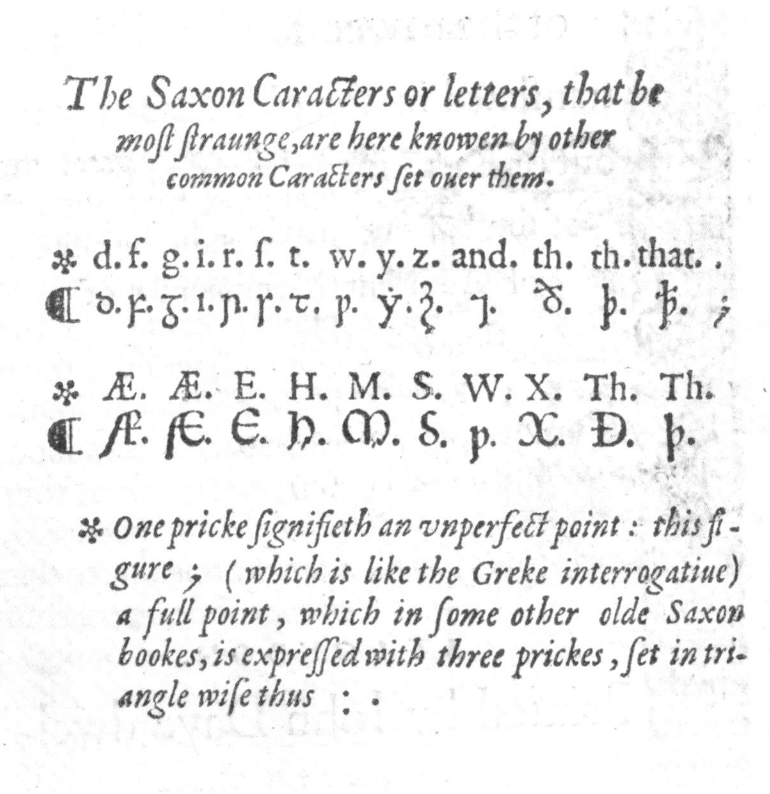

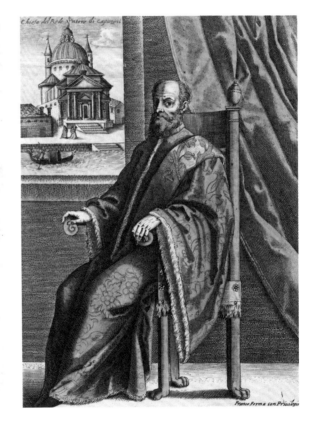

Fig. 112. Detail, *The Gospels of the fower Euangelistes translated in the olde Saxons tyme out of Latin into the vulgare toung of the Saxons* (London: John Daye, 1571), title page verso. Ic B48 d571

Fig. 113. Giacomo Franco, "I Procurati di S. Marcho," in *Habiti d'huomeni et donne venetiane* (Venice, 1609). J18 F8475 +609. Engraved plate-books illustrating European handwriting and fashion were eagerly consumed by English audiences.

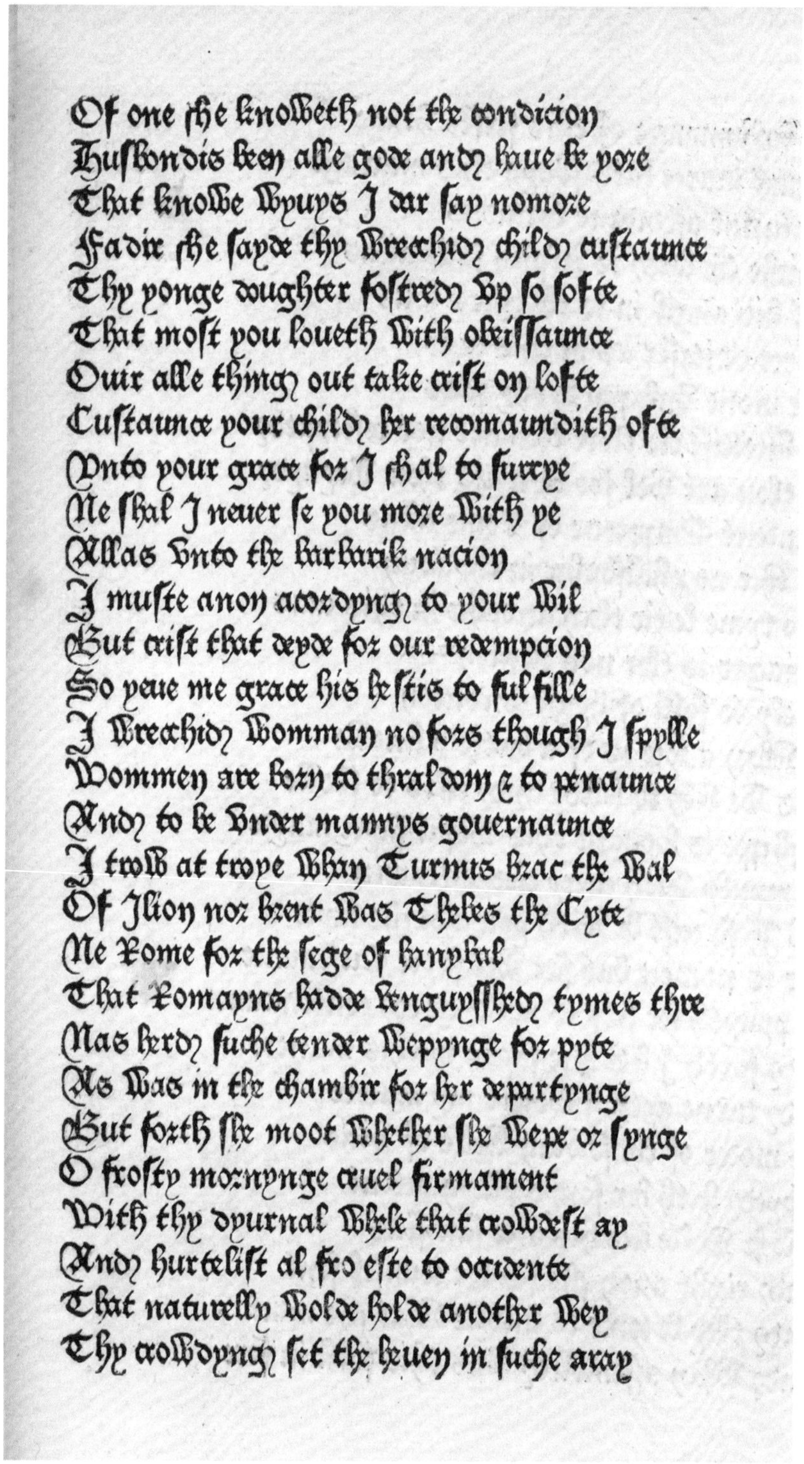
Of one she knoweth not the condicion
Husbondis ben alle gode and haue be yore
That knowe wyuys I dar say nomore
Fadir she sayde thy wrecchid child custaunce
Thy yonge doughter fostred up so softe
That most you loueth with obeissaunce
Ouir alle thing out take crist on lofte
Custaunce your child her recomaundith ofte
Unto your grace for I shal to surrye
Ne shal I neuer se you more with ye
Allas unto the barbarik nacion
I muste anon accordyng to your wil
But crist that deyde for our redempcion
So yeue me grace his hestis to fulfille
I wrecchid womman no fors though I spylle
Wommen are born to thraldom & to penaunce
And to be under mannys gouernaunce
I trow at troye whan Turmis brac the wal
Of Ilion nor brent was Thebes the Cyte
Ne Rome for the sege of hanybal
That Romayns hadde venguysshed tymes thre
Nas herd suche tender wepynge for pyte
As was in the chambir for her departynge
But forth she moot whether she wepe or synge
O frosty mornynge cruel firmament
With thy dyurnal whele that crowdest ay
And hurtelist al fro este to occidente
That naturelly wolde holde another wey
Thy crowdyng set the heuen in suche aray

Fig. 114. Incipit, Sergeant-at-Law's tale. Geoffrey Chaucer, *The Canterbury tales* (Westminster: William Caxton, 1477). Zi 9626

literary book production in Europe among an emergent middle class of book owners and readers. This shift coincided with two additional developments: first, the use of cursive scripts for textual purposes beyond the administrative; second, the increasing availability of paper as a less expensive alternative to parchment in book production.[107]

Early modern English readers and writers lived in a world in which print, paper, and an English vernacular had increasingly, and still only recently, become the textual norm. In 1476 William Caxton had established a printing press in the city of Westminster in London, embarking on a career as an influential publisher and printer in England. His publication of vernacular English texts, both in translation and in his first edition, for instance, of Chaucer's *Canterbury tales* (1477; fig. 114), mirrors the production of similar texts in manuscript (fig. 115) over the course of the fifteenth century.[108] By 1500, early modern English readers lived in a world in which text was produced and consumed in hybrid form by readers and writers moving with increasing ease between manuscript and print.

To the eighteenth-century English reader, the medieval manuscript and early printed book had also come to signify the archaic. The text hand, or textura, had acted as a formative influence on early type design. As a typeface, textura—or, as it was later described by the English, black letter (fig. 114)—became shorthand for the old, difficult, or arcane.[109]

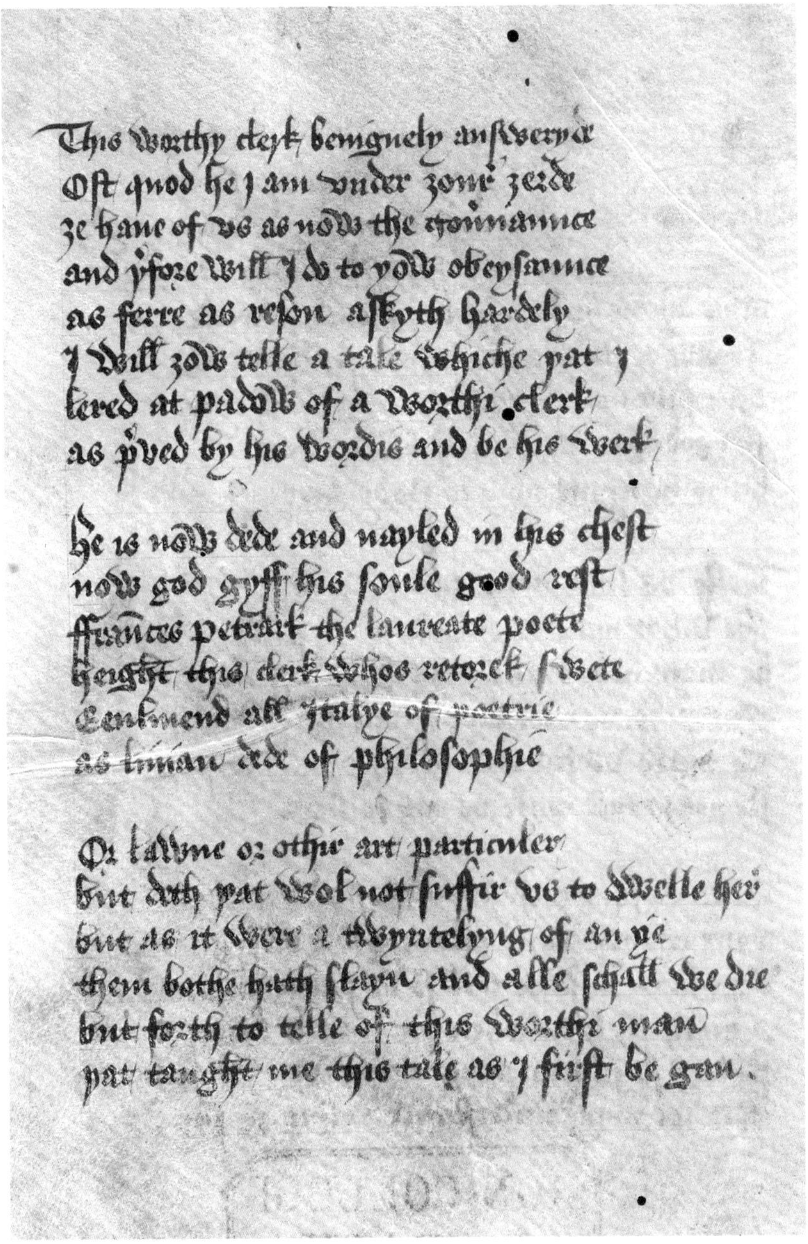

Fig. 115. Geoffrey Chaucer, Canterbury Tales, f. 1v
(from "The Clerk's Tale"). England, ca. 1460–90.
Takamiya MS 22

This worthy clerk benignely answeryde
Oft quod he I am under your yerde
Ye haue of us as now the goũnaunce
and ỹfore will I do to yow obeysaunce
as ferre as reson askyth hardely
I will yow telle a tale whiche ỹat I
hered at padow of a worthi clerk
As p̃ved by his wordis and be his werk

ANGLICANA

Our first manuscript hand, Anglicana, is also that of Caxton's printed Chaucer (see fig. 114). Anglicana derived from a Continental book hand, widespread in England from the middle of the thirteenth century. The paleographer Malcolm Parkes coined the term "Anglicana," arguing that the hand had consistent and recognizable characteristics distinguishing it from similar Continental forms.[110]

Anglicana has several distinctive features, as can be seen in this detail from "The Clerk's Tale" in a late-fifteenth-century manuscript of Chaucer (fig. 115). Four letterforms, characteristic of Anglicana, can be found in the first two lines:

a, in distinctive double-lobed form;

h, with a hooked ascender, and descender below the baseline;

d, with an ascender slanting to the left;

w, with hooked ascenders.

On the second line of the second stanza, *g* also takes a distinctive double-lobed form.

Several features of this manuscript's construction transcend the use of any particular hand and recur in examples throughout this book. The manuscript is ruled, the lines demarcating the space for the text and the opening initial. It is written on parchment, the texture of which is just visible in the example shown here. The text has been written in an iron gall ink, fading in some points from black to brown.

SECRETARY HAND

Anglicana was displaced almost entirely over the course of the fifteenth century, overtaken in popularity by the cursive script known since the early modern period as "secretary hand" (figs. 116–118). Secretary hand originated in Italy and was introduced to England from France in the late fourteenth century. By 1500 secretary hand had become the dominant script in England for books and documents. Over the course of the sixteenth century, secretary hand and italic became the predominant faces of English writing.

Secretary hand offers a striking example of print fixing a manuscript culture in place. Beau-Chesne's *A booke containing diuers sortes of hands* (1570)

consisted almost entirely of plates, elegantly depicting secretary hand and other scripts. The earliest known surviving English penmanship copybook, it marks the emergence of the copybook as a popular genre in English textual culture, one in which the writing master came to achieve a particular prominence in advertising types of handwriting. The visual technologies of print—woodcut and copperplate engraving, among them—shaped the face of secretary hand in early modern England.[III]

Fig. 116. Detail from a manuscript roll. Alchemical text, after Arnold of Villanova. Attributed to George Ripley. England, 16th century. Mellon MS 41

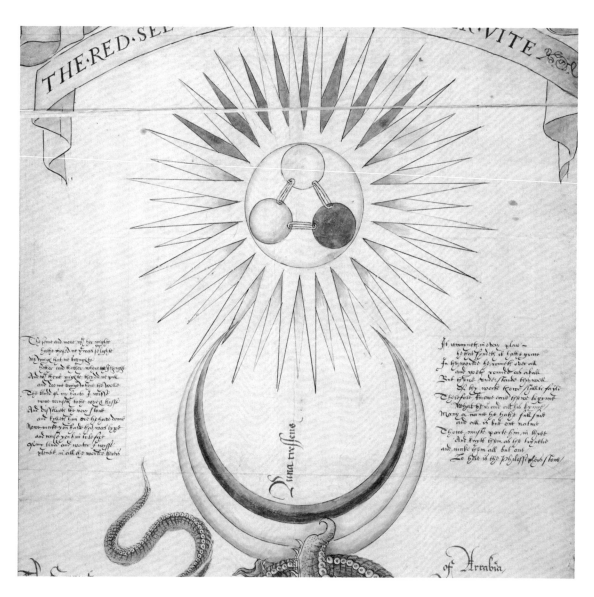

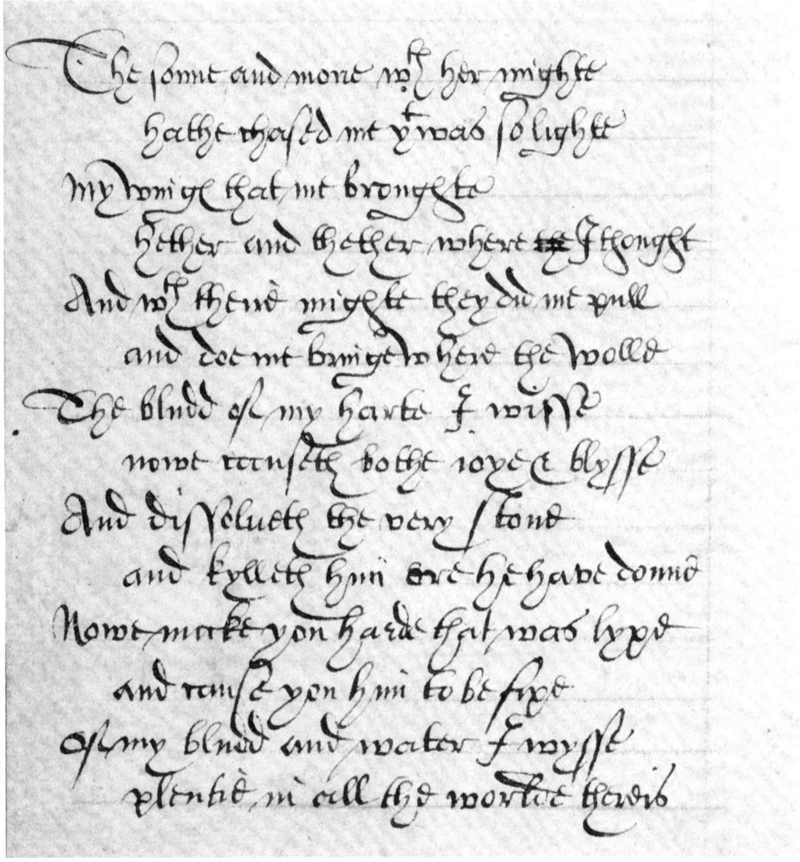

Fig. 117. Detail of fig. 116

The sonne and mone wth her mighte
hathe chased me y^t was so lighte
My wings that me broughte
hether and thether where I thought
And wth there might they did me pull
and doe me bringe where the wolle

Fig. 118. Detail, Elizabeth I, the 23rd heir to the throne.
Morgan Colman, Genealogies of the kings of England.
England, 1592. Osborn fa56. See also fig. 257.

23./
Elizabeth.
The yongest daughter of Kinge
Henrie the eight borne 1533. Beganne her
most blessed Raigne, and was crowned
Queene of England Fraunce, & Irelande,
1559 whome the devine Favours untill this
present, hath continewed happie, in her most
Royall, triumphant, and victorious governe-
ment; the felicitie whereof, the Almightie in
the greatnes of his mercie continewe longe
to the never dienge ioye, and comforte,
of all faithfull subiects, And to the
confussed shame of all
Her Maties Enemies.

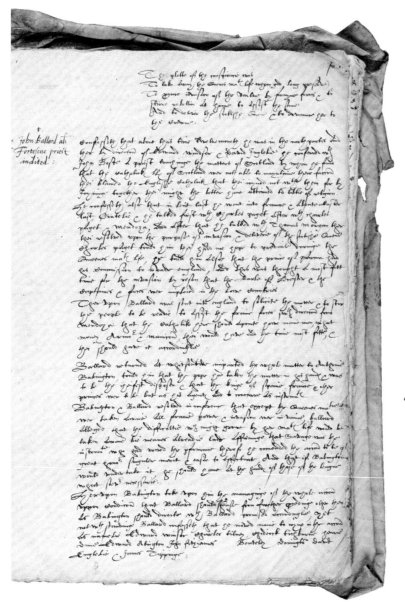

Fig. 119. An examination of the confessions of the conspirators in the Babington Plot, f. 1r. England, 1586. Osborn fa10. The volume holds a copy of the confessions of the conspirators in the plot against Queen Elizabeth, with particular interest in the role played by Mary, Queen of Scots.

Fig. 120. Detail of fig. 119

The plotte of the conspiracie was
To take away the Quenes ma^ts life whom god long preserve
To p̄cure invasion of the realme by forayne forces & to
stirre rebellion at home to assist the same
And to deliver the scotishe Quene & to advaunce her to
the crowne.

This example from 1586, an administrative description of the confessions of the conspirators against Elizabeth in the Babington Plot (figs. 119–120), introduces some of the characteristic features of secretary hand. The hand is cursive, in every way designed to maximize the scribe's speed in writing. As can be seen in the first and second lines, a comparison of the letterforms for *a, h, r,* and *w* reveals some contrasts with those forms in Anglicana:

a has a single lobe;

h has changed form entirely, with a strikingly prominent dropped descender;

r resembles a modern *w* far more than its resemblance to a *v* or *l* in Anglicana;

w has lost its looping ascenders.

Some additional characteristics can be observed. In secretary hand, *s* has two forms: medial *s,* as in "conspiracie" of the first line, in which it has a long ascending flourish, occurring either at the start or in the middle of a word; and finial *s,* as in "was" of the first line, with its looped form. *C,* as in "conspiracie," has a surprisingly deceptive form, closely resembling a modern lowercase *t*. Secretary *e,* in its most formal iteration, is a closed loop, not unlike a modern cursive *o;* in its quickest rendering, the entire letterform might be hastily left open, as in "The" or "plotte" in the first line.

In other ways, Anglicana and secretary hand are not dissimilar. Some letterforms are consistent: *k* is one example (see "take" in the second line); the intensely left-leaning ductus of the *d* is another, as seen in "And to deliver" in line five.

The plotte off the conspiracie was
To take away the Queenes ma(jes)tie life (whom god long preserve)
To procure invasion off the Realme by forraine forces to
stirre rebellion at home to Assist the same
And to deliver the Scotishe Queene & to advaunce her to
the Crowne.

Confesseth that about this time Twelvemoneth he was in the north partes And
ther by direction off Edward Windsor & David Inglebie he conferred with
John Boste a priest touchinge the matters off Scotland by whom he founde
that the Catholike the off Scotland wer nott able to mayntaine their faction
their blamed the Englishe Catholike that they ioyned nott with them for by
ioyninge togither they might the better have attained to libtie off religion.
He confesseth also that in lent last he went into fraunce & abowte Easter
last Gratlie & he talked first with Charles paget After with Charles
paget & Mendoza, And After that he talked with Thomas Morgan there
they resolved vpon the purpose off invasion & deliuerie off the Scotishe Queene
Charles paget tould him thei thei wer not happie to prevent duringe the
Queenes ma(jes)tie life, he tould him also that the prince off Parma had
his commission to invade england, And this was thought a most fitt
time for the invasion by reson that the Earle of Leicester & the
Deputies & forces wer imploied in the lowe Cuntries.

Therupon Ballard was sent into england to solicite the matter & to stir
the people to be readie to Assist the forraine forces throgh direction from
Mendoza that the Catholike here should appointe howe manie men what
money Armes & munition they would have And the time most fitte, &
they should have it accordinglie.

Ballard retorned & accordinglie imparted the wogle matter to Anthonie
Babington, tould him that the pope had taken the matter in his hande & was
to be the chieffest disposer & that the kinge off spaine, fraunce & other
princes wer to be but as his Agents and to concurr As instrumentes

Babington & Ballard resolved in conference that except the Queenes ma(jes)tie
wer taken Awaie All forraine power & invasion wer in vaine, Ballard
alleged that the difficultie which might growe by her ma(jes)tie life would be

Fig. 121. Carolingian minuscule. Pseudo-Isidore, Decretals. France, ca. 850–875. Beinecke MS 442

ITALIC HAND

When, in 1554, Elizabeth I wrote her half-sister, Mary, from the Tower of London to plead her innocence of any involvement in the treasonous rebellion led by Thomas Wyatt, she chose to write in a clear italic hand.[112] The hand carried with it a particular range of associations. Italic hand was closely aligned with humanist learning. It was a relatively recent invention, and like secretary hand it was an outgrowth of the late fourteenth century and the Renaissance. Also like secretary hand, it originated in Italy. Its creation is credited to two scholars, Petrarch and Coluccio Salutati, and their reclamation of an earlier script, the Carolingian minuscule (fig. 121), as superior to the Gothic text hand of their contemporaries.

A new humanistic script—the "littera antiqua," or "letters of antiquity"—was developed and popularized by Poggio Bracciolini and Niccolò Niccoli.[113] Over the course of the fifteenth century, this hand was adapted as a formal cursive, in the "cancellaresca corsiva" used as an administrative hand by the Papal chancery courts. It was in this form, widely used in Italy (fig. 122), that it made its entry into England in the early sixteenth century. Named for its Italian origin, the italic hand was closely affiliated with Italian humanist learning, and with the grace and civility associated with the Renaissance recovery of classical texts.

Elizabeth learned her italic hand from her French tutor, Jean Belmain, who also taught Edward VI.[114] Other aristocratic children learned the italic hand from their tutors, and the hand carried an association with the nobility.[115] Italic was also increasingly gendered: by the mid-seventeenth century it had become specifically associated with women, on the grounds of its ease and simplicity (by contrast, for instance, with textura or secretary hand).[116] Elizabeth's hand changed after she succeeded to the throne: as Henry Woudhuysen notes, she adopted a mixed hand,

Fig. 122. Italian humanist hand. Francesco Martini, Tratti de architettura ingegneria e arte militare. Italy, early 16th century. Beinecke MS 491

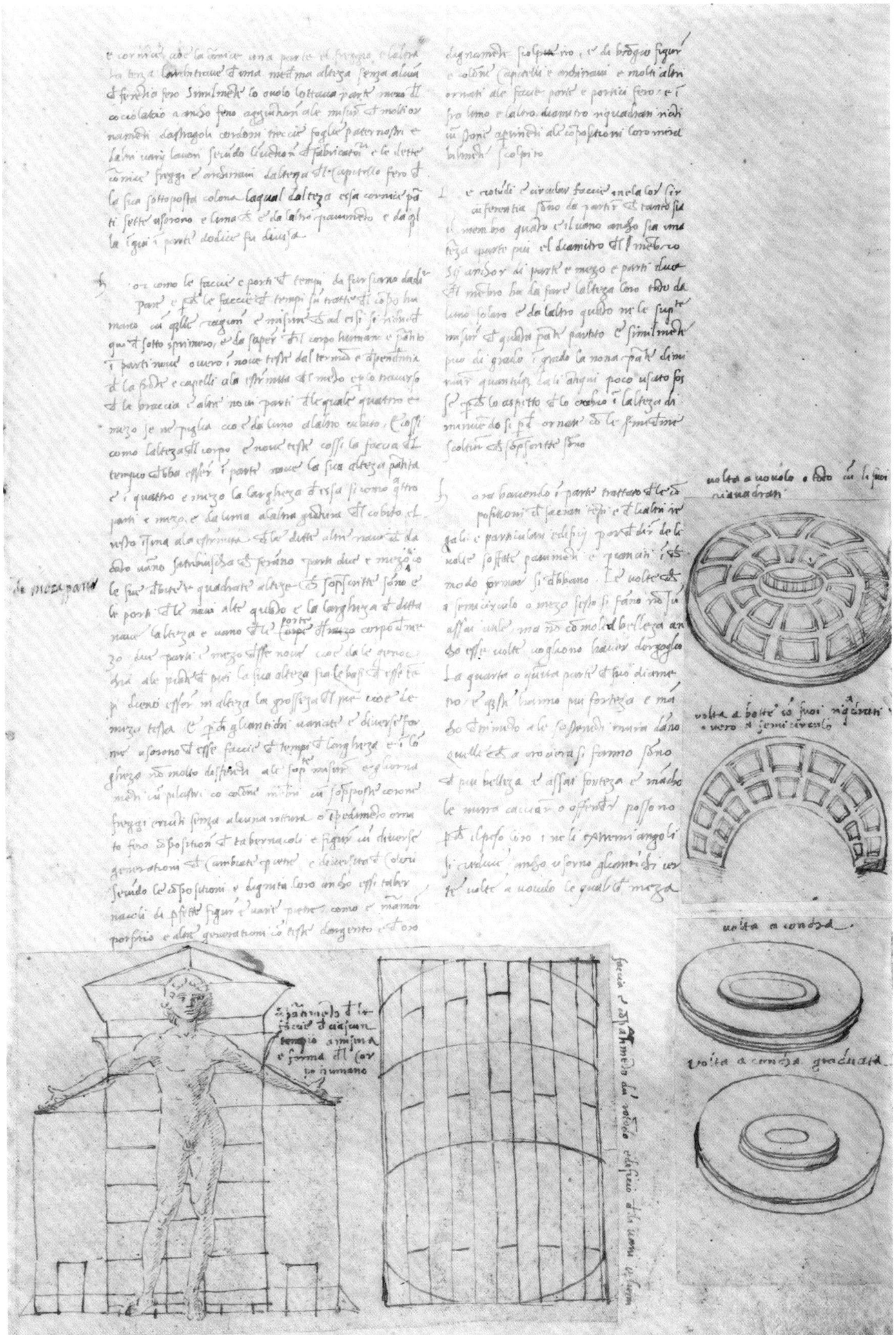

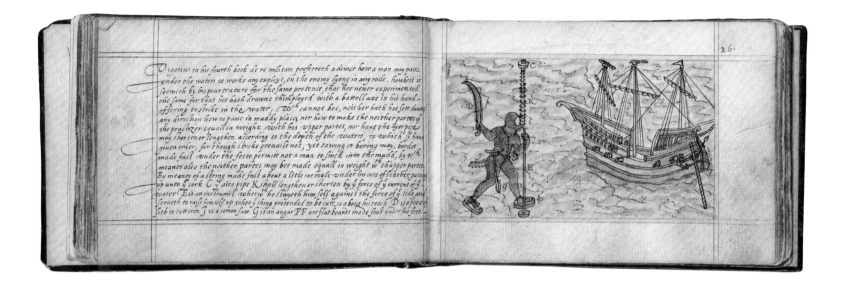

combining italic and secretary hand, an idiosyncratic combination she described as her "skrating hand" in a letter to James VI.[117] Jonathan Gibson suggests that the change marks a self-conscious distancing by Elizabeth from an earlier, and more girlish, persona.[118]

Elizabeth's distinction between her italic and her "skrating," or scribbling, hands highlights the nuanced coexistence of hands in sixteenth-century England, and their use by writers for different social ends. The italic hand could be found in copybooks like Thomas Vautrollier's—labeled "Italian" hand—alongside the secretary and court hands, as well as a study of the Roman capital letters.

Italic hand is characterized by several features. In this presentation copy of a book of technological inventions (figs. 123–124), the writer (and likely author) has adopted a beautiful italic hand. This is a formal presentation copy, a work written to be given as a gift, seeking patronage. The conscientious nature of the layout, the clarity of the text, the use of red ink to refer the reader to notes in the illustrations: these and other characteristics indicate that this is not a manuscript draft, filled with corrections or blank spaces. It is a self-conscious preparation, designed to delight its recipient.

The hand is also intended to convey an overarching impression of grace and regularity. It is not, for the most part, cursive: individual letters have been created with care, with a single stroke of the pen,

Fig. 123. Attributed to Ralph Rabbards, Notebook [Inventions of military machines and other devices]. England, 16th century. Osborn a8

which the writer has meticulously lifted from the page before starting the next letter. Exceptions occur with regularity: note the approach to *s* in the first line, "Vigesius in his." The slight flourishes to the ascenders and descenders—as to the *f, h, b,* and *k* in "fourth book" in the first line—mark the end of the pen stroke, with a slight accumulation of ink.

Note the distinctive appearance of the *a, e, h, r,* and *w,* all letters with very particular, very different forms in Anglicana and secretary. In italic, the *a* has a single-lobe; the *e* takes a simple loop. Compare the *w* in "how" (line one) and "waters" (line two) to see the relative simplicity of the letterform, when read with the *w* of Anglicana or secretary hand in mind. The overall sloping grace, the delicacy and precision of the italic hand, also distinguish it from the haste which could accompany business documents written at speed by a scribe in secretary hand, the "skrating" which Elizabeth ascribed to her business hand. At its best, italic was a courtly hand, an autograph performance of a humanist, learned self.

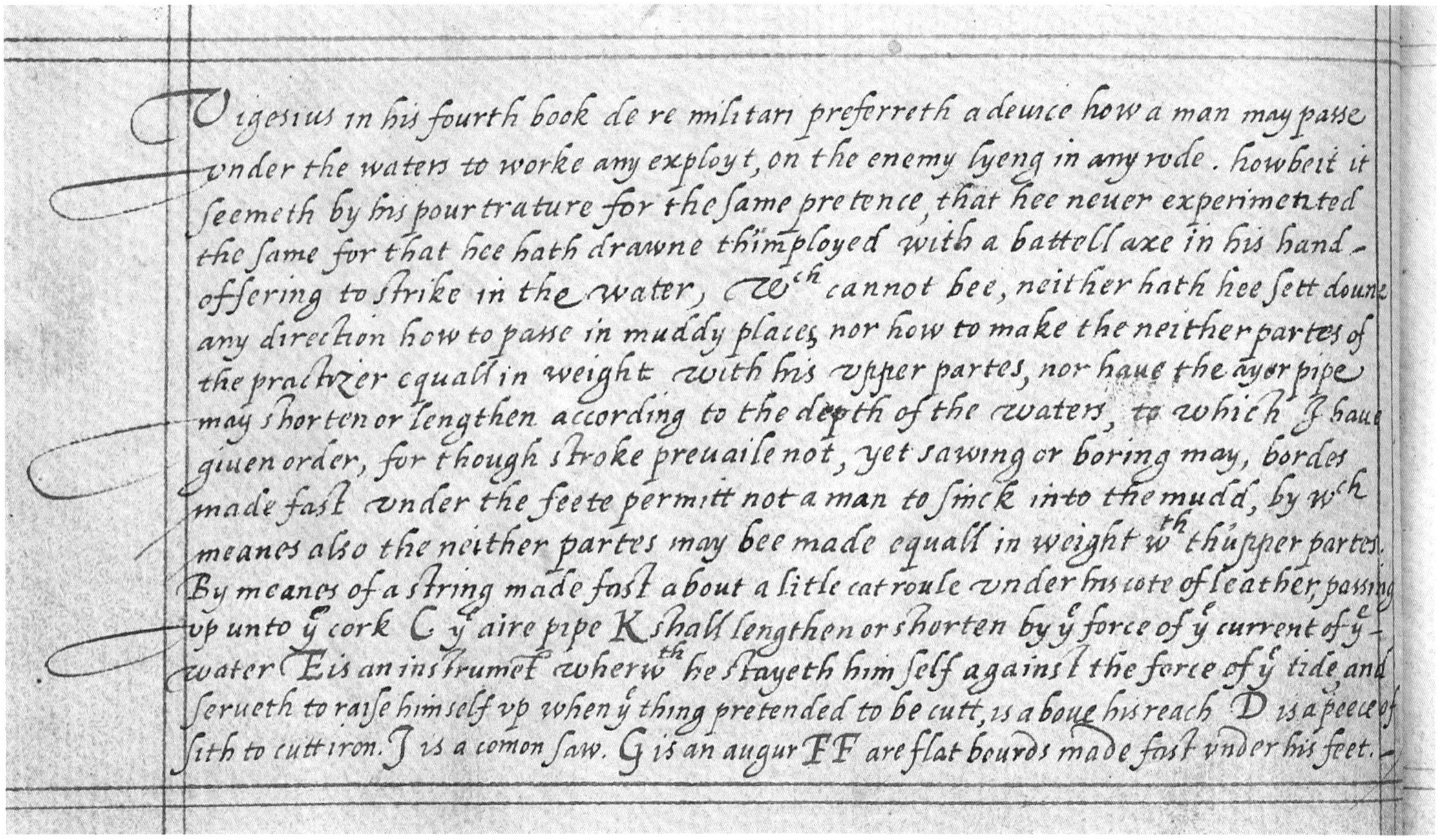

Vigesius in his fourth book de re militari preferreth a deuice how a man may passe
vnder the waters to worke any exployt, on the enemy lyeng in any rode. howbeit it
seemeth by his pourtrature for the same pretence, that hee neuer experimented
the same for that hee hath drawne th'imployed with a battell axe in his hand –
offering to strike in the water, w[ch] cannot bee, neither hath hee sett doune
any direction how to passe in muddy places, nor how to make the neither partes of
the practizer equall in weight with his vpper partes, nor haue the ayer pipe
may shorten or lengthen according to the depth of the waters, to which I haue
giuen order, for though stroke preuaile not, yet sawing or boring may, bordes
made fast vnder the feete permitt not a man to sinck into the mudd, by w[ch]
meanes also the neither partes may bee made equall in weight wth th'vpper partes.
By meanes of a string made fast about a litle cat roule vnder his cote of leather, passing
vp vnto y[e] cork C y[e] aire pipe K shall lengthen or shorten by y[e] force of y[e] current of y[e]
water E is an instrumet wherw[th] he stayeth him self against the force of y[e] tide and
serueth to raise himself vp when y[e] thing pretended to be cutt, is aboue his reach D is a peece of
sith to cutt iron. I is a comon saw. G is an augur FF are flat bourds made fast vnder his feet.

Fig. 124. Detail of fig. 123

Vigesius in his fourth book de re militari preferreth a deuice how a man may passe
under the waters to worke any exployt, on the enemy lyeng in any rode. howbeit it
seemeth by his pourtrature for the same pretence, that hee neuer experimented
the same for that hee hath drawne th'imployed with a battell axe in his hand –
offering to strike in the water, w[ch] cannot bee, neither hath hee sett doune
any direction how to passe in muddy places, nor how to make the neither partes of
the practizer equall in weight with his upper partes, nor haue the ayer pipe
may shorten or lengthen according to the depth of the waters.

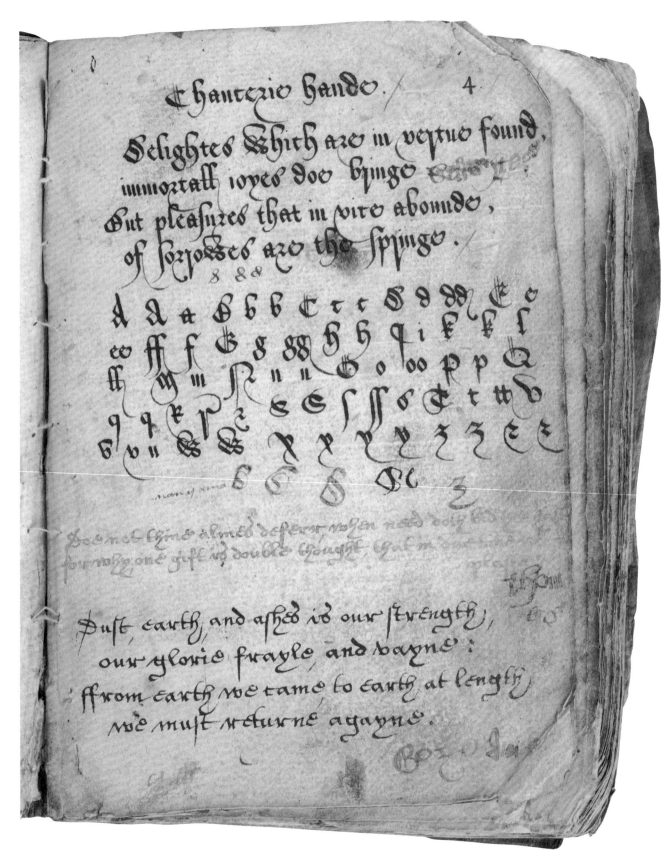

Fig. 125. A student example of "Chancerie hande."
Hill, Notebook, p. 9. Osborn b234

CHANCERY HAND

"Ah! 'twas a fine time for our trade," wrote the anonymous author of *A new case put to an old lawyer* (1656), commenting satirically on the confusion surrounding the "Court-hand writing" once used for legal documents.[119] So impenetrable was the hand, and Latin legal forms, to its county audiences that it was received as "a spel made by an old conjurer," frightening its audience, their wives, and the cows in the fields. What seems a commentary on the archaic quality of court hand is in fact a deeply partisan political statement: in 1650, under the Protectorate of Oliver Cromwell, Parliament had banned the use of court hand and Latin for English legal and administrative documents, declaring that England's records were to be "written in an ordinary, usual, and legible hand and character." Three years after this work was published, when Charles II was restored to the English throne, the set of hands known as "court hand" was reinstated.[120]

Chancery hand (fig. 125), as one category of court hand, was closely intertwined with the political evolution of the English language as the native tongue of the English realm. Before the fifteenth century, the English aristocracy conducted its administrative and other business in Latin, French, and English. By the end of the fifteenth century, English had become the dominant tongue for civil administration. As J.H. Fisher observes, the change is documented through Parliamentary records: over the course of the fourteenth century, members of Parliament increasingly presented their arguments in English. After 1400, when Parliamentary petitions were required to be set in writing, they were also documented with increasing frequency in English, rising from none in English at the start of the fifteenth century to more than a hundred per decade from 1430.[121]

As we have seen, the major departments of the early modern English government often possessed their own distinctive hands, or set hands. Of these, chancery hand was the longest-lived, surviving as the formal hand by which the Acts of Parliament were "enrolled," or officially recorded, on Parliament rolls until 1836.[122]

Chancery English became the standard form for civil administration from the fifteenth century. The Chancery court derived from the court chaplain's management of the King's seal, and from there the oversight of the royal administration. Chancery English and chancery hand therefore reflect the emergence of an English royal administration and its bureaucracy.

Over the course of the fifteenth century, chancery hand became the documentary standard used by clerks in the Chancery court. These clerks were trained through apprenticeships, initially in the Chancery houses and later in the Chancery Inns, where they were taught both the chancery hand and the appropriate forms of legal documents. As these apprentices became clerks—or writing masters, in households or universities—the chancery hand became synonymous with a particular type of formal documentary English. Both the language and the hand were normalized by Chancery clerks in rendering documents for approval by the Chancery administration. As Fisher argues, "until the end of the fifteenth century, Chancery comprised virtually all of the national bureaucracy of England except for the closely allied Exchequer."[123] As English increasingly became the language of Parliament, Chancery English and chancery hand became the formal language and hand of the English parliamentary and legal archive.

Chancery hand has several distinctive characteristics. This example shows a formal Elizabethan rendering of chancery hand (figs. 126–127): it is a mock charter, a stage prop presented to William Cecil, Lord Burghley, by Elizabeth I in 1591, in a pageant staged at Theobolds, his house, to mark his retirement. Theatrically structured as a formal document of the Chancery court—"in oour high court of Chancery"—it emphasizes many of the characteristic features of chancery hand. Note the double-lobed *a* and other characteristics resonant of Anglicana: the two-compartment *g* and looping ascender on *d;* the curved ascenders on the *h* and *s;* the looped ascender on the *v* and *w*. Take note as well of *r*—seen in "retyred" at the start of line two—made with a single hooked stroke; also the sigma form for *s* in "spryte," following.

Fig. 126. Mock charter. England, May 10, 1591.
Elizabethan Club, Yale University. Eliz MS Vault

Fig. 127. Detail of fig. 126

The document is performing formality.[124] It is written on parchment, pricked and ruled in graphite, and signed by the Lord Chancellor, Christopher Hatton; the initials for *E* and *h* are elaborately decorated; headings and section breaks are highlighted in darker ink, with capitals, and further marked by wider spacing than the rest of the text. It is issued with the "Great Seal," the matrix for which was engraved by Nicholas Hilliard. Elizabeth can just barely be made out in the wax impression of the seal: standing in her gown and ruff, holding the orb and scepter of state. One section of the inscription, "dei gracia," can be made out of the whole: "Elizabetha dei gracia Anglie Francie et Hibernie Regina Fidei Defensor," or, "Elizabeth, by grace of God, Queen of England, France and Ireland, Defender of the Faith."[125]

Elizabetha Anglor̃, id est autore et Angelor̃ Regina formosissima & felicissima. Too the disconsolate / & retyred sprite; the hermyte of Tyboll: and to all oother disaffected soules claming by, from or under the sayd heremite: sendeth greeting. / Whear in oour high coourt of Chancery it is gyven us too understand: that yoow sir, heremyte the abandonate of Natures fayr coort, / and servaunt too heavens woonders: have (for the space of two yeer & two moonths) possessed yourself of fayr Tybollt, with hir sweet rosary, / sumtyme the recreacon of our right trusty & right welbelooved Sir William Sitsilt knyght: leaving too him, the olld rude repose...

BASTARD OR MIXED HANDS

Like their writers, hands can be complex and idiosyncratic. A writer might be proficient in several different hands, using them in distinct contexts. A writer might incorporate certain features of one hand into another. The writer of an otherwise characteristic Anglicana might adopt some letterforms from secretary hand, perhaps using both a double-lobed and single-lobed letterform *a* within the same document. Equally, a writer might keep the hand he or she learned as a schoolchild, writing in old age with the hand used in childhood.

Hands also change. Anglicana and secretary hand coexisted as cursive book hand scripts for more than

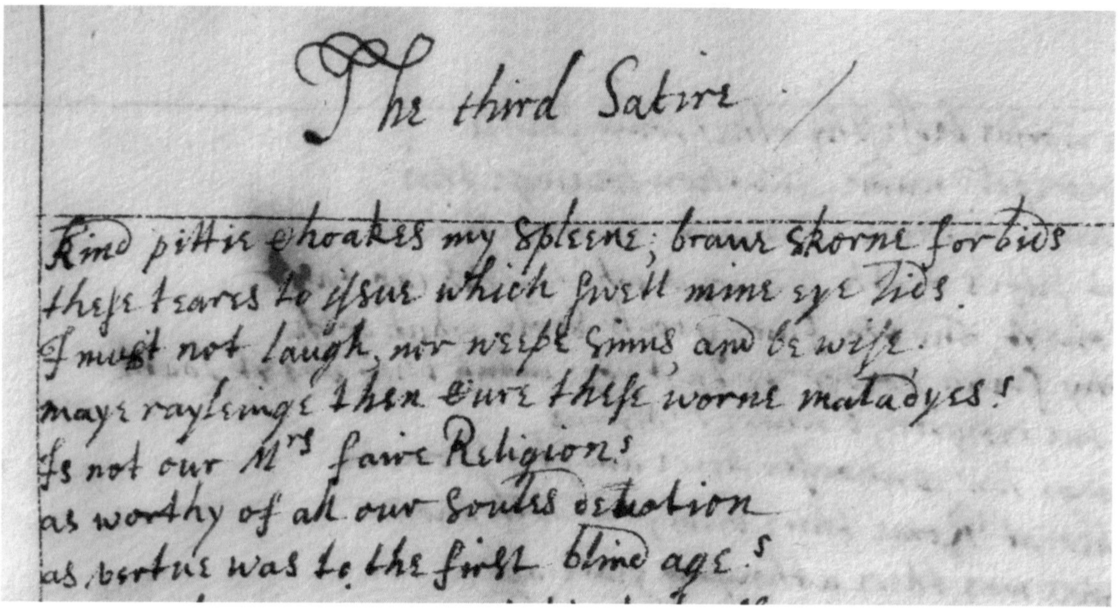

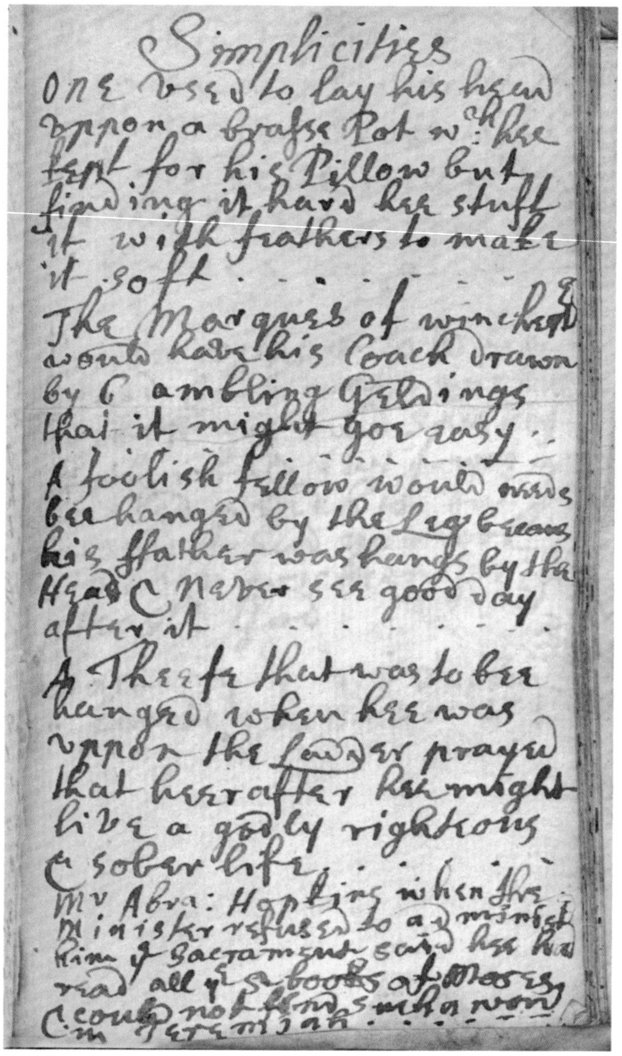

Fig. 128. Detail, "The third Satire," written in a mixed hand in a copy of John Donne's Satires and poems. England, ca. 1613. Osborn b458. Note the use of punctuation; also the stain where the manuscript clearly became wet.

The third Satire

Kind pittie choakes my Spleene; braue skorne forbids
these teares to issue which swell mine eye lids
I must not laugh, nor weepe sins and be wise
maye raylinge then cure these worne maladyes?
Is not our M^{rs} faire Religion
as worthy of all our soules deuotion
as vertue was to the first blind age^s?

Fig. 129. "Simplicities," written in a mixed hand in a tiny, pocket-sized notebook. Jestbook. England, 1640s. Osborn b430

Simplicities
One used to lay his head
uppon a brass Pot wch hee
kept for his Pillow but
finding it hard hee stufd
it with feathers to make
it soft . . . .

a century. Over that period, as the usage of secretary hand gradually became more widespread, the form of both hands also changed. Secretary hand looked different in the early sixteenth century than it had in the late fourteenth: the hand had evolved. Over the course of the early modern period, mixed or "bastard" versions of secretary hand were also used by scribes, eliding features of italic hand with secretary hand, or of secretary with round hand. As Denholm-Young observed, "the best efforts of the writing-master in teaching the distinct styles of writing (Secretary, Roman, Italic, and the Court hands) could not prevent the average man from mixing them up in practice."[126]

Mixed hand, when referring to manuscripts in early modern England, generally refers to penmanship incorporating some aspects of italic hand with secretary hand (fig. 128). In copying jokes and riddles into this pocket-sized notebook (fig. 129), a mid-seventeenth-century reader has retained some features of secretary hand (the left-rising ascender of the *d,* as one example) while rejecting others (most notably, the closed loop of the secretary *e* and the dropped descender of the secretary *h*). Secretary hand steadily declined in use over the course of the seventeenth century. Individuals increasingly wrote in mixed hand and, by the later seventeenth century, in round hand or copperplate.

ROUND HAND

Through most of the early modern period, England was a consumer of Continental hands. From the fourteenth century through the end of the seventeenth, England followed the fashions of Italian and French hands, adapting them to particular English contexts. Anglicana, secretary, and italic—or, Italian—hands show the intertwining of English manuscript culture with Continental fashion.

This was to change in the late seventeenth century. In precisely the period of the Glorious Revolution, when England was emerging as an international commercial and naval power, English penmanship came to dominate first national and then international handwriting. When the young student Mary Serjant

learned about the arithmetic of commodities in her 1688 copybook (figs. 130–131), she did so by copying an exercise on the fees paid to a smith, carpenter, rope maker, and others by a merchant fitting out the hull of a ship. The same page shows her copying an exercise on the cost of the textiles—"Holland," "dutty," "broad cloth," and ribbon—that circulated in the same world of mercantile commerce.

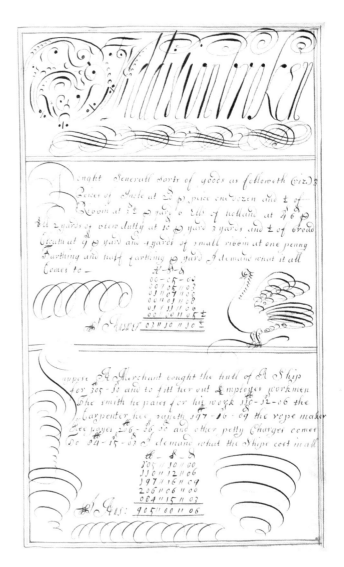

Fig. 130. Serjant, Arithmetic and penmanship notebook. England, 1688. Osborn fb98. Not all manuscript can be easily translated into print. Note the elegance of Serjant's use of superscript, abbreviation, and punctuation in her arithmetic, and the difficulty of conveying these in typographic form.

Bought Severall Sorts of goods as followeth (viz.) 3 Peices of Incle at 20d ℘ peice one dozen and ½ of Ribbin at 3½d ℘ yard 6 Ells of holland at 4s 6d ℘ Ell 2 yards of blew dutty at 10d ℘ yard 3 yards and ½ of broad Cloath at 9s ℘ yard and 4 yards of small ribbin at one penny Farthing and half farthing ℘ yard I demand what it all Comes to —

li.	s.	d.
00	05	00
00	05	03
01	07	00
00	01	08
01	11	06
00	00	05½
Answer 03	10	10½

Suppose A Merchant bought the hull of A Ship for 305li-10s and to fitt her out Employes workmen The smith he paies for his work 110li-12s-06d the Carpenter hee payeth 197li-16s-09d the rope mak Hee payes 206li-06s-00d and other petty Charges comes To 84li-15s-03d I demand what the Shipe cost in all

li.	s.	d.
305	10	00
110	12	06
197	16	09
206	06	00
084	15	03
Ans: 905	00	06

Fig. 131. Detail of fig. 130

Bought Seuerall sorts of goods as followth (viz.) 3
Peices of Incle at 20^d p̃ peice one dozen and ½ of
Ribbin at 3^d ½ p̃ yard 6 Ells of holland at 4^s 6^d p̃
Ell 2 yards of blew dutty at 10 p̃ yard 3 yards and ½ of broad
Cloath at 9^s p̃ yard and 4 yards of small ribbin at one penny
Farthing and half farthing p̃ yard I demand what it all
Comes to—

```
        £ – s – d
        00 – 05 – 00
        00 || 05 || 03
        03 || 07 || 00
        00 || 01 || 08
        01 || 11 || 06
        00 || 00 || 05½

Answer  03 || 10 || 10½
```

Round hand, also known as copperplate, circulated prolifically in plate-books, engraved on copperplate by writing masters (fig. 132). John Ayres's *The accomplished clerk, or, accurate pen-man* (1683?) promises "usefull examples shewing ye most natural and clerk like way of writing all the usual hands of England." In his dedication of the book to Francis Beyer, "Book-keeper and Acomptant to the Hon[ble] East India Company," Ayres touts his own "Endeavours in fitting Youth's for the service" with the East India Company.[127] In 1743 the engraver and writing master George Bickham published *The British monarchy: or, a new chorographical description of all the dominions subject to the king of Great Britain* (fig. 133), engraved

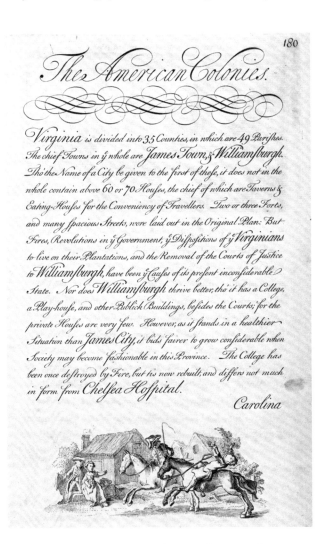

Fig. 132. George Bickham, *Penmanship in its utmost beauty and extent* (London, 1731). Yale Center for British Art. Folio A Z1

Fig. 133. George Bickham, *The British monarchy; or, a new chorographical description of all the dominions subject to the king of Great Britain* (London, 1743). Ede +743

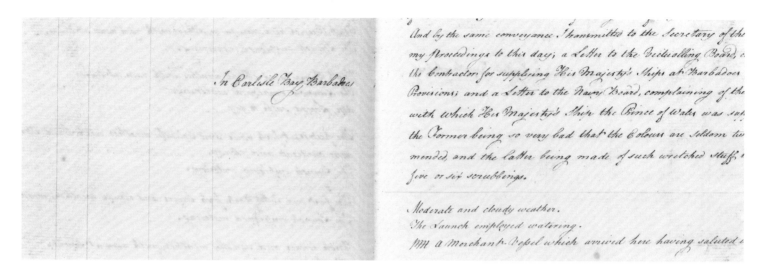

In Carlisle Bay, Barbadoes

And by the same conveyance I transmitted to the Secretary of the
my proceedings to this day; a Letter to the Victualling Board, a
the Contractor for supplying His Majesty's Ships at Barbadoes
Provisions; and a Letter to the Navy Board, complaining of the
with which His Majesty's Ship the Prince of Wales was sup
the Former being so very bad that the Colours are seldom tw
mended, and the Latter being made of such wretched stuff,
five or six scrubbings.

Moderate and cloudy weather.
The Launch employed watering.
PM a Merchant Vessel which arrived here having saluted

Fig. 134. "In Carlisle Bay, Barbados," detail of Samuel Barrington, A journal of the proceedings of the Hon. Samuel Barrington, rear admiral of the red and commander in chief of his majesty's ships and vessels… England, 1778–79. Osborn fc147

lb 8 Woods, 1/2 Flour lb 2 White Argols lb 1 1/4 Logwood oz 4 Brazill oz 10 Crocus oz 4 Crop Madder Shot with oz 2 Coppras oz 4 Allom Lye in	18509
lb 1 Flour oz 8 Shumach lb oz 1. 7 Red Argols oz 6 Fustick lb oz 1. 6 Brazill oz 3 Sanders lb oz 1. 3 Crop Madder, Shot with oz 4 Coppras lb 1 Allom Lye in	18515
lb 1 1/4 Grain lb 10 Tartar, boil 10 Minutes, pump up lb 1 1/4 Allom, six Hours Lye in	18520
lb 1 Grain lb 8 Tartar lb 10 Allom all put into the above Pink Liquor boil six Hours Lye in	18522
The above Pink Wool finisht with lb 40 Crop Madder lb 40 Umbro Madder a 5 1/2 boil 12 Minutes & Landed.	18522

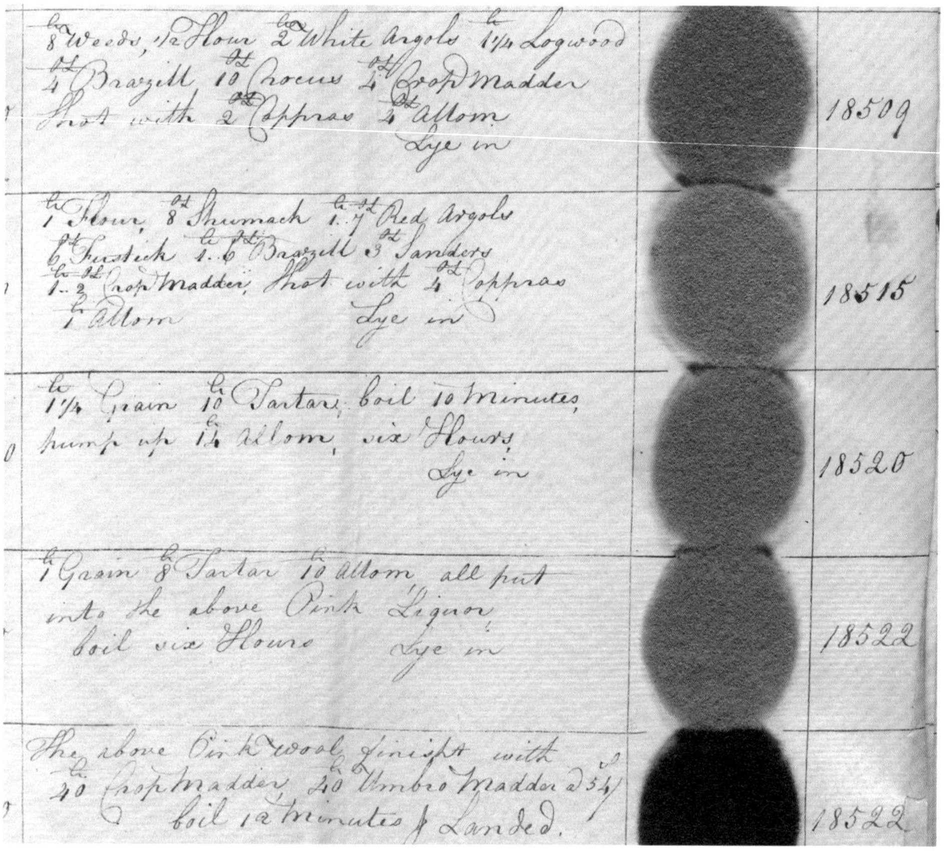

Fig. 135. Detail, William Butts' Dye Book. England, 1768–86. Osborn fc173

in the same beautiful round hand in which he had published *Penmanship in its utmost beauty and extent* (1731; see fig. 132) and multiple editions of his *The universal penman; or, the art of writing made useful to the gentleman and scholar.* For Bickham and his readers, copperplate was increasingly the public demeanor of a universal penman in the service of British empire. From the outset, writing masters like Bickham or Ayres focused on the market for youth entering into the Indies trade and on the professional viability of the clear, graceful, commercial round hand. Round hand fills this late-eighteenth-century logbook of the British navy (fig. 134), as it does this industrial recipe book for the manufacture of textile dyes (fig. 135).[128]

Copperplate became the hand of the professional classes and of Britain's emergent empire. The paperwork of Britain's political and commercial culture was, over the course of the eighteenth century, increasingly completed in round hand, often on a printed form (fig. 136).

Fig. 136. Certificate of entrance into the East-India Company for Nathaniel Helly of Nuneaton, Warwickshire, aged 27 Years, 5 Feet 9 Inches high, Labourer. London, November 13, 1769. Osborn Manuscript File 19652

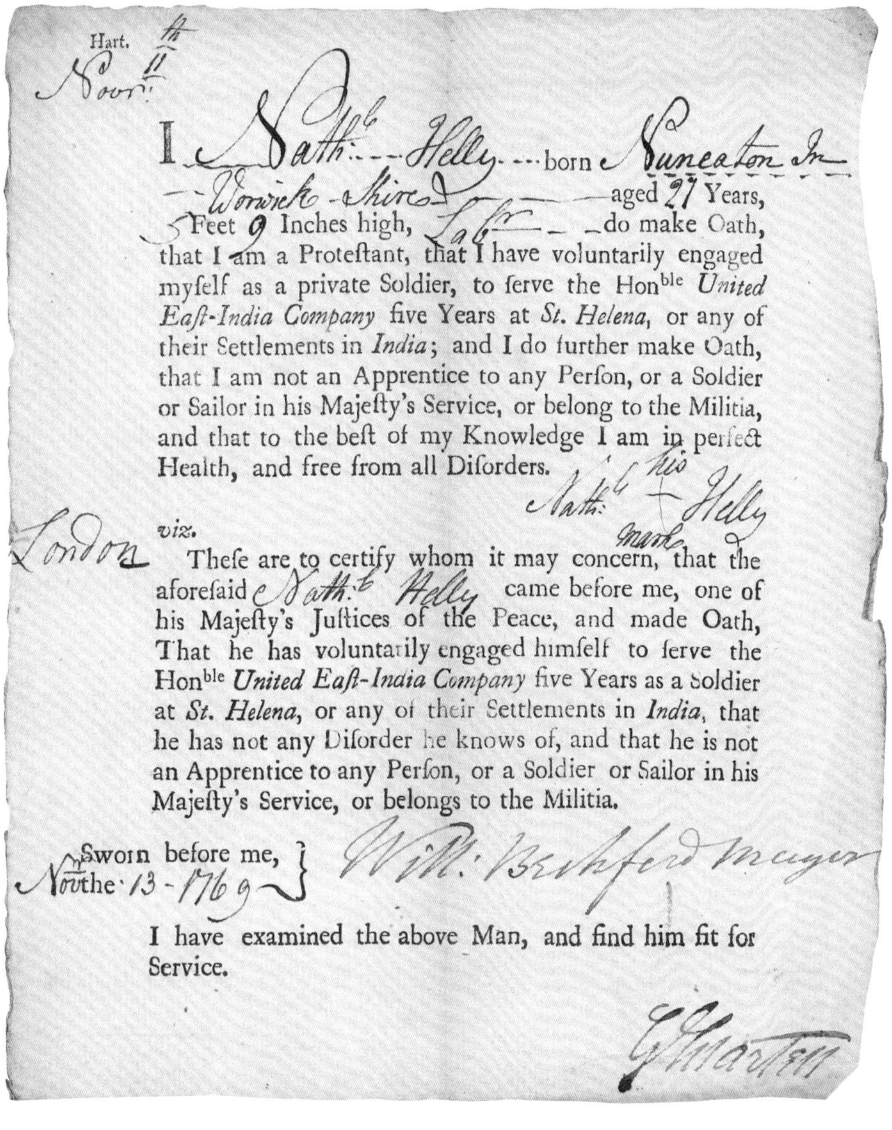

Hart. 4th

11 Novr.

I Nathl. Helly ---born Nuneaton In --Warwick-Shire Labr ---aged 27 Years, 5 Feet 9 Inches high, Labr --do make Oath, that I am a Proteſtant, that I have voluntarily engaged myſelf as a private Soldier, to ſerve the Honble *United Eaſt-India Company* five Years at *St. Helena*, or any of their Settlements in *India*; and I do further make Oath, that I am not an Apprentice to any Perſon, or a Soldier or Sailor in his Majeſty's Service, or belong to the Militia, and that to the beſt of my Knowledge I am in perfect Health, and free from all Diſorders.

Nathl. his + mark Helly

London *viz.* Theſe are to certify whom it may concern, that the aforeſaid Nathl. Helly came before me, one of his Majeſty's Juſtices of the Peace, and made Oath, That he has voluntarily engaged himſelf to ſerve the Honble *United Eaſt-India Company* five Years as a Soldier at *St. Helena*, or any of their Settlements in *India*, that he has not any Diſorder he knows of, and that he is not an Apprentice to any Perſon, or a Soldier or Sailor in his Majeſty's Service, or belongs to the Militia.

Sworn before me, Novthe 13-1769 } Willm. Beckford mayor

I have examined the above Man, and find him fit for Service.

ABBREVIATION AND PUNCTUATION

Abbreviation

Abbreviation was a habitual practice within medieval scribal culture, one surviving into the early modern period. Contractions and other forms of abbreviation helped scribes to compress Latin forms and endings in a consistent manner, comprehensible to readers and other scribes. Regularly repeated features of the language and content were normalized and abridged by writers and readers. Some forms of abbreviation were a response to Latin endings; others to the names of Christ or other religious figures. While medieval Latin abbreviation practices do not apply uniformly to early modern vernacular works, early modern English writers and readers relied on a consistent and pervasive set of textual abbreviations from the fifteenth through the seventeenth century.

Some abbreviations are still so pervasive that they are difficult to recognize as such. Several of these survived from imperial Roman rule through medieval European culture and are still in use today. An example can be found in the Roman "note juris," or legal signs, in which words were shortened to capitals, separated by full stops: B.C. (before Christ) or B.C.E. (before the Common Era) are examples of this practice in modern usage. Another example can be found in the Tironian symbols used by Tiro, Cicero's secretary: e.g., the "Tironian et," in which the symbol ⁊ is used for "and" (in Latin, "et").[129]

Abbreviation takes two major forms in English language documents: suspension, in which letters are omitted from the ending of a word, and contraction, in which letters are omitted from the middle of a word, often taking the form of a superscript, e.g., S^r [Sir]. Suspension is often marked by a colon, used to alert the reader to an absent ending. Both suspension and contraction are often also marked by the use of a "tittle" or tilde (from the Latin *titulus*), a straight or waving bar across the abbreviated section. A third form of abbreviation is the "special" mark or sign, also called brevigraph, in which a symbol was used to refer to particular letters or words, e.g., & for "and" in English or "et" in Latin.

Several common forms occur in early modern English usage (figs. 137–138):

L^p	Lordship or Ladyship
M^r	Master
M^{rs}	Mistress
M^{tie}	Majesty
Rec^d	received
S^r	Sir
W^t	what
W^{ch}	which
Y^e, or the	the y is a remnant of the Old English "thorn" letterform, pronounced "th," with a superscript e
Y^u or y^w	you
Y^r	your
Y^{rs}	yours
Y^t	that
&	and
⁊	and, a precursor of the ampersand, &
X	Jesus Christ

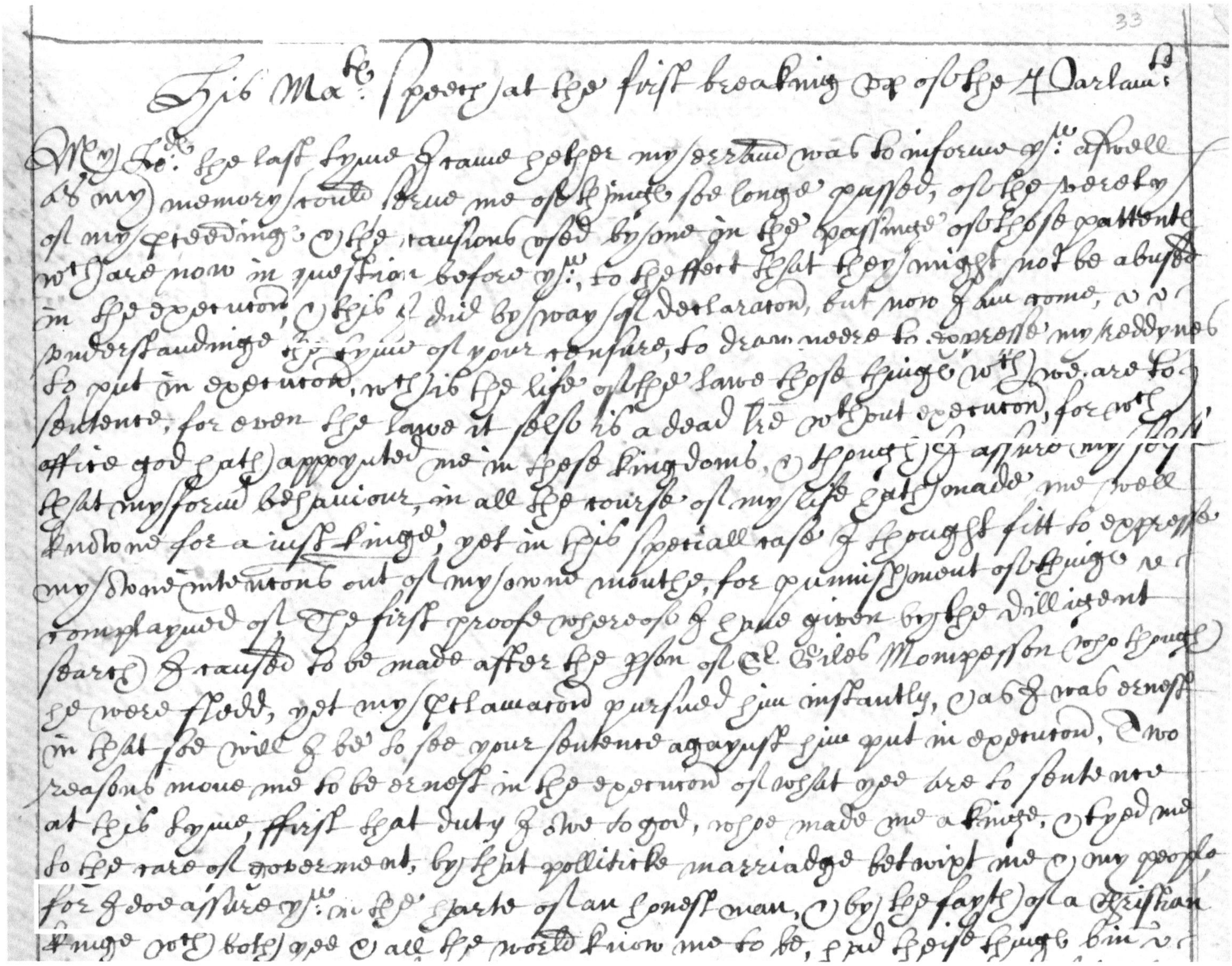
33

His Ma:te speech at the first breaking up of the Parlam:

Fig. 137. Detail, showing the abbreviation Ma^{te} for "Majestie"; et, a precursor to the ampersand; wch and wth for "which" and "with" ["Those things wch we are to/… wthout execucon, for w^{ch}"]; y^{u} for "you" ["for I doe assure y^{u}"]. Volume of political papers, p. 33. England, ca. 1620–39. Osborn fb57

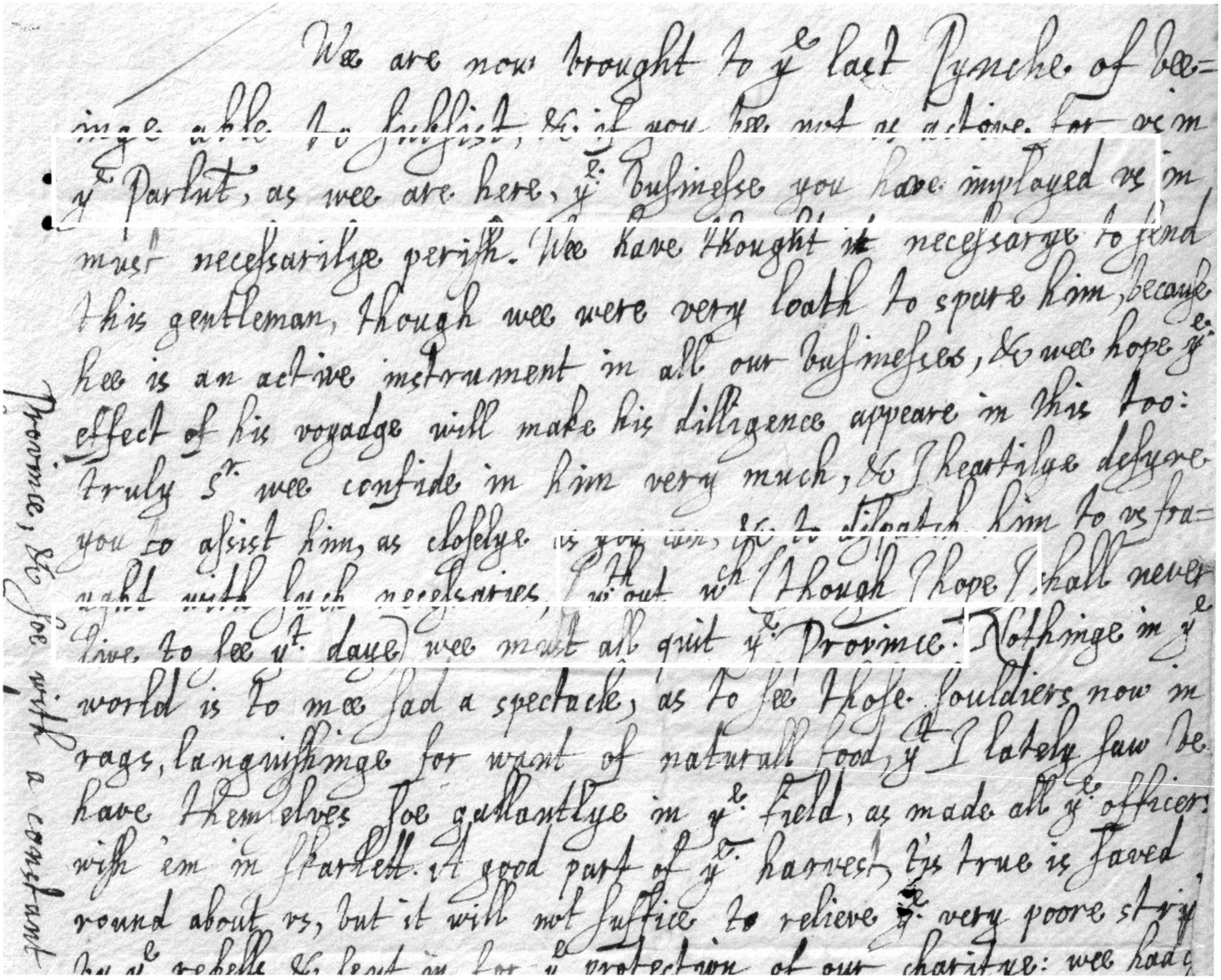

Wee are now brought to ye last Pynche of bee-
inge able to subsist, & if you bee not as active for vs in
ye Parlmt, as wee are here, ye businesse you have imployed vs in
must necessarilye perish. Wee have thought it necessarye to send
this gentleman, though wee were very loath to spare him, because
hee is an active instrument in all our businesses, & wee hope ye
effect of his voyadge will make his dilligence appeare in this too:
truly Sr wee confide in him very much, & I heartilye desyre
you to assist him, as closelye as you can, & to dispatch him to vs fra-
ught with such necessaries, wthout wch (though I hope I shall never
live to see yt daye) wee must all quit ye Province. Nothinge in ye
world is to mee sad a spectacle, as to see those souldiers now in
rags, languishinge for want of naturall food, yt I lately saw be-
have themselves soe gallantlye in ye field, as made all ye officers
wish em in skarlett. A good part of ye harvest, tis true is saved
round about vs, but it will not suffice to relieve ye very poore stript
by ye rebells & sent in for ye protection of our charitye: wee have

Province, & soe with a constant

Fig. 138. Detail, showing the abbreviation y^e for "the" and the use of the tilde to abbreviate Parliament ["ye Parlñt, as wee are here, ye businesse you have imployed us…"]; w^{th}out and wch for "without" and "which" ["w^{th}out w^{ch} (though I hope I…"]; y^t and y^e for "that" and "the" ["live to see y^t daye wee must all quit ye Province"]. William Jephson to John Pym. Cork, October 15, 1642. Osborn fb94, Folder 6

Punctuation

While similar in the marks and symbols employed, early modern punctuation differs significantly from modern usage. Many of the same forms are used—the period or full stop; the comma; the colon; the quotation or speech mark; the question mark—but they serve a slightly, but distinctly, separate function in marking the divisions, spacing, pronunciation, breath marks, or other rhetorical functions of the early modern text (figs. 139–140).

Punctuation marks in a mid-sixteenth-century astronomical treatise (fig. 141) include:

Virgule (fig. 142): this slash seen at the end of lines, particularly in verse, works as the equivalent to a modern full stop or comma; it was also used to mark the end of a stanza.

Colon (fig. 143): the colon serves as one of the major stops in early modern punctuation, acting both as pause and as full stop.

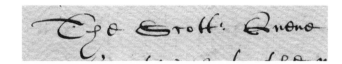

Fig. 139. Detail, showing the use of a colon to mark a suspended ending: "The Scott: Quene," or the Scottish queen. Copy of a narrative of the trial of Mary, Queen of Scots. England, ca. 1600. Osborn fb32

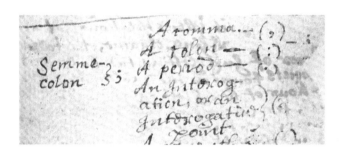

Fig. 140. John Rose, punctuation listed in a notebook. England, 1676. Osborn b227

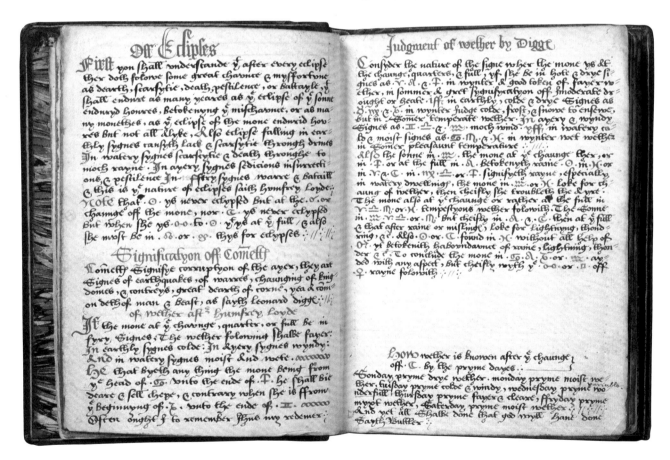

Fig. 141. "Off Eclipses," Significatyon off Cometts," and "Judgment of wether by Diggs," f. 4v–5r. England, mid-16th century. Beinecke MS 558

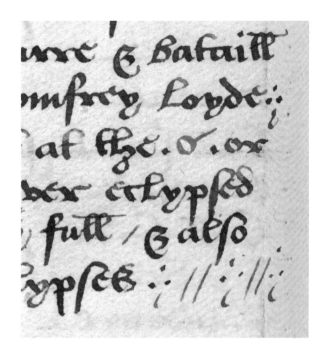

Fig. 142. Detail of fig. 141, showing the virgule

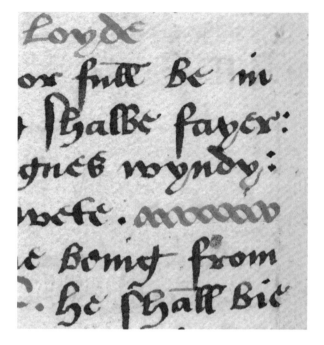

Fig. 143. Detail of fig. 141, showing the colon

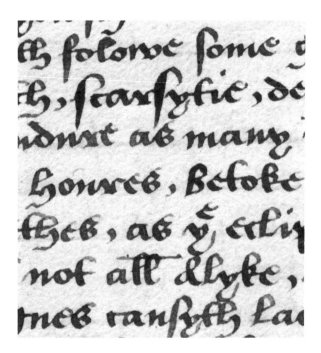

Fig. 144. Detail of fig. 141, showing the comma

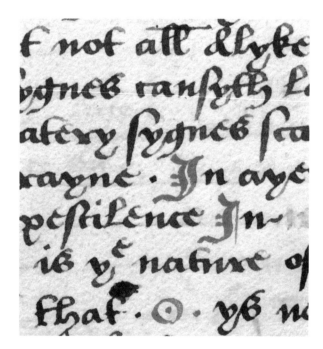

Fig. 145. Detail of fig. 141, showing the period or full stop

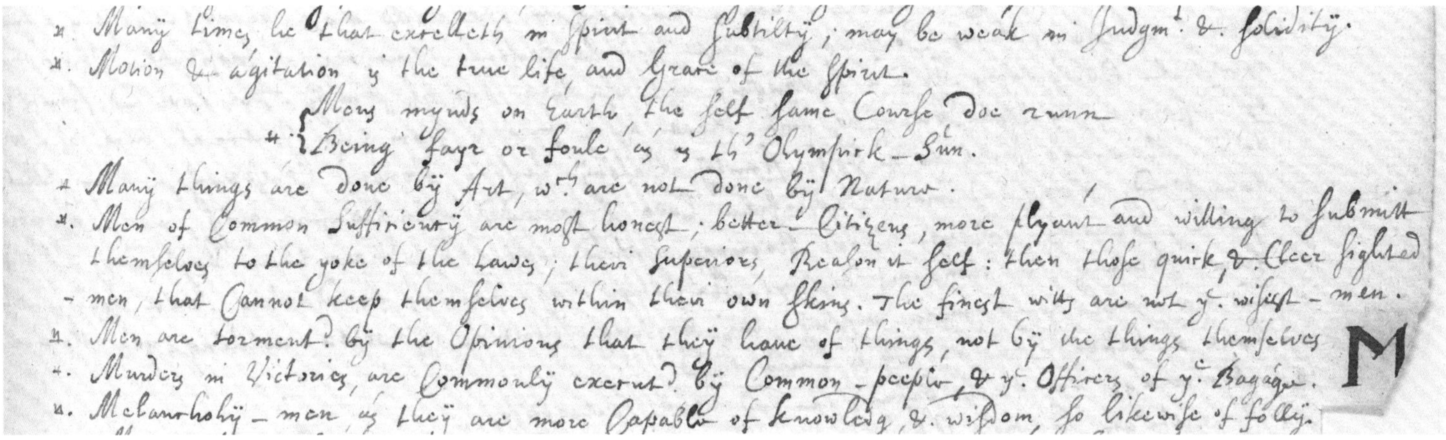

Many times he that excelleth in Spirit and Subtility, may be weak in Judgmt. & Solidity.
Motion & agitation is the true life and Grace of the Spirit.
Many mynds on Earth the self same Course doe runn
Being fayr or foule as is th' Olympick Sun.
Many things are done by Art, wch. are not done by Nature.
Men of Common Sufficiency are most honest; better Citizens, more plyant and willing to submitt themselves to the yoke of the Laws, their Superiors, Reason it self: then those quick & Cleer sighted men, that Cannot keep themselves within their own skins. The finest witts are not ye. wisest men.
Men are torment. by the Opinions that they have of things, not by the things themselves.
Murders in Victories, are Commonly execut. by Common people, & ye. Officers of ye. Bagage.
Melancholy men, as they are more Capable of knowledg, & wisdom, so likewise of folly.

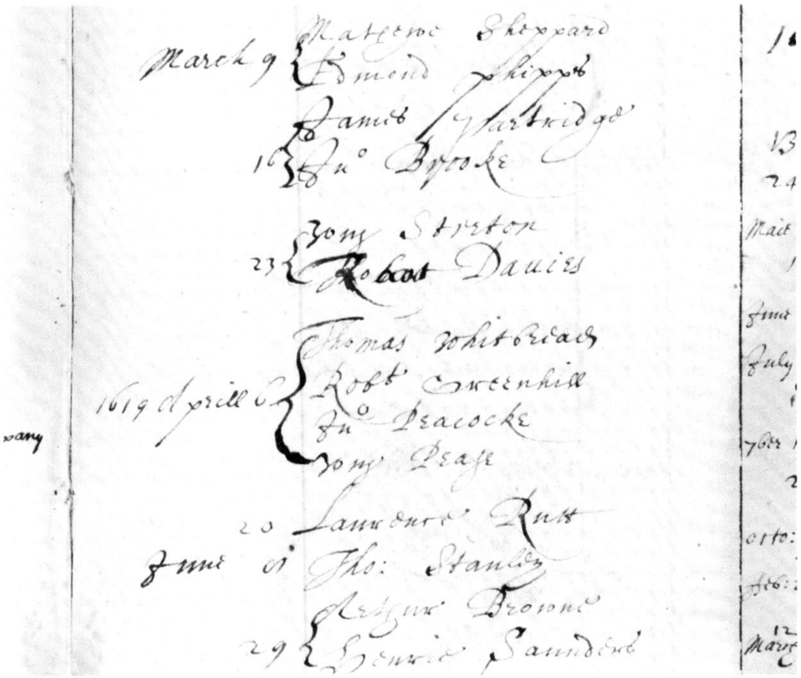

March 9 Mathew Sheppard
Edmond Shipps
16 James Partridge
Jno Brooke
23 Jony Streton
Robert Dauies
1619 Aprill 6 Thomas Whitbread
Robt Greenhill
Jno Peacocke
Jony Peale
June 20 Laurence Rutt
01 Tho: Stanley
29 Arthur Browne
Henrie Saunders

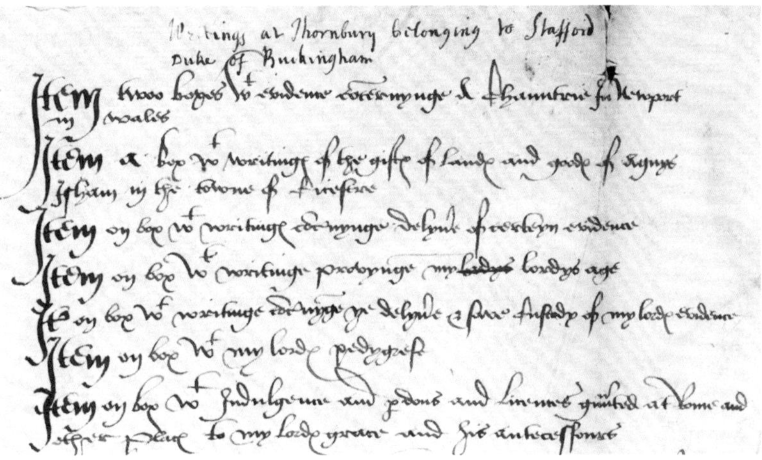

Writings at Thornbury belonging to Stafford Duke of Buckingham

Comma (fig. 144): the comma was an early-sixteenth-century introduction into English culture, acting in its modern role by the seventeenth century and eventually replacing the virgule.

Period (fig. 145): like the colon, the early modern full stop, prick, or point was used to mark a pause of some weight. It was only later in the seventeenth century that it took on its modern usage, denoting a significant pause, break, or end of sentence.

Quotation marks were seldom used in early modern English manuscript. Textual citations or excerpts were often marked by inverted commas in the margins (fig. 146).

Other marks acted to designate the relationships at work within a text. Brackets offer one example, used to articulate the existence (although not necessarily the nature) of a connection (fig. 147). Another example would be the Latin phrase "item," used extensively in inventories, account books, and other sources to demarcate the components of a list (fig. 148).

Fig. 146. Detail, showing quotation marks in a collection of aphorisms. Collection of English proverbs, f. 43r. England, ca. 1654. Osborn fb77

Fig. 147. Detail, showing brackets in Marmaduke Rawdon, Commonplace book. England, ca. 1629–32. Osborn fb150

Fig. 148. Detail of a list, "Writings at Thornbury belonging to Stafford Duke of Buckingham." England, ca. 1520. Osborn fa41.2

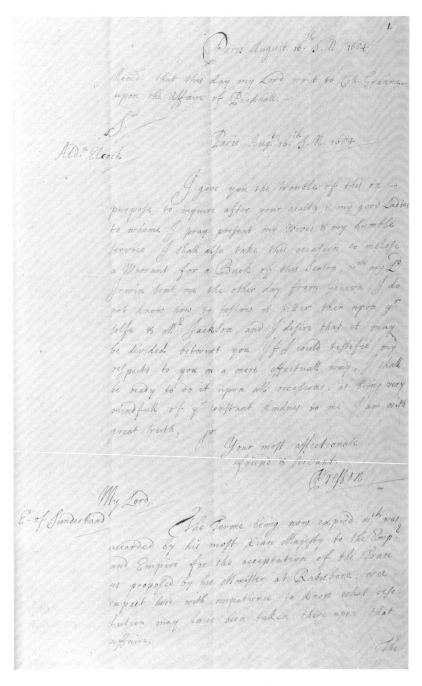

Fig. 149. In a secretary's careful hand: "Paris August 16th S.N. [or stile nouveau, "new style"] 1684," with a note that "this day my Lord writ to Coll. Graham upon the affaire of Pickhall." Richard Graham, Viscount Preston, Letter book. Paris, 1684. Osborn fb83

DATES

March 25—or Lady Day, for the Annunciation—was the start of the year in early modern England. This put England at odds with other countries: on the Continent, Roman Catholic countries switched from the Julian calendar to the Gregorian in 1582, beginning the new year on January 1. Scotland followed suit in 1600. Until 1752, when England adopted the Gregorian calendar, the English year did not align with the Scottish or Continental calendar.[130]

As a result, dates in early modern England were commonly understood to be open to some confusion. "New style" (i.e., according to the Gregorian calendar) and "old style" (according to the Julian) were often used in correspondence and other formats to distinguish between the Catholic and the Protestant calendars. The dates between January 1 and March 25 were also often marked with a dual year, to alert the reader that January 15 might fall, for instance, in 1661 (old style) but in 1662 (new style). Dual-dating allowed the reader to toggle between the complexities of the different calendars.

Writers also filed their correspondence, sometimes docketing (or, making notes for filing) a letter with some combination of information on the sender, the date received, and sometimes the content and whether the recipient had replied. The letter-writer might record the date in the text itself, before the address or after the signature. Sometimes writers might use the Latin months; sometimes Roman numerals for the date, sometimes Arabic; sometimes write "new style" or "old style" by the year, or "n.s." or "o.s." as abbreviation (fig. 149). Writers might also specify that a date was in the current month or year by using the word "instant," often abbreviated as "ins[t]." In this example from a manuscript newsletter, the phrase "letters from Paris of the 28. ins[t]" is used to refer to letters on the 28th of the current month (fig. 150).

Dates could also be interlocked with the legal or religious year. Affidavits often incorporate the mechanisms by which witnesses or participants in a court proceeding might cite a particular date in memory. An event might be situated before or after Lady Day, or a festival day two years past. Printed almanacs, often annotated by their owners and used as diaries, often record the organization of the fiscal or professional year around the law terms of the Inns of Court or university: Michaelmas (Fall); Hilary (Winter); Easter (through Easter Trinity); Trinity (Spring and early Summer). Other dating systems include the assizes and the sitting of Parliament. This manuscript almanac, kept by George Dew in 1692, documents the calendrical, legal, and astrological year (figs. 151–152).

Astrology was another important measure of time. Early modern almanacs offered guides to the influence of the zodiac on their readers, as important and useful advice on when to undertake certain types of action or how to interpret and plan treatment for medical conditions. The horoscope was a widespread table

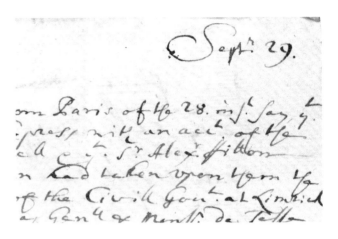

Fig. 150. Detail, showing the abbreviation ins[t] for "instant." OSB MSS 60. See also fig. 221.

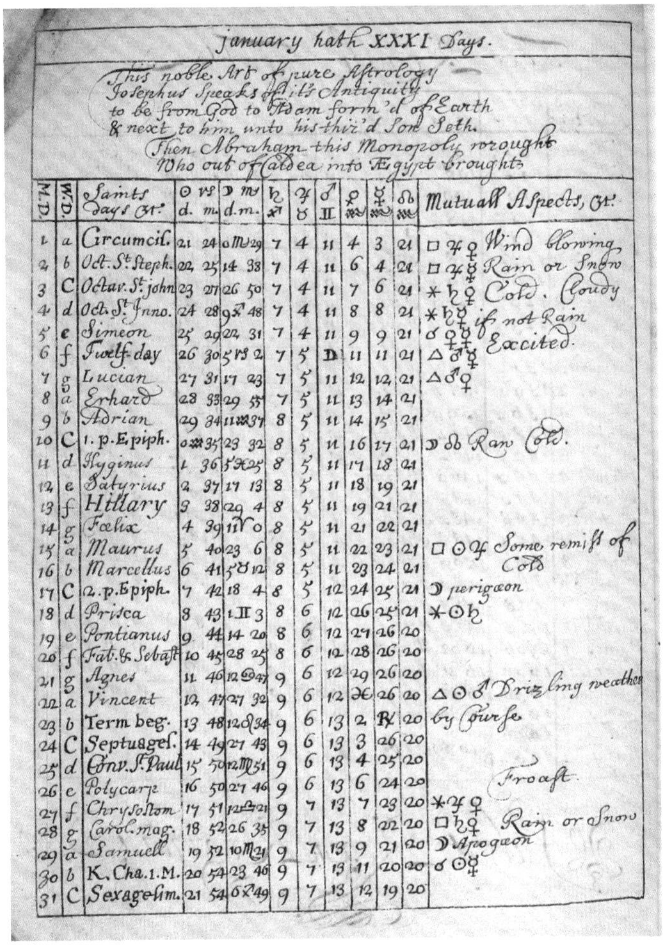

Fig. 151. Almanac table, including the start of Hilary term, in George Dew, "Ephemeris astrologikos, or an Almanack" for the year of the Redemption 1692. England, 1692. Osborn Manuscript File 19212

Fig. 152. "The moon her dominion, over man's body," in George Dew, "Ephemeris astrologikos, or an Almanack" for the year of the Redemption 1692. England, 1692. Osborn Manuscript File 19212

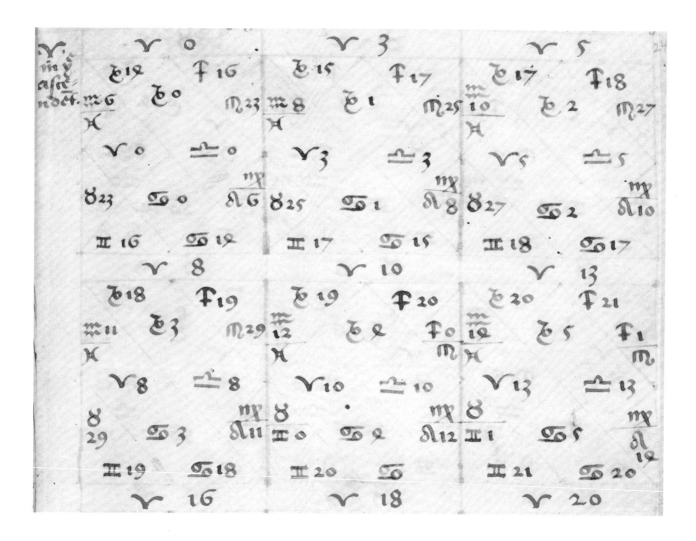

of reference, and early modern readers can be found charting their horoscopes and the particular zodiacal influences in their notebooks and annotated almanacs. This example shows a reader charting a zodiacal table (fig. 153).

The following details (fig. 154), all from Beinecke MS 558, offer a key to some of the more common astrological signs and symbols, shown in two columns as below.

Fig. 153. Detail, Zodiac table. From "Judgment of wether by Diggs," f. 24r. England, mid-16th century. Beinecke MS 558

Aries	Sagittarius
Taurus	Capricorn
Gemini	Aquarius
Cancer	Pisces
Leo	Sun
Virgo	Moon
Libra	Mars
Scorpio	Venus

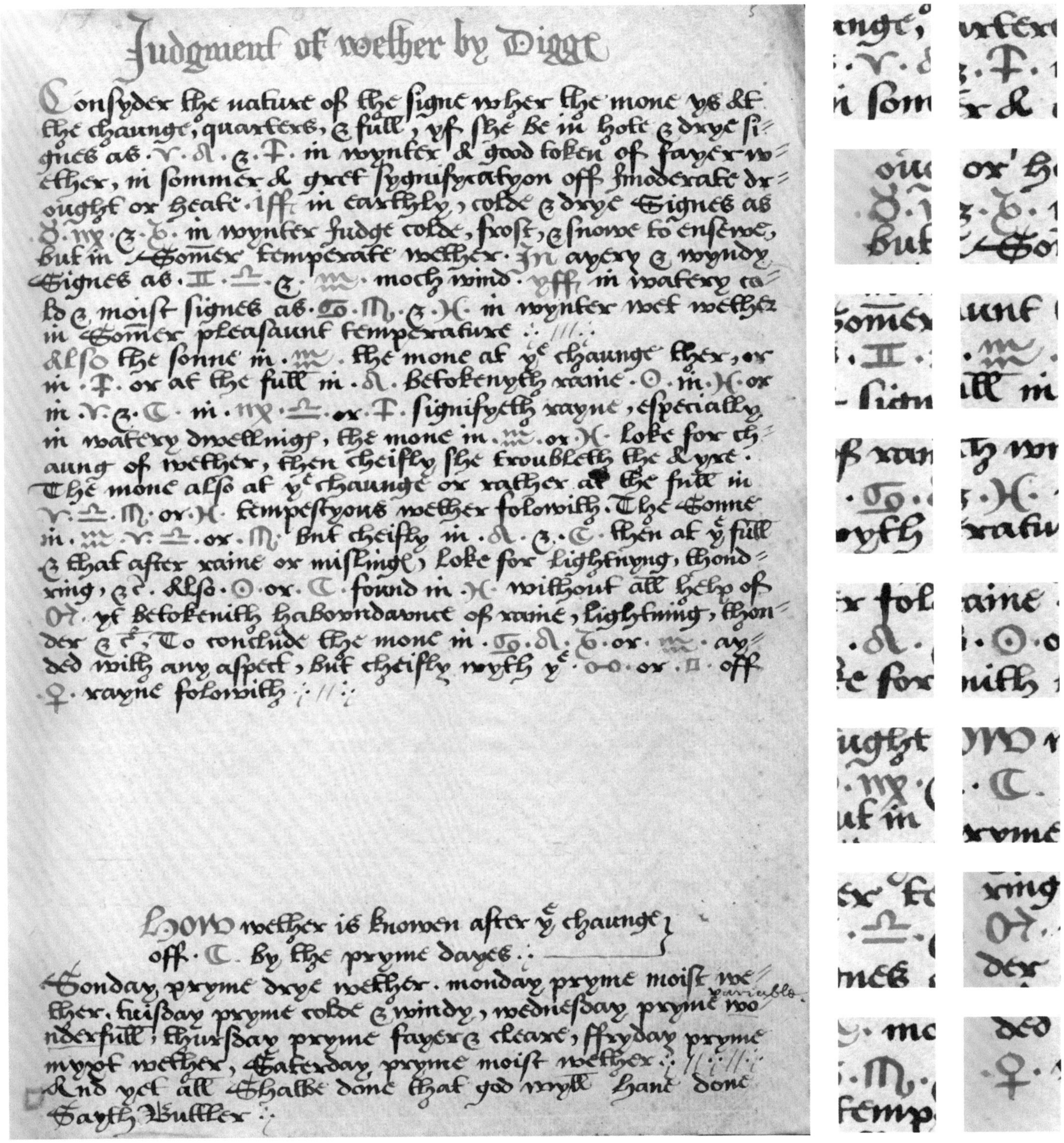

Judgment of wether by Digge

Consyder the nature of the signe wher the mone ys at
the chaunge, quarters, & full, yf she be in hote & drye signes as ♈ ♌ ♐ in wynter a good token of fayer wether, in sommer a gret sygnifycatyon off imoderate dr-
ought or heate. Iff in earthly, colde & drye Signes as
♉ ♍ ♑ in wynter Judge colde, frost, & snowe to ensewe,
but in Somer temperate wether. In ayery & wyndy
Signes as ♊ ♎ ♒ moch wind. yff in watery colde & moist signes as ♋ ♏ ♓ in wynter noch wether
in Somer pleasaunt temperature.
Also the sonne in ♍ the mone at ye chaunge ther, or
in ♐ or at the full in ♌ betokenyth rayne. ☉ in ♓ or
in ♈ & ♐ in ♍ ♎ or ♐ signifyeth rayne, especially
in watery dwellings, the mone in ♍ or ♓ loke for ch
aung of wether, then cheifly she troubleth the ayre.
The mone also at ye chaunge or rather at the full in
♈ ♎ ♏ or ♓ tempestyous wether folowith. The Sonne
in ♍ ♈ ♎ or ♏ but cheifly in ♌ ♐ then at ye full
& that after raine or misting, loke for lightnyng, thond
ring, &c. Also ☉ or ☽ found in ♓ without all help of
♂ yt betokenith habowndaunce of raine, lightning, thon
der &c. To conclude the mone in ♋ ♌ ♑ or ♏ as-
ded with any aspect, but cheifly noyth ye ☌ or ♊ off
♀ rayne folowith.

How wether is knowen after ye chaunge
off ☽ by the pryme dayes.

Sonday, pryme drye wether. monday pryme moist we
ther. tuisday pryme colde & windy, wednesday pryme wo
nderfull, thursday pryme fayer & cleare, ffryday pryme
myyot wether, Saterday, pryme moist wether.
And yet all shalbe done that god wyll have done
sayth Butler.

Fig. 154. Details (16), Astrological symbols.
From "Judgment of wether by Diggs," f. 5r.
England, mid-16th century. Beinecke MS 558

NUMBERS

Three systems of counting coexisted in early modern England: Roman, Arabic, and counters. Roman numerals were the primary numbering system in use through the sixteenth century, particularly for accounting. Arabic numeration, or "algorism," was introduced into England in the sixteenth century, bringing with it the new concept of the zero. Last, counting on counters, or an abacus, as seen in William Hill's seventeenth-century notebook (figs. 155–156), was a common way to count or keep accounts well into the seventeenth century.[131]

In 1543, when Robert Recorde published his *Ground of artes,* a mathematical primer, he could still describe "algorism" or "ciphering" as "arithmetike with the pen."[132] While authors like Recorde, Leonard Digges, or Thomas Digges published works on practical mathematics in the vernacular from the 1550s, instruction in practical mathematics was not at all a common facet of formal education in England until the late seventeenth century. Nor were numbers a common feature of instruction in writing. As Hilary Jenkinson suggests, the shifting forms of numbers might have been stabilized only through the influence of print.[133]

Figs. 155–156. Hill, Notebook, pp. 50–51. Osborn b234

How to vse this Table.

Looke the age of the moone in anie Almanack for the year presente, or for any year to come, then seek the same in this table, which you shal find eyther in the increasing or decreasing, and their in the middle column you shal without further labour find set downe the true time of her shining.

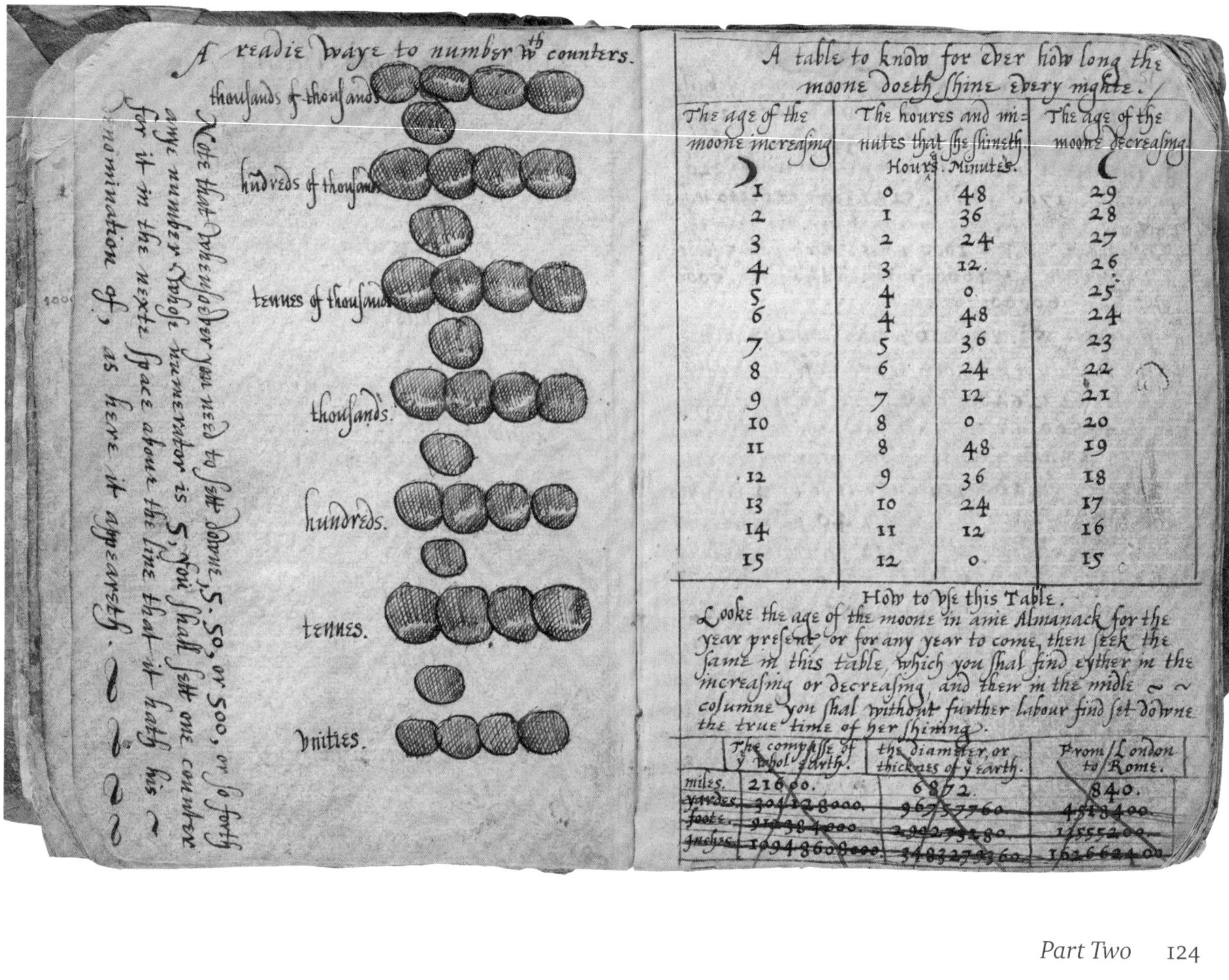

The age of the moone increasing ☽	The houres and minutes that she shineth. Hours.	Minutes.	The age of the moone decreasing ☾
1	0	48	29
2	1	36	28
3	2	24	27
4	3	12	26
5	4	0	25
6	4	48	24
7	5	36	23
8	6	24	22
9	7	12	21
10	8	0	20
11	8	48	19
12	9	36	18
13	10	24	17
14	11	12	16
15	12	0	15

How to vse this Table.

Looke the age of the moone in anie Almanack for the year present, or for any year to come, then seek the same in this table, which you shal find eyther in the increasing or decreasing, and then in the midle ~ ~ columne you shal without further labour find set downe the true time of her shining.

The compasse of y whol earth.	the diameter, or thicknes of y earth.	From London to Rome.
miles. 21600.	6872.	840.

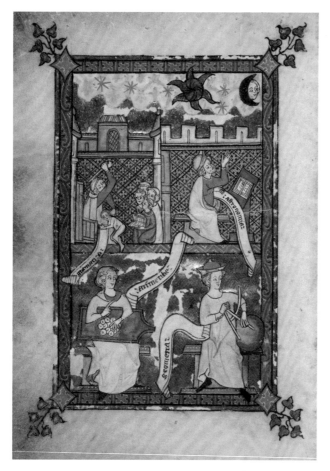

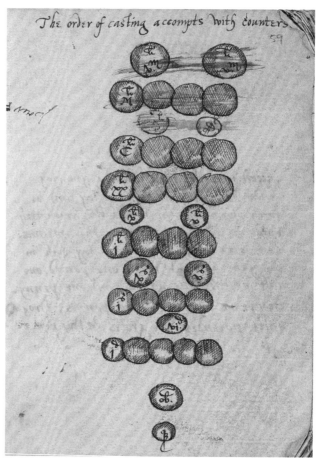

Fig. 157. The Rothschild Canticles, 6v. Flanders or northern France, early 14th century. Beinecke MS 404. A scholar uses his counters in this illustration of the quadrivium, or four liberal arts. Above, students struggle with grammar in a classroom.

Fig. 158. "The order of casting accompts with counters." A second illustration in Hill, Notebook, p. 59. Osborn b234

Medieval and early modern English writers might work across mathematical systems, toggling between counters, arithmetic, and other mathematical arts (fig. 157). In 1635 Gervase Markham could still express distrust of Arabic numerals and arithmetic, writing that

> there is more trust in an honest score chaulkt on a Trencher, then in a cunning written scrowle, how well so ever painted on the best Parchment. … I had rather be my Mans *Amanuensis* to register his Truthes, then a Witnesse of his Learning in finding out false Reckonings. And there is more Benefit in simple and single Numeration in Chaulke, then in double

Multiplication, though in never so faire an hand written.[134]

For our purposes, this lack of familiarity with arithmetic means only that, in early modern English manuscripts, numbers might be encountered in Roman, Arabic, or both forms within a document. Dates, as one example, might combine both Roman and Arabic, in a description of the day in Roman numerals and the year in Arabic.[135] While William Hill might be found copying "The order of casting accompts with counters" in his notebook (fig. 158), his familiarity with Arabic numeration is clear from his copying of tables (see fig. 156). Equally, a reader of

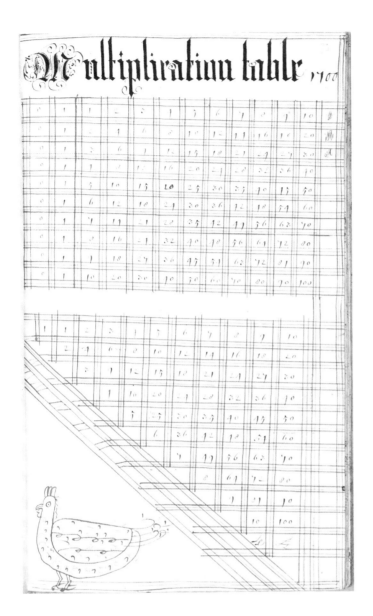

Fig. 159. Multiplication table. Matthew Wood, Arithmetic notebook. England, 1700. Osborn fb179

Gervase Markham, like Hill, could easily be conversant with Arabic numerals, in reading dates and page numbers, while remaining unfamiliar with the idea of the arithmetical calculations, or algorism "by the pen" that Arabic numeration allowed.

The language of mathematics was one learned by students like Hill in the early modern period. It was practiced, like penmanship, in arithmetic and account notebooks kept by students, male and female, like Mary Serjant (see figs. 130–131), Matthew Wood (fig. 159), and John Webb (figs. 160–161). It can also be found in the sums and numerical pen trials by which early modern writers tallied their thoughts in the margins and endpapers of their books (figs. 162–163).

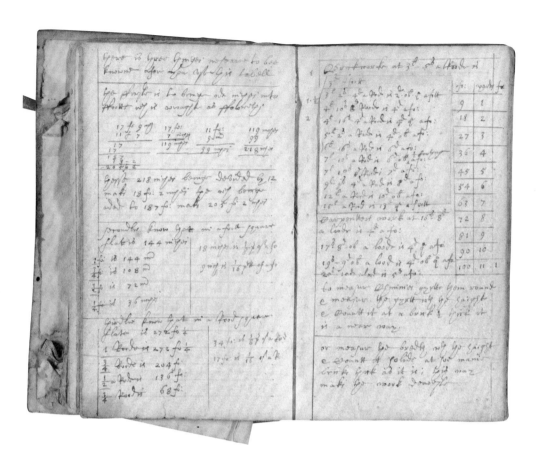

Figs. 160–161. John Webb, Account book. England, 17th century. Yale Center for British Art. NA 25 W43 1630

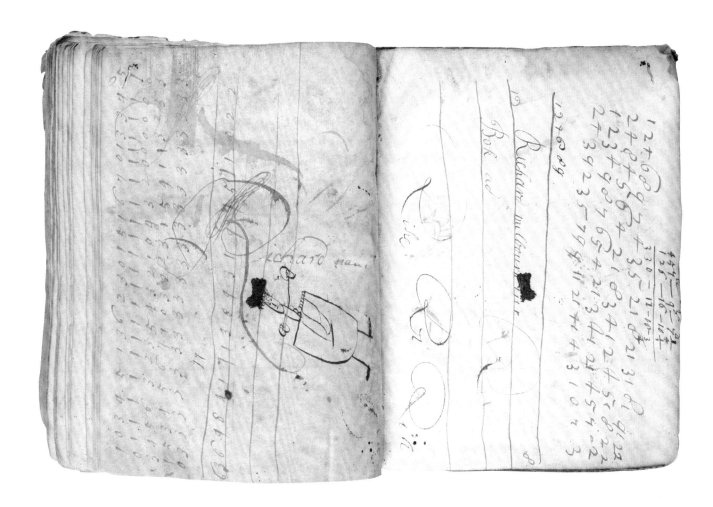

Fig. 162. Student notes in the endpapers of a Latin grammar. John Brinsley, *The posing of the parts: or, a most plain and easie way of examining the accidence and grammar* (London, 1653), rear free and fixed endpaper. Gk4 3

Fig. 163. Detail, tangle of numbers and letters in a pen trial. State papers, p. 246. England, ca. 1620–39. Osborn fb57

PART THREE: CASE STUDIES

"Inhuman Wretch, where's now thy faith and truth?" asks the heroine of her lover in scene V of Lewis Vaslet's satirical series, "The Spoiled Child" (fig. 164). The display of documentary disarray serves only to highlight the disorder of the family and their household.

The image recalls the satire by John Nixon, just a few years earlier, of the Ireland family, shown recklessly consuming (and producing) the documentary abundance of the Shakespeare forgeries (see figs. 2–4). Both scenes call on a familiar textual culture for their satirical effect. A textually ordered household is the understood counterpoint to Vaslet's scene of disarray, just as the latent possibility of Shakespearean documents informed the reception of the Ireland forgeries by their audience.

Part Three explores the habitual and familiar in early modern English manuscript culture, in a series of case studies focused on particular manuscript formats and genres. From penmanship books to waste fragments, this section examines the types of manuscript that early modern English readers and writers might have expected to encounter and understand in the context of their daily lives.

Fig. 164. Detail, a documentary altercation in Lewis Vaslet, "The Spoiled Child, Scene V." England, ca. 1802. Watercolor. Yale Center for British Art. B1977.14.4345

Penmanship and Copybooks

"Duty Fear and Love, we owe to God above. 1234," writes John Hancock in 1753, repeating both the copytext and his signature over the page of his copybook (figs. 165–166). Hancock was sixteen years old, soon to enroll in Harvard College, still twenty-three years from the signing of the Declaration of Independence that, for centuries to follow, would render his name the catchphrase for a signature. Like an embroidered sampler, the exercise uses the text as visual content: the text's meaning is secondary to its visual performance as handwriting on the page. Writing self-consciously, marking the space of the columns over the page, Hancock writes in the copperplate hand of British merchant culture, the hand of the importing firm owned by his uncle and patron. In his adolescent copybook, John Hancock performs the "John Hancock" of the British mercantile self.

Handwriting was a form of style, and writing manuals were a visual genre. From at least 1570, English readers were able to buy illustrated guides to writing published in London. Beau-Chesne's *A booke containing diuers sortes of hands: as well the English as French secretarie with the Italian, Roman, chancelry & court hands* (1570) displayed a fashionable array of hands on plates engraved by John Baildon and published by the émigré printer Thomas Vautrollier.[136] Penmanship, as the subtitle suggests, evoked French and Italian court culture and carried some of the currency of fashion books or city views.

The engravers who rendered the writing masters' hands in copperplate also produced the illustrations for other plate-books. John Sturt, engraver for the writing master John Ayres, made a career from his work on frontispiece portraits and plates. Sturt's particular specialty was miniature text, a fashion in the late seventeenth century. His miniature engravings

Fig. 165. Cover, John Hancock, Workbook for penmanship exercises. Boston, 1753. Gen MSS 764, Box 23, Folder 424

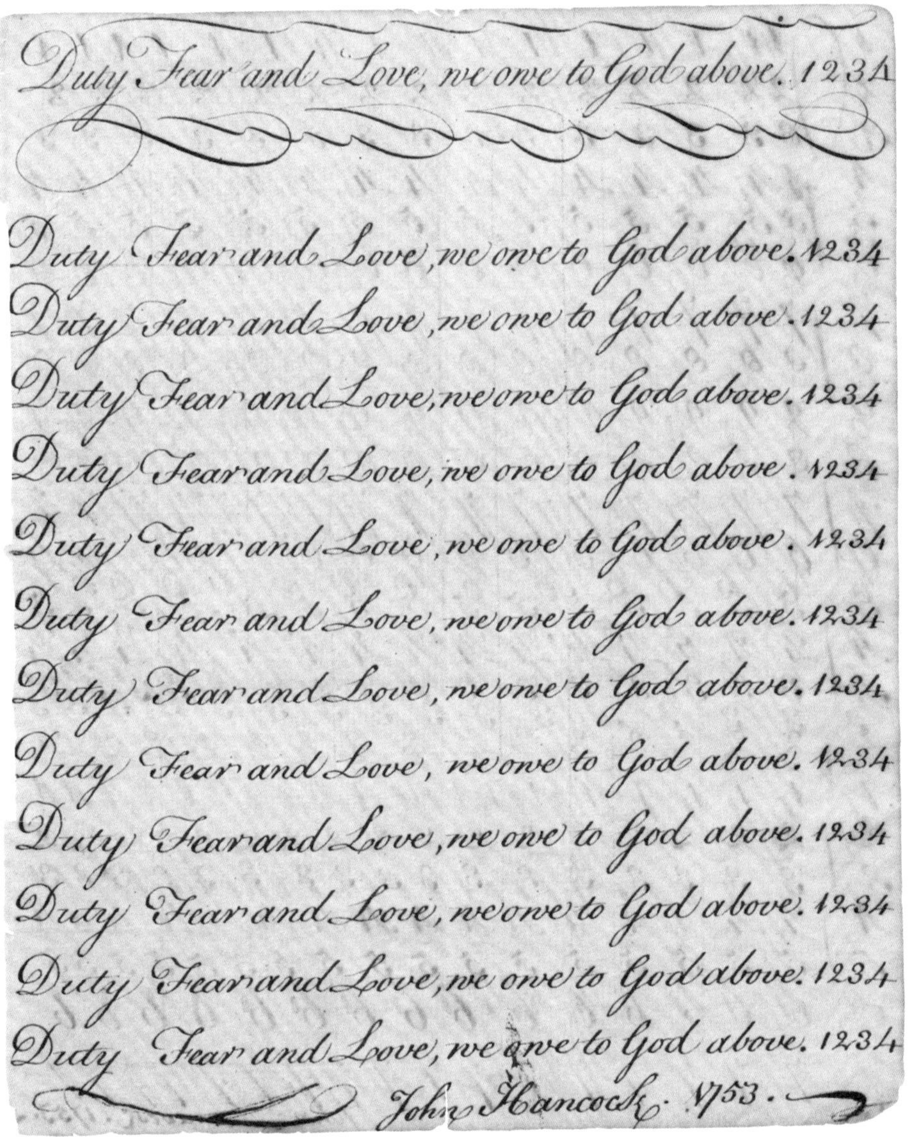

Fig. 166. "Duty Fear and Love." John Hancock, Workbook for penmanship exercises (see fig. 165)

of the Lord's Prayer and elegies for Queen Mary and King William were sold as curiosities for six pence at "the Blew Boar on Red Cross street an Apothecary." Samuel Pepys collected them in the three folio volumes of his "Calligraphicall Collection."[137] In the copybook, as in the curiosity album, handwriting was made visible through engraving: the manuscript hand was published only through the mediations of print and engraving.

Thinking of writing as style allows us to examine more closely the purpose of the text in writing manuals. To be legible, to be more than form or shape, writing required matter; the copybook required copy. In one mid-seventeenth-century schoolbook, *The English schole-master* (1646), a student explains to a colleague that he cannot write because he lacks not only pen-knife, ink, and paper, but also copy. "Rehearse before me some proverbe that I may learn some thing in the mean time," he says to his colleague, as they mix ink. His colleague complies: "Experience (as men commonly say) is the mistres of things," he says. "Have you it? doe you understand it?" The two quibble a bit over the merits of this text, before the friend concludes: "The matter wil appeare better when the writing is dry": that is to say, the act of writing would render the content more valuable.[138]

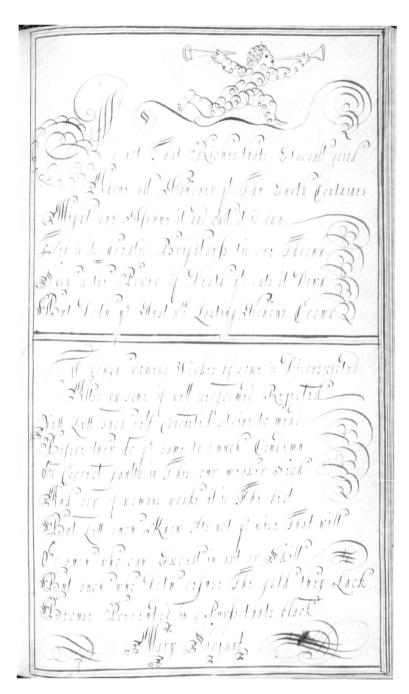

Fig. 167. Serjant, Arithmetic and penmanship notebook, f. 169r. Osborn fb98

Copy was the content of the schoolroom, to be repeated by rote or in writing until it had been absorbed. It was in copying copy, in writing or learning to write with the pen, that the young mind was brought to an understanding of the abstract. In 1646 the educational theorist Ezekias Woodward wrote that "The use of the pen is great, almost universall; It helps the little thing [the child] to judge of artificiall things; what *substance* is, what *formes* or *fashions* are."[139] Copy-text was understood to influence the writer, for good or ill, as he wrote. Woodward therefore enjoins the writing master to "consider well, what *Copy* hee sets before the Child; his own *example* in point of behavior must be straight and exact, for the Child frames after that also, most of all, for there is life in it. And the dead *example,* the copy in his booke I meane, the Master must see to also; and not so much to its *forme,* I doubt not but there he is exact enough, but to the *matter* thereof, that it savour of piety, … so fashioning the *life,* as well as the *hand.*"[140]

To what extent did students respond to the injunctions of copy, in copying their copy-text? Student notebooks, like any manuscript, are often curiously opaque as sources: the writer's hand might be visible, but not their interior lives. In her copybook, a young Mary Serjant has signed her name at the foot of one of the many elaborately written pages of arithmetic and penmanship, decorated with cherubs, dragons, and ornamental flourishes (fig. 167; see also figs. 107, 130–131). Serjant was one of several students of the writing mistress Elizabeth Bean. The Folger Shakespeare Library holds a book by another of Bean's students, in which we find the same cherubs hovering on either side of the student's name, the same flourished snake eating its tail around the title: "Her Book, Scholler to Elizabeth Beane M[rs] in the Art of Writing. Anno 1685."[141] Both books are beautiful and ornate volumes, clearly designed to be kept by their owners: Mary Serjant's book has been bound in elegant black morocco, her initials gilt-stamped on the front panel.

Although they might convey an impression of originality, the notebooks represent an exercise in conformity. The pages, including ornament and text, were copied from a template and show the girls hard at

Fig. 168. "To make inke" and "Romayne hande."
Hill, Notebook, pp. 4–5. Osborn b234

work, attempting (with some individual variations) to replicate a common source. Charles Dickens described a similar scene, in quite a different context, in "A Visit to Newgate" in his *Sketches by Boz* (1833–36). In the women's prison ward, in which the inmates work and sleep, Dickens's narrator finds the tools of copy-text: "Over the fireplace was a large sheet of pasteboard, on which were displayed a variety of texts from Scripture, which were also scattered about the room in scraps about the size and shape of the copy-slips which are used in schools."[142] The sheet of pasteboard, displaying passages of scripture, regulated both the students and their hand.

In this early-seventeenth-century manuscript, a young student, William Hill, can be found learning to write. Hill's notebook is pocket-sized, a small square quarto (fig. 168; see also figs. 17, 98, 125, 155); it is scruffy, stitched into a vellum wrapper. Where Serjant's book is strictly regulated in its presentation on the page, Hill's volume is a work in progress. He writes in the margins; he checks his quill, practices his initials, the alphabet, his flourishes. Like Serjant, Hill learns to write through copying a copy-text. "A monster vile is envie sure," begins his section on secretary hand, "a plague that rageth felle" (see fig. 98). For Hill, as for Mary Serjant, copying is child's play: the playful yet highly regulated engagement with writing and exemplar that served to form the hand.

The Hornbook
and Writing Tables

THE HORNBOOK

The hornbook was an instrument for teaching the alphabet, one used by children over the course of the early modern period (figs. 169–171). It was named for horn, a hard, translucent material made from animal horns or hooves. The copy-text—often consisting of the alphabet, numbers, and the Lord's Prayer—was written on paper or parchment and attached to a wooden or metal paddle (fig. 172). This was then covered with a protective layer of translucent horn.

The hornbook was so closely associated with the schoolroom, and children learning to write, that it could serve as comic shorthand for early modern readers and authors. Thomas Dekker often made use of the hornbook to mock a character's rudimentary literacy. In *Newes from Hell; brought by the Diuells carrier* (1606), a character is described as "having no skill but in his owne *Horne-booke*," forced to look for "a pen-man fit for his tooth to scribble for him." In *The guls horne-booke* (1609), his satirical guidebook for the aspirationally urbane, Dekker writes that "I know that most of you (O admirable *Guls*!) can neither write nor reade. A *Horne-booke* have I invented, because I would have you well schooled."[143]

Dekker's satire reinforces the curious set of tensions inherent in the hornbook as instrument: designed for children and for the hard work of learning to read and write, the hornbook is meant to be both intellectually consumed and abandoned. Its readers are meant to leave it behind as they enter into a more self-sufficient literacy. The horn in the hornbook protects the copy-text from its readers, and the destructive intensity inherent in the process of learning to write and read.

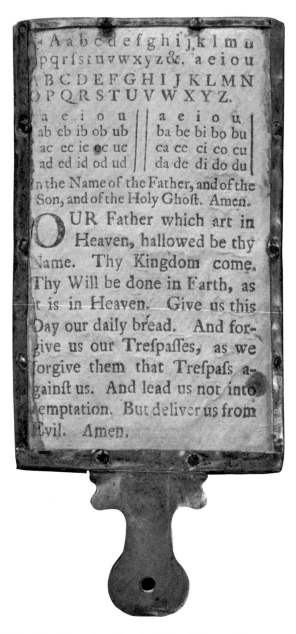

Fig. 169. Silver hornbook. United States (?), ca. 1750–75. Shirley +196

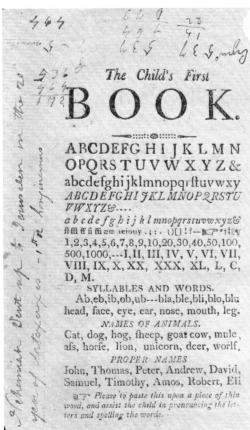

Fig. 170. Hornbook, showing the alphabet, syllables, and Lord's Prayer. United States (?), ca. 1725–50. Shirley 2565

Fig. 171. Verso of fig. 170, showing the image of a child holding the primer

Fig. 172. "Please to paste this upon a piece of thin wood, and assist the child in pronouncing the letters and spelling the words." *The Child's First Book.* England (?), 18th century. 1977 1994

Fig. 173. Scratches on a leaf of reusable card stock, bound in with a guide for the Grand Tour. Notebook. England, ca. 1725. Osborn c593

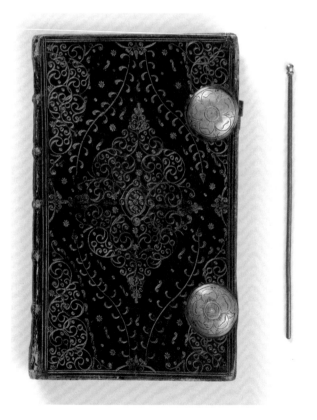

Fig. 174. Stylus and exterior of this pocket-sized notebook (see fig. 173)

WRITING TABLES

In the pageant celebrating the inauguration of Thomas Campbell as Lord Mayor of London in 1609, the figures of Vigilance and Memory are displayed at the feet of the figure of Majesty. Memory is there to record the realm's events for posterity, for which she has been equipped with "a Table Booke with a siluer pen still ready to write."[144]

The table book was a portable notebook, often carried in public to gather notes (figs. 173–177). The table book was often made of sheets of treated parchment and was written on with a wooden or metal stylus, the "siluer pen" that Memory used to record her observations at the Lord Mayor's inauguration.

Table books appeared on the Elizabethan and Jacobean stage: they can be found in satirical guise, as the accessories of the would-be cognoscenti, often desperately seeking help in situations where they felt outwitted. In *Haue with you to Saffron-Walden* (1596), Thomas Nashe makes mock of "Proctors and Registers as busie with their Table-books as might bee, to gather phrases."[145] And Shakespeare brings Polonius to his table-book, in his interview with the King and Queen on Ophelia's relationship with Hamlet:

> But what might you think,
> … what might you,
> Or my dear Majesty your queen here, think,
> If I had played the desk or table-book
> Or given my heart a winking, mute and dumb,
> Or looked upon this love with idle sight?

"No, I went round to work," Polonius says, "And then I prescripts gave her."[146] Work, in this passage, stands in opposition to the table-book, to mute dumbness and inaction, to the inert furniture of learning. With an anxiety familiar to us in the age of the smart phone, Nashe and Shakespeare comment on the table-book as receptacle, where the phrases of lived experience are recorded and stored rather than being turned, as instruments, to action.

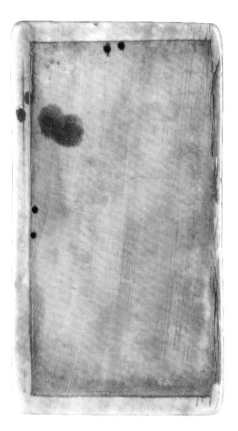

Fig. 177. Ivory table, to be filled with wax, for an erasable writing tablet. Paris, ca. 1350. Beinecke MS 817

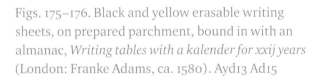

Figs. 175–176. Black and yellow erasable writing sheets, on prepared parchment, bound in with an almanac, *Writing tables with a kalender for xxij years* (London: Franke Adams, ca. 1580). Ayd13 Ad15

Notes and Bound Notebooks

Early modern readers were avid collectors of text. Excerpts were often gathered from what was read, but could also be collected from what was heard or observed in sermons, ballads, jokes, plays, and daily life. These manuscript assemblages were often written in bound notebooks, ranging from the pocket-sized, small and easily carried, through the folio book, more readily housed and consulted in the study or library.[147]

Bookseller inventories indicate that notebooks could be bought readymade and bound, along with other materials, such as ready-ruled paper.[148] Readers might also keep quires of paper, folded and ready to be written on, then later stitched together in rough books, often bound in a paper wrapper (fig. 178). This practice continued through the eighteenth century and was a straightforward way for a reader to make his or her own running notebook.

Early modern readers differed enormously in their expectations and approach to gathering text. Many, even most, notebooks reflect their writer's changing intentions: some are half-filled, petering out in blank pages; some were turned to other purposes; others were used by later owners. Francis Grosvenor has signed his name to the first page of a notebook written in two separate hands: notes on the fees owed by barons, in a secretary hand; and, in a mixed hand, reading notes on geometry and other subjects, including the entry on succubi below Grosvenor's signature (fig. 179). In another example, the young Dorothy Calthorpe has filled her small pocket notebook with her own verse and prose, including her drawing of "A red marble Chappel errected by my hand" (fig. 180).

Fig. 178. Thomas Thistlewood, Diary. Jamaica, 1751. OSB MSS 176, Box 1, Folder 2. Thistlewood kept his diaries in quires, stitched into paper wrappers organized by the year.

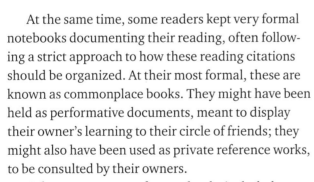

Fig. 179. Francis Grosvenor, Notebook, p. 1.
England, early to mid-17th century. Osborn b349

Fig. 180. Dorothy Calthorpe, Writings, f. 1r.
England, 1684. Osborn b421

At the same time, some readers kept very formal notebooks documenting their reading, often following a strict approach to how these reading citations should be organized. At their most formal, these are known as commonplace books. They might have been held as performative documents, meant to display their owner's learning to their circle of friends; they might also have been used as private reference works, to be consulted by their owners.

Other common uses for notebooks included sermon diaries, joke books, poetic or other miscellanies, and recipe or household books. An early modern reader might begin a new notebook with one intention—and change his or her mind over the course of the notebook. Sometimes notebooks are almost entirely empty. Sometimes a reader might have started with very strict intentions, but later made use of the book for other, more miscellaneous notes and observations. And sometimes, frequently, a later owner might have turned the notebook to an entirely different purpose.

READERS' COLLECTIONS

The early modern compilation drew on the medieval tradition of the florilegium, or gathering of flowers, a term for the collections of proverbs and other textual excerpts kept by learned readers through the fifteenth century.[149] These collections were often described with the metaphor of the garden, and particularly of bees gathering nectar from flowers to make honey in their hives, a metaphor used by classical authors and their Renaissance humanist readers from Seneca through Erasmus.[150] The metaphor also highlights one of the characteristics of early modern reading: like the bee, early modern readers might have to travel to be in the presence of a particular text, or flower. The well-furnished library, in this analogy, acted as the literary equivalent of the well-stocked garden. The reader's collection—whether a printed miscellany of published excerpts or a reader's notebook, assembled in manuscript—acted as an instrument by which a reader could gather the textual flora which she or he wished to retain.

The commonplace book was one form of reader's compendium. Taken in its narrowest sense, the term assumes a particular practice of note-taking associated with humanist readers. Commonplace books often took the form of a gathering of moral or learned excerpts, or sententiae, grouped into categories organized alphabetically or by subject. As a reader noted an observation on, for instance, honesty, he or she might record this passage in the appropriate category in their commonplace book.

More elaborate systems of commonplacing also existed. John Locke devised one of the more complicated, developed while a student at Christ Church College, Oxford.[151] Locke recommends buying a "White Paper Book" and organizing an index, following which the reader would add entries by headings:

> If I would put any Thing in my Common-Place Book, I look a *Head* to which I may refer it, that I may be able to find it when I have Occasion. Every *Head* ought to begin with some Considerable Word that is Essential to the Matter treated of, and of this Word one must carefully observe the First Letter, and the Vowel which follows it; for upon these Two Letters depends the whole Use of our Index.[152]

As Ann Moss has argued, commonplacing can be understood as an instrumental practice requiring a particular type of tool: the commonplace book, with its intellectual categories and expectations mapped upon it by its reader.[153]

As a genre, the commonplace book particularly highlights the tensions between readers' expectations and the reality of their encounters with the set of practices surrounding reading. Commonplace books were often rigorously organized by their owners, in anticipation of the orderly regulation of their reading. The notebooks often show some of the difficulties encountered by readers in managing their reading, over time. Quotations might fall particularly to certain letters, forcing the reader to squeeze more text into the space of the page, or to restructure the rubrics of the notebook. Readers might also move away from the commonplace book as a system of ordering their reading. Many, if not most, commonplace books have unfilled pages. Readers either stopped reading, stopped commonplacing, or switched to a different system of note-taking.

Commonplacing was always only one of many possible programmatic approaches to reading. Some readers became avid and expert practitioners of commonplacing and the commonplace book. Others developed their own often individual and idiosyncratic approaches to note-taking, designed to suit their own reading practices and goals.

NOTES AND NOTE-TAKING

In a famously forbidding exchange, the historian William Lambarde, Keeper of the Rolls, is said to have presented Queen Elizabeth with

> his Pandecta [or survey] of All her Rolls, Bundells, Membranes, and parcells that bee reposed in her Maties Tower att London; wherof shee hadd given to him the charge 21: Jan. last past. Her Matie chearfully receaved the same into her hands [and]…openinge the booke, sayes, you shall see that I cann reade, and soe, with an audible voice, read over the epistle, & the title, soe readily, & distinctly poynted, that it might perfectly appeare, that she well understood, & conceived the same. Then she descended from the beginning of Kinge John, till the end of Rich: 3^d, that is 64 pages, servinge eleven

kings, containinge 286 yeares: in the 1st Page shee demanded the meaning of Oblata, Clausæ, et Litterae Patentes… [Lambarde] likewise expounded these all according to their original diversities, which shee took in gratious and full satisfaction; so her Matie fell upon the reign of King Rich: 2^d. saying, "I am Rich: 2^d. Know ye not that?"

This image of Elizabeth, quizzing her Keeper of the Rolls and pointedly commenting on her resemblance to Shakespeare's Richard, became an icon of English anecdote—one copied, like the version shown here, well into the eighteenth century (fig. 181). The story also highlights the challenges of working with archival

sources in the early modern period. Lambarde's survey of the contents of the Tower of London records indicates the confusion that might reign in the royal archive, as in others of the period. For scholars like Lambarde in the early modern period, the difficulty of locating a source was a contant and pressing concern; having access to collections was another.

The notes that survive from this period often reflect these difficulties, and the range of circumstances in which early modern readers engaged with textual sources. Readers, then as now, had to come to grips with the problems of gathering and organizing their information, and might vary their system of note-taking to suit their sources. Archival sources, found in manuscript documents and rolls, required their own form of note-taking. Avid commonplacers might draw on a printed miscellany as a source, or follow the marginal marks by which the printer or publisher highlighted particularly useful texts to excerpt. Readers also took notes on things they had heard or encountered in person: jokes, performances, sermons, sights and spectacles, or conversations.

Scholars like the historian William Camden might organize their archival notes in a number of different fashions, none of which would necessarily correspond to the commonplacing system. Camden copied notes from sources in the Tower of London, the College of Arms, and other locations into his notebooks (fig. 182).[154] While he occasionally arranged his reading by heading—usually the subject of a particular document—his notebook also contains lists of names, alphabetical lists, abstracts from documents identified by the source and the document date, and other categories governing Camden's use of the notebook as a reference compilation from his sources.

In this example (fig. 183), Isaac Newton can be found taking notes on his alchemical reading, excerpting textual passages from printed sources, organized

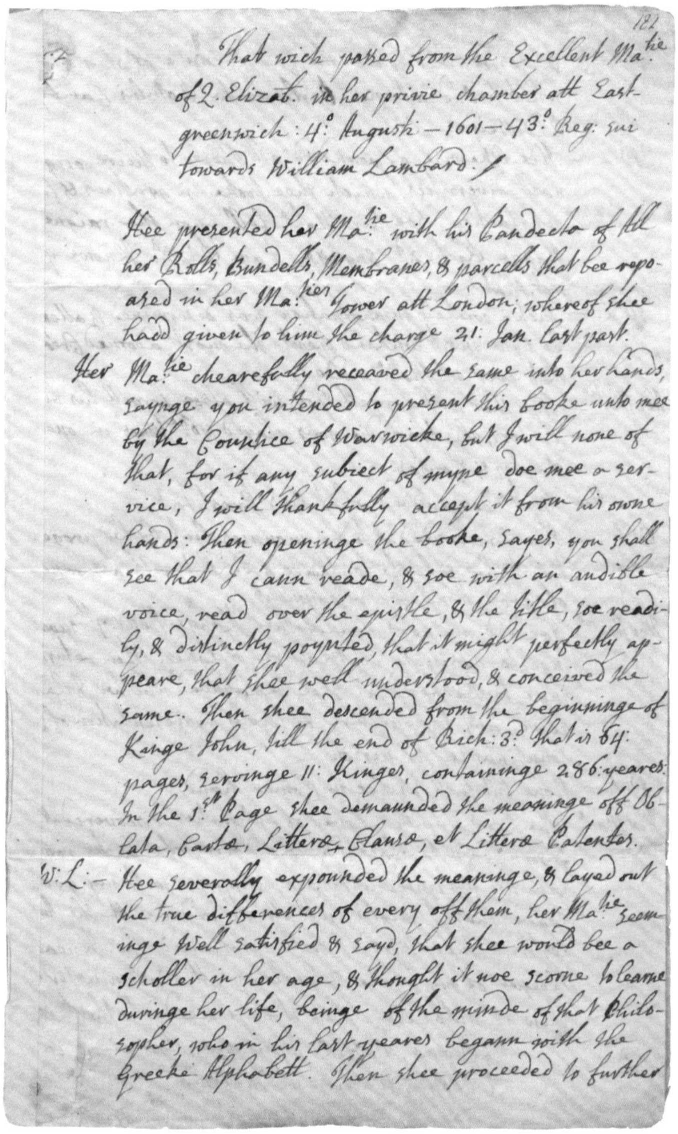

Fig. 181. "That wich passed from the Excellent Matie of Q. Elizab. in her privie chamber att East-greenwich: 4. Augusti—1601—43. Reg: sui towards William Lambard." England, 18th century. Osborn Manuscript File 8519

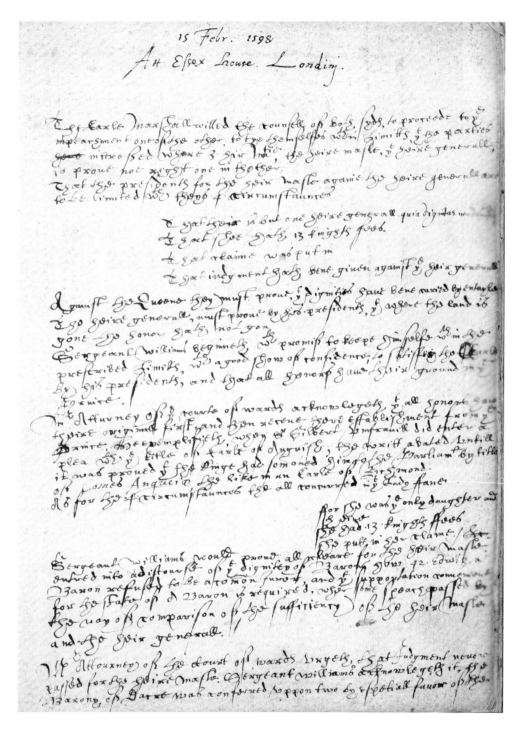

Fig. 182. William Camden, Notebook. England, ca. 1600. Beinecke MS 370

15 Febr. 1598
Att Essex house. Londinij
The Earle Marshall willed the counsell of both syds, to proceede to y^e
impeachment one of the other, to tye themselfes wth in Limitts, y^t the parties
~~here~~ interested where 3 hir M^tie, the heire maste, y^e heire generall,
to proue noe right one in thother.
That the presidents for the heir maste againe the heire generalle are
to be limited wth theyr 4 circumstaunces

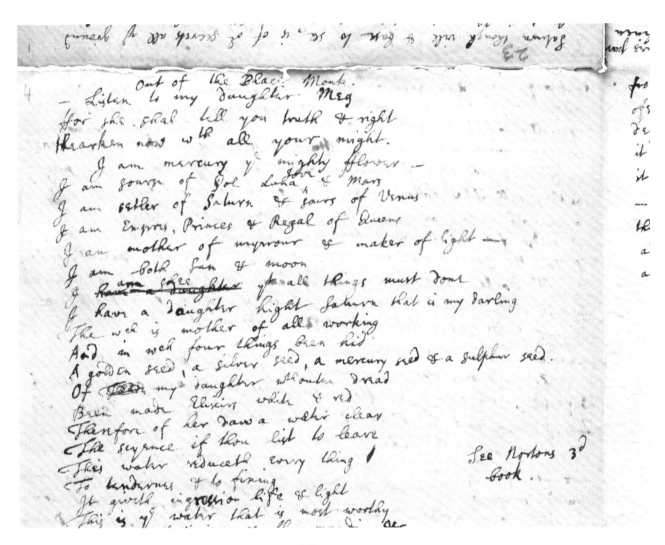

Fig. 183. Detail, Isaac Newton, Reading notes on alchemy, p. 4.
England, ca. 1700. Mellon MS 79

Out of the Black Monk.
    Listen to my daughter Meg
For she shal tell you truth & right
Hearken now wth all your might.
    I am mercury y[e] mighty flower –
I am sourse of Sol Luna ^[Jove] & Mars
I am setler of Saturn & sours of Venus
I am Empres, Princes, & Regal of Queens
I am mother of myrour & maker of light and –
I am both sun & moon
I ~~have a daughter~~ ^[am shee] y[t] all things must done
I have a daughter Light Saturn that is my darling
The w[ch] is mother of all working
And in w[ch] four things been hid
A golden seed, a silver seed, a mercury seed & a sulphur seed.

on loose quires of paper and identified by title. In another example, a mid-sixteenth-century reader painstakingly copies Johann Stoeffler's astronomical work on the phases of the moon (fig. 184), transcribing this in the same notebook in which he has constructed a working model of an astrolabe, a mathematical instrument for astronomical observation (fig. 185).

Fig. 184. "Stoflers Judgement upon ye 28 mansions of ye mone." Astronomical and astrological treatises, f. 7r. England, mid-16th century. Beinecke MS 558

Fig. 185. Working model of an astrolabe, on parchment. Astronomical and astrological treatises, f. 24r. England, mid-16th century. Beinecke MS 558

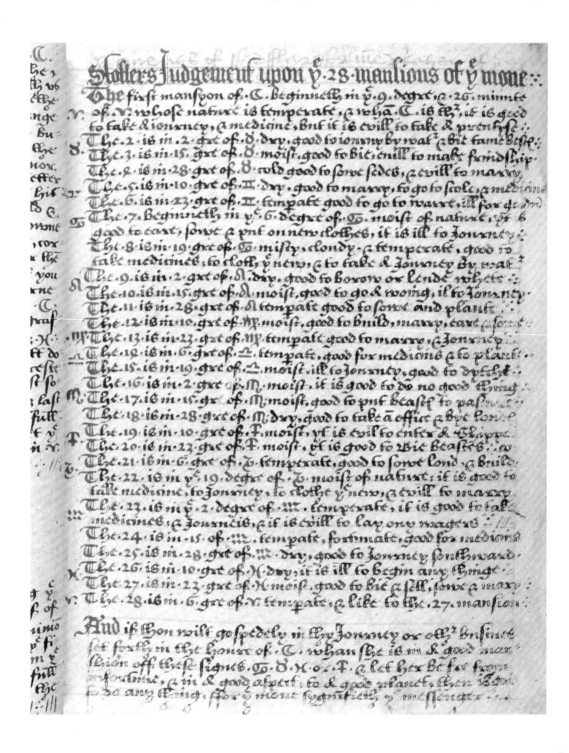

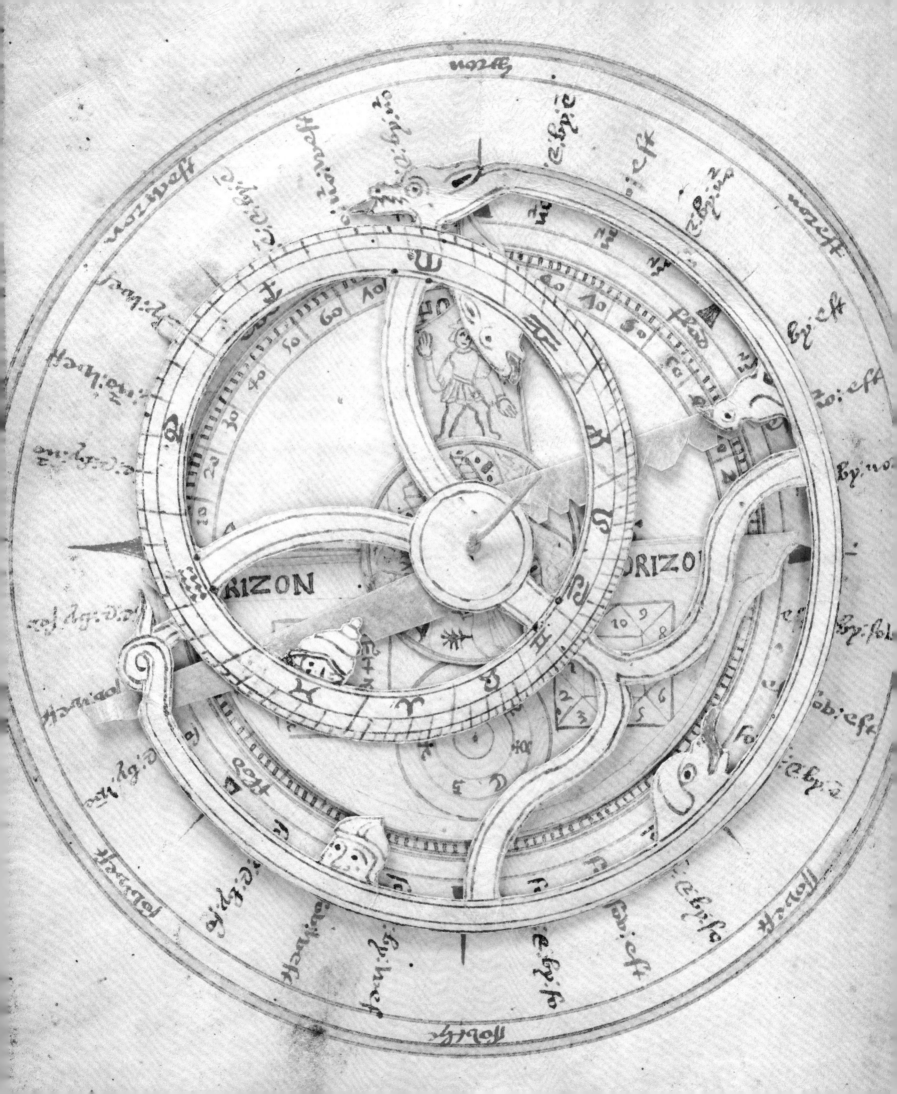

Miscellanies

In a passage in his printed compendium *Palladis tamia* (1598; fig. 186), Francis Meres notes one of the poets of his age:

> As the soule of *Euphorbus* was thought to liue in *Pythagoras:* so the sweete wittie soule of *Ouid* liues in mellifluous & honytongued *Shakespeare,* witnes his *Venus* and *Adonis,* his *Lucrece,* his sugred Sonnets among his priuate friends, &c.[155]

Meres goes on to compare Shakespeare to Plautus and Seneca,

> accounted the best for Comedy and Tragedy among the Latines: so *Shakespeare* among yᵉ English is the most excellent in both kinds for the stage; for Comedy, witnes his *Gētlemē of Verona,* his *Errors,* his *Loue labors lost,* his *Loue labours wonne,* his *Midsummers night dreame,* & his *Merchant of Venice:* for Tragedy his *Richard the 2. Richard the 3. Henry the 4. King Iohn, Titus Andronicus* and his *Romeo* and *Iuliet.*[156]

Meres highlights three entirely separate spheres of publication: staged drama, published poetry, and privately circulated works, in this case the "sugred Sonnets." This manuscript circulation offers us a glimpse of the instability and complexity of text in the early modern period. Readers might copy a text from a printed work, or from another manuscript exemplar; a reader or editor might add a title or change the words, or make a change or error or addition in copying.

On the facing page, Shakespeare's second sonnet has been copied by an early reader in his or her private poetry miscellany, a small pocket-sized informal notebook, written in a single, neat, looping hand throughout (fig. 187). The poem has a title: "To one that would die a maide." It has been gathered alongside other poems, including the poem by Richard Corbett, "On Faireford windowes," below. The reader makes mistakes, crosses out and corrects his or her

Fig. 186. Francis Meres, *Palladis tamia. Wits treasury. Being the second part of wits common wealth* (London, 1598), 281–82. 1993 548

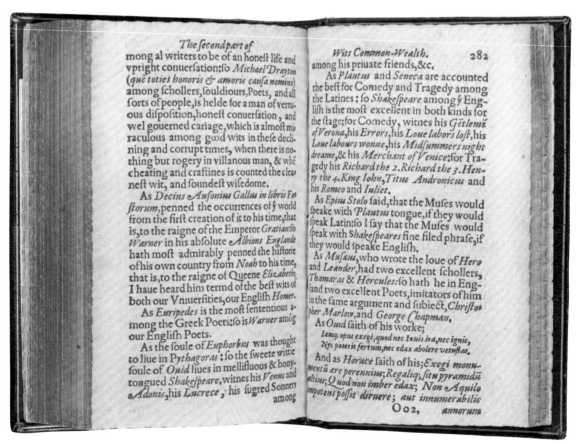

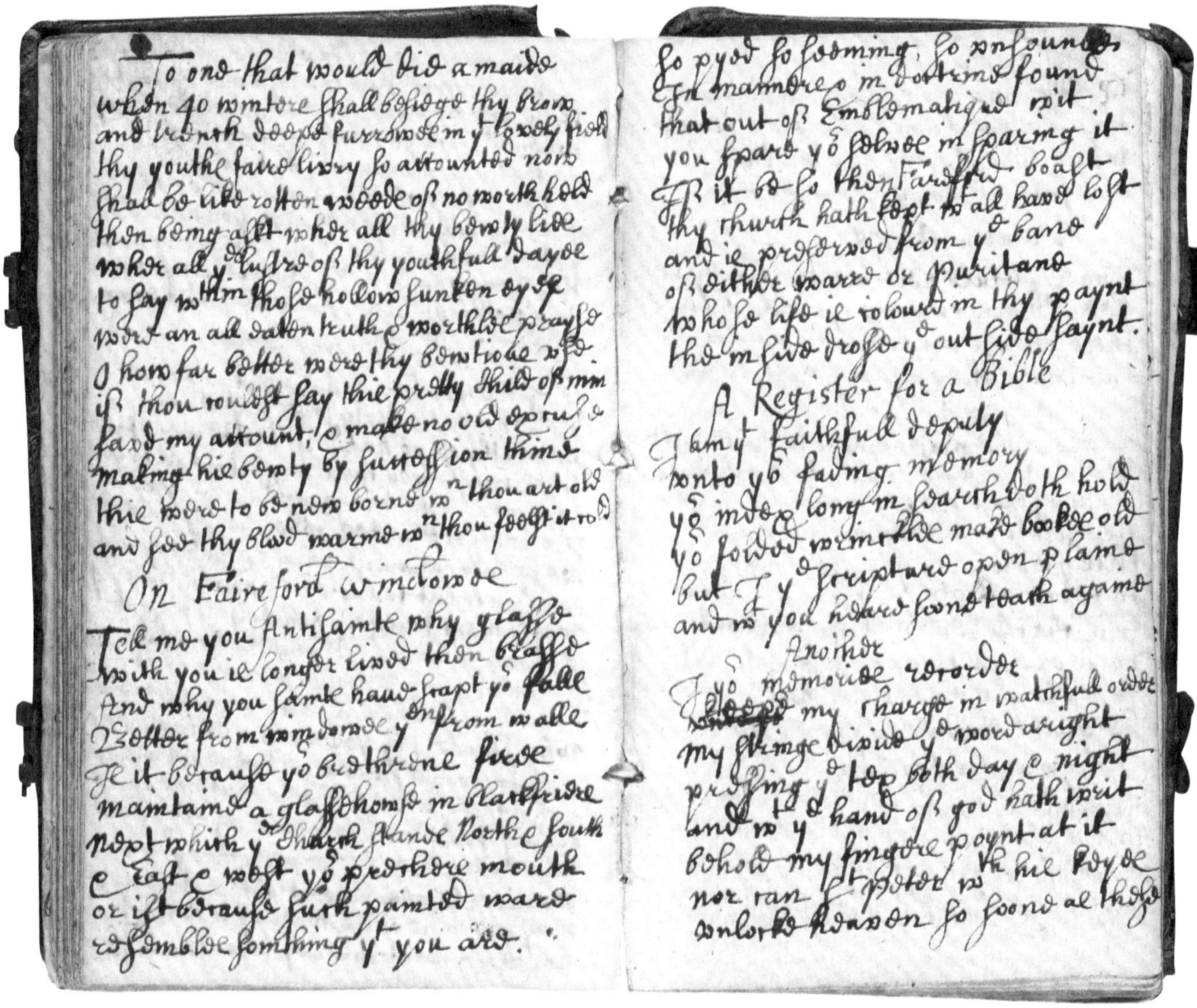

Fig. 187. Notebook, 54v–55r. England, mid-17th century. Osborn b205. Note the *e*-like form of the finial *s* in "dayes" (end, line 7) and "eyes" (end, line 8), as elsewhere through the poem.

To one that would die a maide
when 40 winters shall besiege thy brow
and trench deepe furrowes in y^t lovely field
thy youths faire liury so accounted now
shall be like rotten weeds of no worth held
then being askt wher all thy bewty lies
where all ye lustre of thy youthfull dayes
to say w^thin those hollow sunken eyes
were an all eaten truth & worthless prayse
o how far better were thy bewtious use
if thou couldst say thie pretty child of min
savd my account; & make no old excuse
making his bewty by succession thine
this were to be new borne w^n thou art old
and see thy blood warme w^n thou feelst it cold.

text. This is in every way imaginable a gathering of text for a reader's amusement, and it shows that Shakespeare's second sonnet circulated and was valued in ways that do not necessarily replicate any understanding of the text as a stable authorial creation, housed in a printed edition.

The poem is one of many in the volume, none identified by author. There are four poems in the opening, and all have been given titles. Two, "A Register for a Bible" and "Another [register for a Bible]," are by William Strode, a poet and playwright active at Christ Church College, Oxford, from his matriculation in 1617 through his death in 1645. The third poem, "On Faireford windowes," is by Richard Corbett, from 1620 the Dean of Christ Church and Strode's older contemporary and friend. John Aubrey, in an account of this otherwise somewhat disheveled character, wrote that Corbett's "poems are pure naturall witt, delightfull and easie."[157]

Contrast this with the form of the second sonnet in its first printing in 1609 (fig. 188). In this printed edition, the sonnets are arranged numerically, in sequence; the second sonnet, like the others, lacks a title; the text also varies somewhat from this manuscript copy. Perhaps most importantly, the second sonnet was published in a work presenting the sonnets as a coherent grouping and highlighting Shakespeare's authorship on the title page. By contrast, the copy of the poem in Osborn b205 nowhere mentions Shakespeare as author, nor are any of the other poems in the volume attributed to individual authors. Whatever governing principle might have guided the compiler of this volume, authorship seems not to have been as important as the poems' titles.[158]

While Strode and Corbett might have since fallen into obscurity, they were tremendously popular poets whose work appeared with regularity in seventeenth-century verse compilations. As Adam Smyth has observed, Strode's poetry was among the most commonly transcribed in manuscript collections in the 1630s, also appearing in printed miscellanies "more frequently than the work of any other poet, including Ben Jonson, John Donne, and Thomas Carew."[159] As Smyth argues, Strode's subsequent obscurity might be attributed to the fact that, unlike Shakespeare, his poetry was never published in a

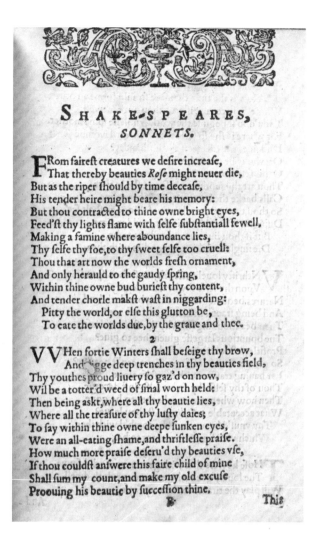

Fig. 188. William Shakespeare, *Shake-Speares sonnets. Neuer before imprinted* (1609), E2v. Elizabethan Club, Yale University, Eliz 194

single-author edition. Shakespeare's "sugred Sonnets" might have circulated for a limited audience in manuscript, but their later coherence and focus as the subject of scholarly attention (and canon formation) is perhaps due to the fact of their independent publication as an edition in 1609.[160]

Verse miscellanies like Osborn b205 straddled the worlds of manuscript and print circulation. Others, like the collection of Anne Wharton's verse (fig. 189) or that of her uncle, John Wilmot, 2nd Earl of Rochester (fig. 190), highlight the manuscript's ability to tread between the private and the public, circulating work that was often left unpublished in the author's lifetime. Manuscript and scribal copies also

To m^rs Behn. on w^t she wrot of
The. Earle. of Rochester

In pleasing transport rapt my thoughts aspire
With humble verse to praise. w^t you. admire.
Few liveing poets may ye laurell claime.
Most passe thrô death to reach a liveing fame.
Fame Phenix like, still rises from a tombe
But bravely you this custome have ore come.
You force an homage from each generous heart
Such as you allways pay to just diserts
You praise'd him liveing whome you dead bemoan.
And now yours tears afresh his laurell crown.
It is this flight of yours excites my art
Weak as it is to take your muses part
And pay low'd thanks back from my bleeding heart
May you in every pleasing grace excell
May bright Apollo in ye bosom dwell
May yours excell ye matchless Saphoes name.
May you have all write without her shame.
Thô shee to Honour gave, a fatall wound
Employ your hand to raise it from ye ground.
Right its wrong'd cause with inticeing straain.
Its ruin'd Temples try to build againe.
Scorn meaner Theam's declining Low desier
And bid you mule maintain a vestall fire.
If you do y^s w^t Glory will ensue.
To all our sex to Poetry and you.
Write on and may y^r number ever flow
Soft as the wishes y^t I make for you.

Fig. 189. Anne Wharton, "To Mrs Behn, on w^t she wrot of The Earl of Rochester," in this compilation of twenty-four poems by Wharton and one by Edmond Waller. England, ca. 1700. Osborn b408

To Mrs Behn on w^t she wrot of
The Earle of Rochester

In pleasing transport rapt my thoughts aspire
With humble verse to praise w^t you admire
Few liveing poets may y^e laurell claime
Most passe thrô death to reach a liveing fame
Fame Phenix like still rises from a Tombe
But bravely you this custome have ore come

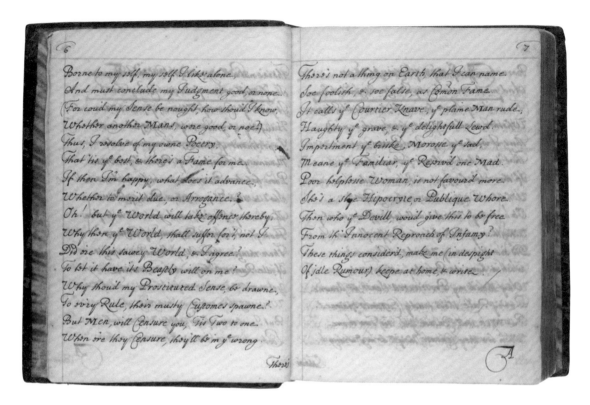

Fig. 190. Notebook containing copies of poems by John Wilmot, Earl of Rochester, Aphra Behn, John Dryden, and others. England, ca. 1680. Osborn b105

circulated within social and institutional networks, such as the tremendously active literary circle of the Inns of Court in the late sixteenth and early seventeenth centuries, in which so much of John Donne's poetry was read and circulated (see fig. 85). As Arthur Marotti writes,

> Verse was transmitted between particular individuals (often on single sheets suitable for enclosure in letters); it was circulated in bifolia and quires or booklets of poetry within restricted social groups; individual or group collecting produced compilations of poems within a particular environment, combined often with poems from other milieux. The circulation of manuscript verse within familial, collegial, or other social circles led to the creation of larger collections—either blank codices filled by a scribe or scribes or combinations of booklets or fascicles in volumes bound either in their own time or later.[161]

This kind of manuscript circulation within communities has been understood as a form of coterie publication.[162] It was also a form of labor. Copying manuscripts in scribal assemblages might have been the work of the reader-owner, sometimes over decades.[163] As Marcy North suggests, it was also the work of the intellectual servants—the tutor, secretary, companion—of the early modern household.[164]

Sermon Notes and Diaries

> And, in some places, the Boyes doe write on the Communion Table, the Table being prepared for the Communion, and remove the vessels of Wine that be on the Table prepared for the communion to make roome for their writing, fouling and spotting the linen and table at the same time with inke…

> Ephraim Udall, *To prepon emchariotichòn i.e. Communion comlinesse* (London, 1641), 12

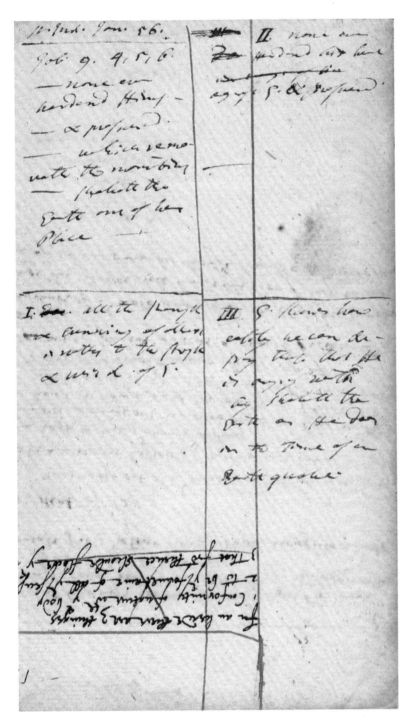

Fig. 191. Jonathan Edwards, Notes for a sermon on Job 9:4–6. January 1756. Gen MSS 151, Box 13, Folder 948

Ephraim Udall's complaint in 1641 about boys "fouling and spotting" the communion linens with their ink reveals the awkwardness and impracticality of the manuscript culture surrounding early modern sermons. Sermon notes and sermon diaries often survive as bound notebooks; these notes were often taken as loose notes or in informal booklets, stitched in paper wrappers and bound later. One example can be seen here, in the sermon notes kept by the eighteenth-century American evangelical preacher Jonathan Edwards (fig. 191). Edwards devoured every scrap of paper in his household for his notes, whether paper slips or paper fan scraps stitched together into quires (see fig. 28).

Sermon notes could take several different forms: notes made by preachers for their own sermons; notes for the later publication of sermons; or notes taken by those present, listening to a sermon. Whatever purpose the notes served, the structure of the early modern English sermon remained consistent. The clergyman chose a scriptural text and organized the sermon around several key headings, or divisions. Mary Morrissey describes the action of the sermon as threefold: first, the explication of a scriptural text for the congregation, unfolding its possible meanings; second, the application of the text's relevance or applicability to the listeners; third, the exhortation to the congregation to absorb and adhere to the lessons of the scripture and sermon.[165] Whatever form a reader's notes might take, they were meant to reflect the essential structure of the early modern sermon around a scriptural text and the headings of an argument. As Morrissey writes,

> The physical layout of many sermon-notes becomes easier to understand when one considers this notion of preaching as the unfolding of a biblical text's meaning through comparison with other biblical commonplaces and in the light of preestablished doctrine.[166]

Jonathan Edwards's notes show the working structure for a sermon (fig. 191). Edwards gives the text, here Job 9:4–6, outlining the sermon's structure in a numbered list of headings, each accompanied by a brief summary of his argument. This unbound, folded quire of paper, palm-sized, could be used as a crib during delivery or as a working outline for later revisions or expansion into textual form.

Osborn b362 represents an example of the latter (fig. 192). The volume is a blank notebook holding a collection of fifteen sermons, preached by Hugh Rawlins between January and July 1655. The shape of the sermon drives the organization of the text. On the right page, the Greek heading for the sermon text accompanies the date. Facing this, Rawlins has given the biblical text, the familiar text somewhat abridged by abbreviations and ellipses: "Exod: 20.17. Thou shalt not covet thy N. house; thou – N. wife, nor Man serv^t nor Mayd s^t nor Oxe, Nor Asse, nor – thy Neigh."/ [Thou shalt not covet thy neighbour's house, thou shalt not covet thy neighbour's wife, nor his manservant, nor his maidservant, nor his ox, nor his ass, nor any thing that is thy neighbour's.]

The manuscript and print cultures of sermons changed over time. Ian Green notes the increase, between the 1660s and the 1730s, in the number of manuscript sermons surviving in archives, alongside an increasing number of printed sermons.[167] The manuscript culture of sermons could also circulate beyond the sermon itself: Anne Sadleir, daughter of Sir Edward Coke, gave scribal copies of Donne's sermons as gifts and received a fair copy (or copy made for presentation) of a sermon as a gift from Andrew Marvell.[168]

Fig. 192. Hugh Rawlins, Sermons. England, January–July 1655. Osborn b362

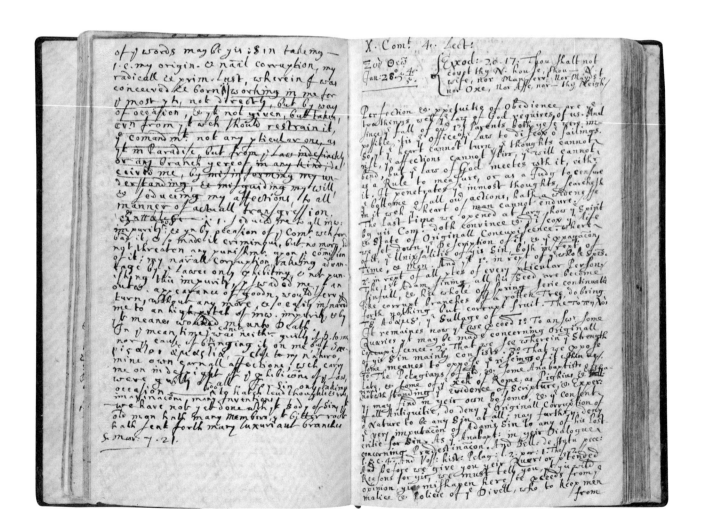

Household or Recipe Books

Recipes for cooking, medicine, and household supplies were gathered in manuscript notebooks, known variously as household, recipe, or receipt books. These were often miscellanies, compiled by one or more owners within a family, sometimes over generations; notebooks were also sometimes adopted as recipe books by later owners. In this late-seventeenth-century example (fig. 193), recipes for ink and vermillion are found alongside an English translation of Machiavelli, puzzles, and multiplication tables. Another can be seen in this late-seventeenth-century notebook, drawing household recipes together alongside satirical verses (figs. 194–196). The notebook is written dos-à-dos, or "back to back"—that is, written in one direction from one end of the volume and then, from the other end, flipped and written the other way. The two sections are written with varying formality: the poems are copied in a slightly neater and more formal round hand; the recipes are copied in a quick, familiar round hand, possibly by the same writer, but with slight variations in the formation of the letters. The compiler of the poetry seems to have been associated with the University of Cambridge, at some point around or after 1693, based on the date of the poems; it is possible that the volume was also used to collect recipes, or that the notebook was co-opted and turned to a different purpose by a later owner.

The recipes offer insight into early modern English household diet and management and into the expansively stodgy nature of English cooking in the early modern period. There are no fewer than three separate recipes for cheesecake, along with recipes for puff pastry, pancakes, white pudding, and many approaches to meat and pickling. As is characteristic

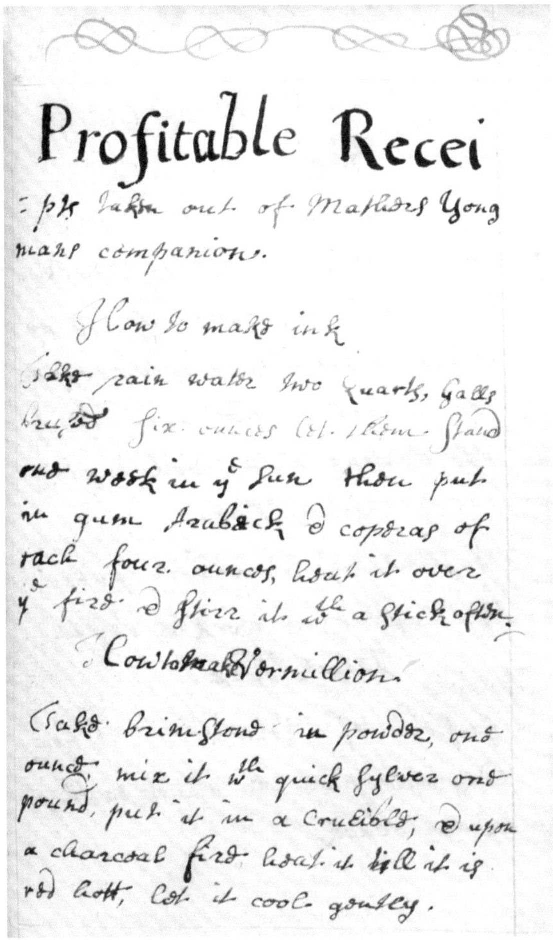
Profitable Recei
=pts taken out of Mathers Yong
mans companion.

How to make ink
Take rain water two Quarts, Galls
brused six ounces let them stand
one week in ye sun then put
in gum Arabeck & coperas of
sack four ounces, heat it over
ye fire & stirr it wth a stick often.

How to make Vermillion.
Take brimstone in powder one
ounce, mix it wth quick sylver one
pound, put it in a Crucible, & upon
a charcoal fire heat it till it is
red hott, let it cool gently.

Fig. 193. "How to make ink," copied from William Mather, *A very useful manual, or, the young man's companion* (1681). England, late 17th century. Osborn b57

Profitable Recei
=pts taken out of Mathers Yong
mans companion.

How to make ink
Take rain water two Quarts, Galls
brused six ounces let them stand
one week in y^e sun then put
in gum Arabeck & coperas of
sack four ounces, heat it over
y^e fire & stirr it wth a stick often.

Fig. 194. "Cheesecakes," "Pancakes," "White Puddings," and "Puff Paste," among other recipes. Notebook of recipes and poems, f. 79r–78v (dos-à-dos). England, late 17th century. Osborn b115

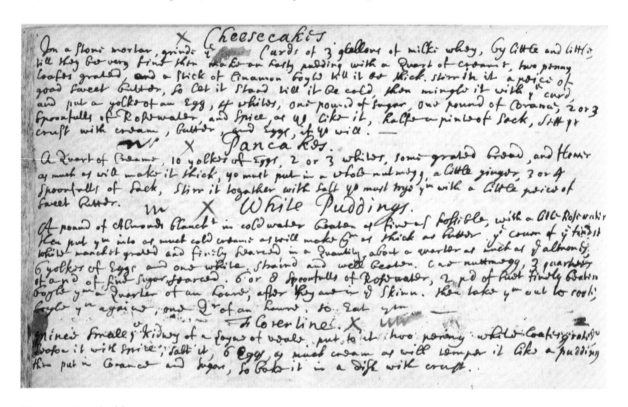

Fig. 195. Detail of fig. 194

Cheesecakes
In a stone mortar, grinde y^e Curds of 3 gallons of milki whey, by little and little,
till they bee very fine then make an hasty pudding with a Quart of creame, two penny
loafes grated, and a stick of Cinamon boyle till it be thick. Stirr in it a peice of
good sweet butter, so let it stand till it be cold, then mingle it with y^r curd,
and put a yolke of an Egg, 4 whites, one pound of sugar, one pound of Corants, 2 or 3
spoonfulls of Rosewater, and spice, as ye like it, halfe a pinte of sack, sett ye
crust with cream, butter, and egge, if ye will.

of early modern recipes, quantities, processes, and durations are often only loosely defined. The recipes in this manuscript seem to have been used at some point: a reader has marked several with a cross, although this could also relate to the book's having been copied.

The book also contains some medical recipes: "Good for weakness either of fundament or mothers"; "For Kibes & chillblanes, A medicine"; "for a Glyster." With these is included one of several recipes for ink (or, in this case, "Excellent Inck") (fig. 196).

Osborn b115 follows the print genre of recipe book, as with the influential *A true gentlewomans delight. Wherein is contained all manner of cookery* published by "W.I., Gent." in 1653 and posthumously attributed to Elizabeth Grey, Countess of Kent (fig. 197). This work is frequently bound with *A choice manual of rare and select secrets in physick and chyrurgery* (1653), also attributed to her. The former lists household recipes, while the latter is primarily medical. Attributions of cookery or medical recipes are common, particularly to aristocratic households. *A true gentlewomans delight* includes the "Lady of Arundels" recipe for manchet, a rich bread loaf that required a bushel of flour, twenty eggs, and three pounds of butter.[169] And in Osborn b115, "The Lord Newberry's white marmolet of Quinces" is detailed, as is "The Lady Manchester[s] Biskett"); Lady Warwick's recipe for yellow biscuits can also be found, alongside recipes for "Paste of Oranges" and "To candy Angellica Roots (fig. 198)."

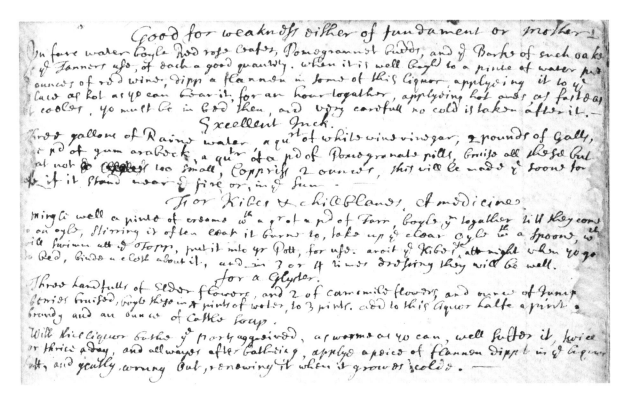

Fig. 196. "Excellent Inck." Notebook of recipes and poems, f. 1r. Osborn b115. A second ink recipe, alongside medical and household recipes

Three gallons of Raine water, a qu[rt] of white wine vinegar, 2 pounds of Galls, one p[d] of gum arabeck, a qu[tr] of a pd of Pomegranate pills, bruise all these but [..at] not too small, Coppriss 2 ounces, this will be made y[e] soone for use if it stand near y[e] fire or, in y[e] sun.

108   *A True Gentlewomans Delight.*

To Boil Cream.

Take a quart of Cream, and set it a boiling with Mace, whilest your Cream is boyling, cut some thin sippets, then take seven or eight yolks of Eggs, beat them with Rosewater, and Sugar, and a little of your cream, when your cream boileth, take it off the fire, and put in your Eggs, and stir it very fast that it curdle not, then put your sippets into the dish, pour in your cream and let it cool, when it is cold, scrape on Sugar, and serve it.

To draw Butter.

Take your Butter and cut it into thin slices, put it into a dish, then put it upon the coals where it may melt leisurely, stir it often, and when it is melted put in two or three spoonfuls of water, or Vinegar, which you will, then stir and beat it untill it be thick.

Lady of Arundels *Manchet.*

Take a bushel of fine Wheat-flower, twenty eggs, three pound of Fresh butter, then

A True Gentlewomans Delight   109

then take as much Salt and Barme, as to the ordinary Manchet, temper it together with new Milk prettie hot, then let it lie the space of half an hour to rise, so you may work it up into bread, and bake it, let not your Oven be too hot.

To boil Pigeons.

Boil them in water and salt, take a handful of Parsley, and as much Thyme stript, two spoonfuls of Capers minced altogether, and boil it in a pint of the same liquor a quarter of an hour, then put in two or three spoonfuls of Verjuyce, two Eggs beaten, let it boil a little, and put to a little Butter, when you have taken it off the fire, stir this altogether, and pour it upon the Pigeons, with sippets round the dish.

A Florendine of *sweet-breads* or *Kidnies.*

Parboil three or four Kidnies, and mince them small, season them with Nutmeg, one stick of Cinnamon, beat as much Sugar as will sweeten it, and a pennie loaf grated, and the Marrow of three bones in good

Fig. 197. "*Lady of* Arundels *Manchet,*" in Elizabeth Grey, Countess of Kent, *A true gentlewomans delight,* bound with *A choice manual of rare and select secrets in physick and chyrurgery* (London, 1653). TS87 K4

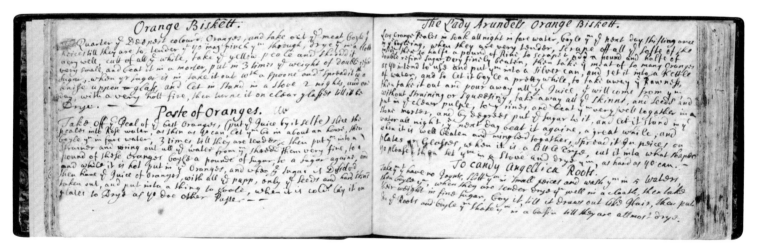

Fig. 198. "The Lady Arundels Orange Biskett." Notebook of recipes and poems, f. 67v–66r (dos-à-dos). Osborn b115

Part Three   158

The Index

Managing information presented difficulties for the early modern reader, as it does for us. Readers might have been enjoined by Erasmus and others to sip, like the bee, the nectar of textual blossom from the abundant garden, but at some point the persistent commonplacer would have to figure out how to find things in his or her notebooks.

As far as John Locke was concerned, readers' anxiety over information retrieval should frame their note-taking from the outset. His instructions on how to commonplace began with the index, the organizational rubric that commonplacers would need to have in place at the outset when gathering citations from their reading. If you waited until you needed something, according to Locke, it was already too late.[170]

Readers often took several different approaches to organizing their notes, sometimes within the same volume. A reader might create an index after a volume was finished, while it was in progress, or sometimes both. Later owners often created retrospective indexes, adding these to printed as well as manuscript volumes; alternately, they might simply list the volume's titles on an endpaper. Equally, readers might add headings to a volume, as they were writing or later, organizing the work around a set of categories.

As William Camden's notebook shows, readers called on a range of approaches to information management (figs. 199–202). Camden has created an alphabetical index for his notebook (fig. 199), copying the entries and page numbers onto a quire of paper, possibly bound in as he had the notes bound into a volume. This was a retrospective effort, almost certainly done from a draft or rough copy, and after the notebook was finished and the contents no longer expanding. Camden demarcated a quire of paper by letter and copied the alphabetized entries and page

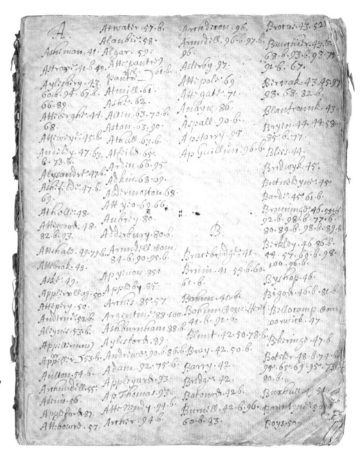

Fig. 199. Index. William Camden, Notebook. England, ca. 1600. Beinecke MS 370. Camden's handmade index is bound in at the front of his notebook.

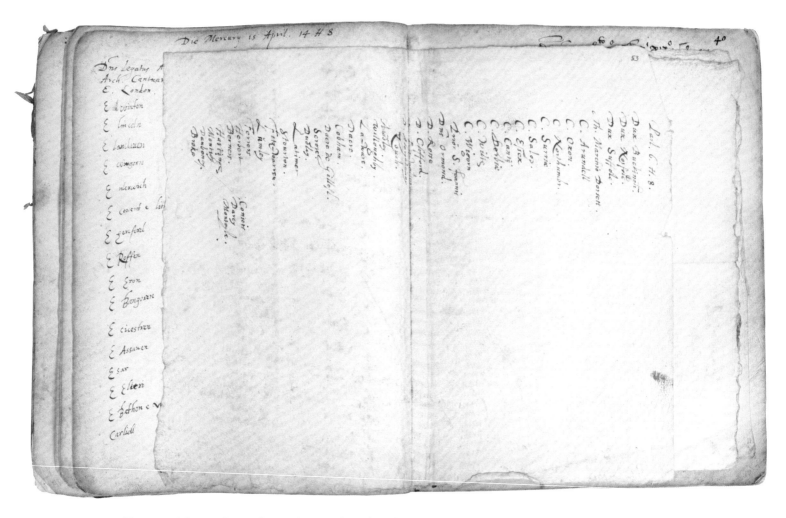

Fig. 200. A loose sheet of notes in Camden's hand, later tipped into the index. Beinecke MS 370

numbers into it. The tidiness of the entire venture—the consistency of the hand, the absence of corrections—indicates that it was done at one sitting. A smaller sheet of notes in the volume (fig. 200) also hints at Camden's overall practice of taking notes on loose sheets that he later organized into notebooks. This sheet, interspersed with his other notes and occasional bouts of pen-trials and jottings (fig. 201), indicates that Camden kept his notes in a working order, imposing a final organization only at a later point.

Camden made headings throughout his notebook, organizing his reading by topic. The notebook has been given a title: Camden has written "Barons" on the parchment of the front cover (fig. 202), and the notebook seems to relate to his administrative work

in the 1590s as Clarenceaux King of Arms, overseeing the research and adjudication of questions relating to hereditary titles.

Other examples show the energetic life of the index, as the reader attempts to impose an external organizational structure on his or her reading, with more or less success. Readers also interacted with their indices after they were completed, marking works, correcting entries, and making additions (figs. 203–204).

Fig. 201. "W W W W William" and "Roma Romæ Romana." Notes, with pen trials, bound in Camden's notebook. Beinecke MS 370

Roma Roma Roma sibimet

Roma Ro Roma. Roma Roma sibimet

Roma

sibimet Ipsa foueris fraude qua foues fraudem

  Ipsa foueris fraude qua foues fraudem

  Ipsa foueris fraude qua foues fraudem

Roma Roma Roma Roma

Roma Roma An. Xpi. Ipsa foueris fraude qua foues

Rob: Ryngborne fraudem

Watton Rome William foueris fraude

Robkus   or Ryngbou Witts

Roma Roma Romana Ryngborne

W Witts Medys tranquillus in undis

W W Ipsa William

William

Ryngbu

qro

qro

Roma

Ipsa foueris fraude que foues fraudem

131 63 Ph

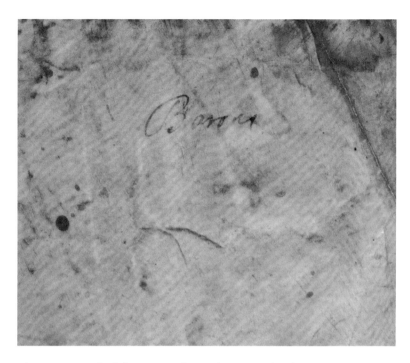

Fig. 202. Detail of the cover of Camden's notebook. Beinecke MS 370

Blotts to take them out of ye paper pag: 15:
Balsome of Cucatilla: pag: 19:
Bruise to heale 22: 34:
Burning to cure itt pag: 27:
Biting of a mad Dog: pag 23:
Breast Poison to heale itt pag: 24:
Bath for ye Dropsy pag: 24:
Barly water: pag: 26:
Brest ye sore pag: 26
Balsome of ye Famory: Pag: 41:
Broth of my mother Clayton: Pag: 44:
Bread to make with a little Cream 78

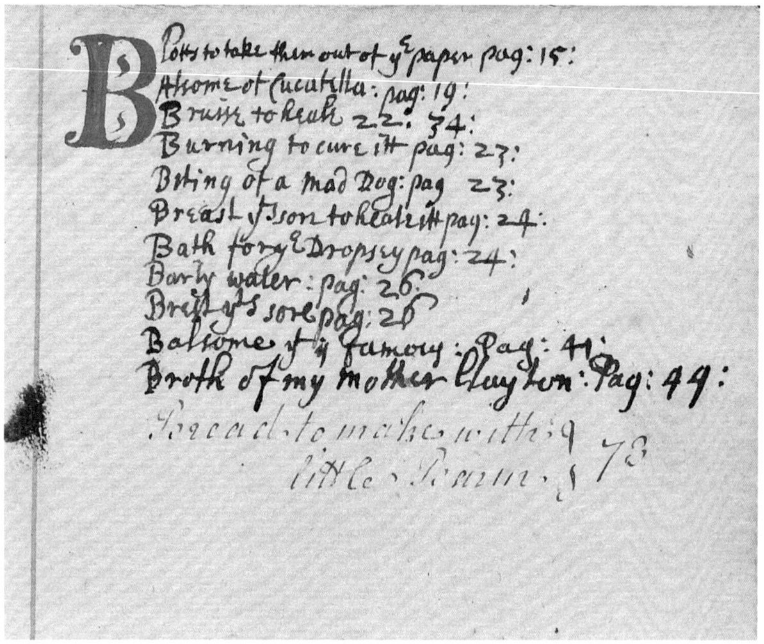

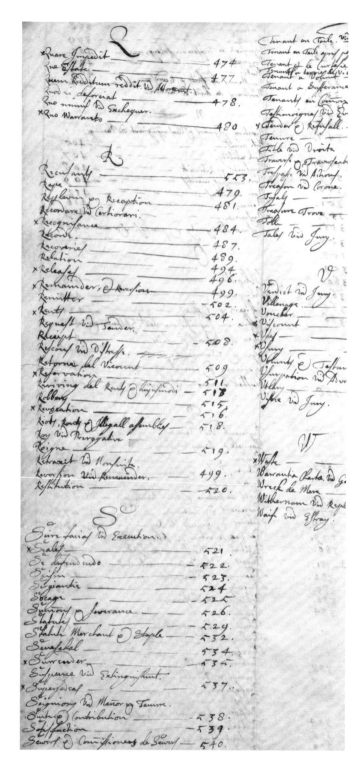

Fig. 203. Detail of index. Robert Paston, Recipe book containing medical, chemical, and household recipes and formulas. England, ca. 1670–83. Osborn fb255

Q
×Quare Impedit — 474
Quo Estate
Quem Redditum reddit vid Attornment — 477
Quod ei deforceat — 478.
Quo minus vid Exchequer.
×Quo Warranto — 480

R
Recusants — 523.
Rape
Replevin & Reception — 479.
Recordare vid Certiorari — 481.
×Recognisance — 484.
Records.
Recoveries — 487.
Relation — 489.
×Release — 494.
×Remainders & Reversions — 496.
Remitter — 499.
×Rents — 502.
Request vid Sanden. — 504.
Receipt
Rescous vid Distress. — 508.
Retorna del Viscount — 509
×Reservation
Reviving del Rents & hereditam — 511.
Robbery — 513
×Revocation — 515.
Riots, Routs & Illegall assemblies — 516.
Roy vid Prerogative — 518.
Reigne — 519.
Retraxit vid Nonsuit
Reversion vid Remainder. — 499.
Restitution — 520.

S
Scire facias vid Execution.
×Scales — 521
Se defendendo — 522.
Seisin — 523.
Sergeantie — 524
Socage — 525
Summons & Severance — 526.
Statutes — 529.
Statute Merchant & Staple — 532.
Seneschal — 534.
×Surrender — 535.
Sufferance vid Extinguishment.
×Supersedeas — 537.
Seigniory vid Mannor & Tenure.
Surplus & Contribution — 538.
Satisfaction — 539.
Sewers & Commissioners de Sewers — 540.

Tenant en Taile vid
Tenant en Taile apres
Tenant a le Curtesie
Tenant a Volunte
Tenant a Sufferance
Tenants en Common
Testimoignes vid
×Tender & Refusall.
Tenure
Title vid Droits
Traverse & Transcript
Trespass vid Action.
Treason vid Corone.
Tryal
Treasure Trove
Tolle
Tales vid Jury.

V
Verdict vid Jury.
Villenage
Voucher
×Viscount
×Use
×Usury
Voluntary & Testam
Usurpation vid Advowson
Utlary
Visne vid Jury.

W
×Waste
Warrantia Charta vid
Wreck de Mere
Withernam vid Replevin
Waif vid Estray.

Fig. 204. Robbery; Revocation; Riots, Routs & Illegall Assemblies. Detail of index, [Legal precedents and procedures]. England, late 17th century. Osborn fb198

Endpapers and Margins

ENDPAPERS

Endpapers and margins are material structures, designed to protect the text of the codex from damage and wear. They also act to create spaces within the volume often inhabited by the books' readers and owners. One example can be seen in Osborn fa50, in which at least three writers are present in the spaces of this late-fifteenth-century manuscript volume of Peter Idle's "Instructions to his son." This opening shows text from two distinct historical time periods, drawn together by the binding structure (fig. 205). On the right is a leaf from a manuscript calendar from the thirteenth century, a medieval manuscript used here as binding waste. Athough calendars were often used for years after their particular date, they were also recycled as scrap, useful parchment or paper for stuffing, padding, wrapping, or other purposes. In the late fifteenth century, when this book was bound, the binder most likely took this leaf from a reserve of similarly discarded texts, valued as a material commodity rather than as text. The leaf is used as a pastedown: a piece of parchment or paper used to cover the wooden boards of the binding.[171]

Fig. 205. Annotated endpapers. Peter Idle, Instructions to his son. England, late 15th century. Osborn fa50

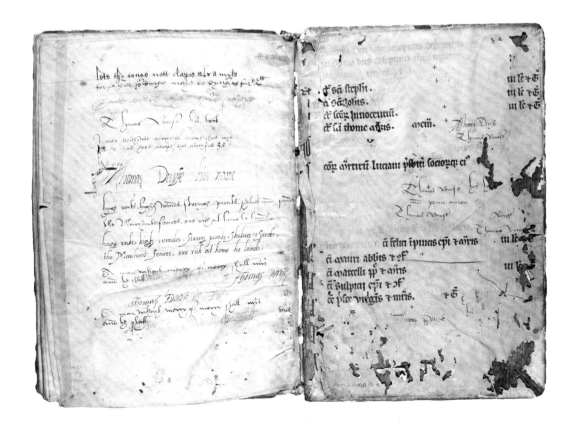

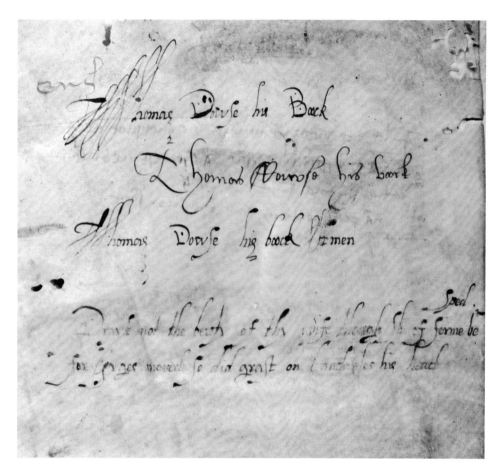

Fig. 206. Detail, front flyleaf of Osborn fa50

On the facing endpaper, in the early seventeenth century, the young reader Thomas Dowse practiced his handwriting, and "Thomas Dowse his hand" can also be found on the wormholed fragment of calendar. Likewise, on the front flyleaf, beneath "Thomas Dowse his Boock / Thomas Dowse his boock / Thomas Dowse his boock Amen," Dowse has copied an excerpt from William Warner's proverbs: "Prayse not the bewty of thy wife though she of forme be sped," at the end mistaking his spacing and cramming the last word above the line (fig. 206). He has also copied an excerpt from Shakespeare's *Lucrece* (1594)—but, as Adam Hooks has observed, Dowse gathered both these excerpts from a ready-made assemblage of learned and witty epithets, the printed commonplace book *Bel-ve-dere* (1600).[172]

MARGINS

The margin, like the endpaper, acts as a space frequently inhabited by a document's or volume's reader. Annotations are often simply straightforward engagements with the text: a reader marking an important passage with a manicule, or pointing finger, to designate a "nota bene" to the self (figs. 207–208).[173]

At other moments, the margin is taken as a type of stage, in which the self is performed, either for itself or for a broader audience. "Gyve me the grace good lord to sett the world at nought," Thomas More wrote in his prayer book, while imprisoned in the Tower of London (fig. 209). And: "a lye," John Stow has written, bitterly and copiously annotating his copy of the history written by his rival (fig. 210).[174]

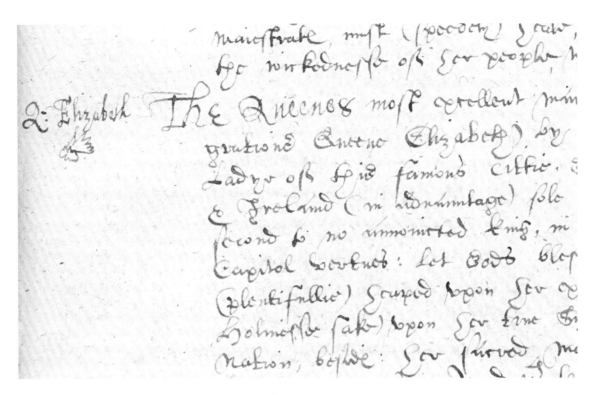

Fig. 207. Manicule, in Richard Ogle, Notebook, 56r.
England, 1586. Osborn a40

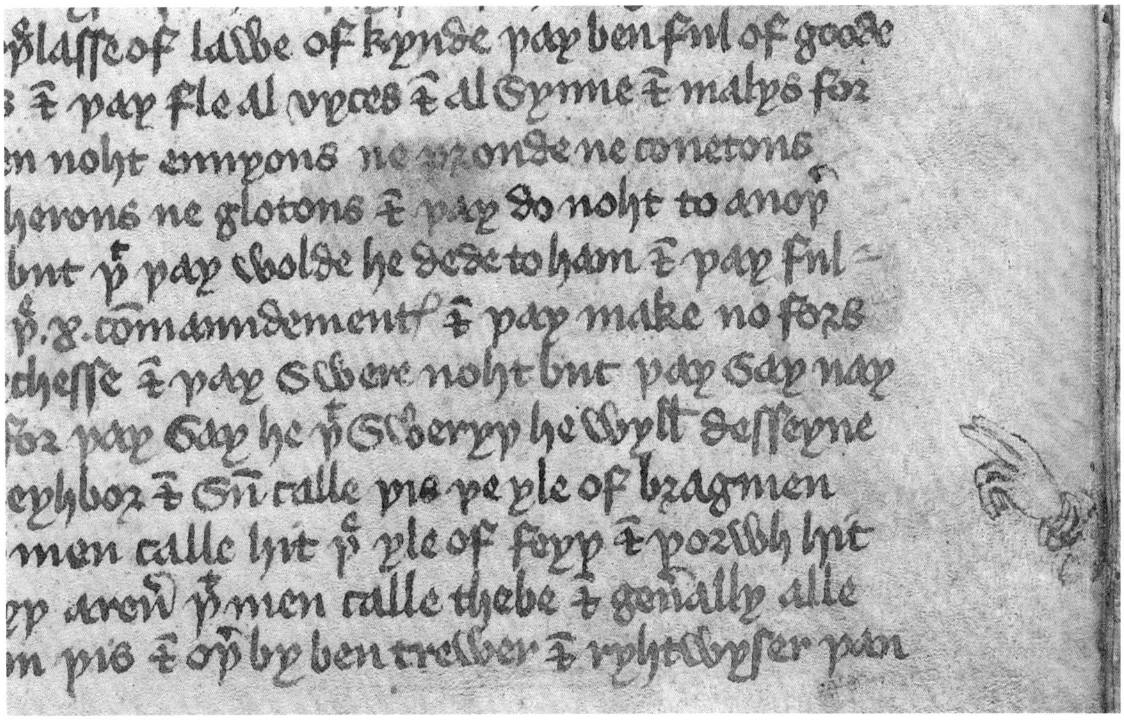

Fig. 208. Manicule, in a copy of John Mandeville,
Travels, 57r. England, ca. 1440. Osborn a55

Fig. 209. Thomas More's notes in his prayer book, from his imprisonment in the Tower of London. Thomas More, annotated copy of *Hore Beate Marie ad usum ecclesie Sarisburiensis* (1530), xvi-v–xvii-r. MS Vault More

Gyve me the grace good lord
to sett the world at nought

Fig. 210. John Stow, annotations in the margins of Richard Grafton, *Graftons abridgement of the chronicles of Englande: newly and diligently corrected, and finished the last of October, 1570* (London, 1570), 1B4v. Osborn pa48

a lye)
stowe saythe some
bodye hathe made
hals cronicle theyr
owne, and namethe
not grafton, There
fore grafton accusythe
hym selfe, when he
sekethe to hyd hym
selfe marke what
shamefull shyfts
he usethe, as he hath
used before in other
matars

To the Reader.

(the vntruthes whereof I will not here detect)
and therin hath charged me bitterly but chief-
ly with ij. thinges. The one, that I haue made
Edward Halles Chronicle my Chronicle, but not
without mangling, and (as he saith) without any
ingenious & playn declaracion therof. The other
thing that he chargeth me withall is . In pray-
sing of Iohn Harding one of his aucthors (who
surely is worthy of great praise, and I wishe
he had folowed in his booke no worsse Auc-
thour) he sayth, that a Chronicle of Hardinges
which he hath, doth much differ from the Chro-
nicle, which vnder the sayde Hardinges name
was printed by mee, as though I had falsefied
Hardinges Chronicle. For aunswere to the first,
I haue not made Halles Chronicle my Chroni-
cle, although the greatest parte of the same was
myne awne Chronicle and written with myne
awne hand. And full little knoweth Stowe of
Halles Chronicle: But this I saye, I haue not
made Halles Chronicle my Chronicle : Neyther
haue I vsed hys Chronicle any otherwise then I
haue all Chronicles, as where Hall spake plain-
ly there I suffer him to tell his awne tale, and in
thende, allege him as my Aucthour as I do all
others, though not in euery place, whiche were
nedelesse, yet in the chiefest places and matters
of weight. And when I found him affected with

many

Margins could be used as a space for counter-publication, in which the reader situated her- or himself in relation to the text and its audiences. In 1799 Hester Lynch Piozzi wrote in her clear round hand in the margins of her copy of the 1789 edition of Joseph Addison's *The Spectator* (fig. 211). She wrote in response to a letter on pin money, originally written in 1712. "The Doctrine of *Pin*-Money is of a very late Date," opines *The Spectator*, "unknown to our great grand-mothers, and not yet received by many of our modern ladies."

Piozzi occupies the space of the margin to rebut Addison's opinions. "The Pin money has however saved many a Woman from being ruined by her

Fig. 211. Hester Lynch Piozzi, annotations in *The Spectator* 4, p. 259. Gen MSS Vol 527

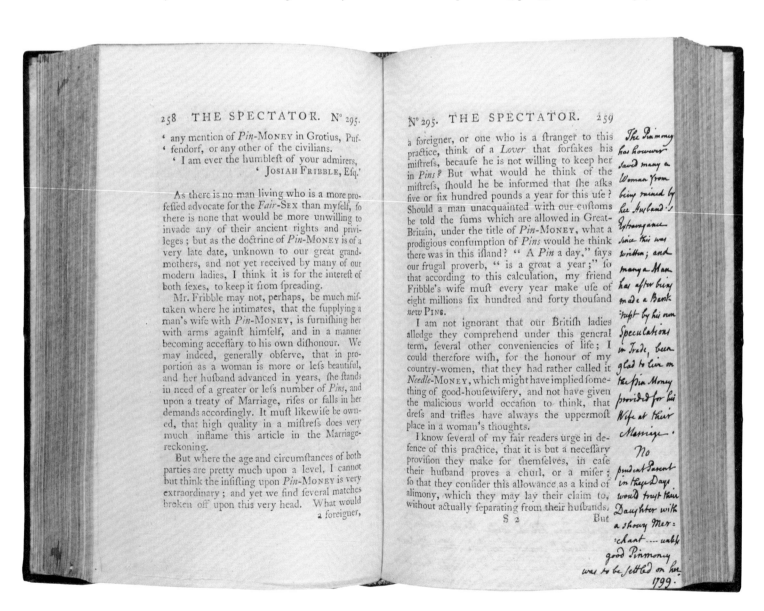

Husband's Extravagance since this was written," she writes,

> and many a Man has after being made a Bankrupt by his own Speculations in Trade, been glad to live on the Pin Money provided for his Wife at their Marriage. No prudent Parent in these Days would trust their Daughter with a showy Merchant ---- unless good Pinmoney was to be settled on her. 1799.

This moment of ascerbic social commentary was one among many inhabiting the margins of Piozzi's copy of *The Spectator.* Piozzi was a habitual and practiced annotator, taking to the margins to offer her witty and often pointed critique. Her copy of the works of Alexander Pope offers her reading of his life and his place in an English literary canon, as articulated in the margin (fig. 212).

Widely read and intellectually engaged, Piozzi was an active note-taker, not only in the margins of her books but also in accompanying notebooks, including the series of bound volumes known as the "Thraliana." This reading and commentary on reading was a sociable activity, and increasingly in her later decades, Piozzi used the margin as a public space, lending her annotated books within her social circle.[175]

The margin might act as a public space, but one whose purposes and audiences remain inscrutable

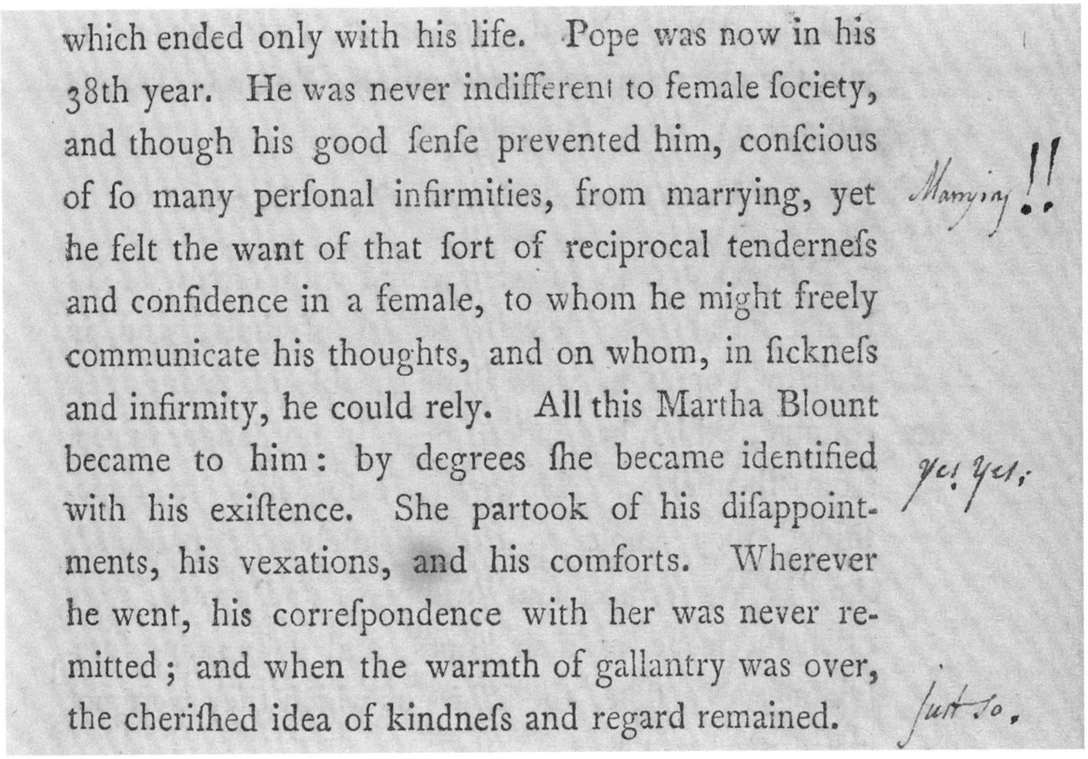
which ended only with his life. Pope was now in his 38th year. He was never indifferent to female ſociety, and though his good ſenſe prevented him, conſcious of ſo many perſonal infirmities, from marrying, yet *Marrying!!* he felt the want of that ſort of reciprocal tenderneſs and confidence in a female, to whom he might freely communicate his thoughts, and on whom, in ſickneſs and infirmity, he could rely. All this Martha Blount became to him: by degrees ſhe became identified *yes! yes!* with his exiſtence. She partook of his diſappointments, his vexations, and his comforts. Wherever he went, his correſpondence with her was never remitted; and when the warmth of gallantry was over, the cheriſhed idea of kindneſs and regard remained. *Just so.*

Fig. 212. Detail, "Marrying!!" Hester Lynch Piozzi, annotations in the *Works of Alexander Pope.* Osborn c661

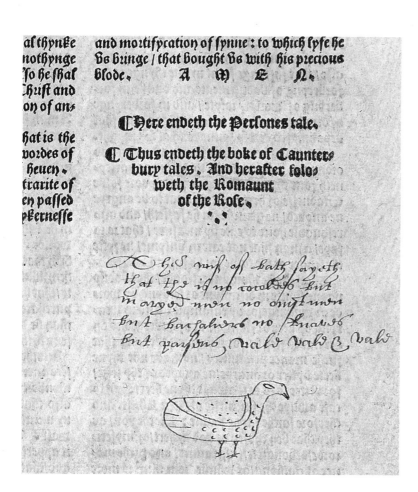

to us as their later recipients (fig. 213). One example can be found in the margin of a copy of William Shakespeare's *Romeo and Juliet* (1599), printed by Thomas Creede for Cuthbert Burby and sold at his shop near the Exchange, in which someone has written, "Anagr. / Elisabeth Rotton / Her lot is to b neat" (fig. 214). All that is known of Elisabeth Rotton's life stems from this punning anagram in the margin of a copy of *Romeo and Juliet,* and from her memorial plaque in a church in Meriden, Warwickshire, where someone, perhaps a family member, has commemorated her to eternity with the anagram "I to a blest throne."[176]

Fig. 213. A reader's annotation in *The workes of Geffray Chaucer newly printed,* ed. William Thynne (London, 1532), f. 82v. Osborn fpa5

Fig. 214. A reader's annotation in William Shakespeare, *Romeo and Juliet* (London, 1599), H3v. Elizabethan Club, Yale University. Eliz 191

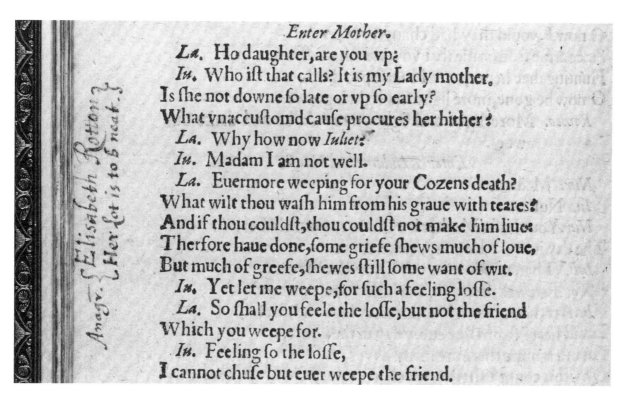

Pen Trials

As an instrument, the quill pen required regular interventions by the writer: it had first to be cut and the nib periodically sharpened and mended. If the writer didn't prepare and maintain his or her pen personally, then that activity had to be outsourced to someone else. According to penmanship manuals, writers might be expected to be in possession of a penknife, ready to mend their quill. In the idealized world of the penmanship manual, writers carried their pen and penknife in a "penner," or pen case, and their ink in an inkhorn, famously carried around the neck. They might buy their pen from a stationer; they might have it cut or mended by a pen-cutter, or a secretary, or another person whose writing skills and labor might be for sale.

It is difficult to know how closely writers' actual practice corresponded with the advice offered them by writing masters. One piece of evidence on how the pen was used can be seen in the example of the pen trial. Peter Beal defines the pen trial as "a piece of scribbling, doodling, or a writing exercise, usually involving only a few words, made by a writer to test his or her freshly trimmed pen or writing style."[177] In English, the term is quite recent: the first *Oxford English Dictionary* reference dates to a 1923 citation in a philological journal: "The patient amassing of data of all kinds from the scribblings and pen-trials of scribes to the character and details of the script."[178] The pen trial's Latin forebear is the *probatio pennae*. In some cases, the *probatio pennae* simply involved writing the words "probatio pennae"; in others, it verged on a genre, a "stylised addition," as Phillip Pulsiano calls it, to the text, playing with the relationships between margin and text, author and writer, reader and scribe.[179]

The pen trial is a catchall term, used to describe a moment of anti-text, or almost-text (figs. 215–219).

It's used to describe something messy, random, or textually irrelevant, written by someone, anyone, by hand. These not- or almost-texts are perhaps best defined through their frequent situation in the waste of a book: in the endpapers, made from another text or its remains, or in an unoccupied space on a page of text. Pen trials take many forms, some verging on text, seeming to hover on the edge of meaning. Writers test their pens, forthrightly, with scratches and scribbling (the description Elizabeth I gave of her handwriting); they might also practice penmanship, copying and repeating a letter or phrase, sometimes varying the hand. Writers might take as sample text their own name, or a married name, testing their pen with their written selves. They might take a trope ("Goe litle booke," as found in Osborn b205 [see fig. 39], with its evocation of Chaucer, Petrarch, and Spenser) or sententiae or excerpts of poetry. A writer might take the space of the endpapers to do a quick sum or tot up his or her accounts (see fig. 79). In all cases these might seem a pen trial to us: seem, that is, random and incoherent, uneasily parsed as a text-act in any way specific to a person or place (the book). Quite how these moments seemed to early modern readers is difficult to say. One of the oddities of the pen trial is its resistance to interpretation, its refusal of meaning: the pen trial carries no expectation of any necessary relationship between writer, reader, and text.

The pen trial is also a term used in catalog descriptions, although not a formal term within the Library of Congress rare book cataloging standard. If used, it is often simply to acknowledge the presence of unattributed and often illegible annotations: marginalia that seem to have little bearing on the work's text or to reveal nothing on the provenance, association, or ownership of the work. In a catalog record, the pen

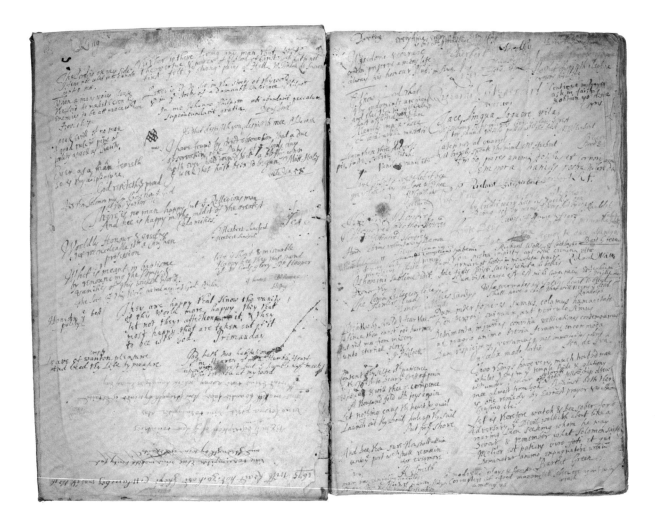

Fig. 215. Richard Fitzherbert, Commonplace book, front endpapers. England, ca. 1630–70. Osborn fb252

trial might be read as a not-description: a writer who is not known; writing that is not coherent or clearly related to the text. Beyond this, one usually finds silence surrounding pen trials, as with other annotations. Until very recently, marks in books (and particularly anonymous marks) were often disregarded, as insignificant or irrelevant to the text, and simply ignored in the catalog record.

The pen trial is therefore a peculiar instance, a moment in which the writing instrument is made visible. In the pen trial, the writer adopts a nominal text—sometimes simply his or her name—as the test of something wholly unrelated to text: the pen. Text, if it is even present, exists only in the guise of handwriting. Sometimes these moments also act as a test of the writer's penmanship, but they are always focused on the pen itself and the writer's handling of it. The pen trial is an anti-authorial act: a moment in which the text becomes the agent of the pen, rather than the pen the agent of the text.

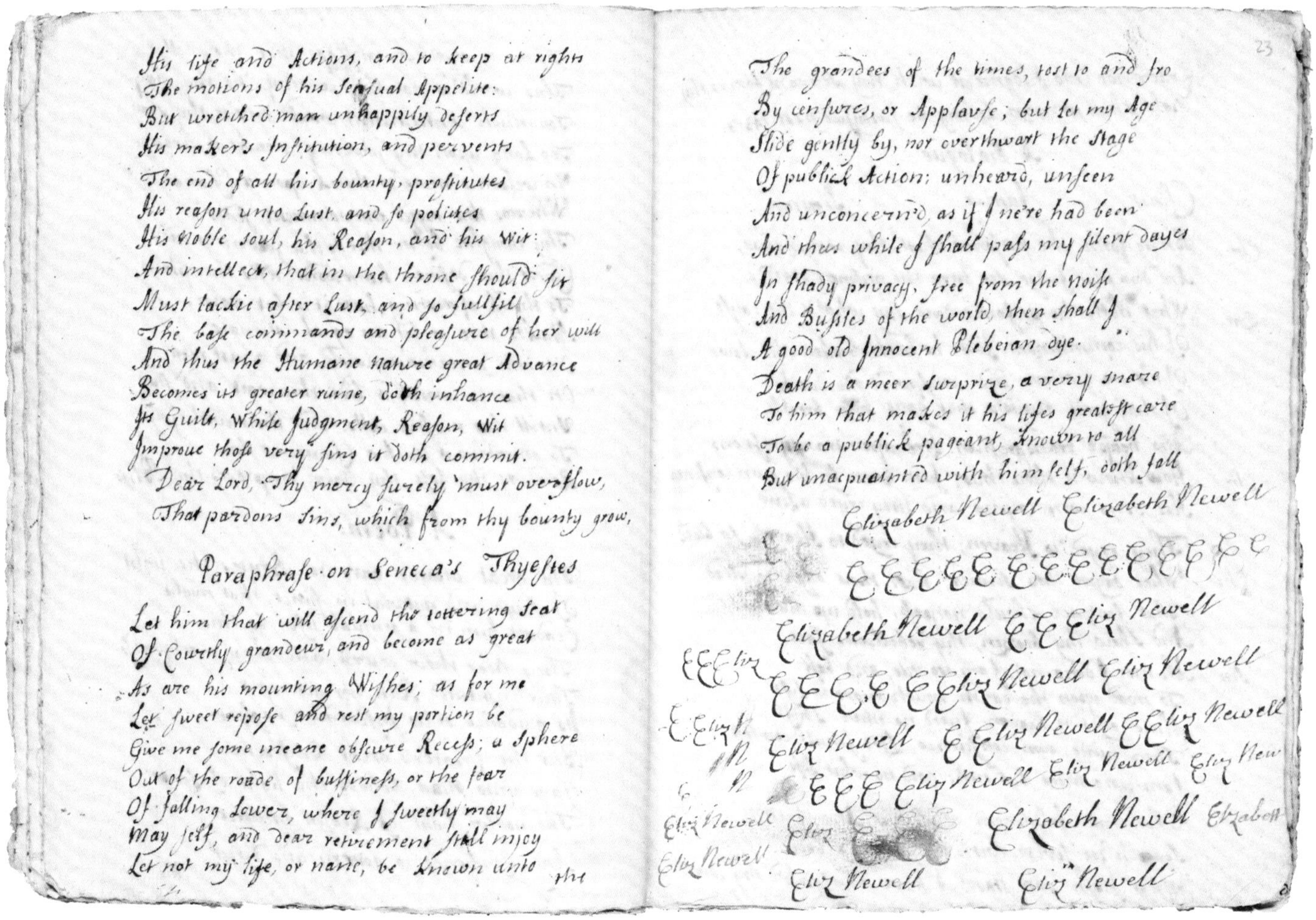

In their immediacy, the promise they seem to offer of the writer's unpolished presence, pen trials offer the suggestion of intimacy. There is an unbuttoned quality to the later reader's encounter with Michael or Elisabeth or Anne in the endpapers of their book, as they practice their names with their pen. It is a moment in which one seems to find the writer or reader amidst unselfconscious practice. They seem clearly visible, even as they are often simultaneously anonymous: often very little is known about the writer other than that he or she once tested their pens and penmanship in the endpapers of a particular manuscript or book. It is precisely in its opacity, its resistance to interpretation, that the pen trial affords us the opportunity to test our expectations of manuscript, and its capacity to allow a glimpse of an interior self in the marks left by a reader's or writer's hand.

Fig. 216. Elizabeth Newell, signature and pen trials in her manuscript copy of eight religious poems. Collection of devotional verse. England, ca. 1655–68. Osborn b49

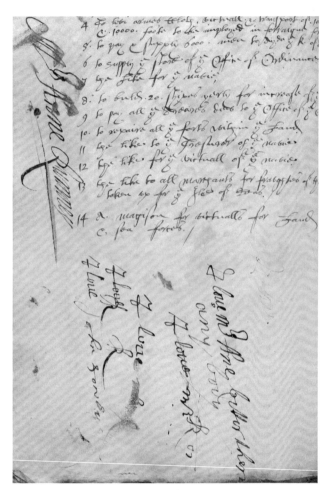

Fig. 217. "I loue Mrs Ane better then any body." A later reader's addition to a notebook containing copies of state papers, p. 250. England, ca. 1620–39. Osborn fb57

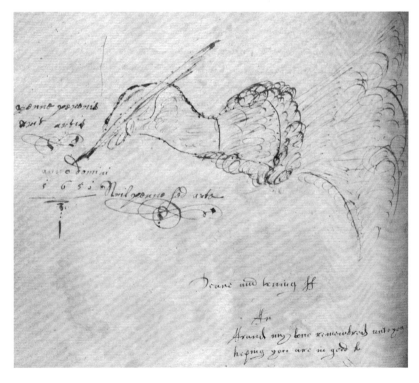

Fig. 218. Detail, pen and pen trial, p. 240. Osborn fb57

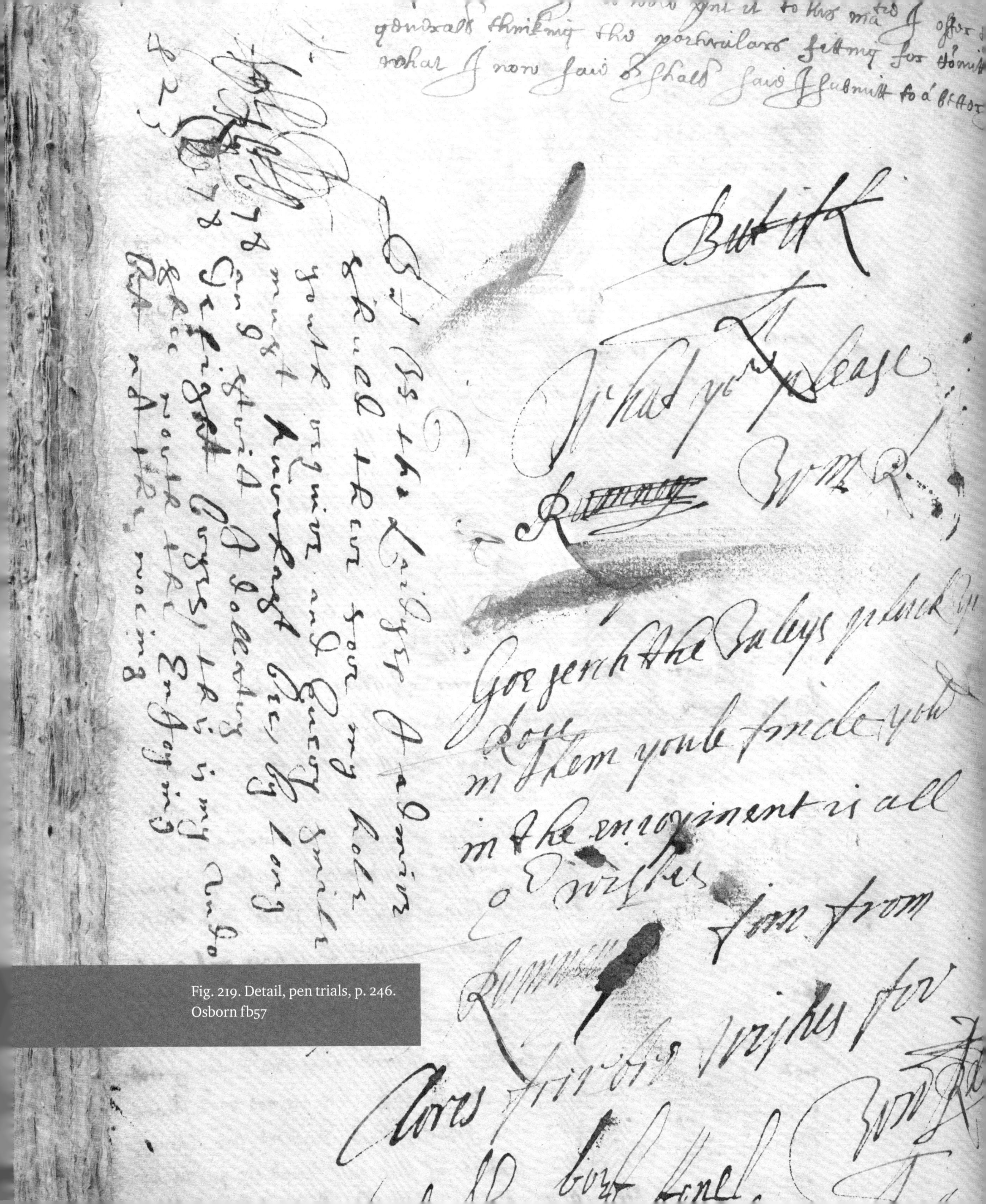

Fig. 219. Detail, pen trials, p. 246.
Osborn fb57

Scribal Publication

Manuscript publication continued long after the advent of the printing press. Shakespeare's "sugred Sonnets" circulating among his "priuate friends" are one example of manuscript publication (see fig. 187). Another might be the circulation of John Donne's poetry, almost entirely published in manuscript in his lifetime (see, for example, figs. 1, 38, 85, 128). News, poetry, and music, like this early-seventeenth-century copy of a lute tablature (fig. 220), were all genres circulating in manuscript in early modern England.[180]

Scribal publication depended on a labor economy of professional writers with a means of distribution. Thomas Nashe hints at the economic infrastructure in the preface to his *Terrors of the night* (1594):

> A long time since hath it line suppressed by mee; untill the urgent importunitie of a kinde frend of mine (to whom I was sundrie waies beholding) wrested a Coppie from me. That Coppie progressed from one scriueners shop to another, & at length grew so common, that it was readie to bee hung out for one of their signes, like a paire of indentures. Whereuppon I thought it as good for mee to reape the frute of my owne labours, as to let some unskilfull pen-man or Nouerint-maker startch his ruffe & new spade his beard with the benefite he made of them.[181]

Nashe's comparison of his play with "a paire of indentures" makes direct reference to the bustling economy of legal copying. The "scriueners" at work on Nashe's copy might as easily have been the clerks or other penmen who made their living copying texts and legal documents for audiences in early modern England.

Fig. 220. Manuscript copy recording the music accompanying "Mr Goodwell his Maske for S^t Jo: Coll: Oxforde." Lute tablature, early 17th century. Osborn fb7

NEWSLETTERS

Newsletters were another form of scribal publication in early modern England. These were commercially copied by professional writers for a subscription list. The newsletters were sent as letters at regular intervals through the week from London to their readers. This late-seventeenth-century newsletter was sent on Tuesday, Thursday, and Saturday to a "Madam Pole of Radbourn near Derby," in the north of England (figs. 221–223).

Scribal newsletters coexisted with those in print: not only did the Pole family receive both scribally published and printed newsletters at Radbourne Hall in Derbyshire, but the printed newsletters often contained a section designed for manuscript additions.[182] The circulation by subscription of both forms, scribal and printed, relied on the emergence in the mid-seventeenth century of a governmentally organized postal system, and the gradual formalization and regularization of the postal service.[183]

Figs. 221–222. Front and reverse of a scribal newsletter, sealed, postmarked, and addressed to Madam Pole "at Radbourn near Derby." England, September 29 [1691]. OSB MSS 60

Fig. 223. Detail of fig. 221

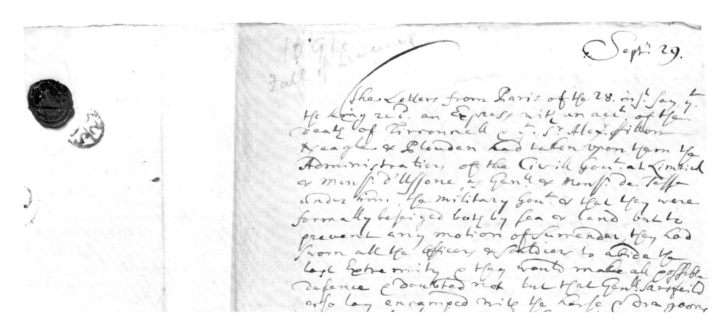

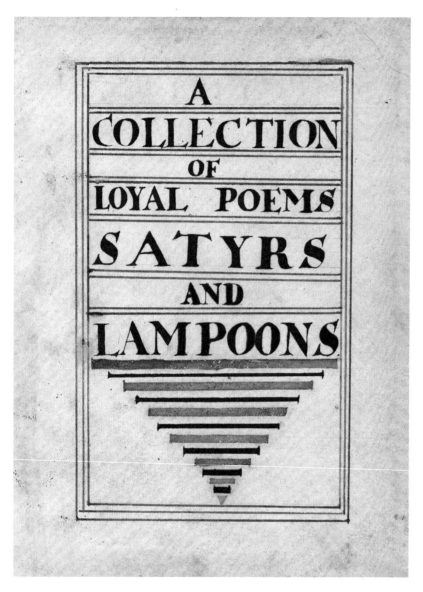

Fig. 224. Title page, A scribal collection of Loyalist poems. England, ca. 1695. Osborn b111

POETRY

Manuscript circulation was a way to publish without publishing in early modern England. Satirical, sexual, political, heretical, written by women: these and other categories of text often circulated in manuscript, either copied by readers themselves or produced by professional writers for sale (fig. 224). Harold Love divides scribal publication into three broad categories: authorial publication, entrepreneurial or commercial publication, and user publication.[184] The categories might overlap, as we have seen in Thomas Nashe's observation on the entrepreneurial appropriation of his work.

Works often circulated in single-author editions, as in the case of the scribal copies of John Donne and Thomas Carew shown here (figs. 225–227). These were copied by professional writers and were likely purchased or commissioned by readers affiliated with one of the Inns of Court. The notebooks themselves are often perfectly ordinary bound blank books, of a kind that could as easily have been filled with recipes and witty epithets by a reader or listed in the accounts of the clerks of the Exchequer (see fig. 36). This type of closed publication, circulating within a limited community, allowed the consumption of works which might otherwise have been too satirical, salacious, or politically problematic to be produced through the more formally licensed and regulated processes of print. It also perhaps worked to normalize certain conventions on the presentation of texts. Professional writers are clearly following certain emergent conventions: the poems are given titles; the pages are numbered; the stanzas are demarcated by spacing or flourishing (or both); each scribe also adopts some form of catchword at the bottom of the page, perhaps both as a scribal convention and as a means to guide the reader from one page to the next.

The labor of copying might also fall to secretaries and amanuenses. This manuscript of Lucy Hutchinson's Miltonic epic, "Order and disorder," is the only copy of the work known to survive (fig. 228); it was given as a presentation copy to Hutchinson's neighbor, Anne Rochester, who has inscribed it as "her book" (fig. 229). Was it copied by Hutchinson, or

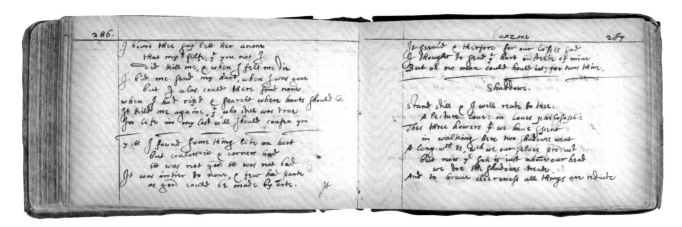

Figs. 225–226. On the right, or recto:
"Shaddowe," copied in a professional hand in
this scribal collection of poems by John Donne,
pp. 286–87. England, ca. 1620. Osborn b114

Stand still & I will reade to thee
A lecture loue: in loues philosophie
Thes three howers y^t we haue spent
in walking here two shadowes went
A long wth us, wch we our selues product
but now y^e sun is iust aboue our head
we doe the shadowes treade
And to braue cleereness all things are reducte

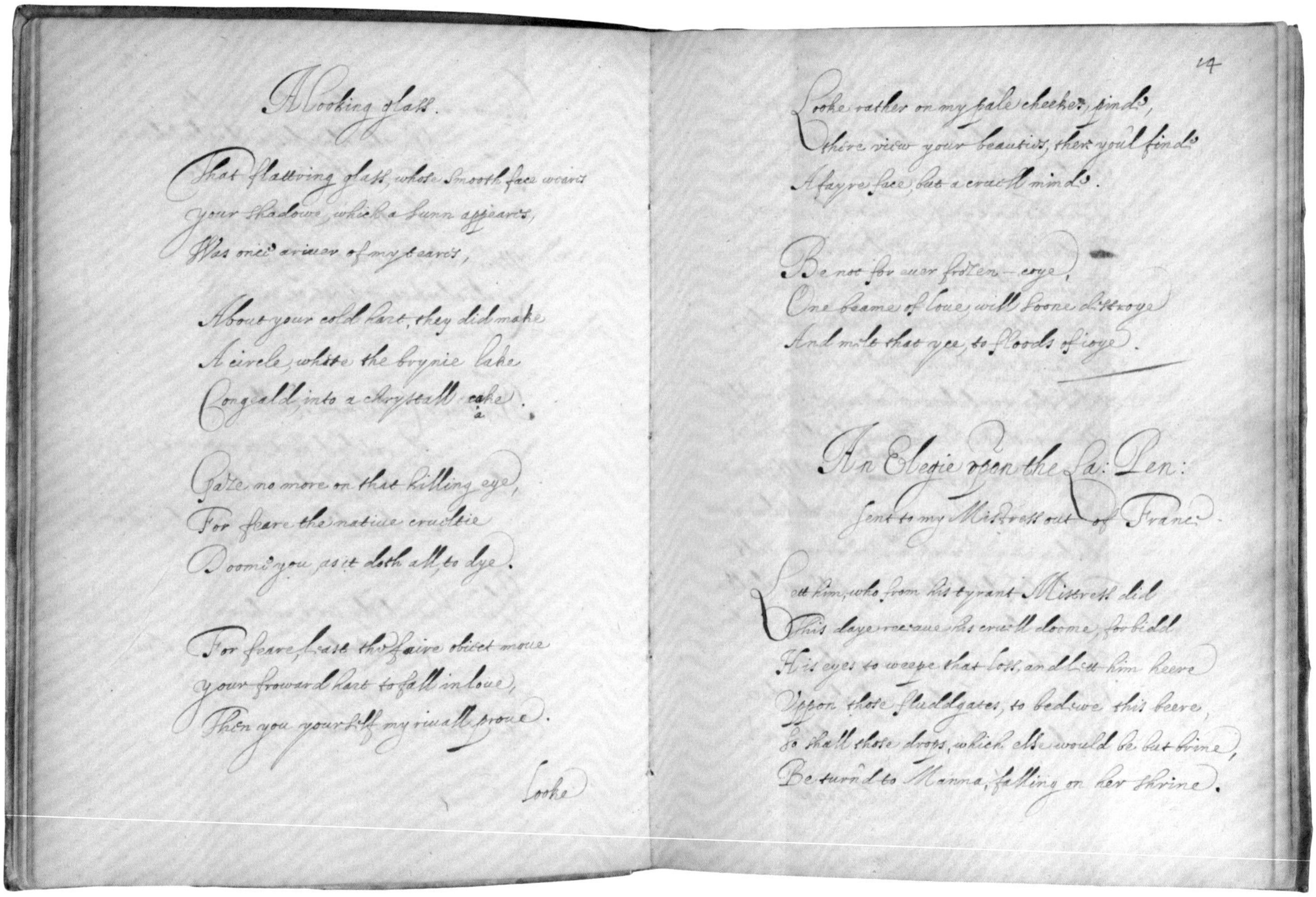
A looking glass.
That flattring glass, whose smooth face weares
your shadow, which a sunn appeares,
Was once a river of my teares,
About your cold hart, they did make
A circle, where the brynie lake
Congeal'd into a Chrystall cake.
Gaze no more on that killing eye,
For feare the native crueltie
Doome you, as it doth all, to dye.
For feare, least the faire obiect moue
your froward hart to fall in loue,
Then you your selfe my riuall proue.
Looke
14
Looke rather on my pale cheekes, pin'd,
there view your beauties, there you'l find
A fayre face, but a cruell mind.
Be not for euer frozen-coye,
One beame of loue will soone distroye
And melt that yce, to floods of ioye.
An Elegie upon the La: Pen:
sent to my Mistress out of France.
Lett him, who from his tyrant Mistress did
This daye receaue his cruell doome, forbidd
His eyes to weepe that loss, and lett him heere
Uppon those fluddgates, to bedewe this beere,
So shall those drops, which else would be but brine,
Be turn'd to Manna, falling on her shrine.

Fig. 227. Two poems by Thomas Carew, "A looking glass" and "An Elegie upon the La: Pen: sent to my Mistress out of France," copied in a professional hand in this scribal collection. England, ca. 1630–39. Osborn b464. Note the use of space on the page: the writer has folded the pages (most visible on the right) to mark the margins.

An Elegie upon the La: Pen:
Sent to my Mistress out of France

Lett him, who from his tyrant Mistress did
This daye receaue his cruell doome, forbid
His eyes to weepe that loss, and let him heere
Uppon those fluddgates, to bed we this beere,
So shall those drops, which else would be but brine,
Be turn'd to Manna, falling on her shrine.

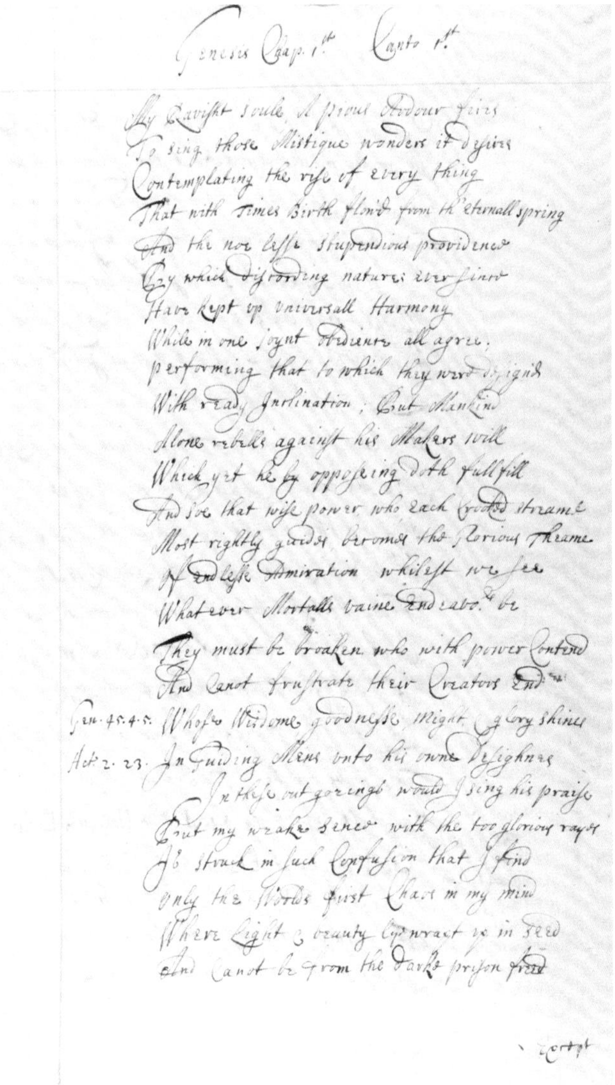

by a secretary or other servant? The question highlights the nebulous quality of scribal publication and how little we know about the mechanisms by which works might have been professionally produced and circulated in manuscript—and the boundaries between professional scribal publication and the copying of manuscript texts within the economy of the household.

Fig. 228. Lucy Hutchinson, Order and disorder: or, the world made and undone, p.1. England, ca. 1664–79. Osborn fb100

Fig. 229. Detail, "Anne Rochester her book," in Lucy Hutchinson, Order and disorder: or, the world made and undone, front free endpaper. England, ca. 1664–79. Osborn fb100

Compositor and Proof Copies

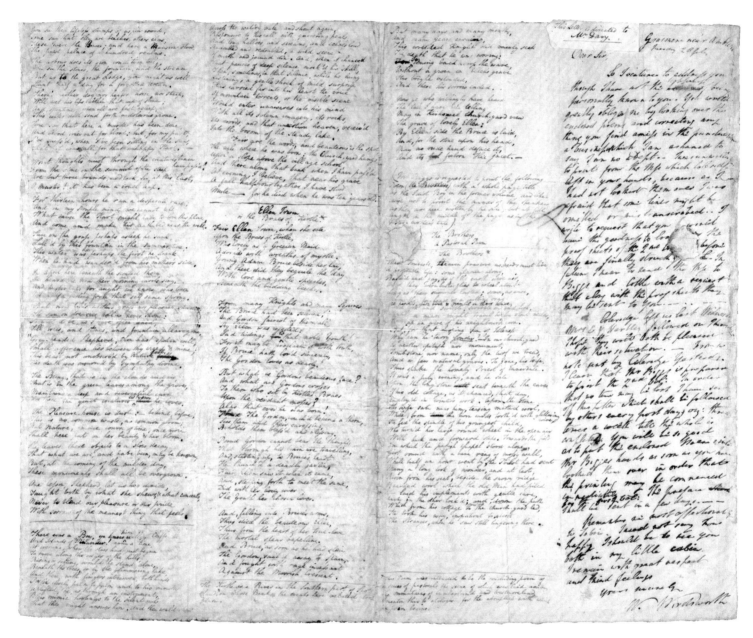

Fig. 230. One of a series of letters from William
Wordsworth to Humphry Davy, with additions by
Dorothy Wordsworth and Samuel Taylor Coleridge,
used by the publishers, Biggs & Cottle, as the
printer's copy for the second edition of *Lyrical Ballads*.
Grasmere, July 28 [1800]. Gen MSS 1261, letter 1

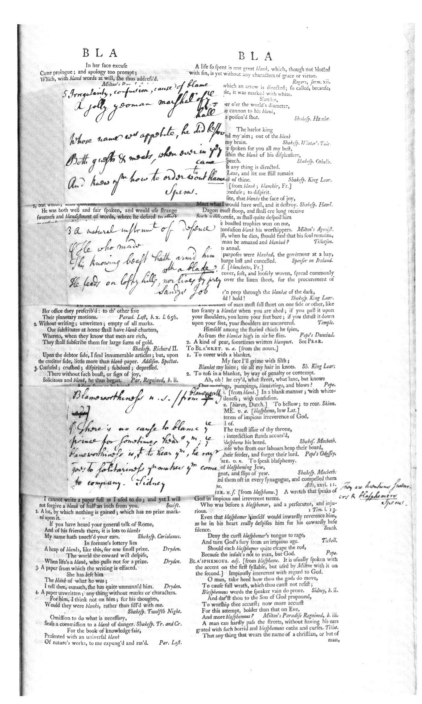

Fig. 231. Additions for a later edition, in Samuel Johnson, *A Dictionary of the English Language* (1755), vol. 1, p. 197. Gen MSS Vol 728

Print culture in early modern England was inseparable from that of manuscript. On a Tuesday in July in 1800, William Wordsworth wrote his friend Humphry Davy from the Lake District to ask him to look over the enclosed poems and make any corrections he thought necessary to the punctuation (fig. 230). The letter was one in a series containing the content for the second edition of *Lyrical Ballads* (1800); the letters show William Wordsworth, Dorothy Wordsworth, and Samuel Taylor Coleridge at work drafting revisions, which were sent as proof copy to the volume's publishers.

In another example, Samuel Johnson used a copy of the first edition of his *A Dictionary of the English Language* (1755) as the archive for his corrections toward a later edition. Together, Johnson and his amanuenses gathered corrections and additions, filing them in the sheets of a printed copy that acted, by default, as one of the manuscript proofs for a subsequent edition (fig. 231).

These citations were collected from printed works: Johnson and his helpers copied these by hand on slips of paper, often cannibalized from letters or administrative documents. The slips find their pairing in printed books, as can be seen in this copy of Francis Bacon's *Works,* owned by Johnson and used by him as the source of Bacon's quotations in the *Dictionary* (figs. 232–233). Johnson (or his aide) can be found in the large graphite marks made in the margins, noting a citation.

The proof copy of the *Dictionary* highlights the inextricability of print and manuscript in the early modern period. Print publication was a process of converting manuscript into typescript, measured in lines of metal type laid in a form on a press bed. Because of the intricacy of this process, a printed copy of a work was often the most convenient form of the text for corrections for a subsequent edition. Manuscript was therefore often the medium for intervention in the printed text: corrections, annotations, additions were made in manuscript, by hand, to be added to the layout of the printed page and volume.[185]

The "compositor's copy" is the term for text used for typesetting. Compositors, the workmen responsible for creating the lines of type to print a page, used

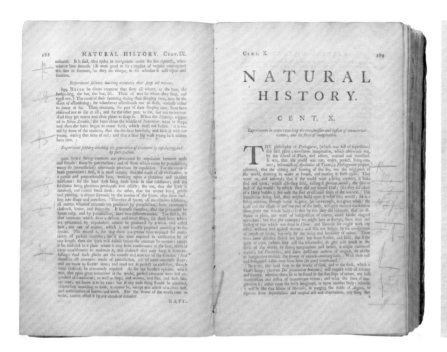

Fig. 232. The copy of Francis Bacon, *The Works of Francis Bacon,* vol. 3 (1740), used by Samuel Johnson in compiling his *Dictionary.* Im J637 +755da

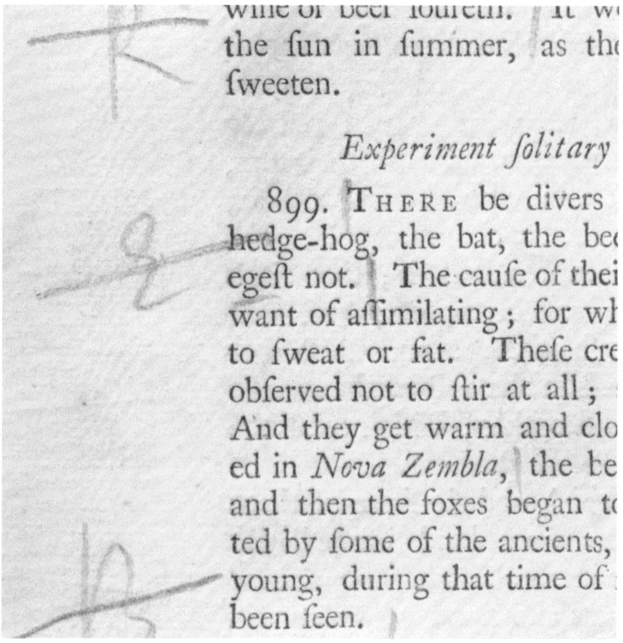

Fig. 233. Detail of fig. 232: "E" for "egest" [or, eat] in a marginal note

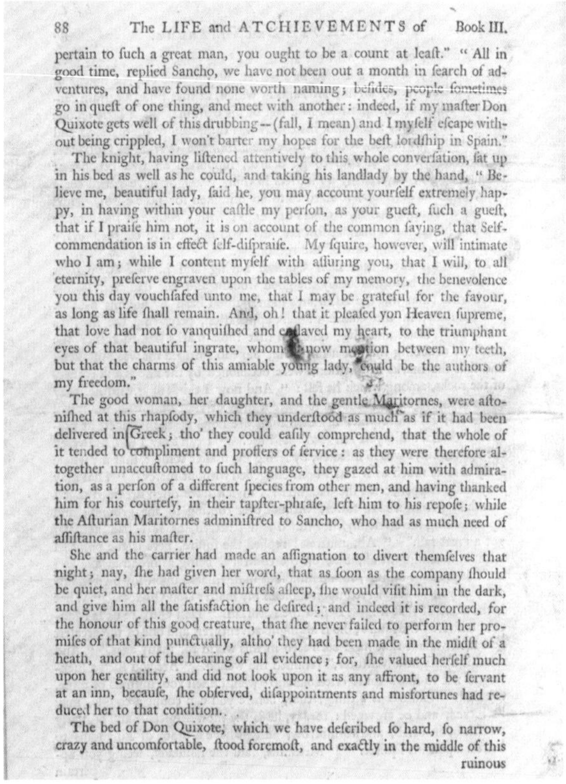

Fig. 234. Editorial fingerprints, in T. Smollett, ed., *The history and adventures of the renowned Don Quixote* (1755). Osborn pc310

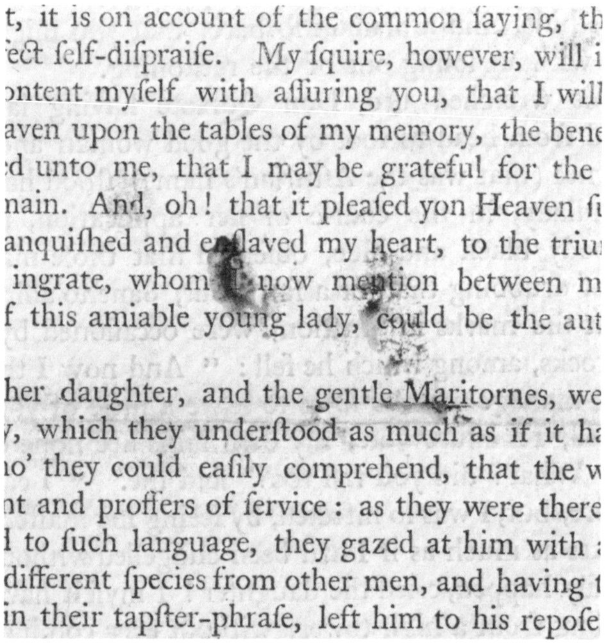

Fig. 235. Detail of fig. 234

different forms of copy-text in typesetting a work. For the first printed edition of a work, some kind of manuscript text would of necessity be the source, whether a fair copy of a completed text or something received in more fragmentary form. For a second or later edition, a compositor might take an annotated or amended printed copy as the copy-text. As the example of the revisions to *Lyrical Ballads* indicates, the printer might also work from an author's manuscript revisions. Composition, or the process of typesetting a work, is a moment of remediation, in which a text might be changed or altered by any of a number of agents: an originating author, editor, publisher, printer, compositor, and others.

The example shown here is of a surviving copy of the 1755 edition of Tobias Smollett's translation of *Don Quixote.* This copy is annotated throughout by the printer, with his marks on the composition of the text (figs. 234–235). In another example, this copy of Simon Segar's *Honores Anglicani* (1712; fig. 236) was used as the compositor's copy for Thomas Banks's 1811 edition of the text, which Banks claimed to have authored, and which he included as a supplement to his 1811 edition of William Dugdale's *Antient usage in bearing of such ensigns of honour as are commonly called arms.*[186]

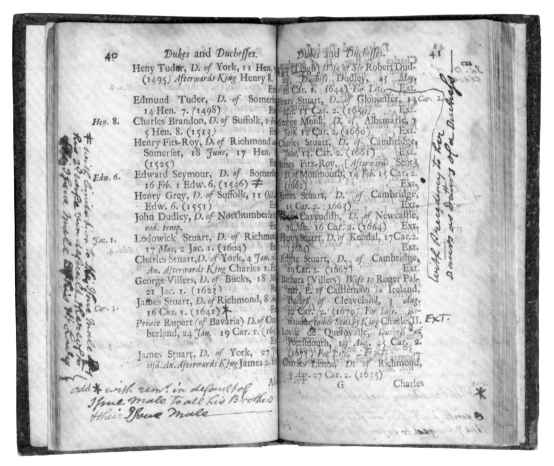

Fig. 236. Simon Segar, *Honores Anglicani: or, titles of honour the temporal nobility of the English nation… have had, or do now enjoy* (London, 1712). Osborn pc312. Both the editor and the compositor have marked this copy of Segar's 1712 work on heraldry, using it to prepare an 1811 edition.

Letters and Letter Books

LETTERS

In Shakespeare's *Hamlet,* shown here in its 1604 edition, Polonius reads a letter written by Hamlet to his daughter (fig. 237). "*To the Celestiall and my soules Idoll, the most beautified* Ophelia," Hamlet has written as salutation. "*That's an ill phrase, a vile phrase,*" Polonius interjects, displeased at the use of the term "beautified." The letter is one of the engines of the play: Hamlet has written a letter to Ophelia, who has given it to her father, who now reads it to the Queen. Letters shape the course of relationships at other points in the play: Ophelia returns Hamlet's letters to him; Hamlet intercepts the letter borne by Rosencrantz and Guildenstern carrying the order for his execution.

The pervasiveness of letters in *Hamlet* only serves to reinforce the sense of a shared understanding of how letters were meant to work—and a shared anxiety at the possibilities for their failure. This reflects the centrality of correspondence to relationships in early modern England: business and personal transactions, both formal and informal, were negotiated by the medium of the letter. Relationships involving any kind of distance—across London, across England, across the Channel or the Atlantic—were transacted through letters and notes.[187]

Letter-writing, at its core, centered on mobility: the movement of a material thought from one person to another, from one place to another, borne from one agent to the recipient, often across the thresholds of occupation, social rank, and gender (fig. 238). The letter traversed the public and private spheres, crossing from the exterior world into the internal life of the household and, in theory, the interior life of the recipient. As such, letters occupied a role that was both pragmatic and highly charged. As Shakespeare made clear in *Hamlet,* the letter could serve both to reinforce and to destabilize all manner of relationships.

Proper letter-writing was the subject of instruction for a popular audience in Elizabethan England (fig. 239). In 1568 William Fulwood—a member of the Merchant Taylors' Company—published *The enimie of idlenesse,* a guide to letter-writing. From the outset, Fulwood emphasizes the role of the letter as a vector crossing between the social status of author and recipient, whether superior, equal, or inferior. He highlights the three points to manage: the salutation, the subscription (or signature), and the superscription, or address, "which must be upon the back syde, the letter being closed, sealed and packed up after the finest fashion."[188]

I haue a daughter, haue while she is mine,
Who in her dutie and obedience, marke,
Hath giuen me this, now gather and surmise,
  To the Celestiall and my soules Idoll, the most beau-
  tified Ophelia *, that's an ill phrase, a vile phrase,*
  beautified is a vile phrase, but you shall heare : thus in
  her excellent white bosome, these &c.
  Quee. Came this from *Hamlet* to her ?
  Pol. Good Maddam stay awhile, I will be faithfull,
Doubt thou the starres are fire,   *Letter.*
Doubt that the Sunne doth moue,
Doubt truth to be a lyer,
But neuer doubt I loue.
O deere Ophelia, I am ill at these numbers, I haue not art to recken
  my grones, but that I loue thee best, ô most best belieue it, adew.
  Thine euermore most deere Lady, whilst this machine is to him.
Pol. This in obedience hath my daughter showne me,   (*Hamlet.*
  And more about hath his solicitings
                                                    A 3

Fig. 237. Detail, Polonius reading Hamlet's letter to Ophelia. *Hamlet* (1604), E4r. Elizabethan Club, Yale University. Eliz 168

Fig. 238. Arthur Devis, "John Orde, His Wife,
Anne, His Eldest Son, William, and a Servant,"
ca. 1754–56. Oil on canvas. Yale Center for British
Art, Paul Mellon Collection. B2001.2.65. In this
family portrait, grouped around the hearth, Orde
sits at the table, by the *Daily Advertiser,* while a
black servant enters the room bearing a letter
addressed to him at Morpeth, his landed estate in
Northumberland. Orde's son, meanwhile, presents
a pheasant to his stepmother, Anne.

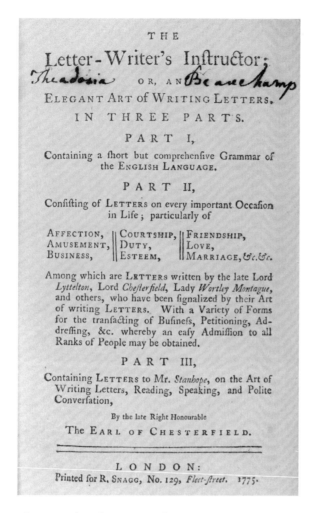

Fig. 239. Theodosia Beauchamp's signature in her copy of *The letter-writer's instructor; or, an elegant art of writing letters. In three parts* (London, 1775). Ia780 775L

In this example, one of a series of letters written during the English Civil War, the Duke of Bedford and seven peers send a letter to the Committee of Safety about the King's refusal to receive a petition (figs. 240–242). The letter is a bifolium, that is, it is written on a single sheet of paper that has been folded in half; this fold is visible at the right edge of fig. 240 and at the left edge of fig. 241. The letter's text is on the recto, or right side, of the fold; the letter's address, or superscription, is on the verso, or left side of the fold. The machinery of the letter—its text and its address— occupies one entire side of the sheet of paper. The other side of the sheet was left blank—even when, as is the case in this example, the author might seem to have needed more space.

At the top, Bedford has begun with a salutation, directed to the Committee of Safety: "My Lords & Gentlemen." He has followed this with a virgule, or slash, dividing the salutation from the body of the text. Bedford's letter fills approximately two thirds of the page, continuing into a postscript in the left margin (fig. 242). The bottom third of the page is dedicated to the subscription, or signature: the letter's seven co-authors have joined Bedford in signing the letter, dated to Worcester on October 18, 1642. We find the superscription, or address, on the verso: "For the Committee of Lords and Coṁons for the safety of the kingdome thes with haste." As the residual fold marks reveal, the letter was folded, sealed, and delivered by a bearer.[189] A recipient or later owner has docketed the letter, visible to the right of the superscription in fig. 240, noting that it concerns the "King's refusal of the petition."

As Jana Dambrogio has observed, there were several methods of folding early modern letters to send. Each of these methods changed the size and shape of the final letter, rendering it larger or smaller, more or less secure from prying eyes, or more or less personal.[190] The recipient of the letter would first encounter its exterior: the size and shape; the hand and address; the seal; floss, if present, and its color, if colored.[191] The recipient would also either meet the letter's bearer or have some level of understanding of how it had been sent. The letter might also be accompanied by other letters, each encountered as one of many. As letters might have been written by a secretary, so might they have been opened by another, and the contents and letter conveyed to the recipient; the secretary's hand would also likely be the hand to docket and file the letter, and oversee the writing and sending of a response.

Often early modern letters will be encountered in an album where they can be read consecutively. For the writer, however, each letter began as a sheet of paper, carefully organized around the relationship between sender and recipient and the means by which the letter would be delivered. Equally, the appearance alone of a letter could lead its recipient to a sense of what to expect: the manner in which it had been sent, the hand, the size of the paper, and the shape of the text on the page would convey a message alongside that of the text.

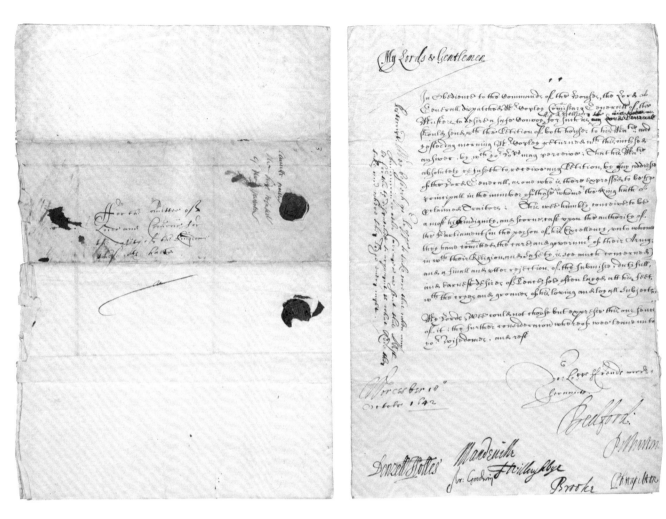

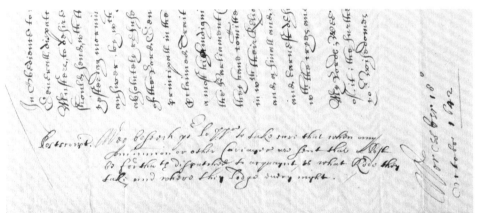

Figs. 240–241. William Russell, 1st Duke of Bedford, with seven co-authors, to the Committee of Safety, of Parliament. Worcester, October 18, 1642. Collection of letters and state papers, apparently from the papers of John Pym. England, 1584–1643. Osborn fb94, Folder 5

Fig. 242. Detail of fig. 241, showing the postscript

LETTER BOOKS

Writers often retained copies of the letters they sent, in case the original went astray or was misdelivered, or simply to keep a personal archive of correspondence. Francis Castillion (1561–1638), Gentleman-Pensioner to James I and MP for Great Bodwyn, 1596–97,[192] kept copies of his letters in a notebook that he also later used for verse and other literary collections. Here Castillion's draft letter to the King is encroached on by the copy of a letter from W: Borough (figs. 243 and 245).

Celebrity letters also often circulated as cultural currency. Castillion's notebook also holds copies of famous letters by others, as in this example of a letter from Sir Walter Raleigh to his wife, shortly before his execution (figs. 244 and 246).

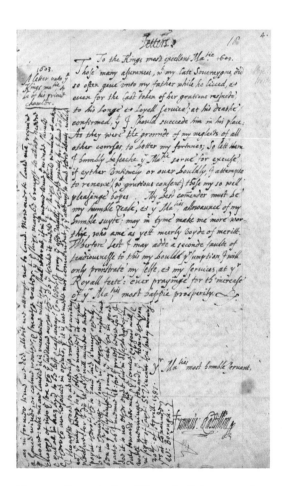

Fig. 243. Francis Castillion, draft letter to the King. Notebook, 4r. England, ca. 1590–1638. Osborn fb69

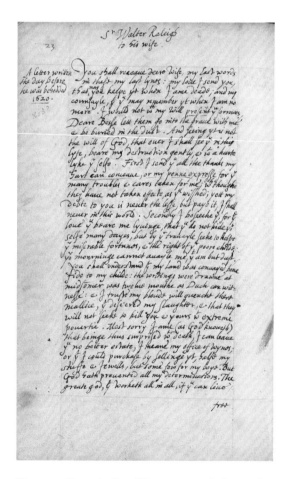

Fig. 244. Francis Castillion, copy of a letter from Sir Walter Raleigh. Notebook, p. 23. England, ca. 1590–1638. Osborn fb69

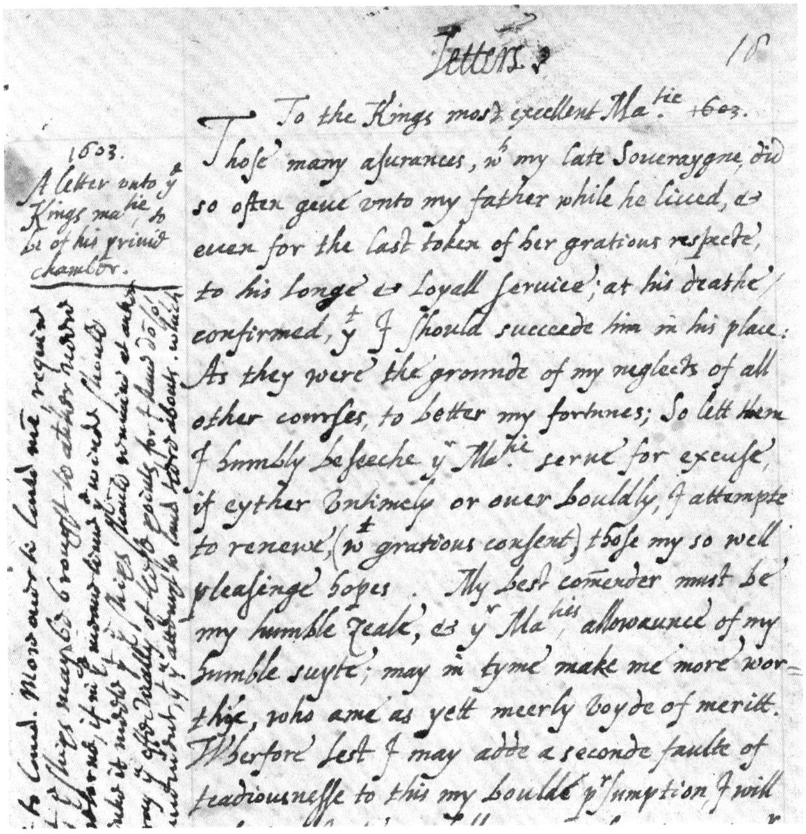

Fig. 245. Detail of fig. 243

Letters
To the Kings most excellent Matie 1603.

1603.
A letter unto y^e
Kings ma^tie, to
be of his priuie
chamber.

Those many asurances, w^h my late Soueraygne, did
so often geue vnto my father while he liued, &
euen for the last token of her gratious respecte,
to his longe & loyall seruice; at his deathe
confirmed, y^t I should succeede him in his place:

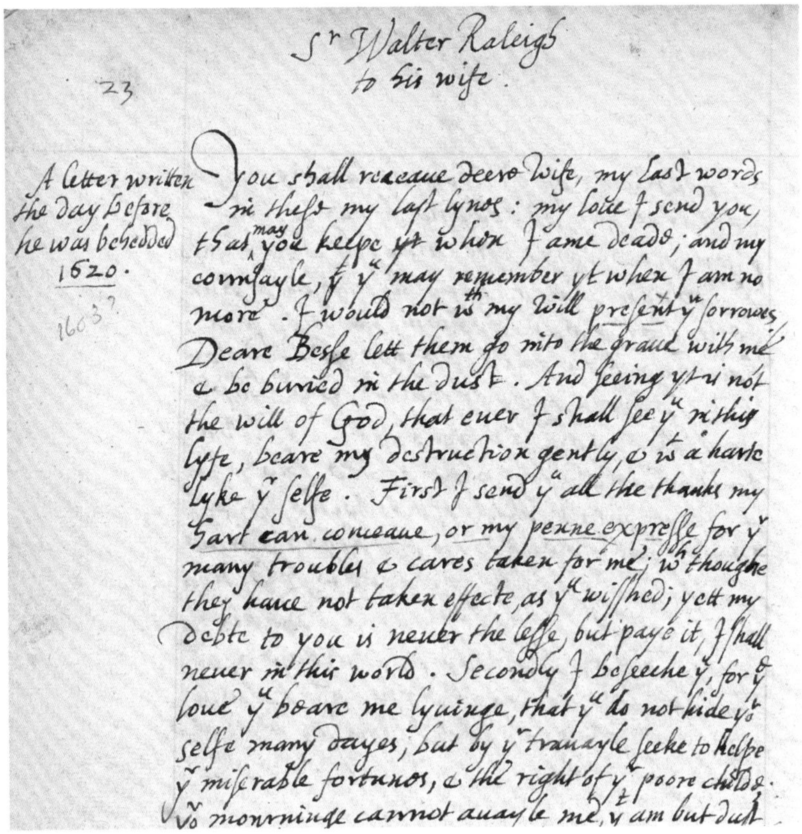

Fig. 246. Detail of fig. 244

Sr Walter Raleigh
to his wife

A letter written
the day before
he was behedded
1620.

You shall receaue deere Wife, my last words
in these my last lynes: my loue I send you,
that ^may you keepe y^t when I ame deade; and my
counsayle, y^t y^u may remember y^t when I am no
more. I would not wth my will present y^u sorrows
Deare Besse lett them go into the graue with me
& be buried in the dust.

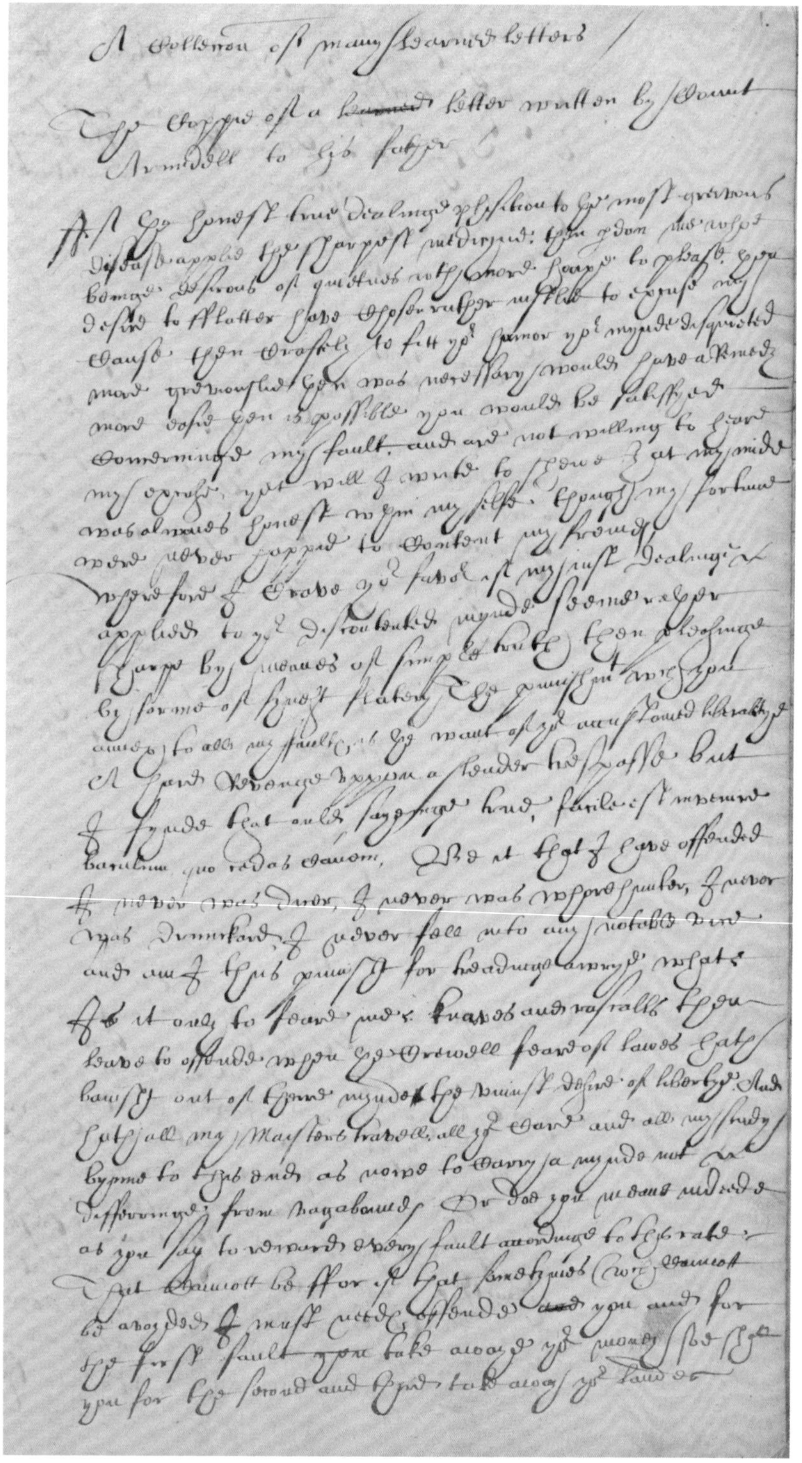

Letters were also copied to be kept and read as historical or literary specimens. An early-seventeenth-century reader has kept copies of a "colleccon of many learned letters," an album of letters from Elizabeth I, Philip Sidney, and other famous (or notorious) figures (fig. 247). As presented here, in this dense secretary hand, the letter has become part of a miscellany, comparable to the verse miscellanies discussed earlier.

In the facing example, also in secretary hand, a writer has made a copy of the proceedings against Mary, Queen of Scots, focusing in this passage on examination of her letters (fig. 248).

Fig. 247. "A colleccon of many learned letters." England, early 17th century. Osborn fb117

The coppie of a ~~learned~~ letter written by Count Arundell to his father

As the honest true dealing phisitan to the most grievous disease applie the sharpest medicine: then pdon me whos beinge desirous of quietness wth more hoape to please then desire to fflatter have chosen rather iustlie to express my cause then crasely to fit yor humor

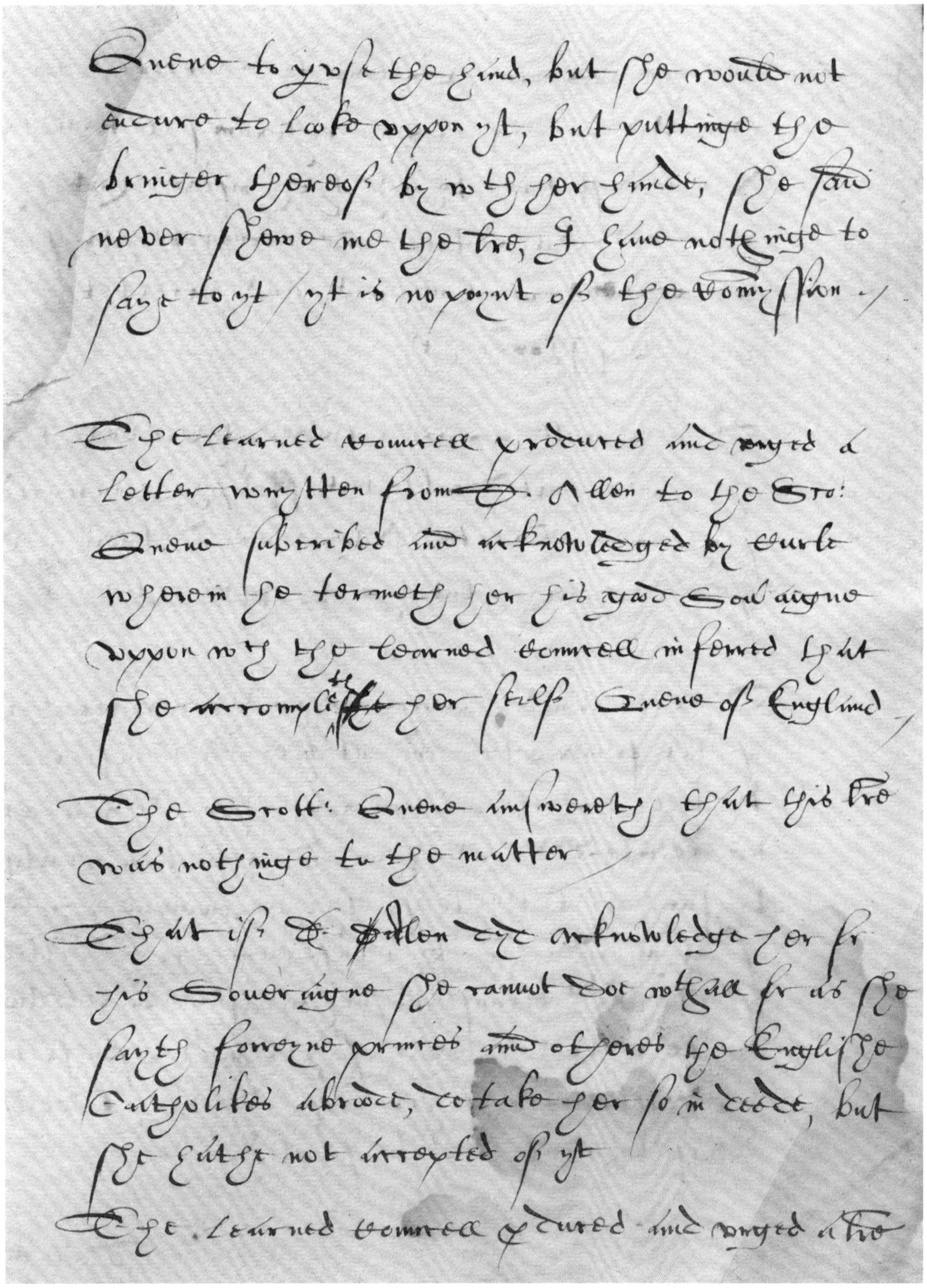

Quene to yuse the same, but she would not
endure to looke vppon yt, but puttinge the
briuier thereof by wth her hand, she said
neuer showe me the lre, I haue nothinge to
saye to yt / yt is no poynt off the Comyssion ./

The learned councell produced and reyd a
Letter wrytten from — Allen to the Sco:
Quene subscribed and acknowledged by Curle
whom he termeth her his good Souaigne
vppon wch the learned councell inferred that
she acknowledgeth her selfe Quene off England

The Scott: Quene ansearoth that this lre
was nothinge to the matter

That iff D. Allen dyd acknowledge her for
his Soueraigne she cannot doe w{th}all fr as the
sayth forreyne prmces and otherob the Englishe
Catholikes abroad, to take her so m reett, but
she doth not acceptid off yt

The learned councell produced and reyd a lre

Fig. 248. Narrative of the trial of Mary Queen of Scots,
at Fotheringay, October 13–15, 1586. England, ca. 1600.
Osborn fb32

Money:
Accounts and Receipts

Like letters and letterbooks, account books document the relationships governing individual lives in early modern England, and the costs by which work, the household, and daily life were measured. The Court offers one example of a household, itemizing the expectations held of its members in the performance of their roles. Each year, the Crown conducted an annual inventory of its expenses, including the salaries paid to its employees. These accounts document the expenses of every office in the Court, from the Lord Chancellor, to the money spent on paper and wax for the clerks, to the money spent on meats and other necessaries for the hunting hounds (hart, buck,

and otter). This volume (Osborn b7) documents the accounts for 1607, under King James VI & I (figs. 249–250). It is known particularly for listing the Players of Enterludes (f. 18r), itemizing the expenses of the company of actors employing Richard Burbage and John Heminge, fellow members of Shakespeare's acting company. The book lists Edward Alleyn and Philip Henslowe as "Keeper of Parrys garden, of beares and Mastyes [Mastiffs]." (f. 37r). Account books like this reveal the complicated structure of the Court and the occupations of its employees as understood by their employer. They also reveal the calendars and material culture that made the Court comprehensible

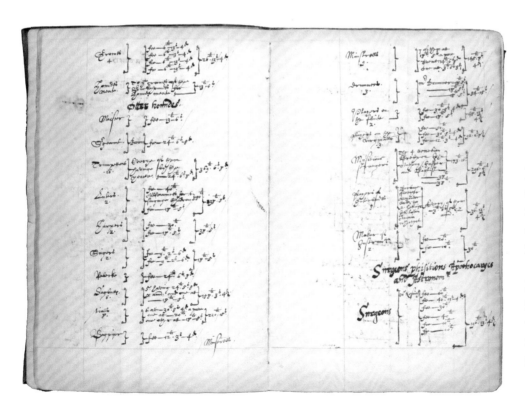

Fig. 249. Account book of the expenses of the English court, ff. 17v–18r. The offices of England collected according to the yeare of 1607. England, 1607. Osborn b7

Fig. 250. Detail of fig. 249 (f. 18r): minstrels, drummers, players on the flute, players on the virginal, musicians strangers, players of interludes, makers of instruments

Minstrolls 9.	7 of them att 18ᵗ. 5ᵇ. a peece one att . 14ᵗ . 6ᵇ 6ᵈ one att . 3ᵗ . 6ᵇ 8ᵈ	145. 8ᵗ 4ᵈ
Drummers 3.	Mr Drummer — 18. 5ᵗ.ᵇ — 18.ᵗ.5ᵇ. — 18 . 5ᵗ.ᵇ	54. 15ᵗ.ᵇ
Players on the flute 2.	for — 30. 8ᵗ.ᵇ 4 dᵈ for — 18. 5ᵗ.ᵇ	48. 13ᵗ.ᵇ 4ᵈ
players on the virginalls 3.	for — 50ᵗ. for — 30ᵗ. 8ᵇ 4 dᵈ for — 12ᵗ. 3ᵇ — 4ᵈ	92. 11ᵗ.ᵇ 8ᵈ
Musitions strangers	The 4 comedian Brethren ffren Anthony, Jasper and Baptist — 38ᵗ. — 38	183. 26ᵗ.ᵇ 296. 6ᵗ.ᵇ 8ᵈ
Players of Enterludes. 8 .	Burbage Alexander Alexander Cooke, the 2. Gohninges John Lowin Armin Nicholas Tooley.	every of them — 3ᵗ. 6ᵇ 8ᵈ R. x and.	26. 13ᵗ.ᵇ 4ᵈ
Maker of Instruments 2.	for — 20ᵗ. for — 10ᵗ.	30ᵗ.

to its participants: the clothing, diet, and materials consumed by the institution and its employees, on its peregrination from location to location.

Osborn b7 is also a household account book, and as such an example of the manuscript genre of accounts and the related genre of inventories. The book is a thin folio volume, in iron gall ink on paper, and stitched into a parchment wrapper. It is written in secretary hand, in a single hand throughout. The writer has not signed the volume at any point, perhaps an indication that it was not meant to act as a formal or public record; the volume is not counter-signed or witnessed in any way. The pages are ruled for accounts: thin at the top and fore-edge, wider on the bottom, and widest in the inner margin.

The volume outlines the Court as a financial structure. Each page is ruled into columns to demarcate the relative value of each office, as well as the relationship of these offices to each other. The accounts are divided into four related categories: the title of the office, the holder of the office, the annual salary to each individual, and the subtotal for the particular office category. In one example, the Lord Treasurer, the Earl of Dorset, is owed a "fee" of £365, in total, with the "Robes out of the wardrobe" accruing to the position, 380 pounds, 7 shillings, and 8 pence. The categories are bounded and made coherent by brackets. Monetary units are broken into the categories of pounds, shillings, and pence.

This format was characteristic of accounts, as can be seen in the three examples that follow. In the first, the cost of the clothing created for John Wilmot, 2nd Earl of Rochester, and his household is itemized in this set of accounts, including the expense for a coat and breeches of striped estamine (a type of worsted fabric), with a lutestring waistcoat (fig. 251). The second notebook lists the pocket expenses of James Compton, Earl of Northampton, on his visits to London when Parliament was in session. These detail his expenses at chocolate houses, at cards, and at the theater, including the cost of a box at Lincoln's Inn (fig. 252). Last, the "Property Bill" for the Drury Lane Theatre lists the granular costs of production over the course of a week, including the bill of six pence for "A Baskett of Garden Mould for yᵉ Grave," in Saturday's performance of *Hamlet* (fig. 253).

Financial transactions were also conducted by correspondence. Early modern English letters are filled with the administrative arrangements surrounding payment for services and the transfer of

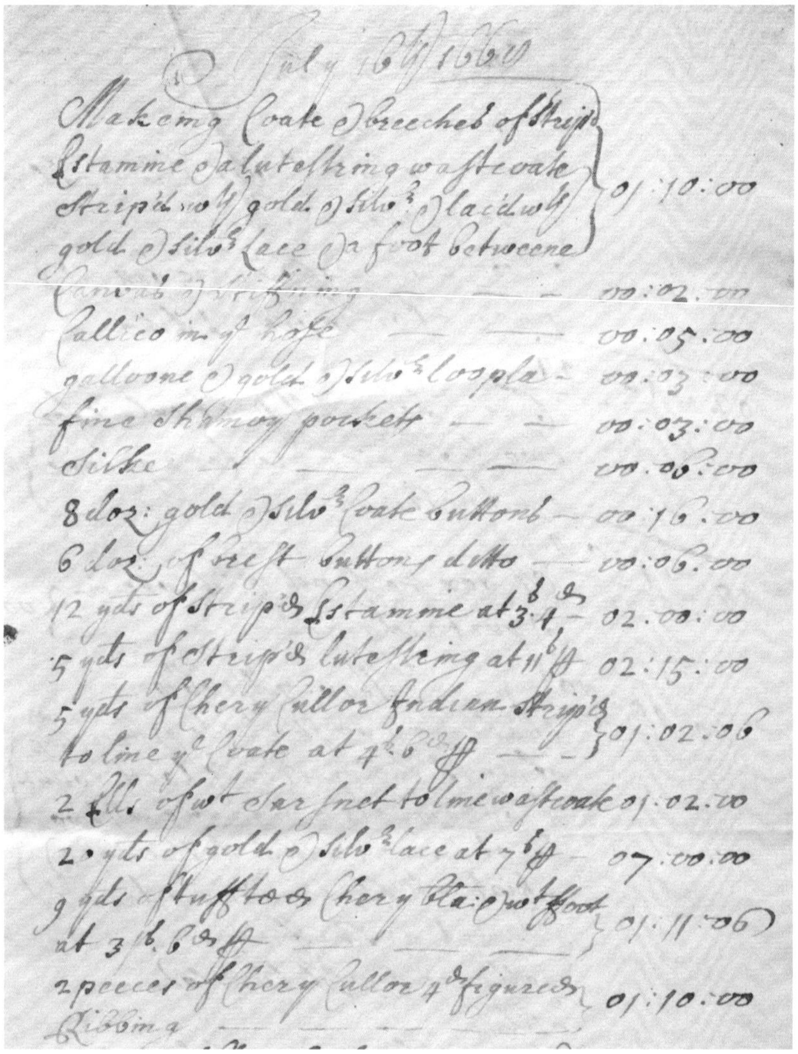

Fig. 251. Detail, Accounts of John Wilmot, 2nd Earl of Rochester, for apparel supplied to him and to members of his household. England, 1667–1671/2. Osborn Manuscript File 15841. Included is a description of Rochester's lutestring waistcoat, striped with gold and silver and laced with gold and silver lace. Note the right column, divided into three categories for pounds, shillings, and pence.

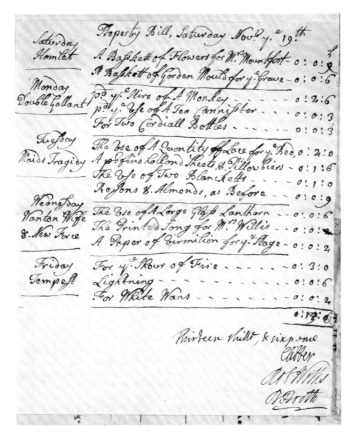

Fig. 252. "Pockett Expences" of James Compton, Earl of Northampton, while in London to take his seat in the House of Lords, May 16–31, 1716. OSB MSS 122. Among the expenses: visits to plays, chocolate houses, and Hyde Park; sums won at cards; and money for chair hire or to the box keeper at Lincoln's Inn Fields play house

Fig. 253. Manuscript property bill for the Drury Lane Theatre. London, November 19, n.d. Ig 6c 676B

Fig. 254. James Huxley, money order, April 23, 1659.
Clayton Papers. England, 1589–1824. OSB MSS 40,
Box 2, Folder 55

Mr Morris
I pray pay unto this bearer my
seruant tenn pounds & this shall be
your discharge witness my hand
this 23^d of Aprill 1659.
James Huxley

For Mr Morris
At the flying horse
In Cornhill or any
Of his clerks there

Mr. Ja: huxley's order
For 10 ^{lb} 1659

money. Transactions frequently take the form of notes requesting payment to the bearer. In this example, from April 1659 (fig. 254), the sender requests the recipient to pay a set sum "unto this bearer," his servant. The document is a money order. James Huxley, the sender, requests that the bearer, his servant, be paid the sum of £10 by the recipient, Mr. Morris. John Morris and his business partner, Robert Clayton, had both apprenticed to Robert Abbott as scriveners but later expanded from the business of copying legal documents into the related fields of money-lending and banking. The money order participates in the documentary tradition of the letter: it is written on a single sheet, folded to be delivered by the bearer. It is addressed to Morris and Clayton, located at the sign of the "flying horse" in Cornhill, a ward in the City of London where Abbott's premises were located. It has also been docketed by Clayton and Morris (or their secretary), to be archived as a record of the transaction.[193] The language is consistent from one document to the next: the money order was a genre followed by

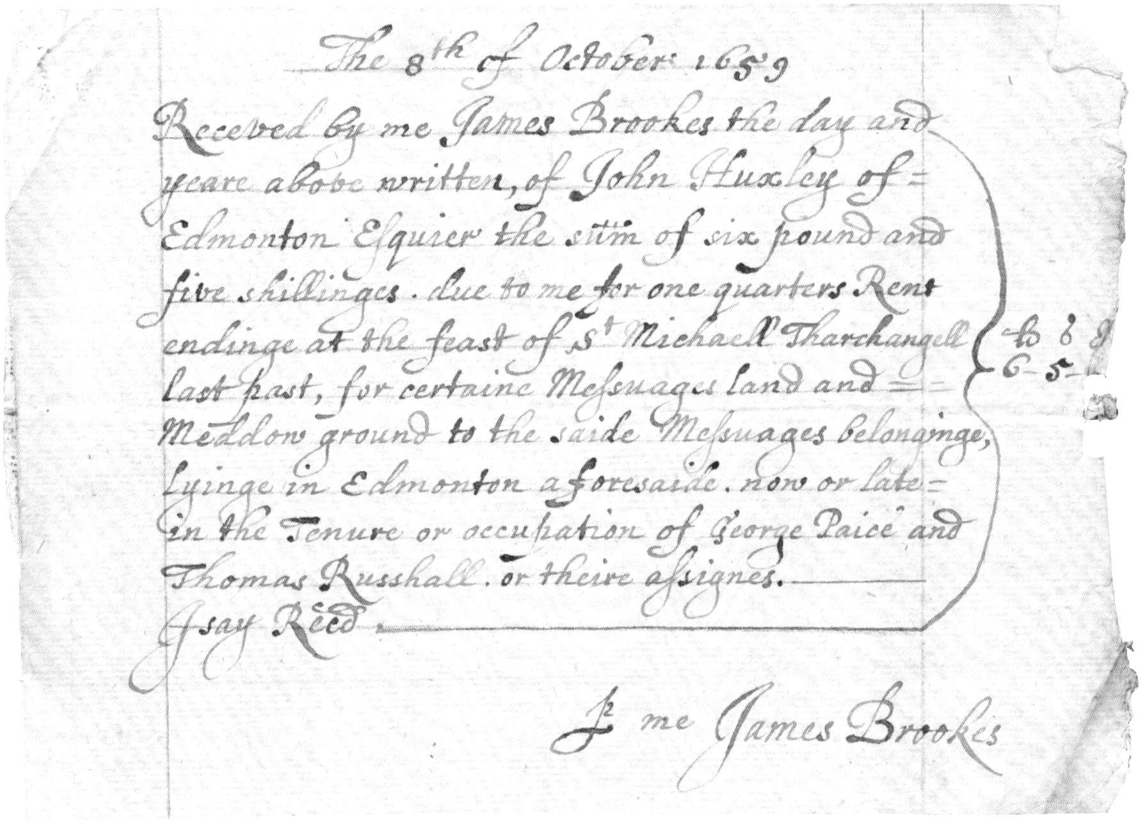

The 8th of October 1659

Received by me James Brookes the day and
yeare above written, of John Huxley of =
Edmonton Esquier the sum of six pound and
five shillinges. due to me for one quarters Rent
endinge at the feast of St Michaell Tharchangell ⎫ li s d
last past, for certaine Messuages land and = ⎬ 6 5
Meddow ground to the saide Messuages belonginge,
lyinge in Edmonton aforesaide. now or late =
in the Tenure or occupation of George Paice and
Thomas Russhall. or theire assignes.
I say Recd

℞ me James Brookes

Fig. 255. Receipt, documenting a payment by John Huxley to James Brookes of six pounds, five shillings, October 8, 1659. Clayton Papers. England, 1589–1824. OSB MSS 40, Box 2, Folder 55

Huxley in his financial transactions with his bankers, rather than a textual form that might need to be reinvented or renegotiated rhetorically in composition.

The receipt was also a genre. As this example shows (fig. 255), receipts conveyed a standard body of information: the names of the payer and payee, the purpose of the payment, and the date. Written in a clear round hand, the receipt documents the payment of £6, 5 shillings by John Huxley to James Brookes, in discharge of a quarter's rent for "certaine Messuages Land and Meddow ground to the saide Messuages belonginge." Huxley is here making the rental payment on a piece of property—the messuage, or portion of land, with its associated buildings and properties—under tenure to George Paice and Thomas Russhall. The document is signed "℞ me James Brookes" and dated "The 8th of October: 1659." Carefully ruled and written, the document is of a size that could fit into a letter as an enclosure, as it was likely conveyed to Huxley's bankers, Morris and Clayton.

On the reverse, the receipt was docketed by Morris and Clayton, noting a payment "for Michaelmas 1659." The payment was made on the date of the Feast of St. Michael, as one of the organizing points of the English legal calendar. The legal year was divided into four legal terms during which the courts were in session: Michaelmas (or Fall, from the Feast of St. Michael through December), Hilary (or Winter, encompassing the Feast of St. Hilary of Poitiers and running through April), Easter (in April and May), and Trinity (from June through July). These terms, and their feasts, governed the calendars for the law courts and the universities.

Heraldry

The message of this portrait of the Tudor dynasty would have been perfectly clear to any early modern English reader of works on heraldry (fig. 256). Henry VIII's children gather around him: his disowned daughter, Mary, stands with her husband, pursued by the allegorical figure of Mars, god of War; to Henry's left, his son, Edward VI, kneels beside him, while the younger daughter he also declared a bastard stands in triumph, clasping the allegorical figures of Peace and Plenty by the hand. This copy, made some eighteen years after the original and in a period of concerted anxiety over the succession to the throne, is assertive in its message of the political destiny of the Tudor dynasty.[194]

In 1592, some two years after the copy of "An Allegory of the Tudor Succession" was created,

Morgan Colman dedicated this ornate, extensively illustrated manuscript genealogy of the monarchs of England to a prospective patron, Francis Bacon (fig. 257). A secretary and heraldic painter who would later achieve success for his genealogy of James VI & I, Colman completed his bid for patronage with an

Fig. 256. Unknown artist, after Lucas de Heere, "An Allegory of the Tudor Succession: The Family of Henry VIII," ca. 1590. Yale Center for British Art, Paul Mellon Collection. B1974.3.7

Fig. 257. Elizabeth I, the 23rd heir to the throne. Morgan Colman, Genealogies of the kings of England. England, 1592. Osborn fa56

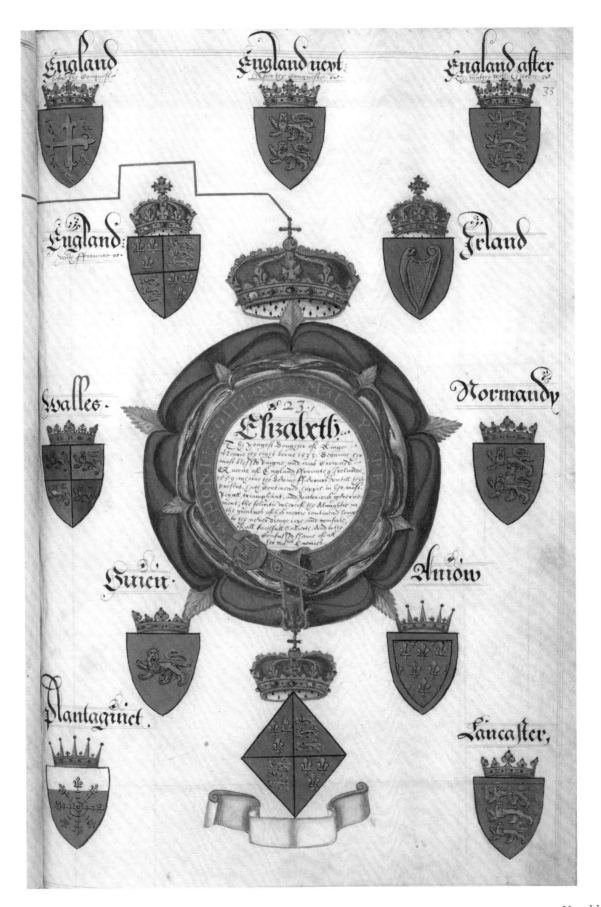

England

England next

England after

England

Irland

Walles

Normandy

Huen

Aniow

Plantaginet

Lancaster

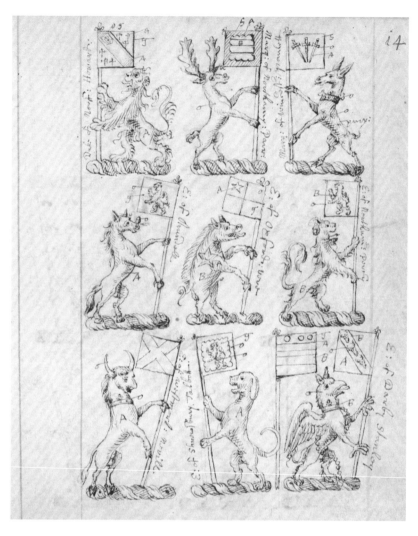

Fig. 258. Robert Glover, Heraldic miscellany. England, ca. 1588. Osborn a19. Letters denote the colors used in this playful illustration of the heraldic devices of the peerage.

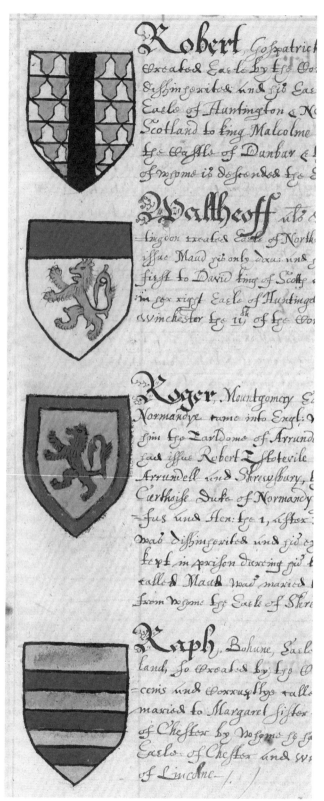

Fig. 259. Detail, Heraldic manuscript of the English kings and peers, p. 13. England, ca. 1620. Takamiya MS 13

illustration of the wild boar, part of Bacon's heraldic device, and the family motto, "Mediocria firma," roughly translating as "Safety in moderation."

Like the "Allegory," Colman's lineage of the English monarchs presented the Elizabethan reign as an inevitability. The document reflected the very anxieties it sought to allay. In 1592 the English monarch was neither married nor possessed of an heir. Colman's genealogy did nothing if not map the strife and uncertainty that followed these conditions through English history, from its origins in the precursor to Egbert of Wessex's succession.

The regulation of lineage was a profession in early modern England. The College of Arms, founded under Richard III in 1484, was the official body overseeing the administration of titles and privileges, effectively regulating the social economy of the realm. The officials, called heralds, were appointed by the Crown to oversee the formal documentation of privileges. Questions of title and precedence dealt with the essentials of power and property, and the right to claim or enforce historically documented claims to title and privileges. Heraldry therefore centered on historical documentation, and there was a long tradition from the Elizabethan period of heralds working in archives as historians.

Heraldry was highly visual. Color—in crests, robes, and other physical manifestations of family, individual, or institutional title—was a critically important focus of study. As can be seen in the facing example, the Elizabethan herald Robert Glover carefully noted the colors accruing to each crest in his miscellany (fig. 258)—colors like those depicted in the heraldic miscellany shown alongside it (fig. 259).

Heraldry offered a particular reading of the English past, one framed around an always linear narrative and organized around the governing principles of inheritance, legitimacy, descendance, and the family as the organizing conveyance for property. This was a genre that was avidly consumed by its early modern readers. Works like this early-seventeenth-century heraldic manuscript chart the history of the British monarchy from its fictional origins in Brutus, descendant of the Trojan Aeneas,

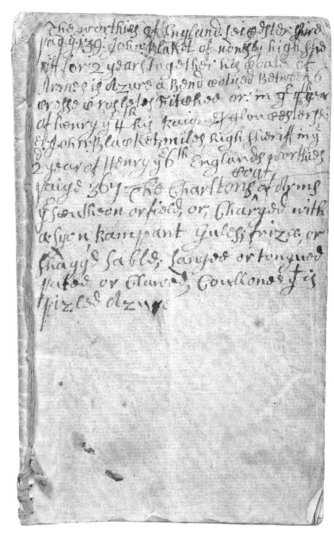

Fig. 260. Detail, paper cover with reader's notes from Thomas Fuller's *The Worthies of England*, originally published in 1662. OSB MSS File 19745

through to the writer's present and the reign of James I (fig. 259). The markers of this history, and its living presence in heraldic devices, were studied and learned by readers like this, copying notes on heraldic devices on the paper cover of this hand-stitched notebook (fig. 260).

Property and Rights: Charters and Deeds

Legal paperwork was an important engine of manuscript culture in early modern England, governing every aspect of life, from the regulation of legal rights and tenures, to professional privileges, contracts, and personal or institutional property ownership and transfer. Considerable anxiety surrounded the production and authenticity of legal documents, as evidenced by responses such as the royal Act of 1563, against the "forgyng of Euidences and Wrytynges," explicitly responding to the "wicked, perniciouse, and daungerous practise of makinge, forging, and publishinge of false and untrue Charters, euidences, dedes, and writynges."[195]

Both as texts and as material objects, legal documents followed consistent, recognizable templates. A law clerk would be familiar with the legal form, or set text, of a given legal document; these were often collected in manuscript reference collections. A clerk would also be expected to be familiar with the customary physical characteristics of a type of legal document, and be able to produce these—often in matched pairs of documents, one for each legal party. As William Henry Ireland understood, law clerks possessed an intimate familiarity with the intricacies of medieval and early modern documents as legal, textual, and material forms.

Charter, as a term, refers to a formal or official document, a "written instrument under seal," by which legal rights or commitments (or "conveyances") were recorded (figs. 261–263).[196] As one example, the Magna Carta—or "great charter"—is the title for a guarantee of rights and privileges to the English people, signed by King John in 1215. "To all free men of our kingdom," asserts the first clause of the 1215 edition

Fig. 261. Pocket-sized copy of the Magna Carta, written in Anglicana, in middle French and Latin, f. 17r. England, 14th century. Osborn a57

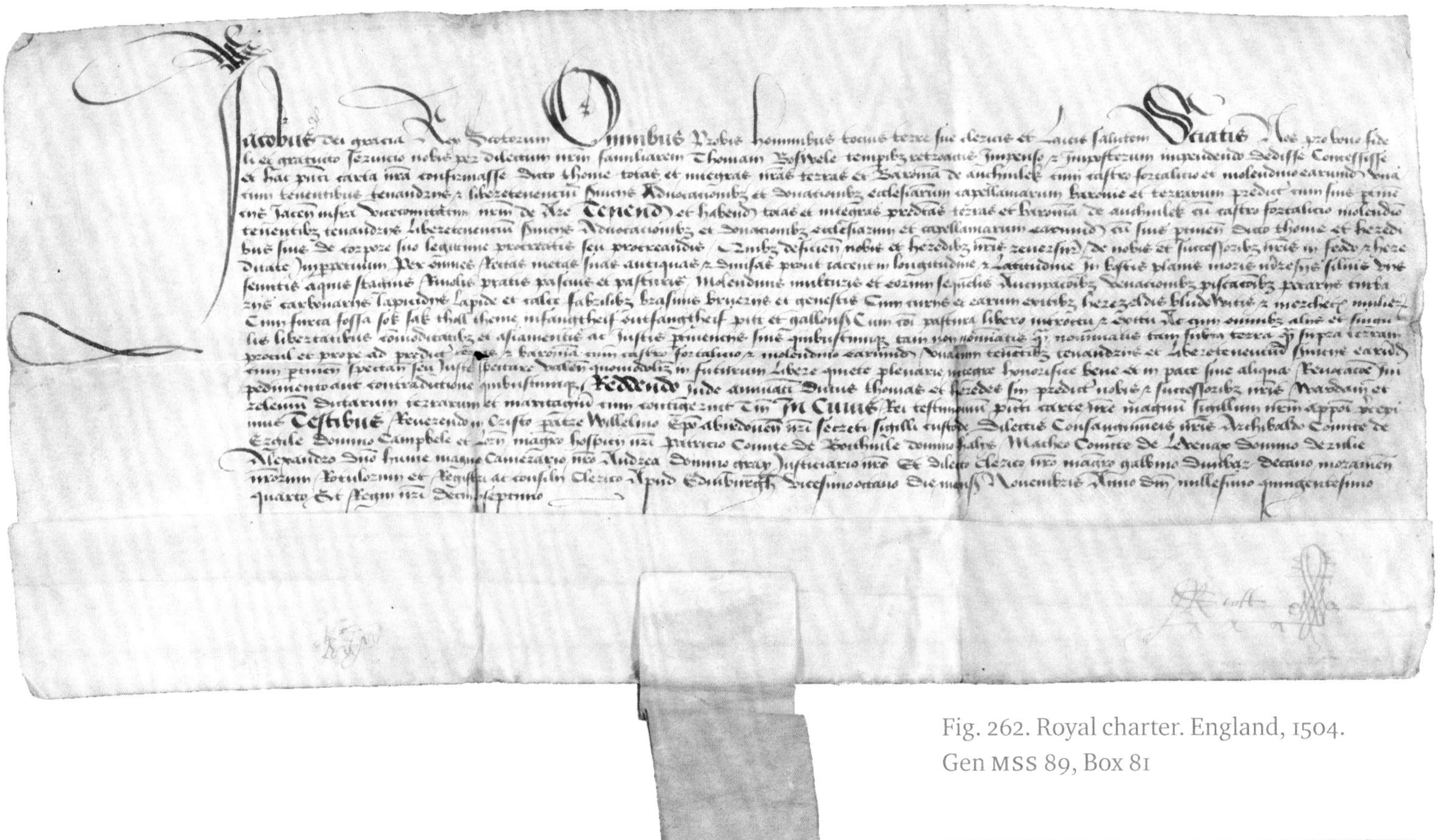

Fig. 262. Royal charter. England, 1504.
Gen MSS 89, Box 81

Fig. 263. Reverse of fig. 262, showing docketing

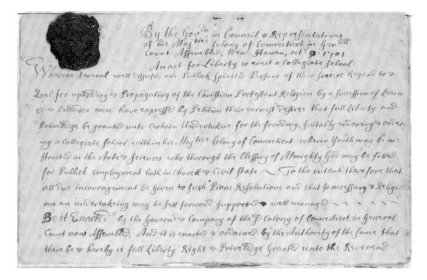

Fig. 264. Charter for the founding of the "Collegiate School." Connecticut, October 9, 1701. Gen MSS 856, Folder 142

By the Gou^rn in Council & Representatives
of his Maj^tie's Colony of Connecticut in Gen^rll
Court Assembled, New Haven, Octr 9. 1701
An act for Liberty to erect a collegiate school.

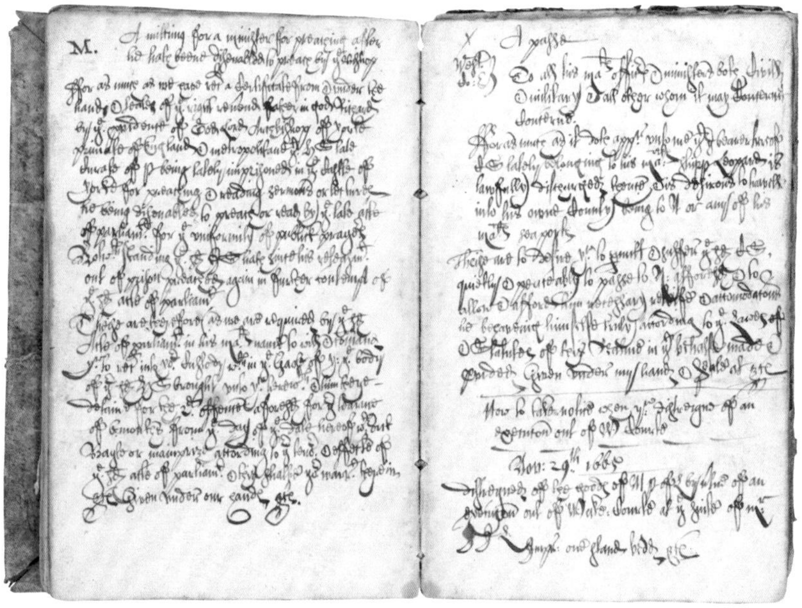

Fig. 265. The form "for a minister for preaching after he hath beene disenabled to preach by ye bishop." Samuel Hemingway, Legal notebook. York, 1683 and later. Osborn b286

of the Magna Carta, "we have also granted, for us and our heirs for ever, all the liberties written out below, to have and to keep for them and their heirs, of us and our heirs."[197]

Another example would be the use of the charter as a founding document, articulating the legal privileges and obligations of an institution, such as the charter in 1701 for the founding of the "Collegiate School" in Connecticut Colony, later known as Yale College (fig. 264).

As a term, charter derives from the Latin, *carta*, referring to paper or papyrus, the substratum of a document. In its very name, then, the charter refers to the type of document on which legal information would be recorded. The term cartulary refers to a collection of charters, often comprising the records of title and property documents kept by a monastic house or other institution, in the form of original documents or formal retained copies of original documents.

A deed refers to a type of legal document concerning the ownership or tenure of property, whether this takes tangible or intangible form.[198] Some examples would include: selling or leasing land or its associated rights; contracts; agreements or covenants. In this manuscript collection of legal forms (fig. 265), a late-seventeenth-century lawyer in York, Samuel Hemingway, has recorded the legal templates for "Three manner of ways of executing a deed of absolute grant bargain, sale and release." In 1690 another reader wrote in this book that: "I sent this Book to Mr. Brown but he shamefully abused it & tore out several presedents [precedents] in the middle of it."

Court Records

In his treatise on memory, John Willis recommended that an attorney say this verse before leaving to meet a circuit judge, to remind himself of everything that he should bring with him:

> Pen-knife. Quills, Ink-horn, Books, Paper,
> Table-Books, Caps; Take
> Wax, Seal and Slippers, Sword, Knife and
> Dagger, safe make
> Purse, Handkerchiefs, Shirts, Rings, Coat,
> and for your own sake,
> Comb, Garters, Stockins, Gloves.[199]

The verse presents us with the image of the well-groomed attorney, writing equipment at the ready. It is also a reminder of the centrality of writing to the workings of English law. Without penknife, quills, inkhorn, books, paper, table books, wax, and seal, the evidence and documentation of the English legal process could not be recorded. The law clerk, with his quill and inkhorn, was himself one of the instruments of the English judicial system.

Court records are one of the most detailed sources of information to be found on the structure of individuals' daily lives in early modern England. The practice of gathering testimony, documenting the presentation of a case, and presenting supporting evidence all leave documentation on how individuals' lives, circumstances, and identities were presented and understood, and how conflict was articulated and resolved within the external power structure of the court system.

That system hinged on the three bodies of law: statutory, common, and ecclesiastical. Statutory law was administered by Parliament. Common law was administered locally through Justices of the Peace, and then regionally through circuit courts, or quarterly meetings of court with a traveling judge. Ecclesiastical law was overseen by the monarch, as the head of state, and administered through the diocese; an appeals system was administered through a hierarchy of courts.[200]

Osborn fb24 houses a single volume of court testimony—the records of ninety-five cases—heard by the Court of Arches beween 1620 and 1635 (figs. 266–267). The Court of Arches is the appellate court (or, court of appeal) for the Archbishop of Canterbury. It originated in the thirteenth century and takes its name from its situation in St Mary Le Bow, London, or *de arcubus*. The volume reveals something of the manuscript culture of the early modern English court. It is an assemblage of documents in different hands, on different sizes of paper. The hands are fast and messy; the paper is of no great quality, intermixed with the occasional leaf of parchment. The documents were gathered and bound later, in the late seventeenth or eighteenth century, in an inexpensive calf binding. The pages are larger than the binding, and the binder has folded the edges down to make them fit. The volume is in every way fragile, difficult to read, ill-kempt, and scruffy.

The court cases it holds bristle with the details of the lives of the parishioners in the diocese of the Archbishop of Canterbury. Each case has been copied by a clerk, in a secretary hand, following a particular form: the title, followed by the articles itemizing the issues addressed in the case, and the docket, or summary of the case. Each document was folded and then docketed on the reverse in the middle fold; this implies that the documents were initially created to be stored as individual documents, perhaps stitched or tacked together, but not necessarily bound.

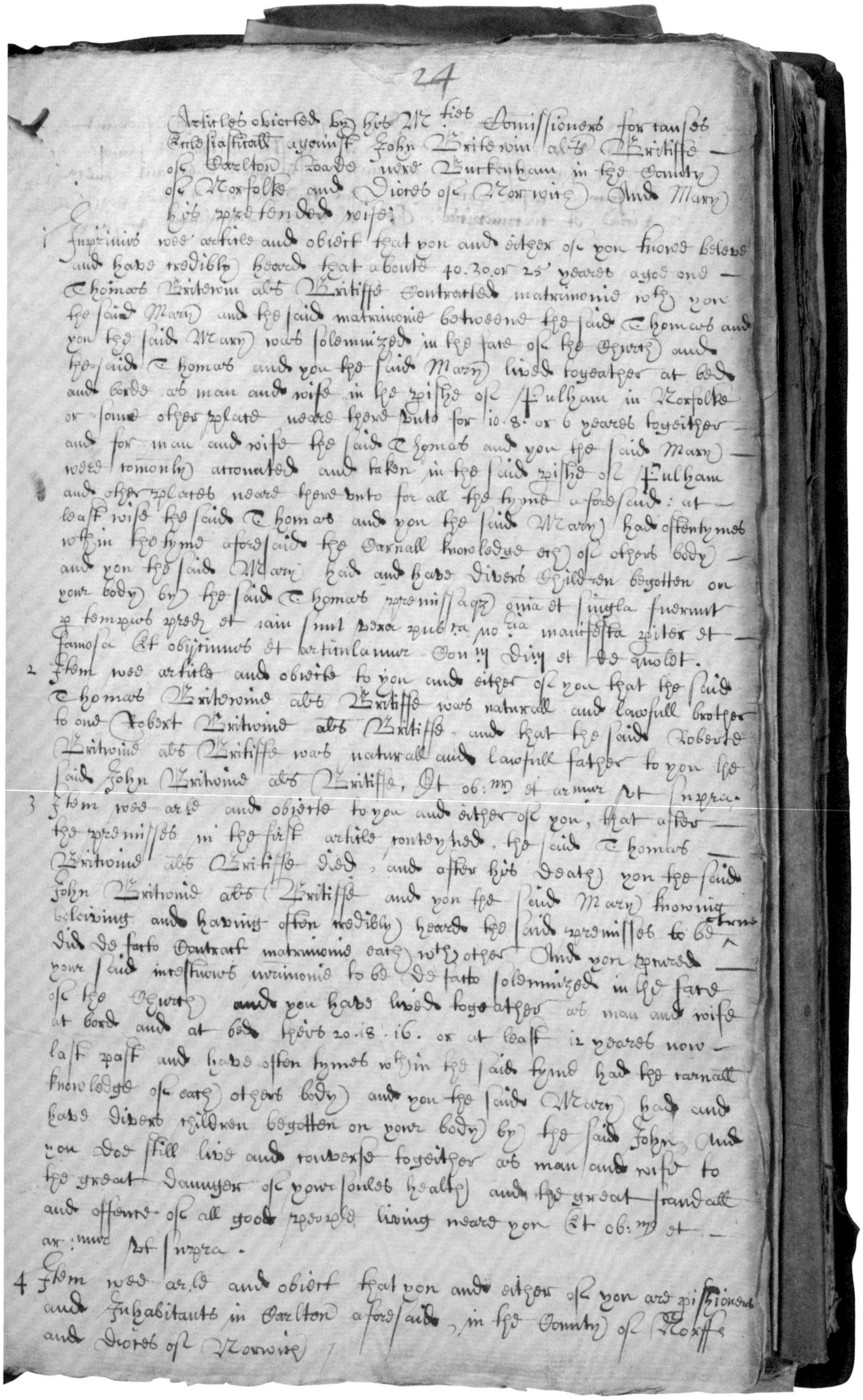

24

Fig. 266. Papers from the Court of Arches. London,
ca. 1620–35. Osborn fb24

Fig. 267. Docket on verso of fig. 266

One of the ninety-five cases is of Thomas (and John) and Mary Britewin (fig. 266). At first glance, the reader can identify this as a secretary hand: the slightly heavier strokes on the ascender of the *d* result in a dark splotch dappling the page at each *d,* looping over to the left above the letterform. The page is ruled with all but an outer margin, where the text runs almost to the edge of the paper, apparently original to the document as the edges still carry a deckle from not having been cut by a later binder.

The title reads: "Articles obiected by her M^ties Commissioners for causes Ecclesiasticall against John Britewin al[ia]s Britisse of Carlton heade near Burkenham in the county of Norfolk and dioces of Norwich And Mary his pretended wife:" The case centers on incest:

> i Inprimis wee article and obiect that you and either of you knowe beleve and have credibly heard that aboute 40.30.or 25 yeares agoe one Thomas Britewin al[ia]s Britisse contracted matrimonie wth you the said Mary and the said matrimonie betweene the said Thomas and you the said Mary was solemnized in the face of the church and the said Thomas and you the said Mary lived togeather at bed and borde as man and wife in the p[ar]ishe of Fulham in Norfolke or some other place neare there unto for 10.8. or 6 yeares togeither and for man and wife the said Thomas and you the said Mary were com[m] only accounted and taken in the said p[ar]ishe of Fulham and other places neare there unto for all the tyme aforesaid: at least wise the said Thomas and you the said Mary had oftentimes w^thin the tyme aforesaid the carnall knowledge ech of others body and you the said Mary had and have divers children begotten on your body by the said Thomas…

The docket on the verso (fig. 267) indicates that the verdict of incest was upheld: "Comess Archi con Johem Britium et eius ux. For an incestuous marriage."

Wills and Inventories

Fig. 268. Probate certificate (and will) of Raphael Holinshed, Prerogative Court of Canterbury, April 24, 1581. Osborn a61

The administrative records surrounding death and the disbursement of property offer a particularly rich set of resources for research. Testamentary documents—wills and inventories—provide information on the identity and possessions of the dead and sometimes on their relationship to those who act as their witnesses, executors, and heirs.

This is particularly the case in England: in 1521, under Henry VIII, Parliament issued a statute requiring an inventory to be made of every individual's property upon his or her death.[201] Like wills, these inventories were reviewed under the probate authority of the diocese and the bishop, unless the individual owned more than £5 in another diocese, in which case they were reviewed under the authority of the archbishop.[202] Property was itemized, both movable goods—furniture, possessions, livestock—and documentary records, tenures and leases, debts, and other immovable goods. Furthermore, it was legally required to be valued by an external auditor. The descriptions are therefore attached to a monetary value. The result is an extraordinarily detailed archive of what was owned by individuals in early modern England, and particularly so in the sixteenth century when the descriptions were at their most detailed.[203]

As the statute outlines, a copy of the inventory was retained by the executor. As a result, copies of inventories are held within the probate records—held (before 1858) by the National Archives—but are also found in other collections. The examples shown here offer an overview of the genre and the types of information it can convey (figs. 268–271).

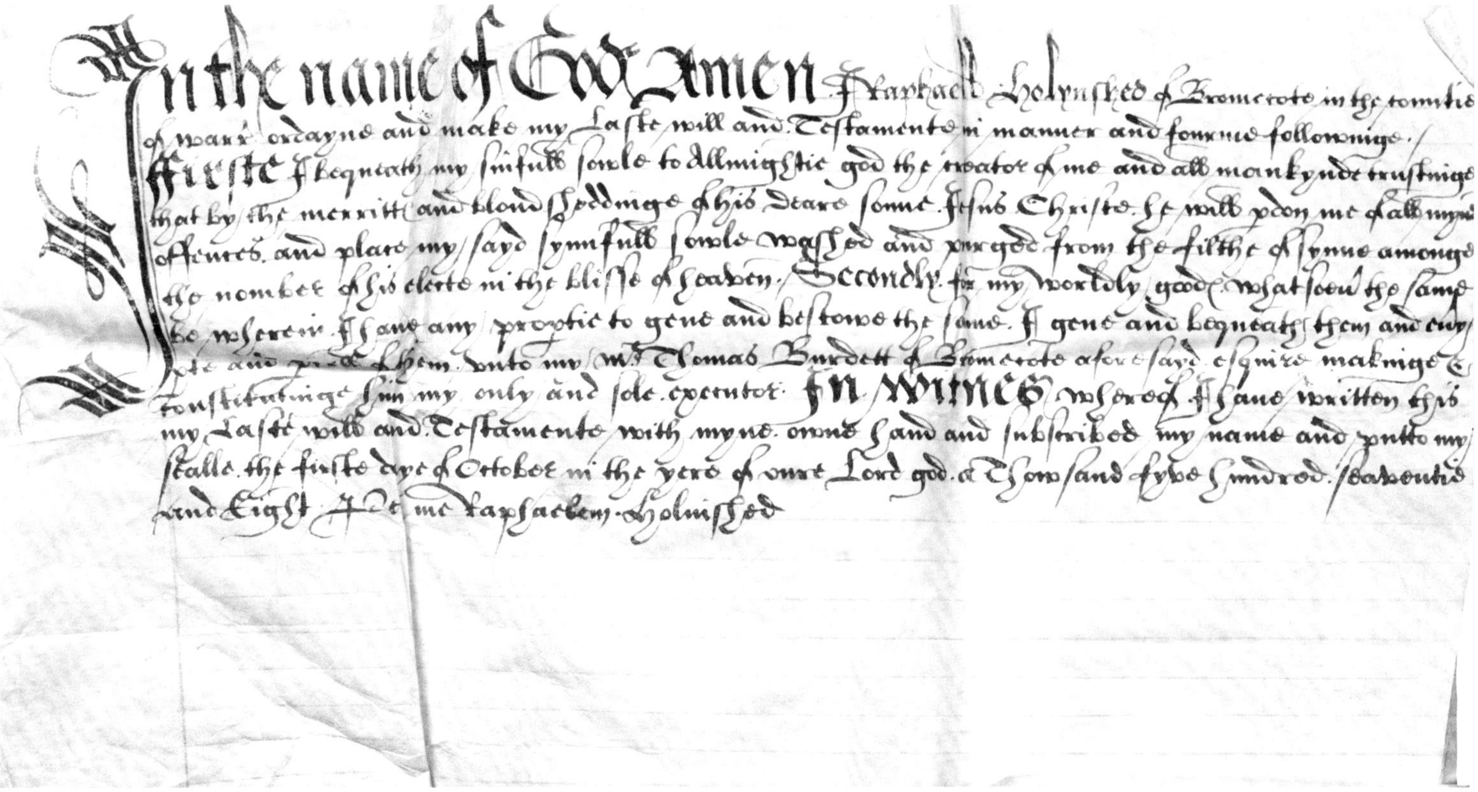

Fig. 269. Detail of will of Raphael Holinshed.
England, October 1, 1578. Osborn a61. See also fig. 59.

In the name of God Amen Raphaell Holynshed of Bromecote in the countie
of Warr ordayne and make my Laste will and Testamente in manner and fourme followinge.
Firste I bequeath my sinfull sowle to Allmightie god the creator of me and all mankynde trustinge
that by the merritts and bloud sheddinge of his deare sonne Iesus Christe he will pdon me of all myne
offences and place my sayd synnfull sowle washed and purged from the filthe of synne amonge
the nomber of his electe in the blisse of heaven.

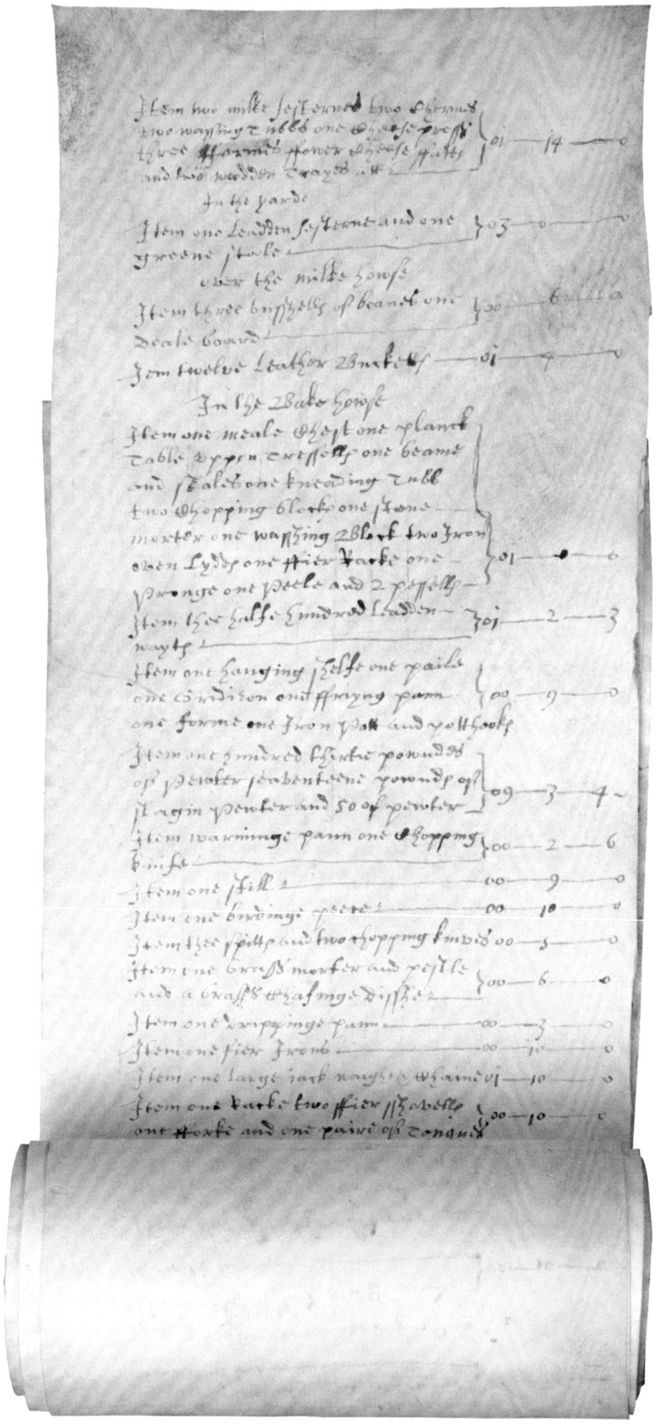

Fig. 270. Detail, "In the yarde," "Over the milke howse," and "In the Bake howse." The inventory of all and singular the goods chattells and debt… belongin unto Michaell Harvie lately deceased. England, April–May, 1643. Osborn b375

Fig. 271. Detail of fig. 270

In the Bake howse
Item one meale chopt one planck
Table upon tressells one beame
And scales one kneading tubb
two chopping blocks one stone
morter one washing Block two Iron
oven Lydds one fier Barke one
pronge one peele and 2 pessells
} 01—0—0

In the Bake howse

Item one meale Chest one planck
Table uppon tressells one beame
and skale one kneading tubb
two Chopping blocks one stone ———
morter one washing Block two Iron
oven Lydds one fier rake one ——— } 01 ———— 0
Pronge one Peele and 2 peffells ———

Item thre halfe hundred Leadden ——— } oj —— 2 —— 3
wayts

Item one hanging shelfe one paile
one Gridiron one ffriyng pann ——— } 00 —— 9 —— 0
one forme one Iron pott and pott hooks

Item one hundred thirtie poundds
of pewter seabenteene poundds of } 09 — 3 — 4
flaggin pewter and 50 of pewter

Item warminge pann one Choppng } 00 —— 2 —— 6
knife

Item one still ——————————————— 00 —— 9 —— 0

Item one bindinge peere ——————— 00 —— 10

Item thre spitts and two chopping knives 00 —— 5 —— 0

Item one brasse morter and pestle
and a brasse chafinge dishe ——— } 00 —— 6 —— 0

Item one dripping pann ———————— 00 —— 3

Item one fier Iron ——————————— 00 —— 10 —— 0

Scrap and Waste

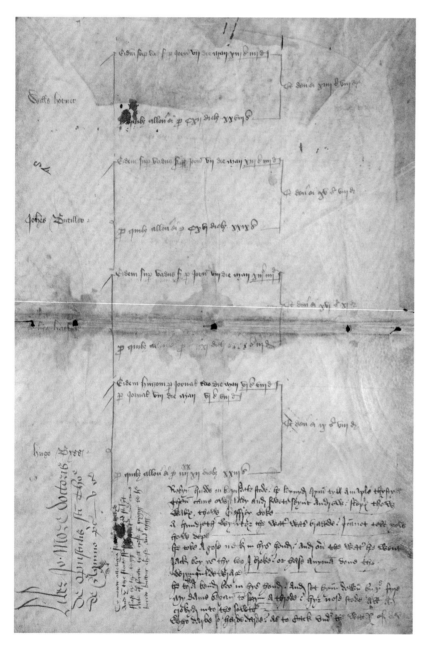

Fig. 272. Fragment in Middle English of Robin Hood. England, ca. 1450. Takamiya MS 51. Note the traces of this fragment's life in the binding of a book.

On July 30, 1560, the radical Protestant John Bale wrote his colleague Matthew Parker, only recently confirmed as Archbishop of Canterbury. When he wrote this letter, Bale was elderly, in poor health, and (as can be heard in his writing) exhausted by the chaos of his repeated flights to the Continent under the changing politico-religious regimes. His subject is the loss of his library following his abrupt departure from Ireland after Mary's accession in July 1553. "And as concernynge bokes of antiquitie, not printed," he writes,

> whan I was in Irelande I had great plenty
> of them, whome I obtained in tyme of the
> lamentable spoyle of the lybraryes of Englande,
> through muche fryndeshypp, labour, and
> expenses. Some I founde in stacyoners and
> boke bynders store howses, some in grosers,
> sopesellars, taylers, and other occupyers
> shoppes, some in shyppes ready to be carried
> over the sea into Flaunders to be solde—for
> in those uncircumspect and carelesse dayes,
> there was no quyckar merchaundyce than
> library bokes, all to destruction of learnyge and
> knowledge of thynges necessary in thys fall of
> antichriste to be knowne.[204]

Bale notes the dystopic landscape following the dissolution of the monastic libraries: textual waste held by book binders and stationers, used to stuff bindings, as tailor's backings, to wrap fish or pies—or, worse than these, in Bale's opinion, carried away in ships to Europe to be sold. He echoes the language used in his edition (1549) of his friend John Leland's *The laboryouse iourney:* manuscripts from the monastic libraries were used "some to serue theyr iakes, some to scoure theyr candelstyckes, & some to rubbe their bootes."[205]

Early manuscripts are now often encountered as binding waste: individual sheets of paper or parchment used to line or stuff the binding of a volume. These stubs or full pages have often been recovered from bindings and recataloged as texts. One example can be found in this fragment in Middle English of Robin Hood, written in the mid-fifteenth century and later used as binding waste (fig. 272).

Waste is the mirror image of the manuscript text. What might be defined as text in one context is, in another, understood as a material commodity: parchment or paper, good for stuffing, or to

Fig. 273. Receipts from the Tellers of the Exchequer. England, 16th–17th century. Osborn fb196. This document was collected by Thomas Phillipps.

polish candlesticks or line a pie pan. The great nineteenth-century book collector Thomas Phillipps habitually acquired "waste" documents (fig. 273), working with a dealer, James Graham, "who held a contract for clearing waste paper out of Government offices and who acquired in this way thousands of deeds and documents." Graham bluntly described the

Fig. 274. Receipt in endpapers. Bible.
England, ca. 1200–1249. Osborn fa57

May y^e 11th 1629 I sould this
bible and one old magna charta
in 8° and thay by bee are warranted
to mee perfett the prise of them
being
viii s viii ^d
by mee Thomas Bayly

14

said ' *It was hard indeed to be whipped for reading.*' "

" Did he ever betray any extraordinary symptoms when young ?"

"No others, sir, than what I have stated; except, indeed, that he was taught his letters from an old black-letter Bible, and would not take his lesson from any book of modern type."

This circumstance very forcibly struck me, and I endeavoured to acquire more knowledge on this head, but she recollected nothing at all interesting.

At the period when the Rowley papers had first come to light (as *he* averred), she informed me as follows :—" My brother, sir, had frequently brought home old parchments, deeds and other things, which were accounted of no value : and one day, having a use for them, I during his absence cut up several of them for threadpapers, and others to cover the schoolbooks of children : and while thus occupied, Thomas Chatterton came home. On perceiving what I had done, he threw himself

Fig. 275. William Henry Ireland, *The confessions of William-Henry Ireland. Containing the particulars of his fabrication of the Shakspeare manuscripts* (London, 1805), 14. Osborn pd138

economy at work: "'every sheet of parchment fit for the printer and the snuff-manufacturers is worth one shilling.'"[206]

Waste, for Phillipps, was a form of textual abundance, allowing him to collect historical documents as scrap, a wholesale commodity purchased at cost. The tension between loss and abundance was reiterated by John Aubrey, writing of his grandfather's account of the sixteenth century:

> In my grandfather's dayes the manuscripts flew about like butterflies. All musick bookes, account books, copie books, &c. were covered with old manuscripts, as we cover them now with blew paper or marbled paper; and the glovers at Malmesbury made great havock of them; and gloves were wrapt up no doubt in many good pieces of antiquity.[207]

And yet: in counterpoint to this litany of lament, one finds a tenacious early modern English culture centered on cutting, recycling, and incorporating scraps into the refurbishment of other objects. Loss was also a form of creation, and sometimes of intensely creative production.[208] In 1629 Thomas Bayley turned the endpapers of his Bible to scrap, in the process recording its sale with a copy of the Magna Carta for later readers (fig. 274). And in his autobiographical confessions, the literary forger William Henry Ireland described his fascination with an earlier forger, Thomas Chatterton, and the old parchments, deeds, and other forms of scrap or waste that Chatterton used to create his false rendition of a lost English literary heritage (fig. 275).

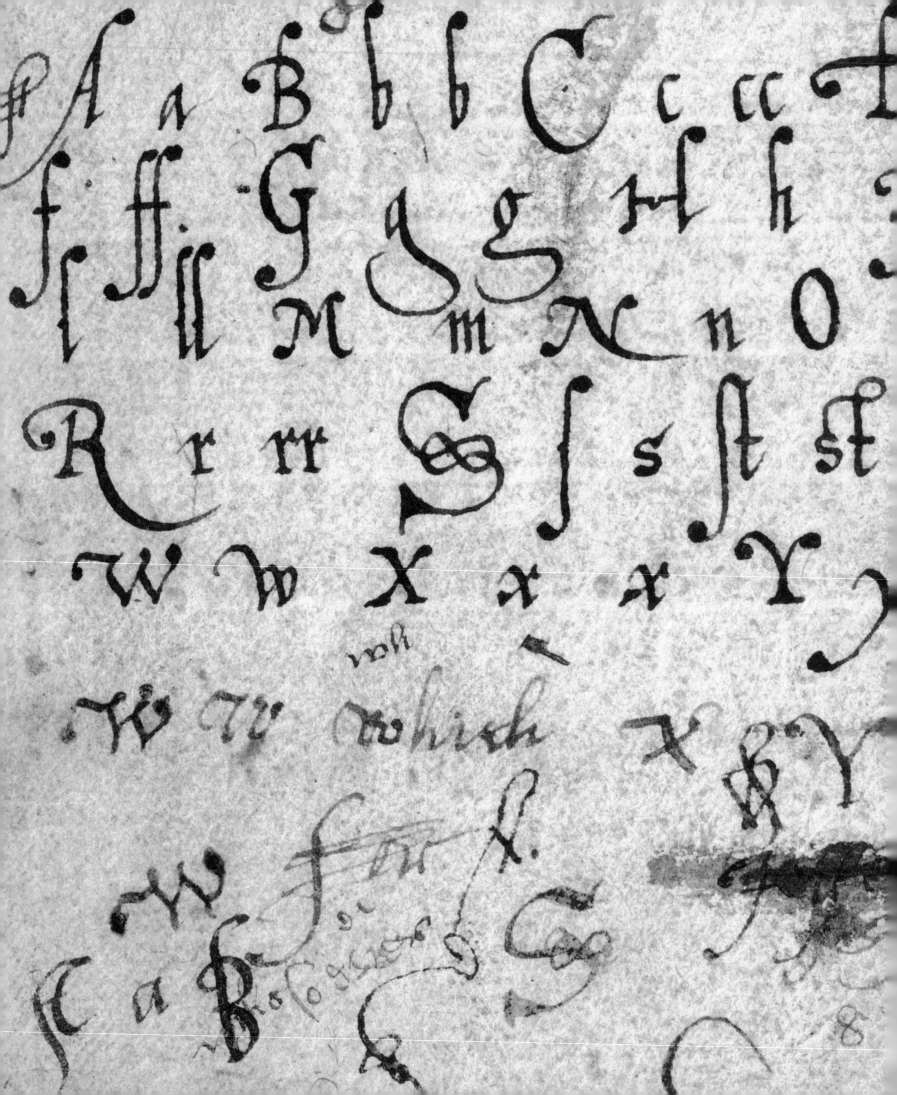

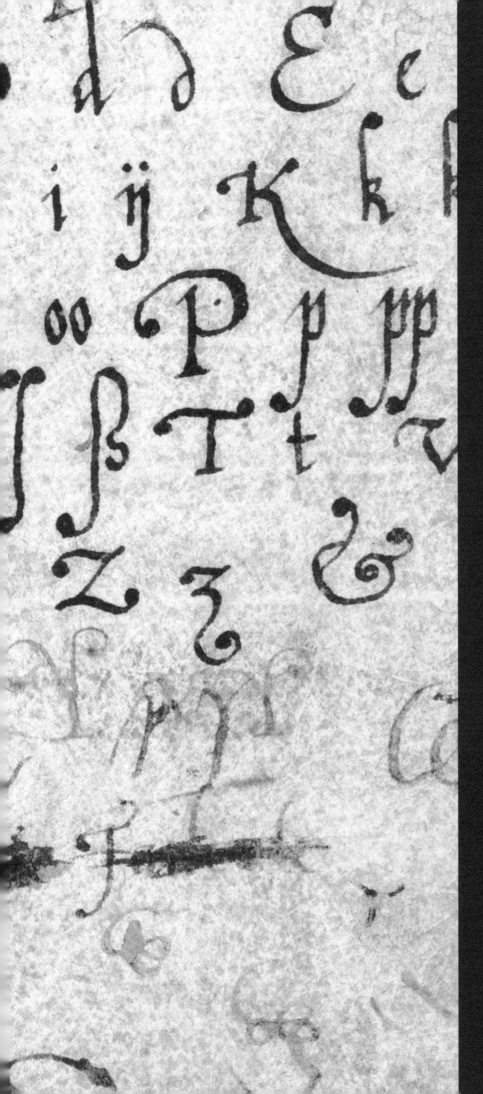

PART FOUR: EXERCISES

How to set writing.

Your Bodye upright stoupe not with youre heade,
Your Brest from the bourde when you haue well fed:
Yncke always good stoore on right hand to stand,
Browne Paper for great hast, elles box with sand:
Dypp Penne, and shake penne, and tooche Pennes
    for heare,
Waxe quilles and penneknyfe see alwayes ye beare:
Who that his Paper dooth blurre or elles blott,
Yealdes me a slouen it falles him by lotte:
In learnyng full slowe write at begynninge,
For greate is your losse, and small your wynninge,
If at the first tyme an ill touch, ye catche,
Use onely is cause of speedye dyspatche.

"Rules made by E.B. for his Children to learne to
    write bye" (1571)[209]

Part Four introduces the principles of transcription as prelude to a set of exercises with which students can practice reading early modern English manuscripts. This discussion of transcription is intended only as a guide: any student needs to develop an individual approach to manuscript research. The role of transcription has also radically altered with the advent of photography in rare book and manuscript reading rooms. For the most part, scholars no longer need to transcribe a manuscript in order to retain access to its contents. They do, however, need to be able to *read* it. What follows is a set of recommendations and guiding questions on transcription practices, followed by twenty exercises with partial transcriptions. These are intended as an introduction to how to read early modern English hands, surviving in these examples from writers who, as in E.B.'s rules for children to write by, centuries ago dipped their pens, shook them, and put them to paper.

Fig. 276. Detail of "Romayne hande." William Hill, Notebook, p. 5. England, early 17th century. Osborn b234

How to Transcribe

Any transcription is an act of witness, a statement of what an observer has seen and understood to be the identity of a document. Like any testimony, it will be imperfect: biased, partial, inaccurate, and vulnerable to vagaries of circumstance. The practical question is not how to make your transcription perfect in its accuracy: it will not be. Even if it were, there are aspects of an original that cannot be conveyed, while other defining characteristics, such as a manuscript's affect or meaning in an originating context, will always remain to some extent inaccessible. The point is to make your transcriptions good enough—good enough that, when you go to use them a day, week, or decade later, you're persuaded that you were an accurate and reliable observer of the original document.

Ultimately, any transcription is only as valuable as the use you are able to make of it. While full or semi-diplomatic transcription formats are necessary in certain circumstances (e.g., editing a text), for the most part researchers use their notes for purposes other than producing publishable editions of early modern English manuscripts. In these circumstances, it is important to remember that you are often the only, and always the primary, audience for your transcriptions. Therefore: take the notes you need, and do so in a way that is consistent and recognizable so that you can have a sense, looking back, of the reliability and limitations of your notes in any given instance.

At minimum, you should include the following:

Name of repository, call number of item

Date of your visit

Page or folio numbers of any passages transcribed

Note of whether your notes or transcription are incomplete, and if so in what way

If time permits, the following might also be helpful:

A brief description of the material object: its format, size, extent, binding, and important and/or memorable characteristics

A summary of the description in the catalog record, including any notes on provenance; failing this, the author, title, location, and date when the manuscript was created or as much of the above as might be known

STANDARDS OF TRANSCRIPTION

Diplomatics originated as a field of study in the seventeenth century in immediate response to the question of how to distinguish between forged and authentic documents. The field's origins are usually dated to the publication of Jean Mabillon's *De re diplomatica libri VI* (1681), in which he proved the authenticity of a discredited diploma, in the process articulating a persuasive series of principles for the examination and authentication of historical documents.[210] Mabillon's *De re diplomatica* was cited by archival scholars through the early modern period as the formative introduction to the study of paleography.

Diplomatic transcription represents an effort to create a copy so complete that it can act as a surrogate for the original. In the diplomatic standard, all text and features of the manuscript are reproduced as they appear. This approach has its disadvantages. As Anthony Petti observes, diplomatic transcription is "laborious to prepare, …costly to print, and tiresome to read."[211]

Semi-diplomatic transcription offers a compromise, in which some aspects of the text are normalized. Following Petti, the protocols for semi-diplomatic transcription are as follows:

1. Start by identifying the manuscript: repository, shelfmark, title, and page or folio number, specifying recto or verso when necessary.

2. Retain spelling, capitalization, word division, and punctuation of the original.

3. Normalize all superscript text and abbreviations, italicizing supplied letters, e.g., y^t should appear as **that**. Deletions can be struck through: e.g., ~~this is a phrase the author deleted~~. Some manuscript practices will be difficult to render typographically or will occur more frequently in particular contexts. Decide before you start how to approach particular circumstances, e.g., whether to normalize u/v/w usage.

4. Place all normalizations or additions to the text in square brackets, e.g., absent folio numbers should be included in square brackets in the left margin.

5. Lost or missing text should be marked by diamond brackets, < >, marking the number of letters thought to be lost with dots.

6. Include notes on any anomalies, later additions or alterations, significant losses to text, changes in hand, or other features that the reader might need to know in order to understand the document.

Regularized, or normalized, transcription simplifies the text still further. In a regularized transcription, abbreviated and superscripted text is normalized, as is spelling. For example:

Diplomatic:
H^r Maties ~~corgye~~ dogge shulde nott sitte on ye sofa:

Semi-diplomatic:
Her Ma*jes*ties ~~corgye~~ dogge shulde nott sitte on the sofa:

Regularized:
Her Majesty's ~~corgy~~ dog should not sit on the sofa:

Capitalization, punctuation, deletions, spacing, and line breaks are retained as in a semi-diplomatic transcription. Corrections and erasures should be noted.

Transcription standards represent a guiding principle; they are always, and only, a guide to the reader's own encounter with a manuscript. In all cases, readers will encounter situations where manuscript offers possibilities not easily represented in print. The manuscript object will also bear the traces of its own history: tears, blots, rebinding, bookplates, bookseller marks, doodles of horses drawn by a later owner, corners chewed by mice or rats, holes where insects once made their homes. It will often have been cataloged and described, but perhaps according to a different set of priorities or standards. Text might also have accrued in layers over time, making it possible for a manuscript to encompass several simultaneous and competing texts. These and other factors will inform the context in which the text is encountered, but also present the reader with the choice of what to document and what to regard as secondary or unimportant. In all these circumstances, a reader has the opportunity to make up her or his own mind on what a text, or text object, is, what it means, and how this should be described and interpreted. This essential uncertainty lies at the heart of manuscript studies: it represents (in the view of this book) a form of intellectual freedom that thrives in the rare book and manuscript library reading room.

Example Transcription

Diplomatic:

Apply thy mind such things to learne
as vertue may advaunce:
soe shalt thou liue in sure estate
not subiecte unto chaunce.
For if thou loose thy worldly wealth
as earthlie thinges are vaine:
Then shall thy science serue thy need
and rayse thy state agayne.

In this case, as there are no abbreviations or super-scripted text, the diplomatic and semi-diplomatic transcriptions are identical.

In a regularized, or entirely normalized transcription, all early modern spellings, abbreviations, and super-scripted text would be effaced. The text would be rendered as follows:

Apply thy mind such things to learn
as virtue may advance:
so shalt thou live in sure estate
not subject unto chance.
For if thou lose thy worldly wealth
as earthly things are vain:
Then shall thy science serve thy need
and raise thy state again.

Figs. 277–278. "Sentences written according to the order of the Alphabet." Hill, Notebook, p. 1. Osborn b234

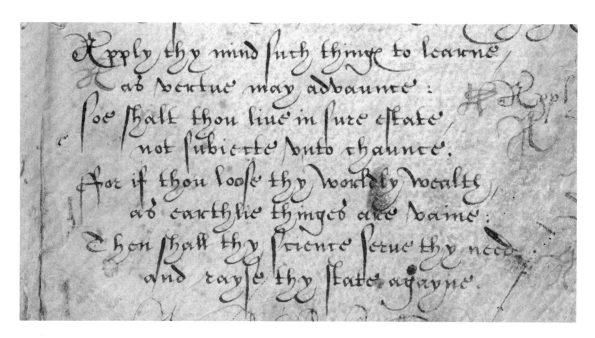

Exercises

Here you will find twenty examples, arranged chronologically, of English manuscripts from the late fifteenth century to ca. 1801. These represent a range of formats, genres, and hands, and offer different challenges as the objects of transcription. Each example is accompanied by a short sample transcription of part of the text, shifting between diplomatic, semi-diplomatic, and regularized forms. The questions here are offered as a guide as you begin to practice how best to read and represent the manuscript text as a transcription.

Questions to bear in mind:

1. What is the format of the document?

2. What is its substratum?

3. How is the document organized on the page or opening? With what was it written?

4. What is the hand? Identify one or several distinguishing letterforms to support your conclusion.

5. Is there more than one hand at work in the document? What differing ends might these serve? Are they by the same writer? From the same time period?

6. Does the hand have unusual or difficult characteristics?

7. Do you think the document was written by a professional writer? Why or why not?

8. Is this a draft or a final text? What might indicate this?

9. What features might indicate the original context of this document, e.g., its creator, purpose, intended audience, and relative value?

10. Are there discernible features of the item's provenance?

11. Bearing all the above in mind, what would be the best approach to transcribing?

1.

Diplomatic and semi-diplomatic transcription
(as this passage has no abbreviated or superscripted
text, there are no variations between these versions):

Aft hym reigned anone ỹan ⎤
the iiij herry a full dougty man ⎦
at Westmest cruned he was ⎤
Wher of all englond mad solac ⎦

Regularized:

After him reigned anon then ⎤
the fourth Harry a full doughty man ⎦
at Westminster crowned he was ⎤
whereof all England made solace ⎦

Fig. 279. Detail of a copy of John Lydgate, The kings
of England sithen William the Conqueror. England,
1475–99. Osborn a14. See also figs. 22, 55.

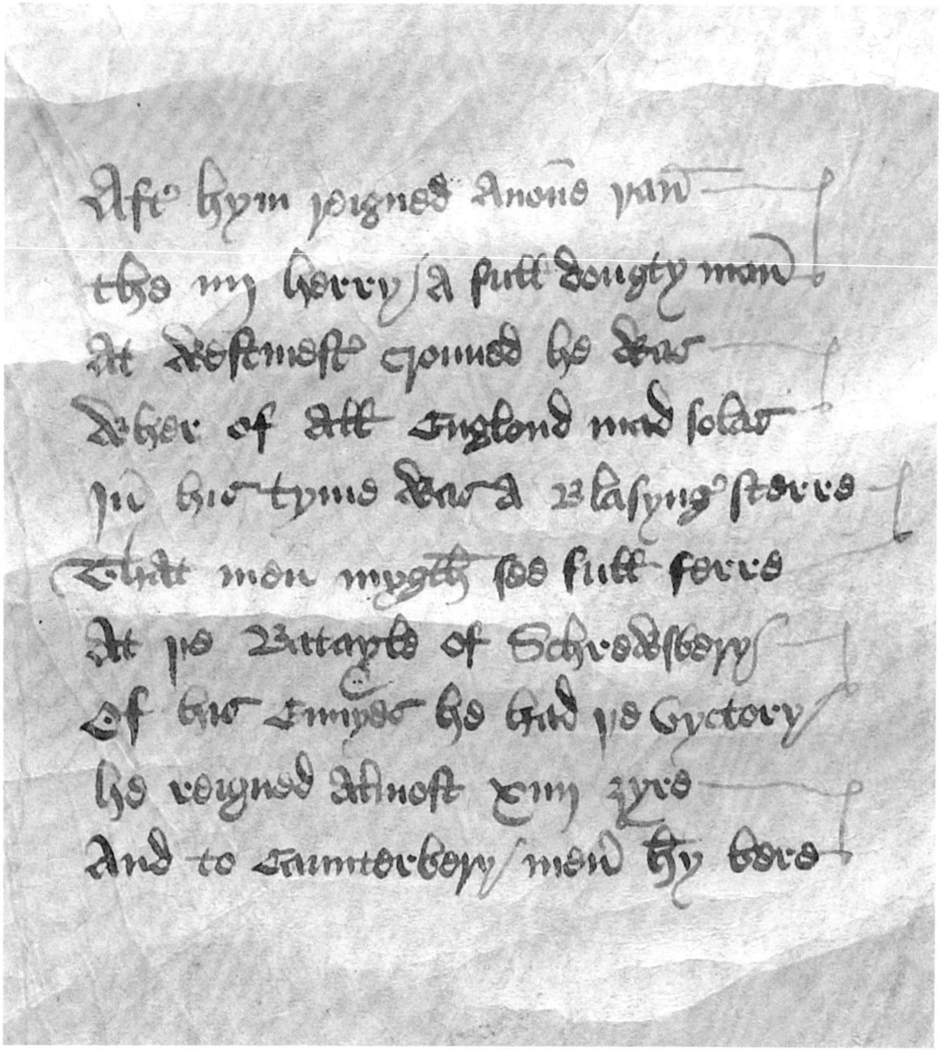

2.

Diplomatic:

That is to saye

Golde plate delyuered
to the kings Matie }

Firste a Crosse of golde plated upon wood garnished w^{th}
dyuerse Emeraldes and perles weuige togithere
Item a Chalice of golde w^{t} a patẽn of golde sett w^{th}
counterfeit stonies weuige togither

Fig. 280. Detail, indenture of receipt by John Williams, Master of the Jewels, for ceremonial plate and jewels collected from religious houses. England, February 27, 1540. Osborn fa37. Note the use of brackets, and the elegance with which these organize text in manuscript (and the difficulty of rendering this typographically). Note also the use of Roman numerals to indicate value, in the three categories of pounds, shillings, and pence (or d, residual from the Roman "deneri.")

3.

Diplomatic:

No dogges to be kepte
in the courte

The kinges highnis also straitlie forbiddeth and inhibith
that no parson what so ever he be p^rsume to kepe any grehounds
mastives, houndes; or other doggs in the court / other then some fewe
smaull spainelles, for laides or other / ne bringe or leade any into
the same excepte it be by the kinges or Quenes cõmaindemente

Regularized:

No dogs to be kept
in the court

The king's highness also straightly forbids and inhibits
that no person whatsoever he be presume to keep any greyhounds
mastiffs, hounds; or other dogs in the court / other than some few
small spaniels, for ladies or other/ nor bring or lead any into
the same except it be by the King's or Queen's commandment

Figs. 281–282. "No dogges to be kepte in the courte."
Bouche of court [an account book for the court], 44r.
England, ca. 1571. Beinecke MS 610

No dogges to be kepte in the courte

The Kinges highnes also ſtraitlit forbiddeth and inhibith that no parſon what ſo ever he be prſume to kepe any grek ounds maſtives, houndes, or other doggs in the Court / other then ſome fewe ſmaull ſpainelles, for laides or other / ne bringe or lead any into the ſame excepte it be by the kinges or Quenes commaundement but the ſaide grekhoundes and doggs to be kept in kennelles and other mete places out oſ the Courte as is convenient ſo as the premiſſes dewlie obſerved, the houſe abrode maie be ſwet holſome clene and well furniſhed / as to a prince's honoꝛ and eſtate doth appertaine

Dynner and ſopper in the hall to be kepte at houres certayne ꞉

And albeit there is no time certaine be prefixede or limited for preparation oſ the kinges meate and the Quenes / but the ſame allwaies to be ordred as ſhall ſtand with their highe pleaſure, yet neverthelesse it is ordened that the houſehold when the houſe is kepte ſhall obſerve times certaine oſ dynner and ſupper as followeth / that is to ſaie, the firſt dynner on eatinge daies / to begine at x oſ the clocke or ſome what afore / and the firſt ſuppꝛ at iiij oſ the clocke on woorkedaies / and one holliedaie the firſt dynner to begine after the kinge be gone to the chappell to his devyne ſervice / and likewiſe at ſupper

4.

Diplomatic:

Questions unto

B.

Who addressed Ballard unto him owt of France?

With whom he conferred upõ the imp̃tinge of Ballards message unto him?

What gentilmẽ they meane, on whose behalf he affixed the Q of S, upõ his owne knowledge, that they meane fitt to be her Lieftenantes?

Who took the fidelities in the Queene of S name, in the west & south p̃tes, Wales Lankashire Darbyeshire & Stafford shire?

What Alphabet he hath receyved of late from the Queene of S?

Semi-diplomatic:

Questions unto

B.

Who addressed Ballard unto him owt of France?

With whom he conferred upon the impartinge of Ballards message unto him?

What gentilmen they meane, on whose behalf he affixed the Q of S, upon his owne knowledge, that they meane fitt to be her Lieftenantes?

Who took the fidelities in the Queene of S name, in the west & south partes, Wales Lankashire Darbyeshire & Stafford shire?

What Alphabet he hath receyved of late from the Queene of S?

Fig. 283. "Questions unto." An examination of the confessions of the conspirators in the Babington Plot, p. 50. England, 1586. Osborn fa10. The chemise binding, a wrapper of soft leather, is just visible here. These bindings are rare survivals, probably because their delicacy led them to be damaged over time and replaced by later bindings.

Questions unto

B.

who addressed Ballard unto him owt off ffraunce

with whom he conferred upp the message off
Ballards message unto him

what gentlemen they meane, on whose behalf
he assured the Q. off S, upp his own know=
ledge, that they meane fitt to be her lieute=
nantes

who toke the fidelities in the Queene off S
name, in the west & southshires, walls
Lankashire Darbyshire & Stafford shire

what Alphabet he hath receyved off late
from the Queene off S
                                    & this followes
what was his ^finall determinacion off the
Q off S, direccions & oppositions

what meanes the Queene off Scots
had for her intelligence wth him

who weare the principalle wth whom
he was to Conferr wth on this side
towching the Q off Sco oppositions

wth whom he was to conferr beyond
the seas, besyde mendozza

of whom these good fellowes made
choise to deale wth mendozze &
others beyond ye seas

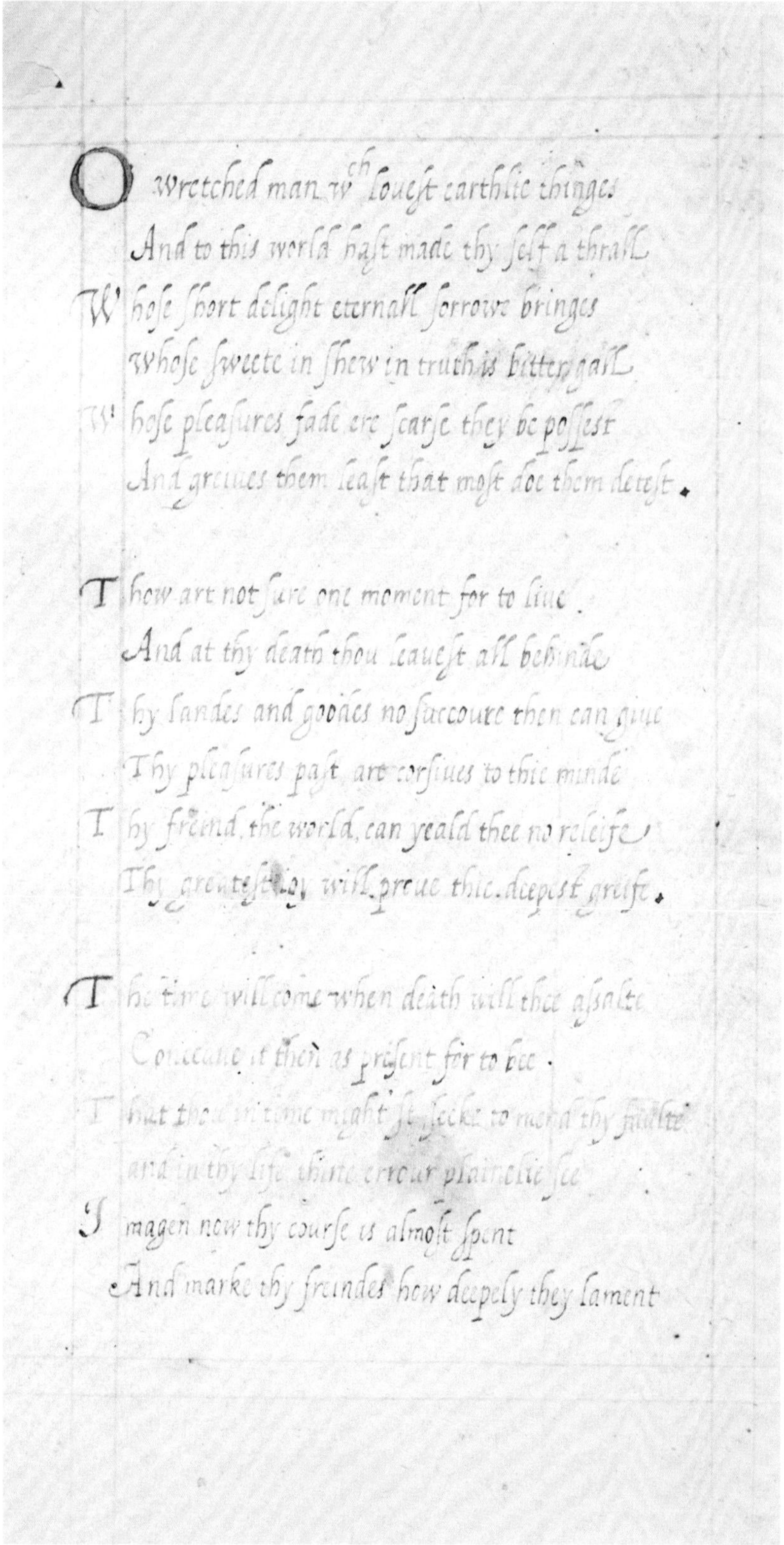

5.

Diplomatic:

O wretched man wch louest earthlie thinges
And to this world hast made thy self a thrall
Whose short delight eternall sorrowe bringes
Whose sweete in shew in truth is bitter gall
Whose pleasures fade ere scarse they be possest
And greiues them least that most doe them detest.

Regularized:

O wretched man which loves earthly things
And to this world has made thy self a thrall
Whose short delight eternal sorrow brings
Whose sweet in show in truth is bitter gall
Whose pleasures fade ere scarce they be possessed
And grieves them least that most do them detest.

Fig. 284. A copy of Philip Howard, Earl of Arundel, The Pathe to Paradise, f. 7r. England, ca. 1600. Osborn a5. The careful layout and use of gold ink for the first initial indicate that this might have been a young writer's exercise, to be presented as a gift.

6.

Diplomatic:

On slip:

They say in heart Let us returne
and soyle them out of hand
they eury sinagogue do burne
of God within the Land

Beneath slip:

[Th] ey saide in hart Let us o'returne
and spoyle them out of hand.
... & ^all the sinagogues ~~of God~~ ~~sinagogues of God~~ they burne ~~up every sinagogue~~
~~are or in~~ ^of God that are all, ^of God wth in the land.

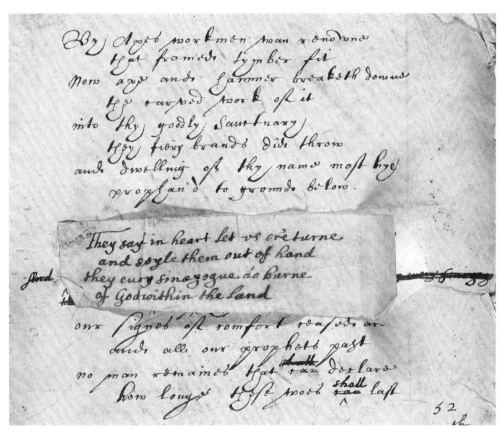

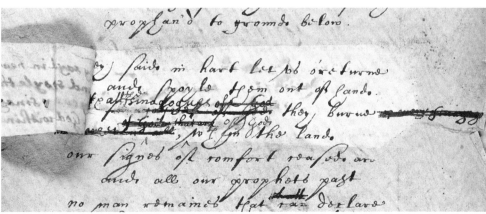

Figs. 285–286. Psalms in English verse, p. 5.
England, early 17th century. Osborn b217.
This manuscript is corrected throughout,
with slips pasted (or "tipped") to show
editorial stages. The exercise highlights
the layered chronologies of the revised
text, presenting any later transcriber or
editor with the choice of how or whether to
represent the multiple iterations of a text.

The named of the five Conquerours of this Island, wth theire sewall Armes viz)

Brutus the sonne of Silvius Posthumus comming out of Italie, wth the Troians, found out this Island, A{o} of the world 2855, and raigned as king thereof, whose heires enioyed the same by the space of 616 yeares about wch time his issue ended in king Ferreus, after he had raigned about 40 yeares.

He gave 4 cots quarterly viz the 1, is Sol, 2{o} Iupit: 3{o} Mars & ye 4th as {the} 2{d} in y{e} ba= gass of y{e} 3 in the 2d L 3, 3 crowns by one in bend ye other in pale in ye 4th a crosse formy fitchy {of} ye 1.

Iulius Casar, a Roman in the yeare before Christ 52 having conquered Fraunce, overcame also Cassibelanus king of Brittaine and made the Island tributarie vnder wch tribute it remayned by the space of 483 yeares. At wch tyme Constantine of Armorica obteyned the kingdome

Sol, an Eagle displaied wth 2 heads Saturne

Hengest a Saxon Duke of the Angles in the yeare after Christ 450 subdued the East part of this realme and first tooke vpon him the kingdome of Kent, whose successors afterwards inhabiting almost the whole Island, gave vnto it the name of England, and replenished the greater part thereof, wth the posteritie.

Quarterly he bare, 1 Iupit a crosse floary betweene 4 martletts Sol the 2d a Saltire Iupit & mars a crosse formy Sol the 3 chequy Sol & mars on a chiefe Sa: a Lion passt gard: of ye 1 & ye 4th as the first

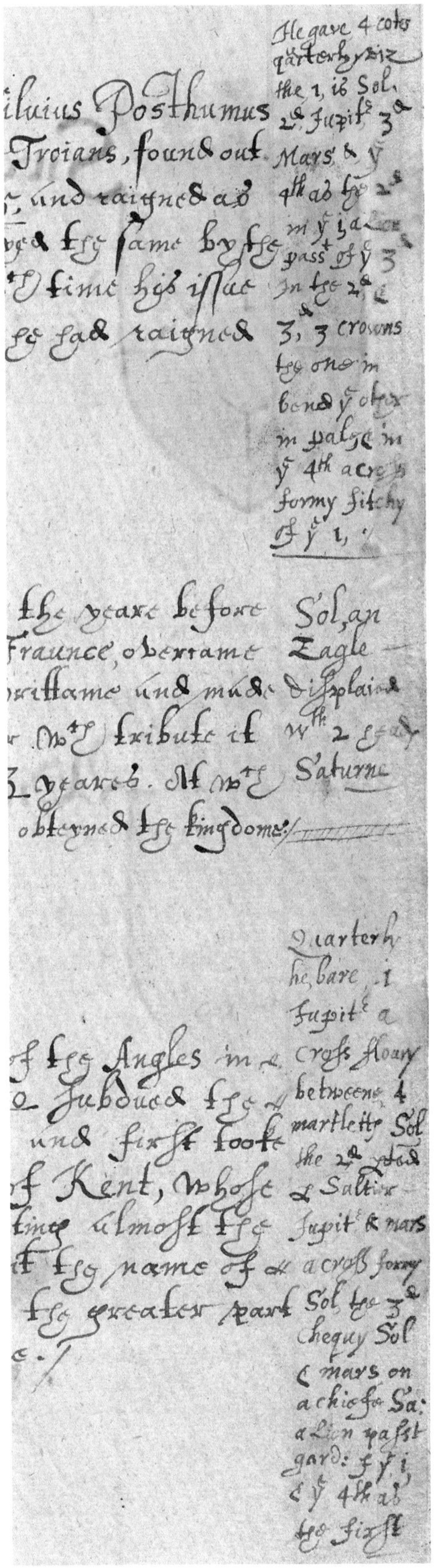

7.

Diplomatic:

Conquerors

The names of the five conquerors of
This island, wth theire seu^rall Armes viz

Brutus the sonne of Siluius Posthumus
coming out of Italie, wth the Troians, found out
this Island, A° of the world 2855, and raigned as
king thereof whose heires enioyed the same by the
space of 616 yeares about wch time his issue
ended in king Feereus. / After he had raigned
about 40 yeares./

> He gave 4 cotes
> q^uarterly viz
> the 1, is Sol,
> 2^d Jupit^r 3^d
> Mars & y^e
> 4th as the 2^d
> in y^e is a Lion
> pass^t of ye 3^d
> in the 2^d &
> 3^d, 3 crowns
> the one in
> bond y^e othr
> in palse in
> y^e 4th acre is
> formy fitchy
> of y^e 1.

Figs. 287–288. Heraldic manuscript of the English kings
and peers, p. 1. England, ca. 1620. Takamiya MS 13

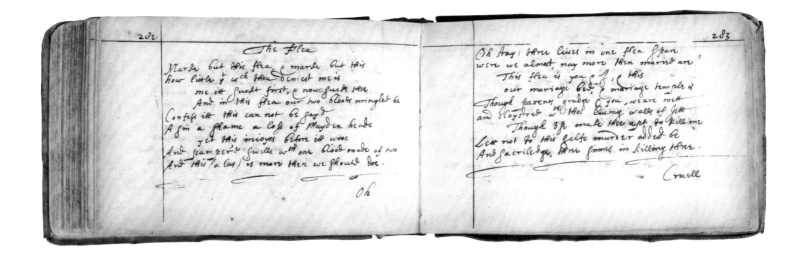

282 · The Flea

Marke but this flea, & marke but this
How litle yt wch thou deniest me is
    me it suck't first, & now sucks thee
    And in this flea our two bloods mingled be
Confess itt this can not be sayd
A sin, a shame, a loss of Mayden heade
    yet this inioyes before itt wooe
And pamper'd swells wth one blood made of two
And this / alas / is more then we should doe.

Oh

283

Oh stay: three liues in one flea spare
were we almost, nay more then maried are
    This flea is you & I, & this
    our mariage bed, & mariage temple is
Though parents grudge, & you, we are mett
and cloystred in thes liuing walls of Iett
    Though vse make thee apt to kill me
Lett not to this selfe murder added be
And sacriledge, three sinnes in killing thee.

Cruell

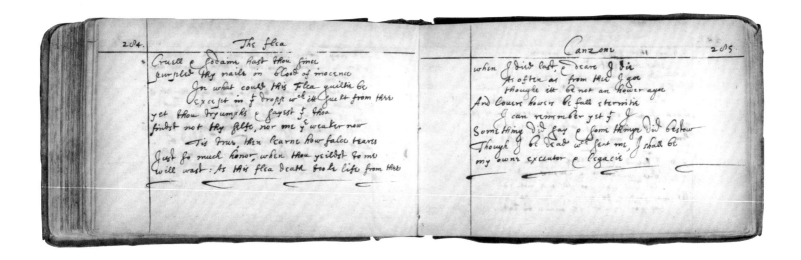

284 · The flea

Cruell & sodaine, hast thou sinee
purpled thy naile, in blood of inocence
    In what could this Flea guiltie be
    Except in yt dropp wch itt suck't from thee
yet thou triumphs't, & sayest yt thou
findst not thy selfe, nor me ye weaker now
    Tis true, then learne how false feares
Just so much honor, when thou yeildst to me
Will wast: As this flea death tooke life from thee

285 · Canzone

when I dyed last, & deare I dye
    As often as from thee I goe
    thoughe itt be not an hower agoe
And Louers howers be full eternitie
    I can remember yet yt I
Some thing did say, & some thinge did bestow
Though I be dead wch sent me, I shall be
my owne executor & legacie

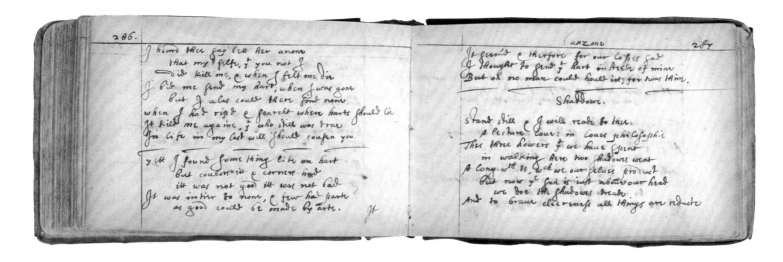

286

I heard thee say lett her anone
    that my selfe, yt you not I
    did kill me, & when I felt me die
I bid me send my hart, when I was gone
    but I alas could there find none
when I had ripd, & searcht where harts should lie
It kild me againe, yt who still was true
In life, in my last will should cousen you

yett I found some thing like an hart
    But coulor'd itt & corners had
    itt was not good, itt was not bad
It was intire to none, & few had parte
    as good could be made by arte.

yf

287 · Canzone

It seem'd & therfore for our losses sad
I thought to send yt hart in steede of mine
But oh no man could hould itt; for twas thine.

Shaddowe.

Stand still & I will reade to thee
    A Lecture loue: in Loues philosophie
Thes three howers yt we haue spent
    in walking here two shadowes went
A long wth us, wch we our selues produc't
    But now ye sun is iust aboue our head
    we doe the shadowes treade
And to braue cleerenes all thinges are reduc't

8.

Diplomatic:

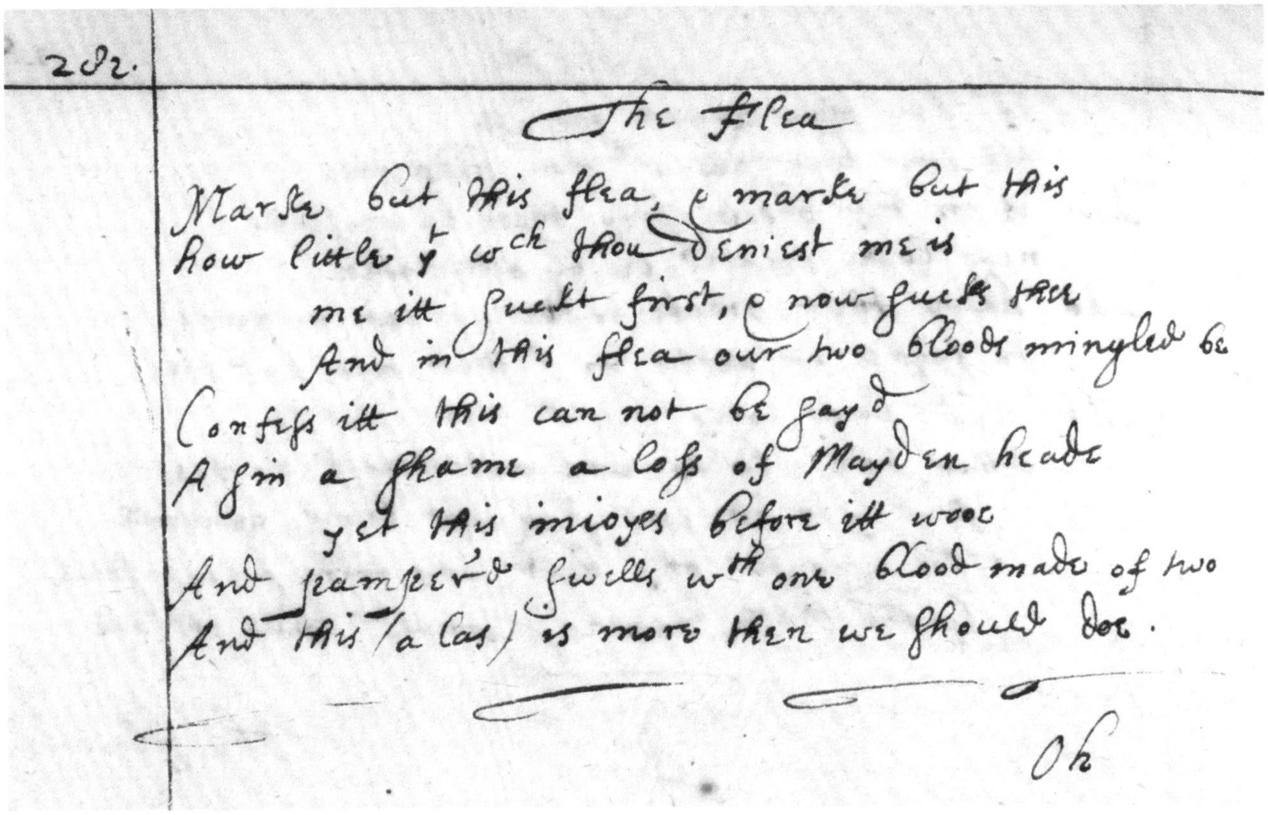

282.

The Flea

Marke but this flea, & marke but this
how little y^t wch thou deniest me is
me itt suckt first, & now suck thee
And in this flea our two bloods mingled be

Regularized:

282.

The Flea

Mark but this flea, and mark but this
how little that which thou denies me is
me it sucked first, & now sucks thee
And in this flea our two bloods mingled be

Figs. 289–292. "The Flea," in a scribal copy of 33 poems by John Donne, entitled Poems, with a few prose problems, pp. 282–87. England, ca. 1620. Osborn b114

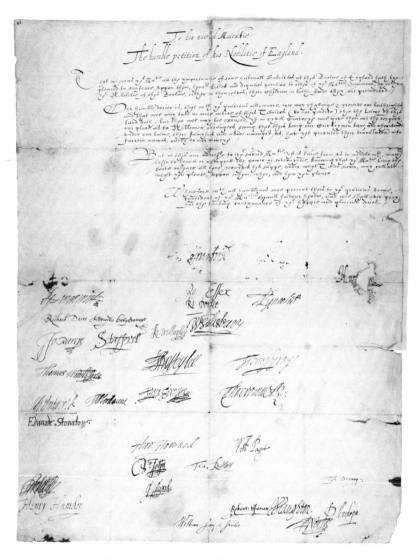

Figs. 293–294. A petition to James I protesting the creation of new Scottish and Irish peers, signed by members of the English peerage. England, 1621. Osborn fb240

9.

Diplomatic [Note my decision to use the virgule to mark line breaks, when addressing long lines of text.]:

To his sacred Maiestie
The humble petition of his Nobilitie of England

That whereas yo[r] Ma[tie] att the ymportunitie of some mutuall Subiectes of this Realme of England hath byn / pleased to conferre upon them, hono[rs] titled and dignities peculiar to other of yo[r] Ma[ties] Commons, by w[ch] ar / yo[r] Nobilitie of this Realme, either in themselves, their children, or bothe, finde they are preiudiced. /

Semi-diplomatic:

To his sacred Maiestie
The humble petition of his Nobilitie of England

That whereas your Majestie att the ymportunitie of some mutuall Subiectes of this Realme of England hath byn / pleased to conferre upon them, honours titled and dignities peculiar to other of your Majesties Commons, by which ar / your Nobilitie of this Realme, either in themselves, their children, or bothe, finde they are preiudiced. /

To his sacred Maiestie.

The humble petition of his Nobilitie of England.

That whereas ye Matie att the ymportunitie of some naturall Subiectes of this Realme of England hath byn pleased to conferre vppon them, hono^{ble} titles and dignities peculiar to other of ye Maties Dominions, by wch the Nobilitie of this Realme, eithe^r in themselves, their Children, or bothe, finde they are preiudited./

Our humble desire is, that wth y^r gratious allowance, wee may challenge & preserve our birthright, and that wee may take no more notice of this Titulers (to our predice) then the Lawe of this land doth, but that wee may bee excused, yf in civill curtesye wee give them not the respect, nor place as to Noblemen strangers, seeing that this being our Cuntrymen borne and inheritance under our Lawe, their familyes and abode amongst vs, have yet procured their translacon into forrein names, onely to our iniurye./

But in this our addresse to y^r sacred Matie yt is farre from vs to meddle wth, much lesse to lymitt or interprett the power of soverayntie, knowing that ye Matie being the roote whence all hono^r receyves his sappe, under what Titles soever, may collate what you please, vppon whom, when, and how you please.

Wherefore wth all humblenes wee present this to y^r gratious viewe, confident of ye Maties equall favour herein, and wee shall ever pray for the lasting contynuance of y^r happie and glorious daies./

[signatures]

Ro: Essex
Ri: Dorset
Lyncolne

Richard Dacre   Edwardes Sergehemye

To: Darcy   S. Stafford   Ro: Willughby   W. Salisbury

Henry Gray

Mordaunt

e. Stourton:

Thos: Howard   Will Paget

10.

Diplomatic:

A songe
Aske me no more whether doe straye
The goulden atomes of the Daye
For in pure Love the Gods prepare
Such powder to enrich your haire.

Aske me no more where Joue bestowes
When June is past the fadinge Rose
For in your beauties orient deepe
All flowers as in their Causes sleepe.

Figs. 295–296. A poem, or song, by Thomas Carew, facing a song, "Cock Lorell," by Ben Jonson, written for *The Gypsies Metamorphos'd* (1621). Manuscript miscellany, pp. 126–27. England, ca. 1640. Osborn b62

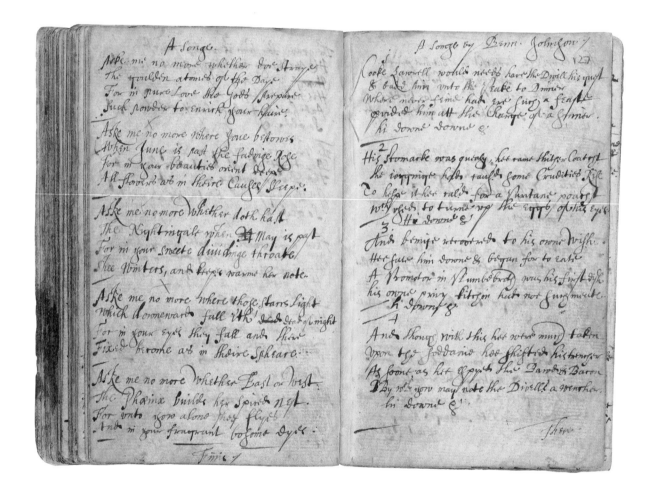

A Songe.

Aske me no more whither doe straye
the goulden atomes of the Daye
For in pure Love the Gods prepare
Such powder to enrich your haire.

Aske me no more where Jove bestowes
When June is past the fadinge Rose
For in your beautie orient deepe
All flowers as in theire Causes sleepe.

Aske me no more whether doth hast
The Nightingale when May is past
For in your sweete diuidinge throate
Shee winters, and keepes warme her note.

Aske me no more where those starrs light
Which donneward fall i'th' dead of night
For in your eyes they fall and there
fixed become as in theire Sphere.

Aske me no more whether East or West

11.

Diplomatic:

I:C: A Pastorall, the Antemaske
          Witches the nomber being fiue
          the Hagg beinge first./

   Hag This a braue world for us now for wee – – –
        metamorphise euery body
   Pre: But I doubt wee are but the Flye of the Cart wheele,
        for wee are but the people that's taulked on, –
        to serue others designes, and our pride to our – –
        selues makes us thinke wee are Actors.

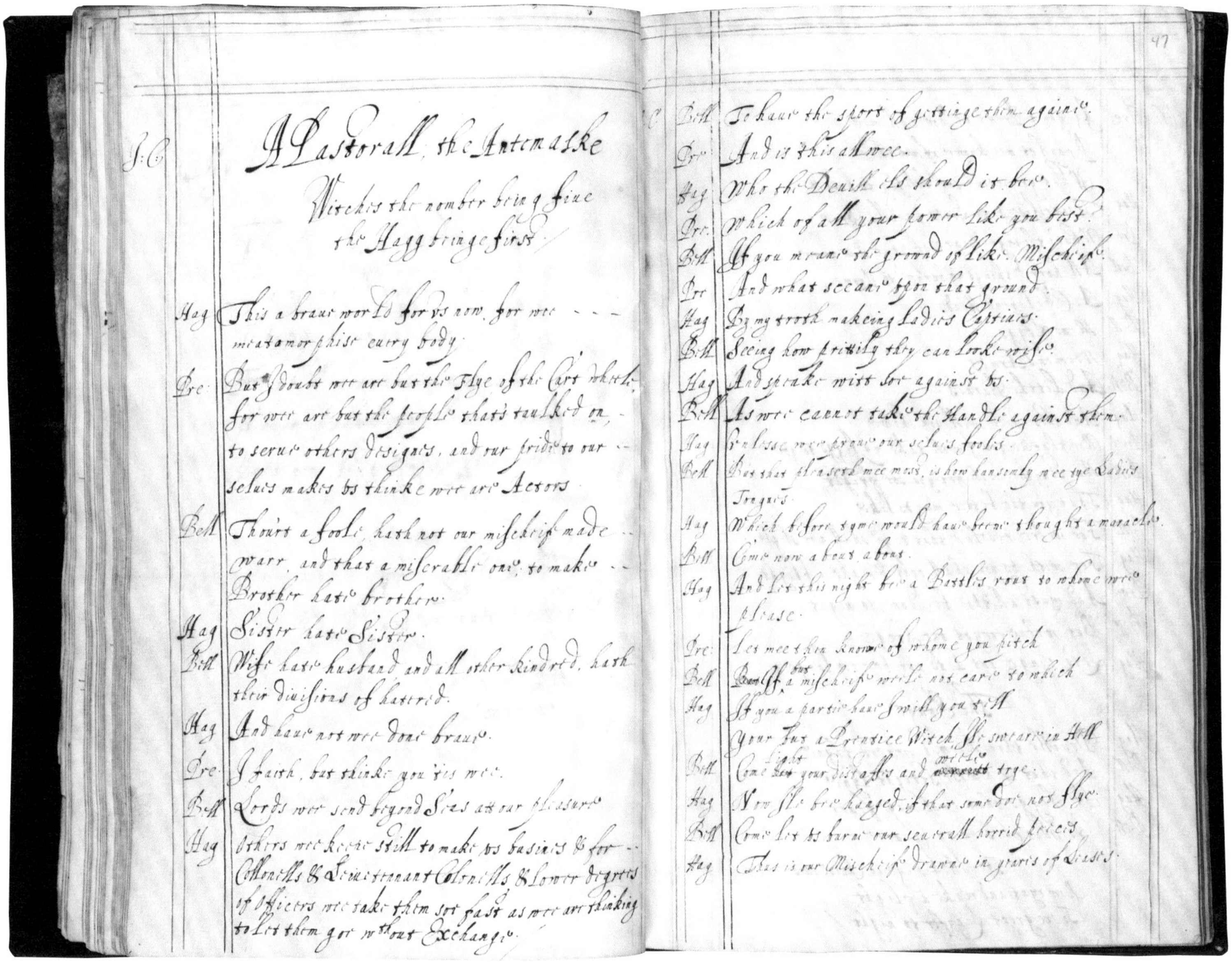

Figs. 297–298. The opening from "A Pastorall,"
a poetic dialogue by Elizabeth Brackley Egerton,
Countess of Bridgewater, copied in a notebook kept
by her sister, Jane Cavendish, pp. [46]–47. England,
mid-17th century. Osborn b233. The manuscript as
a whole is dedicated by Jane to her father, William
Cavendish, Duke of Newcastle.

12.

Diplomatic:

Act 1st: scene: 1st:

B:
Thunder and Lightning
Enter 3 Witches

1: Witch: When shall we three meet againe
In thunder Lightning and in raine
2: When the Hurlyburly's done
When the Battle's lost and won
3: And that will be 'ere sett of sun.

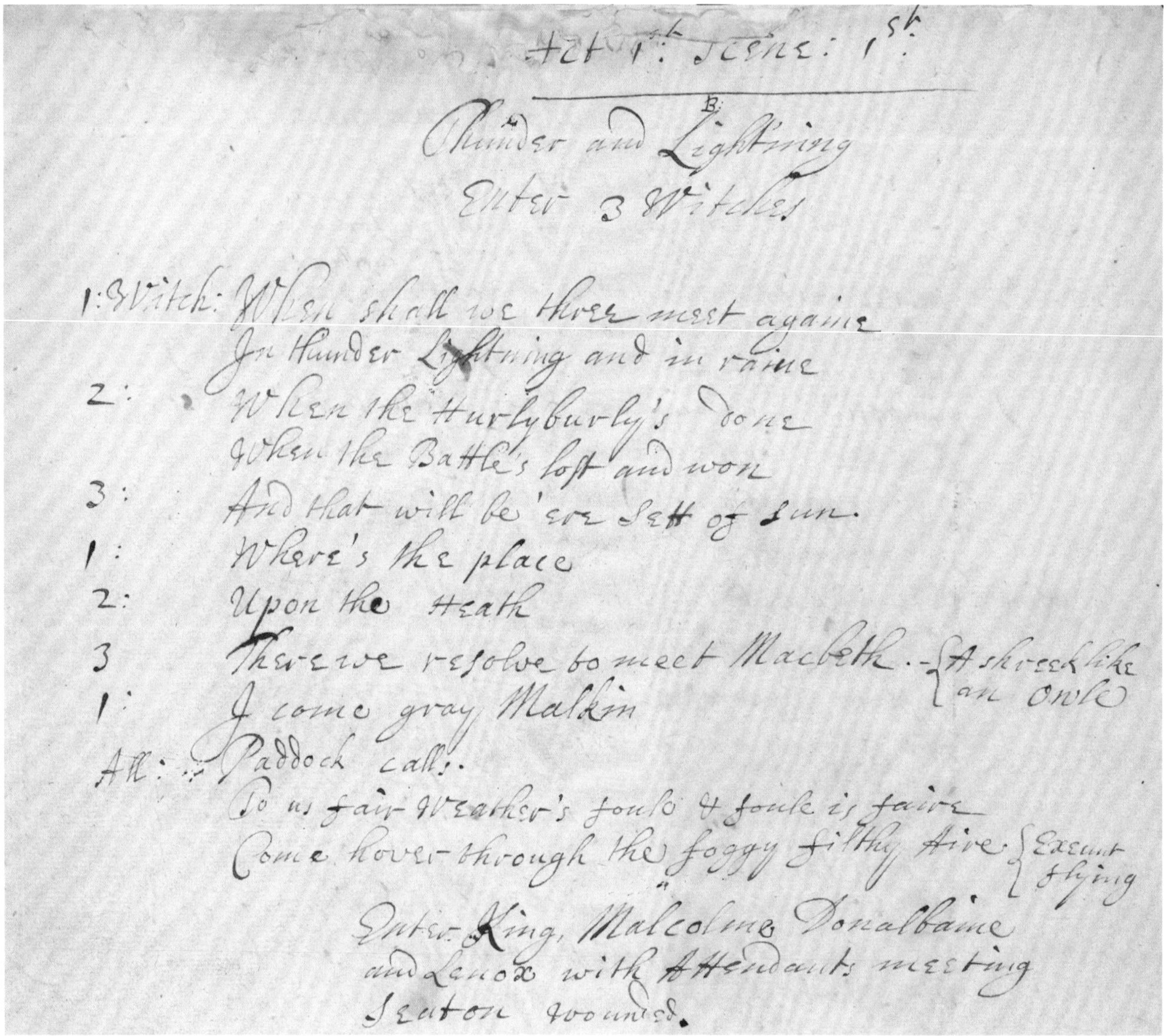

Act 1st: scene: 1st:
B:
Thunder and Lightning
Enter 3 Witches
1: Witch: When shall we three meet againe
In thunder Lightning and in raine
2: When the Hurlyburly's done
When the Battle's lost and won
3: And that will be 'ere Sett of Sun.
1: Where's the place
2: Upon the Heath
3 There we resolve to meet Macbeth. {A shreek like an Owle
1: I come gray Malkin
All: Paddock calls.
To us fair-Weather's foule & foule is faire
Come hover through the foggy filthy Aire {Exeunt flying
Enter King, Malcolme Donalbaine
and Lenox with Attendants meeting
Seaton wounded.

Fig. 299. "Act 1st: scene: 1st:," manuscript copy of William Davenant's adaptation of Shakespeare's *Macbeth,* p. 1. England, 1674. Gen MSS Vol 548

13.

Diplomatic:

December 23 – 1695 Came to fields of Ice Expecting
to be cut asunder Impossible to return to deadmans
Bay the wind fortunately shifted at 3 in the morning

Fig. 300. Thomas Bowrey, Logbook for the ship
London, December 23, 1695, p. [144]. Osborn fc177
(vol. 1)

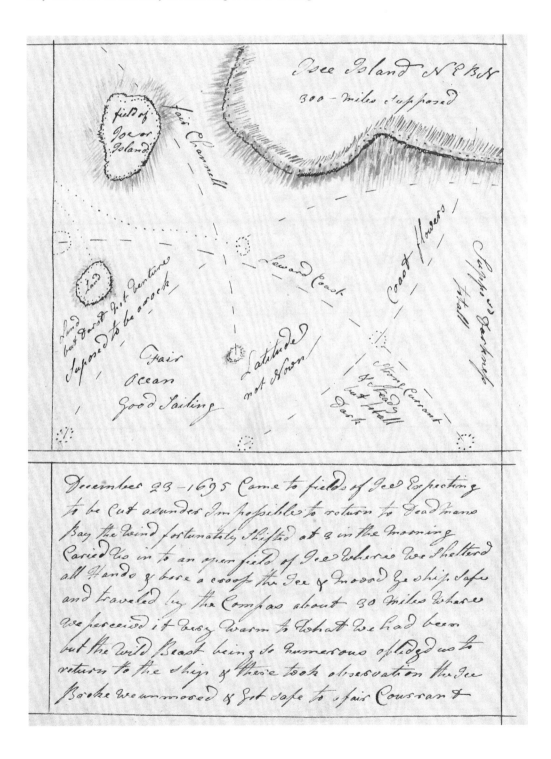

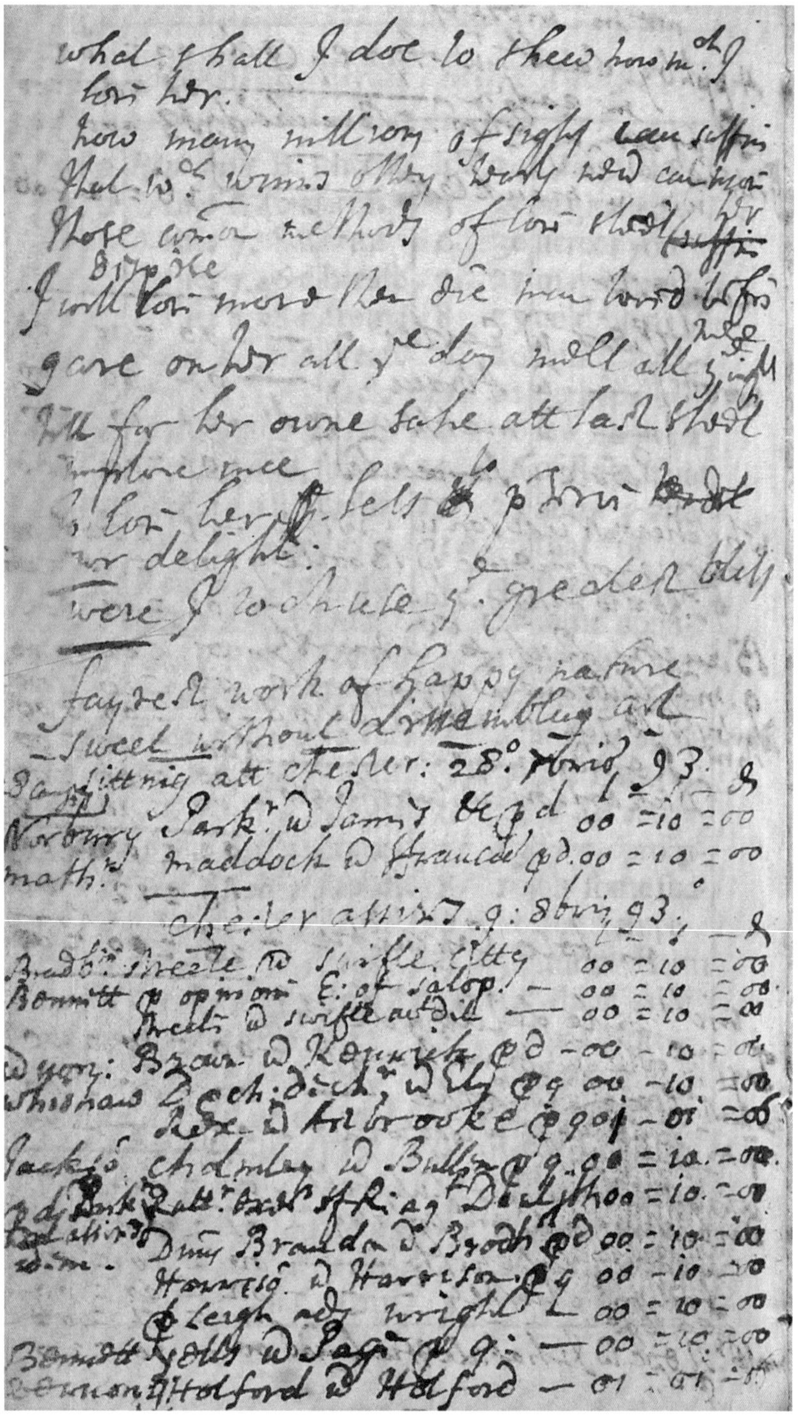

14.

Diplomatic:

what shall I doe to shew how m^ch I
love her.
how many millions of sighs can suffice
that wch wins others hearts nevr can mov her
those comõn methods of love sheel ~~suffis~~
dispise

Regularized:

What shall I do to show how much I
love her.
how many millions of sighs can suffice
that which wins others' hearts never can move her
those common methods of love she'll ~~suffice~~
despise

Figs. 301–302. Notes kept by John Chesshyre in an almanac, *Riders (1699.) British Merlin* (London, 1699), f. 50v–51r. OSB MSS 184, Box 23, Folder 175. This is a libretto, written by Thomas Betterton and set to music by Henry Purcell. It was used in the musical drama *The Prophetess* (1690), which drew on the eponymous play by John Fletcher and Philip Massinger, performed in 1622 and published in the Beaumont & Fletcher folio edition of 1647. Other manuscript copies of the song survive, and this reader might have seen the play, heard the song, and/or copied this as a poem from another manuscript source.

Observations on October.

Last quarter the 6 day, 56 min. past 4 in morn.
New Moon the 14 day, 40 min. past 6 in morn.
First quarter the 22 day, at 5 in the morning.
Full Moon the 28 day, 12 min. past 8 at night.

D.	☉ R	☉ S
1	6 40	5 20
2	6 42	5 18
3	6 44	5 16
4	6 46	5 14
5	6 48	5 12
6	6 50	5 10
7	6 52	5 8
8	6 54	5 6
9	6 57	5 3
10	6 59	5 1
11	7 1	4 59
12	7 3	4 56
13	7 5	4 55
14	7 7	4 53
15	7 9	4 51
16	7 11	4 49
17	7 13	4 47
18	7 15	4 45
19	7 17	4 43
20	7 20	4 40
21	7 22	4 38
22	7 24	4 36
23	7 26	4 34
24	7 28	4 32
25	7 30	4 30
26	7 32	4 28
27	7 34	4 26
28	7 35	4 25
29	7 37	4 23
30	7 39	4 21
31	7 41	4 11

Sow Wheat and Rye, remove young Plants and Trees about the New Moon, observing this as a seasonable secret, that in setting, you carefully place that side to the South and West which were so before you took up the Plant; otherwise the cold kills it. Gather your remaining Winter Fruit, set all kinds of Nuts and Acorns, and cut Rose-trees but once in two years, if you intend to have store of Roses.

The Garments you last Month hung on your backs in jest, now button them close in good earnest. Cloth you now for prevention, for the cold comes insensibly, & Fogs oftimes beget a whole Winters cold. Consult with your Taylors, as well as Physitians.

Advertisement.

15.

Diplomatic:

Multiplication

To know how many barly coarn pukles wil reach one mile

    paces in one mile

    1000

    feet in a pace 5

Books bought att Ed: Decr 1724

	s d
~~Tillotsons works 2 volums~~	—
X Secerit Memoirs from the new Atals	5:2
X History of the Buccaneers 3 vols	3:9
X Tillotsons sermons	5:4
X Sherlock on death	2:6

Figs. 303–304. Mrs. Christian Kerr, "Books bought att Ed [i.e., Edinburgh]: Decr 1724." Notebook, pp. 186–87. England, 18th century. Osborn c102

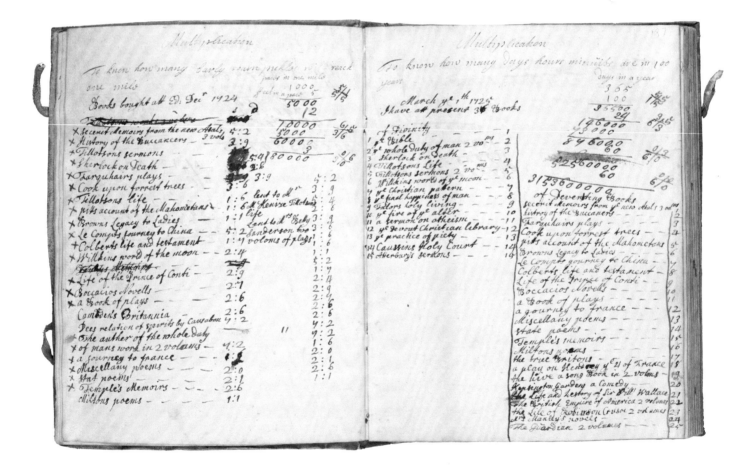

Multiplication

To know how many barly corn prickles will reach
one mile   pace in one mile
                                        feet in a pace   1 0 0 0   5
                                                            5   5/5

Books bought att Ed: Dec.r 1724   5 0 0 0
                                            s   d   12
~~Tillotsons works in 4to~~   1 0 0 0 0   6
✗ secret memoirs from the new Atals   4 : 2   3 0 0 0   3/6
✗ History of the Buccaneers ___ 3 vols 3 : 9   6 0 0 0 0
✗ Tillotsons sermons _____   3
✗ Sherlock on Death _____   5 : 4   8 0 0 0 0   0/6
✗ Farquhairs plays _____   2 : 6   9/10
✗ Cook upon forrest trees ___   3 : 9   5 : 2
✗ Tillotsons life _____   3 : 6   3 : 9
✗ pitts account of the Mahometans   1 : 6   lent to dr   5 : 4
✗ Browns Legacy to Ladies   1 : 6   dr Kenixe Tillotsons   2 : 6
✗ Le Compts journey to China ___   1 : 1   life   3 : 9
✗ Colberts life and testament ___   5 : 2   Lent to drs Betty 3 : 6
✗ Wilkins world of the moon ___   1 : 1   Sanderson two   3 : 6
~~Tychos memoirs~~   2 : 4   voloms of plays   1 : 6
✗ Life of the Prince of Conti ___   1 : 1
✗ Boccacios Novells _____   2 : 9   1 : 2
✗ a Book of plays _____   2 : 1   1 : 4
Camden's Britannia ___   2 : 6   2 : 4
Dees relation of spirits by Causabon 4 : 2   2 : 9
✗ the auther of the whole duty   2 : 6   2 : 4
✗ of mans work in 2 volams ___   4 : 2   2 : 6
✗ a journey to france ___ ___   1 : 1   11 2 : 6
✗ Miscellany poems ___ ___   4 : 2
✗ Stat poems _____   2 : 0   4 : 2
✗ Temples Memoirs ___ ___   2 : 1   1 : 6
Miltons poems ___ ___   2 : 6   2 : 0
                            1 : 1   2 : 1
                                                2 : 6
                                                1 : 1

16.

Diplomatic:

4 --	Mr Chitty for the house — —		2 2 —	
4 —	pd the Scourer for Curtains Cleaned — — — —	]	-- 12 —	
7 --	pd for a bunch of Grapes bought of Mr Edward tomlin at Harpe Alley fleet dich Cort — — —	]	-- 14 —	
8 —	pd Mr Rawlins paviour for diging & putin in a post & for Worck at Mr Artors — — — — —	]	5 —	
7 —	5 bushells of Brown Mault at	]	-- 17 6	
2nd	3s: & 6d p bushell — — — —		3 9	
	& 2 pound ½ of hoops at — —			

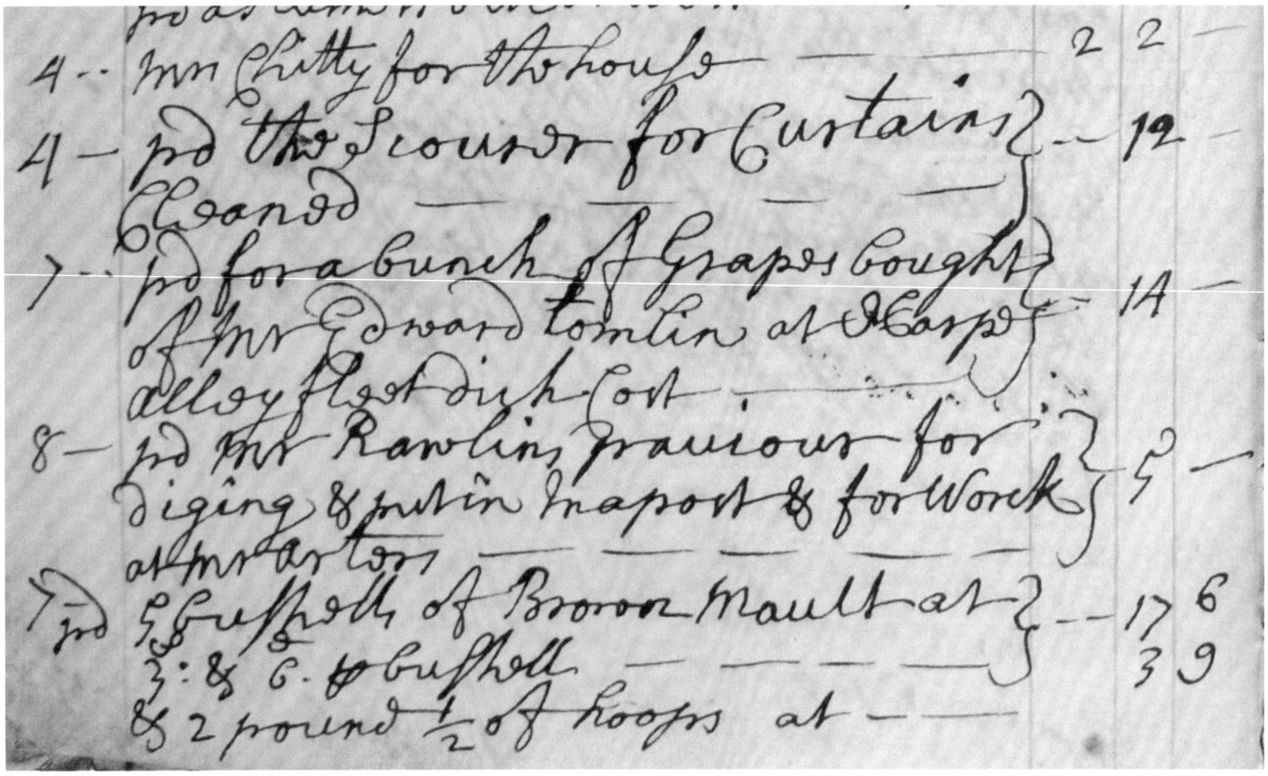

Figs. 305–306. Abraham Chitty, Account book, n.p. London, May 19–June 29, 1737. Osborn fc154

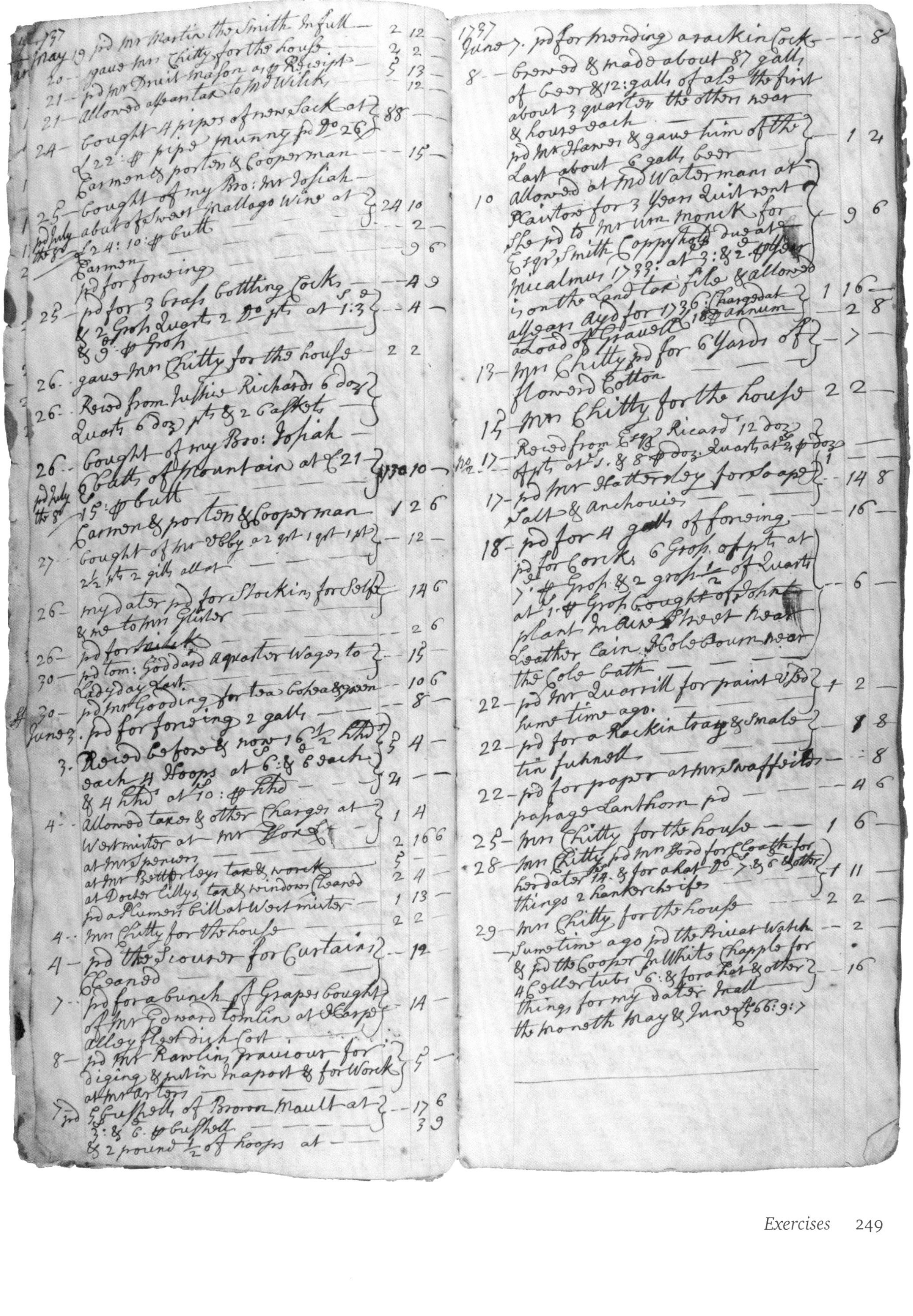

17.

Diplomatic:

A A Manuscript Manuscript

The grand ariostatic globe of M. Montgolfier having
inspired me with a notion ^it might be so improved that
with equal facility we might glide thro' the air, as
sail on the water; laid me much open to the redicale
of my friends, who laughed at my credulity; but their
irony only served to make me adhere to my own opini-
-on.

18.

Diplomatic:

imel & unjust mortification he would suffer, if he
were to think himself misapprehended.
Friday, Aug[st] 25.
To day I had the happiness of seeing my dear Char-
-lotte,—for the first time since I parted with her al-
-most at the Altar.— She came in the afternoon, & I
went into Mrs. Schivillenberg, when she was assembled with
Major Price & General Bude to tea, to make an apology
for not joining her, as I had my sister in my own
Room.

Fig. 308. Detail, Frances Burney, Diary entry. Friday, August 25, 1786. Gen MSS 1429

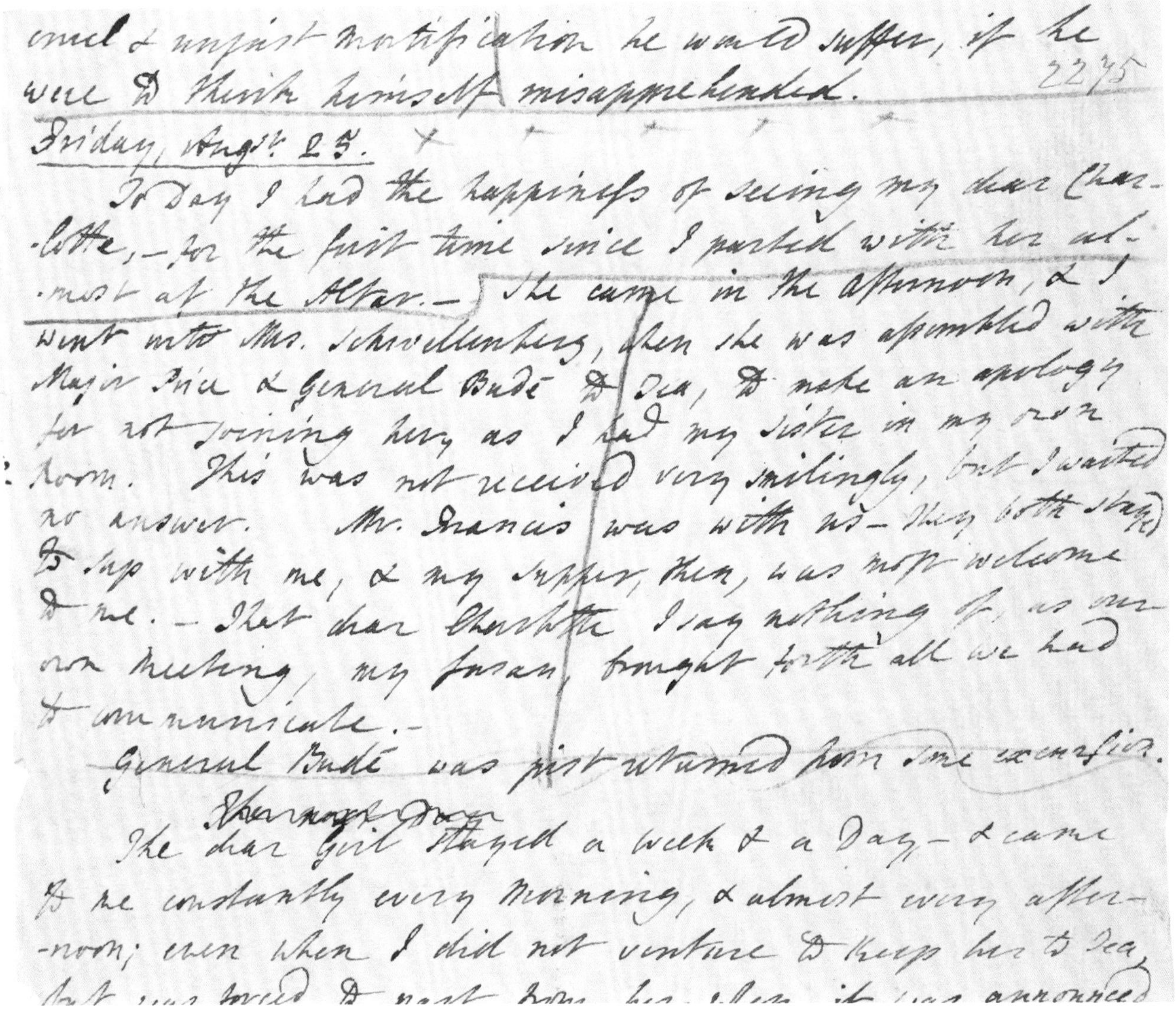
cruel & unjust mortification he would suffer, if he
were to think himself misapprehended.
Friday, Augst 25.
To Day I had the happiness of seeing my dear Char-
-lotte,—for the first time since I parted with her al-
-most at the Altar.— She came in the afternoon, & I
went into Mrs. Schivillenberg, when she was assembled with
Major Price & General Budé to Tea, to make an apology
for not joining her, as I had my sister in my own
Room. This was not received very smilingly, but I waited
no answer. Mr. Francis was with us— they both stayd
to sup with me, & my supper, then, was most welcome
to me.— What dear Charlotte I say nothing of, as our
own meeting, my Susan, brought forth all we had
to communicate.—
General Budé was just returned from some excursion.
The dear Girl stayed a week & a Day— & came
to me constantly every morning, & almost every after-
-noon; even when I did not venture to keep her to Tea,

19.

Diplomatic:

Sir

I sent off a short letter by the last post contain
ing a paragraph concerning Christabell which
I wished to have inserted towards the conclusion
of the Preface. I now write to say that this
paragraph must not be inserted or taken any
notice of, and further that I wish the
first page of the preface to be cancelled
and to, to be in order to be reprinted,
when it [meet to it] there.

Fig. 309. William Wordsworth, letter to his publishers, Biggs & Cottle, with notes on the inclusion of Samuel Taylor Coleridge's poem "Christabel" in the second edition of *Lyrical Ballads* (1800). [Grasmere], October 10 [1800]. Gen MSS 1261, Letter 10

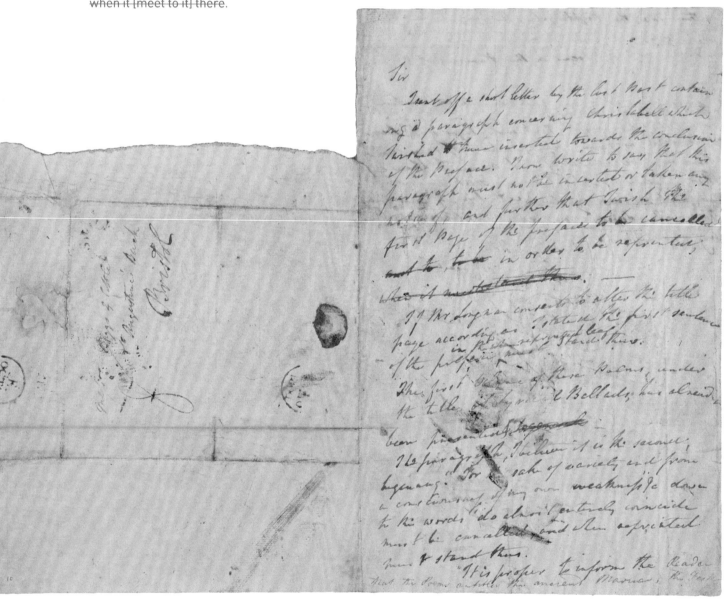

20.

Diplomatic:

a very bad Dinner
when Mr Nisby
came methinks.

Fig. 310. Hester Lynch Piozzi, annotations in *The Spectator,* vol. 4, pp. 412–13. ca. 1801. Gen MSS VOL 527

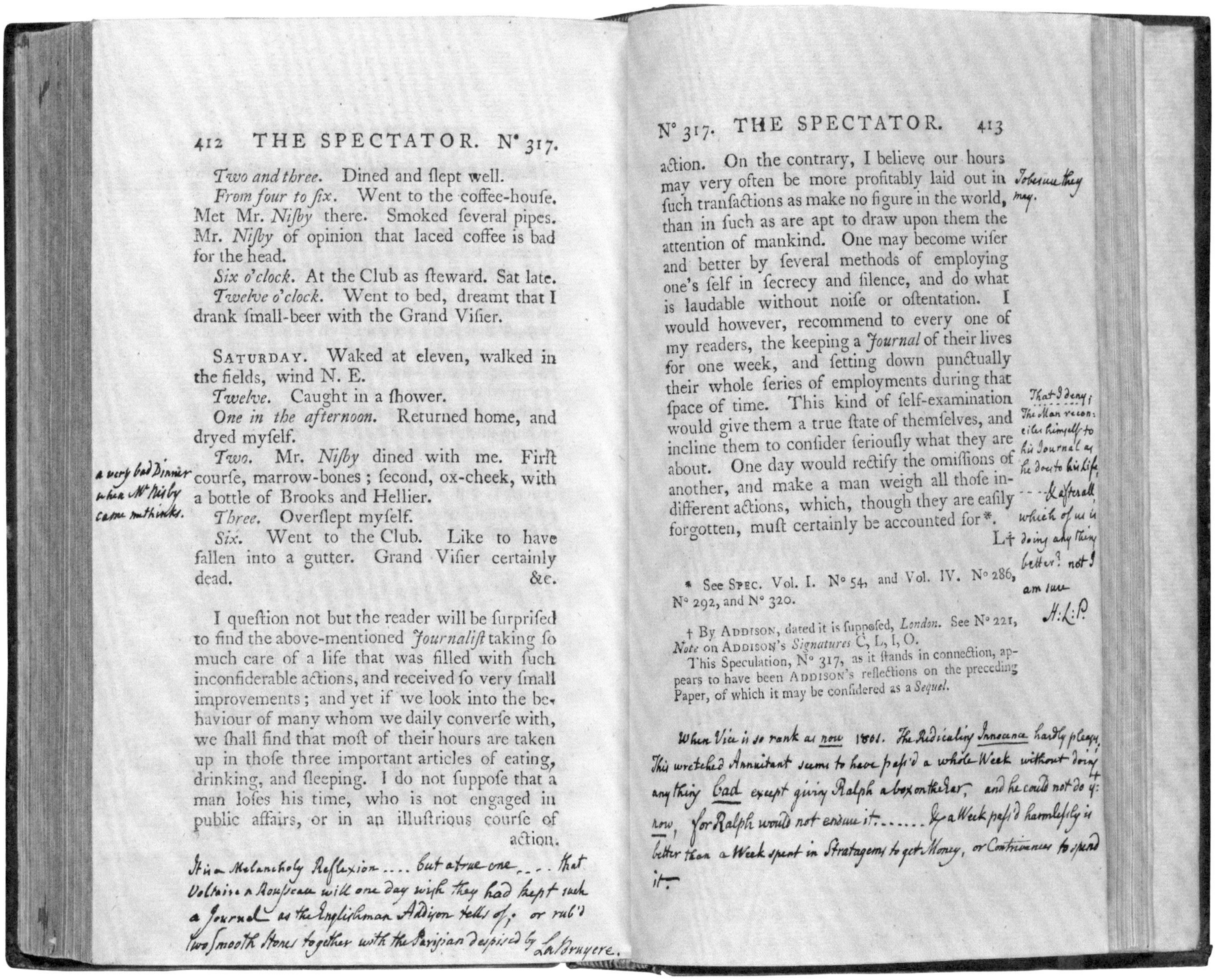

412 THE SPECTATOR. N° 317.

Two and three. Dined and ſlept well.

From four to ſix. Went to the coffee-houſe. Met Mr. *Niſby* there. Smoked ſeveral pipes. Mr. *Niſby* of opinion that laced coffee is bad for the head.

Six o'clock. At the Club as ſteward. Sat late.

Twelve o'clock. Went to bed, dreamt that I drank ſmall-beer with the Grand Viſier.

SATURDAY. Waked at eleven, walked in the fields, wind N. E.

Twelve. Caught in a ſhower.

One in the afternoon. Returned home, and dryed myſelf.

Two. Mr. *Niſby* dined with me. Firſt courſe, marrow-bones; ſecond, ox-cheek, with a bottle of Brooks and Hellier.

Three. Overſlept myſelf.

Six. Went to the Club. Like to have fallen into a gutter. Grand Viſier certainly dead. &c.

I queſtion not but the reader will be ſurpriſed to find the above-mentioned *Journaliſt* taking ſo much care of a life that was filled with ſuch inconſiderable actions, and received ſo very ſmall improvements; and yet if we look into the behaviour of many whom we daily converſe with, we ſhall find that moſt of their hours are taken up in thoſe three important articles of eating, drinking, and ſleeping. I do not ſuppoſe that a man loſes his time, who is not engaged in public affairs, or in an illuſtrious courſe of action.

a very bad Dinner when Mr Nisby came methinks.

It is a Melancholy Reflexion .... but a true one .... that Voltaire & Rouſseau will one day wish they had kept such a Journal as the Englishman Addison tells of; or rub'd two ſmooth Stones together with the Parisian despised by La Bruyere.

N° 317. THE SPECTATOR. 413

action. On the contrary, I believe our hours may very often be more profitably laid out in ſuch tranſactions as make no figure in the world, than in ſuch as are apt to draw upon them the attention of mankind. One may become wiſer and better by ſeveral methods of employing one's ſelf in ſecrecy and ſilence, and do what is laudable without noiſe or oſtentation. I would however, recommend to every one of my readers, the keeping a *Journal* of their lives for one week, and ſetting down punctually their whole ſeries of employments during that ſpace of time. This kind of ſelf-examination would give them a true ſtate of themſelves, and incline them to conſider ſeriouſly what they are about. One day would rectify the omiſſions of another, and make a man weigh all thoſe indifferent actions, which, though they are eaſily forgotten, muſt certainly be accounted for*.

L†

To be sure they may.

That I deny; The Man reconciles himself to his Journal as he does to his Life, ---& after all, which of us is doing any thing better? not I am sure

H:L:P.

* See SPEC. Vol. I. N° 54, and Vol. IV. N° 286, N° 292, and N° 320.

† By ADDISON, dated it is ſuppoſed, *London.* See N° 221, *Note* on ADDISON'S *Signatures* C, L, I, O.

This Speculation, N° 317, as it ſtands in connection, appears to have been ADDISON'S reflections on the preceding Paper, of which it may be conſidered as a *Sequel.*

When Vice is so rank as now 1801. The Ridicaling Innocence hardly pleases; This wretched Annuitant seems to have pass'd a whole Week without doing any thing bad except giving Ralph a box on the Ear, and he could not do y^t now, for Ralph would not endure it....... & a Week pass'd harmlessly is better than a Week spent in Stratagems to get Money, or Contrivances to spend it.

NOTES

1 G.M. Woodward, *Familiar Verses, from the Ghost of Willy Shakspeare to Sammy Ireland* (London: Richard White, 1796), A3r–v.

2 William Henry Ireland, *The Confessions of William-Henry Ireland. Containing the particulars of his fabrication of the Shakspeare Manuscripts* (London: Ellerton and Byworth, 1805). Ireland is an unreliable witness, but describes a journeyman to a bookbinder, Mr. Laurie, who "looking at the manuscript, informed me that he could give me a mixture that would resemble old ink much more than that which I had used; and, in consequence of my request, he immediately mixed together in a phial three different liquids used by bookbinders in marbling the covers of their calf bindings" (39–40).

3 George Steevens, ed., *The plays of William Shakspeare: in ten volumes: with the corrections and illustrations of various commentators: to which are added notes by Samuel Johnson and George Steevens* (London, 1778).

4 Edmond Malone, *An inquiry into the authenticity of certain miscellaneous papers and legal instruments, published Dec. 24, M DCC XCV. and attributed to Shakspeare, Queen Elizabeth, and Henry, Earl of Southampton* (London, 1796), 117.

5 "Began Jany 10.—Began printing Jan. 18. / ^Finished at the press—March. 28. 1796." Edmond Malone's notes in his copy of *An inquiry into the authenticity of certain miscellaneous papers and legal instruments.* Folger Shakespeare Library, PR2950 M32, copy 2, front endpaper.

6 Roger Chartier, "The Author's Hand," in *The Author's Hand and the Printer's Mind*, trans. Lydia G. Cochrane (Cambridge: Polity Press, 2014). Chartier's work deeply informs the approach to manuscript culture taken in this book, as does the often hauntingly resonant work by Margreta de Grazia and Peter Stallybrass.

7 The Columbia University Rare Book & Manuscript Library holds the earliest known extant copy of the first edition, dated 1570 (Plimpton 092 1570 B38). Other early copies are dated 1571.

8 Wrigley estimates London's population to have grown from 200,000 in 1600 to 900,000 in 1800. E.A. Wrigley, "A Simple Model of London's Importance in Changing English Society and Economy 1650–1750," *Past & Present* 37 (1967): 44. See also Roger Finlay and Beatrice Shearer,

"Population Growth and Suburban Expansion," in *London 1500–1700: The Making of the Metropolis*, ed. A.L. Beier and Roger Finlay (London: Longman, 1986), 37–59.

9 For Leedham-Green, see English Handwriting, 1500–1700, an online course (https://www. english.cam.ac.uk/ceres/ehoc); her formative *Books in Cambridge Inventories: Book-Lists from Vice-Chancellor's Court Probate Inventories in the Tudor and Stuart Periods*, 2 vols. (Cambridge: Cambridge University Press, 1986); and Leedham-Green and Teresa Webber, eds., *The Cambridge History of Libraries in Britain and Ireland, vol. 1 to 1640* (Cambridge: Cambridge University Press, 2006). For Wolfe, see especially her Early Modern Manuscripts Online (https://emmo.folger.edu); "Was Early Modern Writing Paper Expensive?" *The Collation* (February 13, 2018; https://collation. folger.edu/2018/02/writing-paper-expensive; and Wolfe and Alan Stewart, *Letterwriting in Renaissance England* (Washington, D.C.: Folger Shakespeare Library, 2004). For Yeandle, see particularly her work with Jean F. Preston, *English Handwriting, 1400–1650: An Introductory Manual* (Binghamton, N.Y.: Medieval & Renaissance Texts & Studies, 1992). For earlier works on English paleography, see L.C. Hector, *The Handwriting of English Documents* (London: Edward Arnold, 1966); Charles Johnson and Hilary Jenkinson, *English Court Hand A.D. 1066 to 1500* (New York: Ungar, 1967), and Jenkinson, *The Later Court Hands in England from the Fifteenth to the Seventeenth Century* (New York: Ungar, 1969); Anthony G. Petti, *English Literary Hands from Chaucer to Dryden* (Cambridge, Mass.: Harvard University Press, 1977).

10 See in particular Albert Derolez, *The Palaeography of Gothic Manuscript Books: From the Twelfth to the Early Sixteenth Century* (Cambridge: Cambridge University Press, 2003); Malcolm B. Parkes, *English Cursive Book Hands, 1250–1500* (Berkeley: University of California Press, 1980) and *Their Hands before Our Eyes: A Closer Look at Scribes* (Aldershot: Ashgate, 2008); Barbara A. Shailor, *The Medieval Book* (Toronto: University of Toronto Press, 1991) and *A Catalogue of Medieval and Renaissance Manuscripts in the Beinecke Rare Book and Manuscript Library*, 4 vols. (Binghamton, N.Y.: Medieval & Renaissance Texts & Studies, 1984–2004); Raymond Clemens and Timothy Graham, *Introduction to Manuscript Studies* (Ithaca: Cornell University Press, 2007).

11 For material studies, this book is indebted to the work of Peter Beal, and particularly his work on the Catalogue of English Literary Manuscripts 1450–1700 (http://www.celm-ms.org.uk); Peter W.M. Blayney, and particularly *The Stationers' Company and the Printers of London, 1501–1557*, 2 vols. (Cambridge: Cambridge University Press, 2013); Mirjam M. Foot, *Bookbinders at Work: Their Roles and Methods* (London: British Library, 2006); James Daybell, *The Material Letter in Early Modern England: Manuscript Letters and the Culture and Practices of Letter-Writing, 1512–1635* (Basingstoke, UK: Palgrave Macmillan, 2012); Burnett Hillman Streeter, *The Chained Library* (London: Macmillan and Co., 1931); Jana Dambrogio on letterlocking (http://www.janadambrogio. com/letterlock); Timothy Barrett et al., "Paper through Time: Nondestructive Analysis of 14th-through 19th-Century Papers," The University of Iowa (http://paper.lib.uiowa.edu/index.php); Cathleen A. Baker, *From the Hand to the Machine: Nineteenth-Century American Paper and Mediums: Technologies, Materials, and Conservation* (Ann Arbor: Legacy Press, 2010); Theresa Fairbanks and Scott Wilcox, *Papermaking and the Art of Watercolor in Eighteenth-Century Britain: Paul Sandby and the Whatman Paper Mill* (New Haven: Yale Center for British Art, 2006); Jesse Meyers, Pergamena (https://www.pergamena.net); Michael Finlay, *Western Writing Implements in the Age of the Quill Pen* (Wetheral, UK: Plains Books, 1990); Karen Jutzi, Ainsley Joe, Marie-France Lemay, Christine McCarthy, Laura O'Brien, and Paula Zyats, "The Traveling Scriptorium," Yale University Library (https://travelingscriptorium.library.yale.edu).

12 This book is particularly indebted to the work of Heidi Brayman, most especially her *Reading Material in Early Modern England: Print, Gender, and Literacy* (Cambridge: Cambridge University Press, 2005); William H. Sherman, *Used Books: Marking Readers in Renaissance England* (Philadelphia: University of Pennsylvania Press, 2008); Ann M. Blair, *Too Much to Know: Managing Scholarly Information before the Modern Age* (New Haven: Yale University Press, 2010); Adam Smyth, especially *Material Texts in Early Modern England* (Cambridge: Cambridge University Press, 2018) and, with Gill Partington, eds., *Book Destruction from the Medieval to the Contemporary* (Basingstoke, UK: Palgrave Macmillan, 2014); Christina Lupton, *Knowing Books: The Consciousness of Mediation in*

Eighteenth-Century Britain (Philadelphia: University of Pennsylvania Press, 2012); Juliet Fleming, *Graffiti and the Writing Arts of Early Modern England* (London: Reaktion Books, 2001); Jonathan Goldberg, *Writing Matter: From the Hands of the English Renaissance* (Stanford: Stanford University Press, 1990).

13 McKenzie defined the sociology of texts as relating to "the composition, formal design, and transmission of texts by writers, printers, and publishers; their distribution through different communities by wholesalers, retailers, and teachers; their collection and classification by librarians; their meaning for, and—I must add—their creative regeneration by, readers" (D.F. McKenzie, *Bibliography and the Sociology of Texts* [Cambridge: Cambridge University Press, 1999], 12).

14 See especially Roger Chartier, *The Order of Books: Readers, Authors, and Libraries in Europe between the Fourteenth and Eighteenth Centuries*, trans. Lydia G. Cochrane (Cambridge: Polity Press, 1994); Margreta de Grazia, particularly *Shakespeare Verbatim: The Reproduction of Authenticity and the 1790 Apparatus* (Oxford: Clarendon Press, 1991) and, with Peter Stallybrass, "The Materiality of the Shakespearean Text," *Shakespeare Quarterly* 44 (1993): 255–83; Peter Stallybrass, both his unpublished work and, in particular, with Roger Chartier, J.F. Mowery, and Heather Wolfe, "Hamlet's Tables and the Technologies of Writing in Renaissance England," *Shakespeare Quarterly* 55 (2004): 379–419.

15 John Foxe, *Actes and monuments of these latter and perillous dayes, touching matters of the Church* (London, 1563), 1714. This was one of two poems written on material surfaces of the gatehouse of Woodstock Palace, where Elizabeth was held without access to writing materials. Although later eyewitness accounts of the second poem survive, this first couplet is only recorded through Foxe's 1563 edition, from which it then circulated in print and manuscript. On the two poems, see Arthur F. Marotti and Steven W. May, "A New Manuscript Copy of a Poem by Queen Elizabeth: Text and Contexts," *English Literary Renaissance* 47 (2017): 2–3. On Elizabeth's writing under house arrest, see Ilona Bell, "Elizabeth Tudor: Poet," *Explorations in Renaissance Culture* 30 (2004): 1–22. Foxe's edition was cited as the source for manuscript renditions of the couplet, which was also published in Raphael Holinshed's *Chronicles* (London, 1587) and Anthony Munday's *A Watch-woord to England* (London, 1584); see Carlo M. Bajetta, "'Most

peereles Poëtresse': The Manuscript Circulation of Elizabeth's Poems," in *Representations of Elizabeth I in Early Modern Culture,* ed. Alessandra Petrina and Laura Tosi (Basingstoke, UK: Palgrave Macmillan, 2011), 108.

16 Ben Jonson, *The diuell is an asse* (London, 1631), 117.

17 Procession, with Ceremony of the Investiture and Installation of his Highness Oliver Cromwell, as by the Parliament appointed to be performed in Westminster-hall, on June 26, 1657, written by me Edmund Prestwick, of the City of London, an eye and ear-witness to all that passed on this Glorious Occasion. Now set forth by me John Prestwick, Esq. No. VI (Supra, p. 311, 425), in "Procession at installation of Cromwell as Lord Protector, June 1657," in *Diary of Thomas Burton Esq: Volume 2, April 1657–February 1658,* ed. John Towill Rutt (London, 1828), 511–15. *British History Online,* http://www.british-history.ac.uk/burton-diaries/vol2/pp511-515 [accessed June 27, 2018].

18 William Caxton, *Here endeth this doctrine at Westmestre by London in fourmes enprinted. In the whiche one euerich may shortly lerne. Frenssh and englissh* (Westminster, 1480), n.p.

19 "Thomas Crosby and John Robinson, at the lower end of Fair-street, upon Horse-ly-down, in Southwark, sell all sorts of carpenters, joyners, painters, and artificers rules" (London, [1740?]). ESTC T150362.

20 Thomas Wetherel, *Five sermons, preached upon several texts* (London, 1635), 48. This work was published by Wetherel's successor to the Suffolk rectory of Newton, Francis Quarles. The sermon is identified as an Assizes sermon, i.e., preached on the occasion of the Assizes court, at its Lent or summer meeting on the Norfolk circuit.

21 See the *Oxford English Dictionary* entry: Substratum, n.

1. An underlying principle on which something is based; a basis, a foundation, a bedrock.

2. *Philos.* A permanent underlying thing or essence in which properties inhere. More commonly called substance (cf. substance n. 2, 4a).

3. The matter out of which something is made or created; the fundamental or basic constituents of something.

4. a. An underlying layer or substance; a layer of something below another.

b. *Geol.* An underlying stratum, *esp.* that beneath the soil or other surface feature.

c. *Biol.* The surface or material upon which a plant, fungus, or other organism grows; = substrate n. 2.

d. A lower class or stratum of society, *esp.* one which is characterized by poverty or criminality. Cf. underclass n.

5. *Linguistics.* Cf. earlier substrate n. 3.

a. A language spoken in a particular area at the time of the arrival of a new language, and which has had within that area a detectable influence on the elements or features of the new language.

b. More generally: a language spoken by a socially subordinate group, which has influenced that of the socially dominant one, or contributed to the formation of a Creole. Cf. adstratum n., superstratum n. 2.

22 Thomas Blount, *Glossographia* (London, 1661), I2v.

23 Robert Farlie, *Kalendarivm hvmanae vitae. The kalender of mans life* (London, 1638), n.p. On writing tables or tablets, see Stallybrass, Chartier, Mowery, and Wolfe, "Hamlet's Tables and the Technologies of Writing in Renaissance England." On writing on walls and surfaces, see Juliet Fleming, *Graffiti and the Writing Arts*; see also William N. West on writing in libraries, "Reading Rooms: Architecture and Agency in the Houses of Michel de Montaigne and Nicholas Bacon," *Comparative Literature* 56 (2004): 111–29.

24 William Shakespeare, *The tragicall historie of Hamlet, Prince of Denmarke* (London, 1604), M2v–M3r.

25 Ephraim Chambers, *Cyclopædia: or, an universal dictionary of arts and sciences,* vol. 2 (London, 1728), 351.

26 Hector, *The Handwriting of English Documents,* 15–16.

27 Jesse Meyer, Pergamena, Montgomery, N.Y.; Ronald Reed, *The Nature and Making of Parchment* (Leeds: Elmete Press, 1975); Alexis Hagadorn, "Parchment Making in Eighteenth-Century France: Historical Practices and the Written Record," *Journal of the Institute of Conservation* 35 (2012): 165–88; Michael L. Ryder, "Parchment—Its History, Manufacture and Composition," *Journal of the Society of Archivists* 2 (1964): 391–99.

28 Jesse Meyer, Class visit, October 2018, to the Meyers' tannery and parchment workshop, Pergamena, in Montgomery, N.Y.; https://www.pergamena.net. Cited with permission of Jesse Meyer.

29 Matthew D. Teasdale et al., "The York Gospels: A 1000-Year Biological Palimpsest," *Royal Society Open Science* 4 (2017): 170988.

30 Sarah Fiddyment et al., "Animal Origin of 13th-Century Uterine Vellum Revealed Using Noninvasive Peptide Fingerprinting," *PNAS* 112, no. 49 (2015): 15066–71.

31 The covers will be printed on vellum. Hannah Jordan and Max Goldbart, "Vellum Acts to be Axed," *PrintWeek* (March 24, 2017), https://www.printweek.com/print-week/news/1160701/vellum-acts-to-be-axed [accessed August 8, 2018].

32 As one example, in the month of September 1568, the *Grace of God* of London imported four shipments of playing cards, sixty-one gross or 8,784 in total, alongside shipments of "coarse paper," "paper," "loose paper," "coarse cap-paper," "writing paper," and other unrelated items, such as prunes, wool-cards, copper nails, combs, and crewel lace. See "London Port Book, 1567–8: No. 827s (Sept 1568)," in *The Port and Trade of Early Elizabethan London: Documents,* ed. Brian Dietz (London: London Record Society, 1972), 129–33. *British History Online,* http://www.british-history.ac.uk/london-record-soc/vol8/pp129-133 [accessed September 25, 2018].

33 Stephen Bredwell, *A detection of Ed. Glouers hereticall confection* (London, 1586), 111.

34 *A pleasant commodie, called looke about you* (London, 1600), F1v.

35 Thomas Dekker, *Newes from Graues-end: sent to nobody* (London, 1604), A4r.

36 C.M. Briquet researched the date and makers of European paper in his now standard reference work, *Les Filigranes: Dictionnaire historique des Marques du Papier* (Geneva: A. Jullien, 1907), 4 vols.

37 I am indebted for this description to the work of Timothy Barrett and Cathleen Baker. See in particular Timothy G. Barrett, "European Papermaking Techniques 1300–1800" (2011) on Tim Barrett, Mark Ormsby, et al., *Paper through Time,* http://paper.lib.uiowa.edu/European.php; Baker, *From the Hand to the Machine.* On British papermaking and mills, see Alfred H. Shorter, *Paper Mills and Paper Makers in England 1495–1800* (Hilversum, Holland: Paper Publications Society, 1957); on the Whatman paper mill, see Fairbanks and Wilcox, *Papermaking and the Art of Watercolor.*

38 Temple Henry Croker, *The Complete Dictionary of Arts and Sciences* (London, 1765), 2:580.

39 William Blades, "On Paper and Paper-Marks," *The Library,* 1st ser., 1 (1889): 220.

40 R.W. Chapman lists the following charges per ream, ranked by size and quality, from sections 32 and 38 of this act, 10 Anne, c. 19: Atlas Fine, 16s; Atlas Ordinary, 8s; Imperial Fine, 16s; Super Royal Fine, 12s; Royal Fine, 8s; Medium Fine, 6s; Demy Fine, 4s; Demy Second, 2s. 6d; Demy Printing, 1s. 8d; Fine Fools Cap, 2s. 6d.; Second Fools Cap, 2s.; Superfine Pot, 2s.; Second Fine Pot, 1s. 6d. See R.W. Chapman, "An Inventory of Paper, 1674," *The Library* 4th ser., 7 (1927): 402.

41 William J. Ashworth, "Quality and the Roots of Manufacturing 'Expertise' in Eighteenth-Century Britain," *Osiris* 25 (2010): 243.

42 Hector, *The Handwriting of English Documents,* 17. Alfred Shorter tracks the emergent English paper industry in *Paper Mills and Paper Makers in England,* 27–31. For an account of the political complexities of importing paper from the Continent, and the founding of the Company of White Paper Makers, a monopoly chartered in 1686, see Allen T. Hazen, "Eustace Burnaby's Manufacture of White Paper in England," *The Papers of the Bibliographical Society of America* 48, no.4 (1954): 325–30.

43 Nos. 613, 625, 677, and 678, July 1568. *The Port and Trade of Early Elizabethan London: Documents* (London: London Record Society, 1972), 98–112. Accessed through *British History Online,* www.british-history.ac.uk/london-record-soc/vol8/pp98-112 [accessed August 8, 2018].

44 "James Whatman," *Oxford Dictionary of National Biography* [henceforth *ODNB*].

45 Fairbanks and Wilcox, *Papermaking and the Art of Watercolor in Eighteenth-Century Britain.*

46 Edward Topsell, *The history of four-footed beasts and serpents* (London, 1658), 1124.

47 Richard Head, *Proteus redivivus: or, the art of wheedling or insinuation* (London, 1675), 340.

48 James Howell, *Paroimiographia. Proverbs, or, old sayed sawes & adages* (London, 1659), 28.

49 "A catalogue of some other books lately printed for Will Marshall, and sold at the Bible in Newgate Street," in Isaac Chauncy, *Alexipharmacon: or, a fresh antidote against neonomian bane and poyson to the protestant religion* (London, 1700), A4v.

50 Edward Cocker, *The pen's triumph: being a copy-book, containing variety of examples of all hands practised in this nation according to the present mode* (London, 1659), B1v–B2r.

51 The authoritative source on early modern pens is Finlay, *Western Writing Implements.* On the British quill trade, see also Joe Nickell, *Pen, Ink, & Evidence: A Study of Writing and Writing Materials for the Penman, Collector, and Document Detective* (New Castle, Del.: Oak Knoll Press, 2003), 3. Quills can be plucked from geese during their annual molting period. For a discussion of farming geese for quills, the supply from Lincolnshire, Norfolk, and Somerset, and the importation of quills from Europe, see Finlay, 3–4.

52 Nickell, *Pen, Ink, & Evidence,* 4. Christopher De Hamel asks whether writers might not also simply have cut the nibs of their pens more finely. See *Scribes and Illuminators* (London: British Museum, 1992), 28–29.

53 Finlay, *Western Writing Implements,* 3–4.

54 Cocker, *The pen's triumph,* B2r.

55 Edward Cocker, *Multum in parvo. Or the pen's gallantrie* (London, 1660), 2.

56 "I send my lady her pen, an Italian book, a book of prayers. Send the silver pen which is broken, and it shall be mended quickly." In his next letter to Elizabeth, Ascham returned the pen, which he had mended. John Allen Giles, ed., *The Whole Works of Roger Ascham,* vol. 1, *Life and Letters* (London: John Russell Smith, 1865), 86–87.

57 "London Port Book, 1567–8: No. 298 (Jan 1568)," in *The Port and Trade of Early Elizabethan London,* 28–45. *British History Online,* http://www.british-history.ac.uk/london-record-soc/vol8/pp28-45.

58 Maygene Daniels, "The Ingenious Pen: American Writing Implements from the Eighteenth Century to the Twentieth," *The American Archivist* 43 (Summer 1980): 2.

59 Cocker, *The pen's triumph,* 23. For further information on iron gall ink and recipes, see Marie-France Lemay, "Iron Gall Ink," https://travelingscriptorium.library.yale.edu/2013/03/21/iron-gall-ink.

60 William Hill, Notebook, p. 22. England, 17th century. Osborn b234.

61 "Rules made by E.B. for his Children to learne to write bye," in Jehan de Beau-Chesne, *A booke containing diuers sortes of hands* (London, 1571). The book was first published in 1570; references here are to this 1571 edition.

62 George Gascoigne, "Certayne notes of instruction concerning the making of verse or ryme in English," in *The posies of George Gascoigne* (London, 1575).

63 Roger Ascham, *The scholemaster or plaine and perfite way of teachyng children* (London, 1570), 43v.

64 Daniel Starza Smith, "Wax seals," Bess of Hardwick's Letters, https://www.bessofhardwick. org; Jana Dambrogio, Daniel Starza Smith, et al., *Dictionary of Letterlocking* (DoLL; 2016; https:// letterlocking.org/dictionary); Daybell, *The Material Letter*, 50–51, 105–7.

65 John Locke, *A new method of making common-place-books* (London, 1706), 4.

66 On the affective significance of manuscript forms, and particularly of letters, see the work of Heather Wolfe and Jana Dambrogio.

67 This is a very cursory introduction to the field of bindings. For further information, see the Selected Bibliography, and particularly the work of Mirjam Foot, David Pearson, Nicholas Pickwoad, Aaron Pratt, and Paula Zyats.

68 Jeffrey Todd Knight, "'Furnished for Action': Renaissance Books as Furniture," *Book History* 12 (2009): 51.

69 Leedham-Green, *Books in Cambridge Inventories* 1:xvi.

70 Burnett Hillman Streeter, *The Chained Library: A Survey of Four Centuries in the Evolution of the English Library* (1931; New York: Cambridge University Press, 2011), xiii.

71 Ibid., "Synopsis," 1.

72 Mateo Alemán, *The rogve: or the second part of the life of Guzman de Alfarache* (London, 1623), 6.

73 Ireland, *Confessions*, 46–48, 105.

74 On the Inns of Court, see Wilfrid R. Prest, *The Inns of Court under Elizabeth I and the Early Stuarts, 1590–1640* (Totowa, N.J.: Rowman and Littlefield, 1972); Jayne Elisabeth Archer, Elizabeth Goldring, and Sarah Knight, eds., *The Intellectual and Cultural World of the Early Modern Inns of Court* (Manchester, UK: Manchester University Press, 2011).

75 Harold Love, *Scribal Publication in Seventeenth-Century England* (Oxford: Clarendon Press, 1993), 225.

76 On Hale, see Alan Cromartie, *Sir Matthew Hale, 1609–1676: Law, Religion and Natural Philosophy* (Cambridge: Cambridge University Press, 1995).

77 On amanuenses and note-taking in particular, see Ann Blair, "Early Modern Attitudes toward the Delegation of Copying and Note-Taking," in *Forgetting Machines: Knowledge Management Evolution in Early Modern Europe,* ed. Alberto Cevolini (Leiden: Brill, 2016), 265–85.

78 Blair, *Too Much to Know*, 104.

79 Richard Mulcaster, *Positions wherin those primitiue circumstances be examined, which are necessarie for the training up of* children (London, 1581), 34.

80 Richard Mulcaster, *The first part of the elementarie which entreateth chefelie of the right writing of our English tung* (London, 1582), *[iv]v.

81 This reading follows the argument of Richard Helgerson, *Forms of Nationhood: The Elizabethan Writing of England* (Chicago: University of Chicago Press, 1992). Jonathan Goldberg covers similar ground, although Jacques Derrida occasionally muscles Mulcaster to one side, in his *Writing Matter: From the Hands of the English Renaissance* (Stanford: Stanford University Press, 1991), esp. 38.

82 The best historical resource on English writing masters remains Ambrose Heal, *The English Writing-Masters and Their Copy-Books, 1570–1800: A Biographical Dictionary and a Bibliography* (Hildesheim: G. Olms, 1931). For a critical analysis, strongly influenced by the work of Jacques Derrida, see also Goldberg, *Writing Matter*, and Goldberg's related work.

83 Lynn Shepherd, "'Our family has indeed been strangely discomposed': Samuel Richardson, Joseph Highmore and the Conversation Piece in *Clarissa*," *Journal for Eighteenth-Century Studies* 31 (2008): 451–72.

84 The Yale Center for British Art impression of the engraving is from the second edition of 1762; the British Museum impression is from the first edition of 1745. See BM 1847,0306.13.

85 Samuel Richardson, *Pamela; or, virtue rewarded* (London, 1741), 1:3.

86 Jan Golinski, "Enlightenment Science," in *The Oxford Illustrated History of Science*, ed. Iwan Rhys Morus (Oxford: Oxford University Press, 2017), 187.

87 "James Woodhouse," *ODNB*.

88 This approach differs somewhat from that taken by authorities such as Albert Derolez, who distinguishes more concertedly between the two, defining "hand" as "the personal shape of a scribe's handwriting, whereas Script is the model

he [the scribe] has in mind" in the glossary to his magisterial *The Palaeography of Gothic Manuscript Books*, xx.

89 "The informal cursive script, called Old Roman Cursive, used for administrative purposes, correspondence and as everyday handwriting, even for graffiti at Pompeii, was also derived from Capitals, written rapidly with a tendency to fragment letters and favouring greater fluidity or angularity of forms depending on whether a pen or a stylus was being used" (Michelle P. Brown, *A Guide to Western Historical Scripts from Antiquity to 1600* [Toronto: University of Toronto Press, 1993], 14).

90 Derolez, *The Palaeography of Gothic Manuscript Books*, 123–24.

91 For a study of a scrivener in Newcastle-upon-Tyne during the 1636 plague outbreak, see Keith Wrightson, *Ralph Tailor's Summer: A Scrivener, His City, and the Plague* (New Haven: Yale University Press, 2011).

92 See Blayney, *The Stationers' Company and the Printers of London* 1:1.

93 "Rawlinson MS. D51: Letters Patent of incorporation, 1616/17," in *Scriveners' Company Common Paper 1357–1628 with a continuation to 1678*, ed. Francis W. Steer (London: London Record Society, 1968), 80–91. *British History Online*, http://www.british-history.ac.uk/london-record-soc/vol4/pp80-91 [accessed June 28, 2018].

94 Petti, *English Literary Hands*, 21.

95 As Peter Blayney observes, scriveners specialized in legal documents: "Although the word *scrivener* was sometimes used as an unspecialized synonym for *writer* and might thus be applied to any professional penman, by the fifteenth century its primary meaning was much the same as modern *solicitor*, and it denoted a writer of legal deeds as distinct from other kinds of manuscript" (*The Stationers' Company and the Printers of London* 1:1).

96 "A Bill of writings made for Col. Thomas Howard," 1666–67. Clayton Papers, 1589–1824. OSB MSS 40, Folder 13.

97 Barbara Shailor highlights the "biting," or overlapping proximity, of letterforms in northern European script in the medieval period, with "a sharp and angular style in which the letters appeared to be woven together to form a line, hence the name given to the script, *littera textura* (Latin: *texere*, to weave)" (Shailor, *The Medieval Book*, 30).

98 Parkes, *Their Hands before Our Eyes,* 45–49. Parkes notes that scribes might be paid either by the quire or by the pecia.

99 Blayney cites the petition in 1403 to the mayor and aldermen of London, from the "good men of the mistery of Writers of Text Letter, those commonly called Limners, and other good people, citizens of London, who used to bind and sell books" (*The Stationers' Company and the Printers of London* 1:4–5).

100 Ibid., 1:4–11.

101 John Stow, "Of orders and customes of the Citizens," in *A Survey of London. Reprinted From the Text of 1603,* ed. C.L. Kingsford (Oxford, 1908), 79–91. *British History Online,* http://www.british-history.ac.uk/no-series/survey-of-london-stow/1603/pp79-91 [accessed June 27, 2018].

102 Thomas Nashe, *Nashes Lenten stuffe* (London, 1599), 9.

103 Gabriel Harvey, *Foure letters, and certaine sonnets: especially touching Robert Greene* (London, 1592), 60.

104 Petti, *English Literary Hands,* 8–9.

105 On Matthew Parker and the recovery of Old English, see Wright, "The Dispersal of the Monastic Libraries," 208–37; Benedict Scott Robinson, "'Darke speech': Matthew Parker and the Reforming of History," *The Sixteenth Century Journal* 29 (1998): 1061–83.

106 Matthew Parker, *A testimonie of antiquitie* (London, 1566), Ciiir.

107 Parkes, *English Cursive Book Hands,* xiii–xiv; Eric Kwakkel, "A New Type of Book for a New Type of Reader: The Emergence of Paper in Vernacular Book Production," *The Library* 4 (2003): 219–48.

108 On the emergence of the vernacular book in fifteenth-century Britain (and, by extension, Europe), see Parkes. On Caxton, see Lotte Hellinga, *William Caxton and Early Printing in England* (London: The British Library, 2010); Paul Needham, *The Printer & the Pardoner: An Unrecorded Indulgence Printed by William Caxton for the Hospital of St. Mary Rounceval, Charing Cross* (Washington, D.C.: Library of Congress, 1986); and, on Caxton's influence as publisher and translator, Blayney, *The Stationers' Company and the Printers of London* 1:28–33

109 On the "Gothic" and typography, see especially the work of Joseph A. Dane, as for instance his, with Svetlana Djananova, "The Typographical

Gothic: A Cautionary Note on the Title Page to Percy's *Reliques of Ancient English Poetry,*" *Eighteenth-Century Life* 29 (2005): 79–97.

110 "This script has never been given a name. Scripts of this kind have usually been referred to in England as 'Court Hands,' or 'Charter Hands.' However, since the several varieties of this script are peculiar to manuscripts produced in England in the fourteenth and the fifteenth centuries, I propose to call it 'Anglicana'" (Parkes, *English Cursive Book Hands,* xvi).

111 On script in handwriting manuals, see particularly Aileen Douglas, *Work in Hand: Script, Print, and Writing, 1690–1840* (Oxford: Oxford University Press, 2017), and the work of Peter Stallybrass.

112 A letter dated March 16, 1554, from Elizabeth I, as princess, to her sister Queen Mary I. National Archives, EXT 11/25. Cited from http://www.nationalarchives.gov.uk/palaeography/doc1/default.htm.

113 B.L. Ullman, *The Origin and Development of Humanistic Script* (Rome: Edizioni di Storia e letteratura, 1960).

114 "Elizabeth I," *ODNB.*

115 James Daybell, *Women Letter-Writers in Tudor England* (Oxford: Oxford University Press, 2006), 65, n.19.

116 Heather Wolfe, "Women's Handwriting," in *The Cambridge Companion to Early Modern Women's Writing,* ed. L.L. Knoppers (Cambridge: Cambridge University Press, 2009), 27–29.

117 Henry Woudhuysen, "The Queen's Own Hand: A Preliminary Account," in *Elizabeth I and the Culture of Writing,* ed. Peter Beal and Grace Ioppolo (London: British Library, 2007), 13, cited in Jonathan Gibson, "The Queen's Two Hands," in *Representations of Elizabeth I in Early Modern Culture,* ed. Alessandra Petrina and Laura Tosi (Basingstoke, UK: Palgrave Macmillan, 2011), 58–59.

118 Gibson, 59.

119 *A new case put to an old lawyer, or, lawyers look about you* (London, 1656), 12.

120 Hector, *The Handwriting of English Documents,* 66–67.

121 John H. Fisher, "Chancery and the Emergence of Standard Written English in the Fifteenth Century," *Speculum* 52 (1977): 875–77. See also Malcolm Richardson, "Henry V, the English Chancery, and Chancery English," *Speculum* 55

(1980): 726–50. For a critical view of Fisher's thesis, see Michael Benskin, "Chancery Standard," in *New Perspectives on English Historical Linguistics,* vol. 2, ed. Christian Kay, Carole Hough, and Irené Wotherspoon (Amsterdam: John Benjamins Publishing Company, 2004), 1–40.

122 See www.nationalarchives.gov.uk/palaeography/pdf/doc_10.pdf.

123 Fisher, "Chancery and the Emergence of Standard Written English," 872.

124 For Burghley's retirement, and the performance in which the mock charter was used, see John Strype, *Annals of the reformation and establishment of religion, and other various occurrences in the Church of England* 4 (London, 1731), 77–78; and E.K. Chambers, *The Elizabethan Stage* 2 (Oxford: Clarendon Press, 1923), 247–48.

125 "The Great Seal of Elizabeth I," http://www.nationalarchives.gov.uk/education/resources/elizabeth-monarchy/the-great-seal-of-elizabeth-i.

126 N. Denholm-Young, *Handwriting in England and Wales* (Cardiff: University of Wales Press, 1954), 75.

127 John Ayres, *The accomplished clerk, or, accurate pen-man: a new copy book containing variety of usefull examples shewing ye most natural and clerk like way of writing all the usual hands of England* (London: sould by ye author, [1683?]), dedication.

128 Aileen Douglas discusses the gender associations of round hand in *Work in Hand: Script, Print, and Writing.*

129 Petti, *English Literary Hands,* 22.

130 Daybell, *The Material Letter,* 102.

131 Keith Thomas, "Numeracy in Early Modern England: The Prothero Lecture," *Transactions of the Royal Historical Society* 37 (1987): 103–32.

132 Robert Recorde, *The grou[n]d of artes* (London, 1543). Hilary Jenkinson, "The Use of Arabic and Roman Numerals in English Archives," *The Antiquaries Journal* 6 (1926): 263–75; Thomas, "Numeracy in Early Modern England"; Kathryn James, "Reading Numbers in Early Modern England," *Journal of the British Society for the History of Mathematics* 26 (2011): 1–16.

133 Jenkinson, "Use of Arabic and Roman Numerals," 267.

134 Gervase Markham, *The English husbandman* (London, 1635), 9.

135 Jenkinson, "Use of Arabic and Roman Numerals," 266.

136 ESTC 6445.5. Works on sixteenth-century English penmanship guides include Simran Thadani, "'For the Better Atteyning to Faire Writing': An Analysis of Two Competing Writing-Books, London, 1591," *The Papers of the Bibliographical Society of America* 107 (2013): 422–66. Thomas Vautrollier was a French émigré who had also worked for a year as a London agent for Christopher Plantin, distributing and selling books from his press. See A.E.M. Kirwood, "Richard Field, Printer, 1589–1624," *The Library,* 4th ser., 12 (June 1931): 2.

137 Pepys Library, Magdalene College, Cambridge, MS 2983, f. 325.

138 *The English schole-master or certaine rules and helpes, whereby the natives of the Netherlandes, may bee, in a short time, taught to read, understand, and speake, the English tongue* (Amsterdam, 1646), 126.

139 Ezekias Woodward, *A light to grammar, and all other arts and sciences* (London, 1641), 50.

140 Ibid, 53.

141 Folger Shakespeare Library V.b.292. Heather Wolfe has identified a third pupil, Anna Dowe, in 1689, whose copybook was offered for sale at Sotheby's, March 27, 1972, lot 23.

142 Charles Dickens, "A Visit to Newgate," in *Sketches by Boz* (London, 1836), 118. Dickens visited Newgate Prison in November 1835, writing his wife about the visit on November 5 (British Library Additional MS 43689; https://www.bl.uk/collection-items/letters-about-newgate-from-charles-dickens-to-his-wife-catherine-1835). His essay was published in February 1836 in *Sketches by Boz* (1836). See Philip Collins, "Newgate," in his *Dickens and Crime,* 3rd ed. (New York: St. Martin's Press, 1994), 27.

143 Thomas Dekker, *Newes from Hell; brought by the Diuells carrier* (London, 1606), B2; and Thomas Dekker, *The guls horne-booke* (London, 1609), A3r.

144 *Camp-bell: or the ironmongers faire field: A pageant at the installation of Sir Thomas Cambell in the office of Lord Mayor of London, 29 Oct. 1609* (London, 1609), B1v.

145 See H.R. Woudhuysen, "Writing-Tables and Table-Books," *Electronic British Library Journal* (2004): 9. On erasable writing tablets, see Stallybrass, Chartier, Mowery, and Wolfe,

"Hamlet's Tables and the Technologies of Writing in Renaissance England."

146 *Hamlet,* Act II, Scene 2, lines 140–48, 151.

147 There is a large and growing literature on early modern reading practices, with particular attention paid to note-taking and notebooks, and this note and the Selected Bibliography refer readers only to a few of the many contributions to this field, as a starting point for further reading. On humanist reading, see the formative essay by Lisa Jardine and Anthony Grafton, "'Studied for Action': How Gabriel Harvey Read His Livy," *Past & Present,* no. 129 (1990): 30–78. On commonplace books, see Ann Moss, *Printed Commonplace-Books and the Structuring of Renaissance Thought* (Oxford: Clarendon Press, 1996), and, for the example of Milton, Thomas Fulton, *Historical Milton: Manuscript, Print, and Political Culture in Revolutionary England* (Amherst: University of Massachusetts Press, 2010). On reading and note-taking habits, see in particular Ann M. Blair, *Too Much to Know*, and her "Early Modern Attitudes toward the Delegation of Copying and Note-Taking," in *Forgetting Machines: Knowledge Management Evolution in Early Modern Europe,* ed. Alberto Cevolini (Leiden: Brill, 2016), 265–85.

148 See H.R. Woudhuysen, *Sir Philip Sidney and the Circulation of Manuscripts, 1558–1640* (Oxford: Clarendon Press, 1996), 45–48; E.S. Leedham-Green, *Books in Cambridge Inventories.*

149 Ann Blair, "The Rise of Note-Taking in Early Modern Europe," *Intellectual History Review* 20 (2010): 309.

150 Randall L. Anderson, "Metaphors of the Book as Garden in the English Renaissance," *The Yearbook of English Studies* 33 (2003): 248–49.

151 Lucia Dacome, "Noting the Mind: Commonplace Books and the Pursuit of the Self in Eighteenth-Century Britain," *Journal of the History of Ideas* 65 (2004): 606–7. Dacome notes that Locke's notebooks show him continuing to adapt his commonplacing system, as he also struggled with the exasperating question of how to make best use of space within the commonplace book categories.

152 *A new method of making common-place-books; written by the late learned Mr. John Lock, author of the Essay concerning Humane Understanding* (London: Printed for J. Greenwood, 1706), 4–5.

153 "Despite, or perhaps because of, their differing emphases, the prescriptions for

commonplace-books to be found in the works of Erasmus, Melanchthon, and Vives were published together as excerpts in manuals *De ratione studii.* Their presence there, together with other examples of good practice in the matter of education, points us to the schoolroom environment within which boys were conditioned to think in ways determined by the instrument they used to probe material they were set to study, store in their memory, and retrieve for reproduction, that is to say, by their commonplace-book" (Moss, *Printed Commonplace-Books,* 134).

154 The set of notes shown in fig. 182 concerns a dispute over claims to the Abergavenny peerage heard before the Court of Chivalry (the legal forum for matters relating to questions of hereditary title or the peerage). William Camden, recently appointed to the office of Clarenceaux herald, was overseeing the proceedings of the case for the court for the Earl Marshal, an office held at that point by Robert Devereux, 2nd Earl of Essex. See Richard Cust, *Charles I and the Aristocracy* (Cambridge: Cambridge University Press, 2013), 21.

155 Francis Meres, *Palladis tamia, wits treasury* (London, 1598), Oo1v–Oo2r.

156 Ibid., Oo2r.

157 John Aubrey, *"Brief Lives," chiefly of Contemporaries, set down by John Aubrey, between the Years 1669 & 1696,* ed. Andrew Clark (Oxford: Clarendon Press, 1898), ; see Project Gutenberg at http://www.gutenberg.org/files/47787/47787-h/47787-h.htm.

158 On anonymity, see Marcy L. North, "Rehearsing the Absent Name: Reading Shakespeare's Sonnets through Anonymity," in *The Faces of Anonymity: Anonymity and Pseudonymous Publication from the Sixteenth to the Twentieth Century,* ed. R.J. Griffin (New York: Palgrave Macmillan, 2003), 19–38, and *The Anonymous Renaissance: Cultures of Discretion in Tudor-Stuart England* (Chicago: University of Chicago Press, 2003).

159 Adam Smyth, "'Art Reflexive': The Poetry, Sermons, and Drama of William Strode (1601?–1645)," *Studies in Philology* 103 (2006): 437. See also Smyth, *"Profit and Delight": Printed Miscellanies in England, 1640–1682* (Detroit: Wayne State University Press, 2004).

160 See Margreta de Grazia, *Shakespeare Verbatim,* for a discussion of the effect of later scholarship on the formation of an early modern English literary canon.

161 Arthur F. Marotti, "The Circulation of Verse at the Inns of Court and in London in Early Stuart England," in *Re-evaluating the Literary Coterie, 1580–1830*, ed. Will Bowers and Hannah Leah Crummé (London: Palgrave Macmillan UK, 2016), 53. See also Marotti, *Manuscript, Print, and the English Renaissance Lyric* (Ithaca: Cornell University Press, 1995); Love, *Scribal Publication in Seventeenth-Century England;* Woudhuysen, *Sir Philip Sidney and the Circulation of Manuscripts.*

162 See also Jason Scott-Warren, "Reconstructing Manuscript Networks: The Textual Transactions of Sir Stephen Powle," in *Communities in Early Modern England: Networks, Place, Rhetoric,* ed. Alexandra Shepard and Phil Withington (Manchester: Manchester University Press, 2000), 18–37.

163 Michelle O'Callaghan examines a professional compilation alongside an owner's long-term assemblage in her "Collecting Verse: 'Significant Shape' and the Paper-Book in the Early Seventeenth Century," *Huntington Library Quarterly* 80 (2017): 309–24.

164 Marcy L. North, "Household Scribes and the Production of Literary Manuscripts in Early Modern England," *Journal of Early Modern Studies* 4 (2015): 133–57. See also Ann Blair, "Hidden Hands: Amanuenses and Authorship in Early Modern Europe," *A.S.W. Rosenbach Lectures in Bibliography* 8 (2014), http://repository.upenn.edu/rosenbach/8.

165 Mary Morrissey, "Sermon-Notes and Seventeenth-Century Manuscript Communities," *Huntington Library Quarterly* 80 (2017): 295.

166 Ibid., 296.

167 Ian Green, "Preaching in the Parishes," in *The Oxford Handbook of the Early Modern Sermon,* ed. Peter McCullough, Hugh Adlington, and Emma Rhatigan (Oxford: Oxford University Press, 2011), 151.

168 Jeanne Shami, "New Manuscript Texts of Sermons by John Donne," *English Manuscript Studies 100–1700* 13 (2007): 112; cited in Shami, "Women and Sermons," in ibid., 165. On the Marvell sermon, see Michael Craze, *The Life and Lyrics of Andrew Marvell* (New York: Palgrave Macmillan, 1979), 3.

169 Elizabeth Grey, Countess of Kent, *A true gentlewomans delight* (London, 1653), 108.

170 Locke, *A new method of making commonplace-books* (London, 1706).

171 The wooden binding boards are tannic (just like the oak galls, for iron gall ink). If not covered, they will, over time, stain whatever is against them. These discolorations on endpapers can often be used to gauge whether a book is in its original boards: if the size and shape of the stains on the facing pages don't match the boards, then the book is likely not in its original binding.

172 Adam G. Hooks, "Re-membering Shakespeare" (April 2012); http://www.adamghooks.net/2012/04/re-membering-shakespeare.html.

173 I am grateful to Dana Kovarik (Ph.D. student in English, University College London) for suggesting these two examples of the manicule. On the manicule, or fist, see also William H. Sherman, "Toward a History of the Manicule," in his *Used Books: Marking Readers in Renaissance England* (Philadelphia: University of Pennsylvania Press, 2008).

174 See David Scott Kastan, "Opening Gates and Stopping Hedges: Grafton, Stow, and the Politics of Elizabethan History Writing," in *The Project of Prose in Early Modern Europe and the New World,* ed. Elizabeth Fowler and Roland Greene (Cambridge and New York: Cambridge University Press, 1997), 66–79. I am grateful to Emily Yankowitz (Yale Ph.D. student in History) for highlighting Stow's comment.

175 H.J. Jackson discusses Piozzi's annotations in *Marginalia: Readers Writing in Books* (New Haven: Yale University Press, 2001).

176 Tiffany Stern (Shakespeare Institute, University of Birmingham), private communication to the Elizabethan Club, Yale University (January 10, 2019).

177 Peter Beal, *A Dictionary of English Manuscript Terminology: 1450 to 2000* (Oxford: Oxford University Press, 2008), 294.

178 *OED,* "pen-trial."

179 Phillip Pulsiano, "Jaunts, Jottings, and Jetsam in Anglo-Saxon Manuscripts," *Florilegium* 19 (2002): 193.

180 Love, *Scribal Publication in Seventeenth-Century England;* Rachel Scarborough King, "The Manuscript Newsletter and the Rise of the Newspaper, 1665–1715," *Huntington Library Quarterly* 79 (2016): 415–16; Marotti, *Manuscript, Print, and the English Renaissance Lyric;* Noah Millstone, *Manuscript Circulation and the Invention of Politics in Early Stuart England* (Cambridge: Cambridge University Press, 2016); Woudhuysen, *Sir Philip Sidney and the Circulation of Manuscripts.*

181 Thomas Nashe, *The terrors of the night or, a discourse of apparitions* (London, 1594), Aij-r–[Aij-v]. Cited from Early English Books Online; original reference from Love, *Scribal Publication in Seventeenth-Century England,* 76–77. A "nouerint" or noverint was a writ (*OED*).

182 Finding aid for the Pole Family News Collection, MS.1951.021, Clark Library, UCLA.

183 On the post before the reign of Charles I, see Daybell, *The Material Letter,* 109–47.

184 Love, *Scribal Publication in Seventeenth-Century England,* 47.

185 For an introduction to composition and printing, see Philip Gaskell, *A New Introduction to Bibliography* (New Castle, Dela.: Oak Knoll Press, 1995). On typography, see Robert Bringhurst, *The Elements of Typographic Style,* 4th ed. (Point Roberts, Wash.: Hartley & Marks, 2012).

186 Eva Guggemos, "Compositor's Copy of Simon Segar's *Honores Anglicani,*" *Yale University Library Gazette* 78 (2004): 164.

187 Jana Dambrogio, "Historic Letterlocking: The Art and Security of Letter Writing," *Book Arts Arts du Livre Canada* 5 (2014): 21–23; Daybell, *The Material Letter;* Daniel Starza Smith, "The Material Features of Early Modern Letters: A Reader's Guide," Bess of Hardwick's Letters, https://www.bessofhardwick.org/background.jsp?id=143; Susan E. Whyman, *The Pen and the People: English Letter Writers 1660–1800* (Oxford: Oxford University Press, 2009).

188 William Fulwood, *The enimie of idlenesse* (London, 1568), sig. [Aviii-v].

189 For more information on seals, postage, and other features of the material letter, see Starza Smith, "The Material Features of Early Modern Letters."

190 Dambrogio has studied the methods used to fold and seal letters to send, using the term letterlocking for "the process by which a substrate such as paper, parchment, or papyrus has been folded and secured shut to function as its own envelope" (Dambrogio, "Historic Letterlocking," 21).

191 See Daybell, *The Material Letter,* 6. See also Heather Wolfe, "'Neatly Sealed, with Silk, and Spanish Wax or Otherwise': The Practice of Letter-Locking with Silk Floss in Early Modern England," in *In the Prayse of Writing: Early Modern Manuscript Studies. Essays in Honour of Peter Beal,* ed. S.P. Cerasano and Steven W. May (London: The British Library, 2012), 169–89. On letter-writing generally, see also Stewart and Wolfe, *Letterwriting in Renaissance England,* and Whyman, *The Pen and the People.*

192 Walter Money, *Collections for the History of the Parish of Speen, in the County of Berks* (Newbury: W.J. Blacket, 1892), 21.

193 On Clayton and banking, see Frank T. Melton, *Sir Robert Clayton and the Origins of English Deposit Banking 1658–1685* (Cambridge: Cambridge University Press, 1986).

194 The original was presented ca. 1572 by Elizabeth to her political minister and secretary, Francis Walsingham. On the portrait, see Margaret Aston, *The King's Bedpost: Reformation and Iconography in a Tudor Group Portrait* (Cambridge: Cambridge University Press, 1994), 128–29; Roy Strong, *Gloriana: The Portraits of Queen Elizabeth I* (New York: Thames and Hudson, 1987); Helen Hackett, "A New Image of Elizabeth I: The Three Goddesses Theme in Art and Literature," *Huntington Library Quarterly* 77 (2014): 225–56; and Lisa Ford, "Art in Context: Lisa Ford on *Allegory of the Tudor Succession: The Family of Henry VIII*" (2012), https://www.youtube.com/watch?v=vpomtLONkUk.

195 "An Acte against the forgyng of Euidences and Wrytynges," *Anno qvinto reginae Elizabethe. At the Parliament holden at Westmynster the xii. of Ianuary, in the fyfth yere of the raigne of our soueraigne lady, Elizabeth* (London, 1564); STC (2nd ed.) / 9464.5, 48v.

196 Alexander M. Burrill, *A New Law Dictionary and Glossary,* Pt. 1 (New York: John S. Voorhies, 1850), 206.

197 "English translation of Magna Carta," The British Library (July 28, 2014); https://www.bl.uk/magna-carta/articles/magna-carta-english-translation.

198 "Introduction to Deeds," Manuscripts and Special Collections, Universiy of Nottingham, https://www.nottingham.ac.uk/manuscriptsandspecialcollections/researchguidance/deeds/introduction.aspx.

199 John Willis, *Mnemonica; or, the art of memory, drained out of the pure fountains of art & nature. Digested into three books* (London: Leonard Sowersby, 1661), 32. Wing W2812

200 R.B. Outhwaite, *The Rise and Fall of the English Ecclesiastical Courts, 1500–1800* (Cambridge: Cambridge University Press, 2006); Bryan A. Garner, ed., *Black's Law Dictionary* (St. Paul, Minn.: Thomson Reuters, 2011).

201 The terms of statute H.8.an.21.c.5 are as follows: "that the (1) executor or executors named by the persons, two at the least, to whom the person dying was indebted, or made any legacy, and upon their refusal or absence, two other honest persons, in their presence, and by their discretions shall make, or cause to be made, a true and perfect inventory (2) of all the goods and chattels, wares, and merchandises, as well movable as not movable, whatsoever they were of the said person so deceased; and the (3) same shall cause to be indented, whereof one part shall be by his said executor upon (4) his oath to be taken before the bishop's *ordinaries,* their officials and *ordinaries,* or other person having power to take probate of the testament, upon the holy evangelists, to be good and true: and the same one part indented, shall present and deliver to the keeping of the said bishop, *ordinary,* or *ordinaries* or other person whatsoever, having power to take probate of testaments; and the other part of the said inventory indented, to remain with the executor: and that no bishop, *ordinary* or *ordinaries,* or other person whatsoever, having authority to take probate of testaments, upon pain in the said statue contained (viz. ten pounds) do refuse to take any such inventory to him or them presented or tendered, to be delivered as is aforesaid" (cited from Henry Swinburne, *A Treatise of Testaments and Last Wills; Compiled out of the Laws, Ecclesiastical, Civil, and Canon; as also out of the Common Laws, Customs, and Statutes, of this Realm,* vol. 2 [London: W. Clarke and Sons, 1803], 764–65). Jayne adds to this that "The relatively haphazard medieval practice of ecclesiastical authorities was thus given the added force of civil law, and at first the law was interpreted fairly strictly; most probate authorities took it to mean that every single book that the person owned must be listed by name. For anyone who died between 1521 and about 1590, therefore, the best chance of finding a detailed list of the books he owned is to find not his will but the inventory of his property at his death" (Sears Jayne, *Library Catalogues of the Renaissance* [Berkeley: University of California Press, 1956], 9).

202 Swinburne, *A Treatise of Testaments and Last Wills,* 790.

203 Elisabeth Leedham-Green studied the probate inventories of Cambridge to compile lists of book ownership, in her monumental *Books in Cambridge Inventories.* Catherine Delano Smith drew on Cambridge probate inventories to study map ownership, in her "Map Ownership in Sixteenth-Century Cambridge: The Evidence of Probate Inventories," *Imago Mundi* 47 (1995): 67–93.

204 John Bale to Matthew Parker, Cambridge University Library Additional MS 7489.

205 John Leland, *The laboryouse iourney [and] serche of Iohan Leylande, for Englandes antiquitees* (London : Printed by S. Mierdman for John Bale, [1549]), B1r.

206 A.N.L. Munby, *The Formation of the Phillipps Library up to the Year 1840,* vol. 3 in *Phillipps Studies* (Cambridge: Cambridge University Press, 1954), 48.

207 John Aubrey, cited in *Gentleman's Magazine* 183 (1847), 529. Aubrey goes on to imagine what had been lost: "Before the late warres a world of rare manuscripts perished hereabout; for within half a dozen miles of this place were the abbey of Malmesbury, where it may be presumed the library was as well furnished with choice copies as most libraries of England; and perhaps in this library we might have found a correct Pliny's Naturall History, which Canutus, a monk here, did abridge for King Henry the Second."

208 Smyth, *Material Texts in Early Modern England.*

209 In Beau-Chesne, *A booke containing diuers sortes of hands,* n.p.

210 Mabillon responded to Daniel Van Papenbroeck, the editor of the second volume (published in 1675) of the *Acta sanctorum,* a study of the documentary evidence underpinning the histories of saints' lives. Papenbroeck had disputed the authenticity of a Merovingian diploma, in the process casting doubt on the category overall. See Luciana Duranti, *Diplomatics: New Uses for an Old Science* (Lanham, Md.: The Scarecrow Press, Inc., 1998), 13.

211 Petti, *English Literary Hands,* 34.

... of ... tale in watter & then rule it in
... & so ... him

Or boyle ... in ... & rule it ...
... watter or ... & so ...

To make a good Red ruling Inke

Take fyne Brasill steepid to ponder and
seethe it in stronge stale lye and then
put a small quantitie of Alom therto &
use it

for wormes in dogge

Take mylke warme & put brimston
in ponder therto & so gyve it

for Cotton & [?]

Steepe Bay Salte in colde watter
to make it of a good Saltnes & put
therto so mee of other thynges to make
in dyvers colours & so gyve it twyse in
ij dayes & it will save him untill new may

Let peaches have barke upon them

LIST OF ILLUSTRATIONS

Unless otherwise noted, all illustrations are from works in the collections of the Beinecke Rare Book and Manuscript Library, Yale University.

Frontispiece

Detail, writing in reverse. William Hill, Notebook, p. 15. England, early 17th century. Osborn b234

Acknowledgments

Fig. 1. Scribal copy of 33 poems by John Donne, entitled Poems, with a few prose problems, p. 256. England, ca. 1620. Osborn b114

Introduction

Fig. 2. John Nixon, "The Oaken Chest or the Gold Mines of Ireland a Farce," 1796. BM Satires 8884. British Museum K,64.72. Reproduced with permission from the collections of the British Museum

Fig. 3. Detail of fig. 2

Fig. 4. Detail of fig. 2

Fig. 5. Sylvester Harding, "The Spirit of Shakspere appearing to his Detracters," 1796. BM Satires 8883. British Museum J,4.100. Reproduced with permission from the collections of the British Museum

Fig. 6. William Henry Ireland's forgery of Shakespeare's annotations in a copy of Edmund Spenser's *The faerie qveene* (1590). 2014 160

Fig. 7. Engravings of Shakespeare's signatures. From George Steevens, ed., *The plays of William Shakspeare* (London, 1778). 2000 3141

Fig. 8. Tracings and forgeries of Shakespeare's signature. From William Henry Ireland, An album of "The Shakespearian productions," 1805. Osborn fd83

Fig. 9. Document signed by Elizabeth I, on April 7, 1593, directing Sir Thomas Heneage to pay 133 6 s 8d to Richard Fletcher, Bishop of Worcester. Osborn fa64

Fig. 10. Engraving of Elizabeth's signatures and a comparison of her "spurious" and "genuine" Alphabet. From Edmond Malone, *An inquiry into the authenticity of certain miscellaneous papers and legal instruments* (London, 1796), facing p. 111. Tinker 1520

Fig. 11. "The mape off Ynglonnd." Astronomical and astrological treatises, f. 47v–48r. England, mid-16th century. Beinecke MS 558

Fig. 12. Two binding fragments of Aelfric, Catholic homilies. England, 11th century. Osborn fa26

Fig. 13. Detail, annotations in red crayon, probably by Matthew Parker (1504–1575). Chronicles of England, f. 13r. England, ca. 1420–50. Takamiya MS 29

Fig. 14. Detail, a reader's account of expenses. Annotations in a copy of *Riders (1699.) British Merlin* (London, 1699), front free endpaper. OSB MSS 184, Box 23, Folder 175

Fig. 15. Detail, "God saue the kynge," by a professional writer, and copied by a student. Contemporary copy of a charter granted by Edward VI to the burgesses of Devizes. England, [Nov. 27, 1547]. Osborn a64

Fig. 16. Accounts, pen trials, and writing practice. Collection of accounts, receipts, memoranda, letters, and other documents, nearly all relating to Devonshire. England, ca. 1679–1716. Osborn b124

Part One: Writing Materials & Writers

Fig. 17. "To make inke" and an excerpt of the decorative "Cloven hande." Detail, William Hill, Notebook, pp. 12–13. England, early 17th century. Osborn b234

Fig. 18. Detail, John Foxe, *Actes and monuments of these latter and perillous dayes, touching matters of the Church* (London, 1563), p. 1714. Mey34 F83 +1563

Fig. 19. John Florio, *Florios second frutes* (London, 1591), p. 89. Hb50 3

Fig. 20. Detail, Thomas Blount, *Glossographia: or, A dictionary, interpreting all such hard words of whatsoever language, now used in our refined English tongue*, 2nd ed. (London, 1661), f. 12v. Ia742 656B

Fig. 21. Detail, William Shakespeare, "King John." From *Mr. William Shakespeares comedies, histories, & tragedies* (London, 1623), b5v. 1978 +83

Fig. 22. The end of a parchment roll, containing a copy of John Lydgate, The kings of England sithen William the Conqueror. England, 1475–99. Osborn a14

Fig. 311. "To make a good Red rulin Inke" and "For wormes in doggs." The Fawkners' Glasse, inside rear cover. England, ca. 1590–1620. Beinecke MS 100

Fig. 118. Detail, Elizabeth I, the 23rd heir to the throne. Morgan Colman, Genealogies of the kings of England. England, 1592. Osborn fa56

Fig. 119. An examination of the confessions of the conspirators in the Babington Plot, f. 1r. England, 1586. Osborn fa10

Fig. 120. Detail of fig. 119

Fig. 121. Carolingian minuscule. Pseudo-Isidore, Decretals. France, ca. 850–875. Beinecke MS 442

Fig. 122. Italian humanist hand. Francesco Martini, Tratti de architettura ingegneria e arte militare. Italy, early 16th century. Beinecke MS 491

Fig. 123. Attributed to Ralph Rabbards, Notebook [Inventions of military machines and other devices]. England, 16th century. Osborn a8

Fig. 124. Detail of fig. 123

Fig. 125. A student example of "Chancerie hande." Hill, Notebook, p. 9. Osborn b234

Fig. 126. Mock charter. England, May 10, 1591. Elizabethan Club, Yale University. Eliz MS Vault

Fig. 127. Detail of fig. 126

Fig. 128. Detail, "The third Satire," written in a mixed hand in a copy of John Donne's Satires and poems. England, ca. 1613. Osborn b458

Fig. 129. "Simplicities," written in a mixed hand in a tiny, pocket-sized notebook. Jestbook. England, 1640s. Osborn b430

Fig. 130. Serjant, Arithmetic and penmanship notebook. England, 1688. Osborn fb98

Fig. 131. Detail of fig. 130

Fig. 132. George Bickham, *Penmanship in its utmost beauty and extent* (London, 1731). Yale Center for British Art. Folio A Z1

Fig. 133. George Bickham, *The British monarchy; or, a new chorographical description of all the dominions subject to the king of Great Britain* (London, 1743). Ede +743

Fig. 134. "In Carlisle Bay, Barbados," detail of Samuel Barrington, A journal of the proceedings of the Hon. Samuel Barrington, rear admiral of the red and commander in chief of his majesty's ships and vessels... England, 1778–79. Osborn fc147

Fig. 135. Detail, William Butts' Dye Book. England, 1768–86. Osborn fc173

Fig. 136. Certificate of entrance into the East-India Company for Nathaniel Helly of Nuneaton, Warwickshire, aged 27 Years, 5 Feet 9 Inches high, Labourer. London, November 13, 1769. Osborn Manuscript File 19652

Fig. 137. Detail, showing the abbreviation Ma^te for "Majestie"; et, a precursor to the ampersand; wch and wth for "which" and "with"; y^u for "you." Volume of political papers, p. 33. England, ca. 1620–39. Osborn fb57

Fig. 138. Detail, showing the abbreviation y^e for "the" and the use of the tilde to abbreviate Parliament; w^thout and wch for "without" and "which"; y^t and y^e for "that" and "the." William Jephson to John Pym. Cork, October 15, 1642. Osborn fb94, Folder 6

Fig. 139. Detail, showing the use of a colon to mark a suspended ending. Copy of a narrative of the trial of Mary, Queen of Scots. England, ca. 1600. Osborn fb32

Fig. 140. John Rose, punctuation listed in a notebook. England, 1676. Osborn b227

Fig. 141. "Off Eclipses," Significatyon off Cometts," and "Judgment of wether by Diggs," f. 4v–5r. England, mid-16th century. Beinecke MS 558

Fig. 142. Detail of fig. 141, showing the virgule

Fig. 143. Detail of fig. 141, showing the colon

Fig. 144. Detail of fig. 141, showing the comma

Fig. 145. Detail of fig. 141, showing the period or full stop

Fig. 146. Detail, showing quotation marks in a collection of aphorisms. Collection of English proverbs, f. 43r. England, ca. 1654. Osborn fb77

Fig. 147. Detail, showing brackets in Marmaduke Rawdon, Commonplace book. England, ca. 1629–32. Osborn fb150

Fig. 148. Detail of a list, "Writings at Thornbury belonging to Stafford Duke of Buckingham." England, ca. 1520. Osborn fa41.2

Fig. 149. In a secretary's careful hand: "Paris August 16th S.N. [or stile nouveau, "new style"] 1684," with a note that "this day my Lord writ to Coll. Graham upon the affaire of Pickhall." Richard Graham, Viscount Preston, Letter book. Paris, 1684. Osborn fb83

Fig. 150. Detail, showing the abbreviation ins^t for "instant." OSB MSS 60

Fig. 151. Almanac table, including the start of Hilary term, in George Dew, "Ephemeris astrologikos, or an Almanack" for the year of the Redemption 1692. England, 1692. Osborn Manuscript File 19212

Fig. 152. "The moon her dominion, over man's body," in George Dew, "Ephemeris astrologikos, or an Almanack" for the year of the Redemption 1692. England, 1692. Osborn Manuscript File 19212

Fig. 153. Detail, Zodiac table. From "Judgment of wether by Diggs," f. 24r. England, mid-16th century. Beinecke MS 558

Fig. 154. Details (16), Astrological symbols. From "Judgment of wether by Diggs," f. 5r. England, mid-16th century. Beinecke MS 558

Figs. 155–156. Hill, Notebook, pp. 50–51. Osborn b234

Fig. 157. The Rothschild Canticles, 6v. Flanders or northern France, early 14th century. Beinecke MS 404

Fig. 158. "The order of casting accompts with counters." Hill, Notebook, p. 59. Osborn b234

Fig. 159. Multiplication table. Matthew Wood, Arithmetic notebook. England, 1700. Osborn fb179

Figs. 160–161. John Webb, Account book. England, 17th century. Yale Center for British Art. NA 25 W43 1630

Fig. 162. Student notes in the endpapers of a Latin grammar. John Brinsley, *The posing of the parts: or, a most plain and easie way of examining the accidence and grammar* (London, 1653), rear free and fixed endpaper. Gk4 3

Fig. 163. Detail, tangle of numbers and letters in a pen trial. State papers, p. 246. England, ca. 1620–39. Osborn fb57

Part Three: Case Studies

Fig. 164. Detail, a documentary altercation in Lewis Vaslet, "The Spoiled Child, Scene V." England, ca. 1802. Watercolor. Yale Center for British Art. B1977.14.4345

Fig. 165. Cover, John Hancock, Workbook for penmanship exercises. Boston, 1753. Gen MSS 764, Box 23, Folder 424

Fig. 166. "Duty Fear and Love." John Hancock, Workbook for penmanship exercises (see fig. 165)

Fig. 167. Serjant, Arithmetic and penmanship notebook, f. 169r. Osborn fb98

Fig. 168. "To make inke" and "Romayne hande." Hill, Notebook, pp. 4–5. Osborn b234

Fig. 169. Silver hornbook. United States (?), ca. 1750–75. Shirley +196

Fig. 170. Hornbook, showing the alphabet, syllables, and Lord's Prayer. United States (?), ca. 1725–50. Shirley 2565

Fig. 171. Verso of fig. 170, showing the image of a child holding the primer

GLOSSARY

I have made every effort to define all terms used in this book in as clear and useful a fashion as possible. Readers are also referred to the works listed in the Selected Bibliography for further discussion.

A

Abbreviation a formal shortening of a word or series of letters, used by scribes to write more quickly

Anglicana (court hand) a cursive hand prominent in England from the twelfth through the mid-fifteenth century, eventually overtaken in the early sixteenth century by secretary hand

Annotation a mark or note left by a reader on a book or document

Ascender (supralinear stroke) stroke rising above the baseline (e.g., *b, d, h* in modern English)

Autograph written in the author's own hand

B

Back the spine of a letter, as in *b, d, h*

Baseline a line, written or imagined, marking the bottom of the main section of the letterform

Bastard hand a hand mixing different forms of script

Bifolium a sheet folded in two

Binding structure the means by which the text block has been formed and attached to the exterior binding

Bite the point of contact between the lobes of two letters

Black letter a reference to the appearance of textura (a formal script in use from the thirteenth through sixteenth century) when used as a typeface in printing

Blotting paper paper not treated with sizing, and used as a blotting agent

Body the main part of a letterform

Book hand a category of hand associated with text, usually contrasted with documentary hand, or hands used for charters, contracts, and other legal forms

Bookplate a personal or institutional ownership statement on paper, usually affixed to the front fixed endpaper on a book

Buckle the response of parchment documents or bindings to humidity changes, stiffening and arching

Bundle a unit of measurement for paper, equal to 40 quires or 960 sheets

C

Calligraphic written in a formal, ornamental manner

Carbon ink ink made from soot, sourced either from lamp-black or another form of carbon, and mixed in a binding agent with gum arabic

Cartulary a collection of charters, often comprising the records of title and property documents kept by a monastic house or other institution

Chain line the impression left on a sheet of paper by the support wires of the paper mold

Chained binding a binding attached by a chain to a library book press or other reading stand

Chancery hand a hand associated with the clerks of Chancery court

Charter a type of formal legal document, usually granting a royal or legal privilege or incorporation

Chirograph a document separated into two interlocking parts, to be held by separate parties as evidence of a legal or other agreement (see fig. 50)

Club the broader end of a stroke, where ink has gathered

Codex a textual structure created by gatherings, stitched or attached at one side

Commonplace book a form of note-taking, usually in a bound notebook, in which notes are organized by topical headings and an index

Contraction a form of abbreviation, in which letters are omitted in a word, usually from the middle, e.g., Mrs, for mistress

Coppresse a term for iron sulfate, used in iron gall ink. "All gall, and coppresse, from his inke, he drayneth," Ben Jonson, *Ben: Ionson his Volpone or the foxe* (1607), A4v

Copybook a writing manual, often engraved, teaching how to write through exemplar hands and copy-texts

Copy-text "the text used as the basis of mine" (see Ronald McKerrow); the source text used by a scribe or printer in producing a copy

Fig. 312. Edward Collier, "A Letter Rack." England, 1695. Yale Center for British Art, Paul Mellon Fund. B2018.6. The Dutch painter Edwaert Colyer moved to London in 1693, later anglicizing his name to Edward Collier. He specialized in trompe l'oeil depictions of writing materials and texts, like this still life painting of a quill, penknife, seal, sealing wax, and comb, alongside a sealed parchment document, a sealed and unopened letter (stamped and dated by the penny post), and printed copies of a London newspaper and Parliamentary speech. On Collier, see Dror Wahrmann, *Mr. Collier's Letter Racks: A Tale of Art & Illusion at the Threshold of the Modern Information Age* (Oxford: Oxford University Press, 2012).

Coucher the worker transferring the sheet from the paper mold to the felt

Court hand any one of a set of hands used by particular English law courts

Cross-stroke a horizontal stroke to or across the stem of a letter

Cursive a style of writing in which the pen or writing instrument is lifted from the page as little as possible

D

Deckle the rough, uncut edge of a sheet of paper, formed by the thin tray of wood fitted around the paper mold

Decorate to add ornamental strokes, often in colored ink, to initials or other parts of the page

Deed a type of formal legal document, usually noting the ownership or tenure of property

Descender the stroke below the baseline on a letterform

Docket to identify or label a document on its exterior, for filing

Document a structure or format for a text, usually consisting of a single sheet of paper or parchment

Dos-à-dos a manuscript written "back to back," or in a different direction from each end of the volume

Downstroke a stroke of the pen downwards, usually thicker than the upstroke

Dry point marks or writing made, without ink, by pressure with a stylus or other instrument

Ductus the characteristic way in which an individual writes his or her hand

E

Endpapers the blank leaves placed at the beginning and end of a book (*OED*); usually described as fixed (pasted down to the rear board of the binding) and free (able to be turned)

Engrossing the process of creating a formal legal document

Exemplar the text (in whatever relationship to an original) used by a scribe

Eye-skip a common form of scribal error, in which a scribe skips a word when copying a text

F

Fair copy a perfect copy of a manuscript made for presentation

Felt the material on which a newly made sheet of paper is laid

Fist (see Manicule)

Flourish an ornamental stroke of the pen

Foliate (see Folio)

Folio a leaf, made from folding a sheet of parchment or paper once; text is usually written on the front (recto) and reverse (verso)

Fore-edge the front edge of the binding on a book, sometimes painted or decorated and displayed facing outward from a shelf or press

Format the defining structure and material character of a text object, e.g., folio, quarto, roll, codex

Furniture the guards, clasps, and other attachments to a volume

G

Gall (see Oak gall)

Gathering the unit made by a single sheet of paper, folded

Genre a type or category of text, e.g., indenture, sermon, drama, associated with particular textual characteristics or structure and recognizable to its intended audiences

Gilt a thin layer of gold leaf

Gothic a style of writing or printing associated (in the early modern period and later) with the medieval, sometimes also a negative association with the barbaric; for print, synonymous with black-letter

Graph a letter or character formed by the pen

Gum arabic a binding agent used in carbon ink and other ink recipes

Gutter the inner margin of a text, extending into the text block and binding

H

Hair side the outer side of a sheet of parchment, dehaired during the course of processing

Hand a term sometimes used interchangeably with *script*, to denote a style of writing, e.g., italic, and the ideal form of that style understood by a writer; more often used to describe the manner in which an individual writer manifests that style in his or her writing

Head/tail/body/foot terms referring to the parts of letterforms: the head, or central lobe, of a letter such as *a*; the tail, or trailing line of a letter such as *p*; the body, or main or central section, of a letterform; the foot/feet, or anchoring section(s), of a letter such as *m*

Headline in conjunction with the *baseline*, the real or imagined line at the top of the main body of a letterform or row of letters

Historiated decorated with figures or scenes, technically "given a story"; often used of initials

Holograph a manuscript written in the author's hand

I

Illuminate to paint or decorate with color or metallic leaf

Infralinear literally, below the line; denoting the lower line of letters such as *p* and *q*

Initial/medial/finial terms usually referring to the shape of the letter *s*, as it changes with its position in a word. A medial *s* will often take a long form, like the German Eszett (*ß*), by contrast with the short form of the initial/finial *s*

Inkhorn a portable container used to hold ink

Inkwell or ink stand a container for ink; by the mid-sixteenth century, sometimes a decorative piece or item of furniture

Iron gall ink a common form of ink for writing, produced from four primary ingredients: iron sulfate, gall nuts, gum Arabic, and water

Italic hand a fifteenth-century cursive hand, sometimes described as Italian or Italianate

L

Laid lines the impression left on a sheet of paper by the fine wires of the paper mold

Leaf the front and reverse of a page, formed by folding a sheet of paper

Letterform the shape of a letter

Ligature the stroke joining two letters, or two connected letters together forming a single letterform or character: e.g., *æ*

Lobe the rounded section of letters with round sections: e.g., *a, b, d*

M

Majuscule capital letter, as opposed to minuscule, or lowercase letter

Manicule a marginal note, in the shape of a hand or pointing finger, used as a nota bene

Margin the space (usually consistently measured and demarcated) framing the text in a page or opening

Marginalia a manuscript note, usually written in the margin of a book by a reader

Medial s an archaic form of s, taking elongated form; often the first in a double s

Membrane a piece of section of substrate, stitched with others into a length to form a roll, or scroll

Minim a single stroke of the pen

Minuscule at its most basic, a lowercase or small letter (as opposed to a majuscule, or capital letter)

Miscellany a gathering of separate texts, either of one genre (e.g., poetry) or several

Mold the frame, with a mesh of wire chain lines and laid lines, used to make paper

Morocco leather made from goatskin, used in book-bindings

N

N.S., New style dates dates calculated by the Gregorian calendar, which started on January 1; Europe switched to this calendar in 1582; England formally retained the Julian calendar, with a March 25 new year, until 1752. Dates between January 1 and March 25 are often demarcated as "N.S." or "O.S.," particularly by correspondents.

O

Oak gall (also gall or gall nuts) a spherical growth found on oak trees, formed in response to insects; used as a tannin in iron gall ink

Oblong a horizontal format

Octavo the text unit created when a sheet of paper is folded into eight

Opening the visual unit created by two pages of a codex, when opened

Ornament non-textual decoration added to a manuscript

O.S., Old style dates (see N.S., New style dates)

P

Page the basic unit within the codex, forming one side of an opening

Paginated the successive numbering of pages in a codex

Palimpsest layers of older text, overwritten on parchment or another substrate after it has been scraped to be reused or to erase mistakes

Paper mold the wooden frame, clad with mesh, used in hand papermaking

Papermaker's tears small spots, visible on sheets of paper, created when drops of water fall onto the sheet after it has been dipped

Paratext the textual and visual material that surrounds the main body of a published work, e.g., advertisements, footnotes, introduction, etc.

Parchment a writing substrate made from animal hide, usually sheep, cow, or goat, through being stripped, dried under tension, scraped, and polished

Pastedown a piece of parchment or paper used to cover the interior boards of a binding, and often of recycled manuscript or printed text

Pen trial the marks or textual excerpts made by writers testing the cut of their quill pens

Penknife a knife kept to shape and sharpen the nib of a quill pen

Pen-man a late-seventeenth-century term for a writing master or other form of professional writer

Penner a portable case used to carry pens and penknife

Pigment a substance, usually colored, prepared from mineral or organic substances, and with liquid to form a paint or dye

Pounce a fine powder used to prepare surfaces for writing, to prevent ink from spreading or sinking into the substrate

Pricking in the preparation of the substratum for writing, the holes made to rule lines on a page

Q

Quarto the text structure formed when a sheet of paper is folded into a unit of four

Quill pen a writing instrument made from the flight feather of a goose, swan, raven, or other bird

Quire sheets of paper or parchment folded to form a gathering of leaves; also used as a measurement, equal to 24 sheets or one twentieth of a ream

R

Ream a unit of paper measurement, equal to 20 quires

Recto the right or first side of a leaf of paper or parchment

Retted, retting the fermentation breaking down rags in the papermaking process

Roll (also scroll) a structure or format for a text, created of pieces (or membranes) of a material, usually parchment or paper, attached together in a linear textual structure that must be unfurled to be read

Round hand a hand emerging in the mid- to late seventeenth century, also known as copperplate; a recognizably modern or contemporary hand, the antecedent of twentieth-century formal scripts such as the Palmer cursive

Rubricate/rubrication to mark or color a writing surface in red

Ruling using graphite or ink to draw the boundaries and lines of a page

S

Salutation the greeting or opening of a letter

Sandarach gum-sandarach, or "sand," a resin added to pounce to stop the spread of ink

Script a particular style of handwriting

Seal the metal or stone instrument, often engraved, used to impress heated sealing wax to authorize or close a document

Sealing wax originally made from beeswax and resin; by the early modern period, made from imported shellac; melted, applied to a document, and impressed with a seal; used to authorize or close a document, such as a folded letter

Secretary hand a cursive script, most prominent in England from the mid-sixteenth century, and particularly advertised by writing masters

Serif the finishing strokes or cross strokes of a letter, often used in descriptions of typefaces or fonts

Set hand one of several possible types of formal script, used by formal or legal bodies

Sheet the basic unit of paper, as it is produced from the paper mold

Sink, sinking ink being absorbed into paper without the correct sizing

Size, sizing the gelatinous mixture used to coat paper and prepare it for manuscript, drawing, or print

Skin side the side of a leaf of parchment originally facing into the animal

Spur a gathering of sheets of paper (usually 7–8) hung to dry

Stab stitch a simple, straight stitch used to sew paper wrappers as a binding or to bind quires into a binding structure

Standish an inkwell; sometimes a table, with writing materials and ink (*OED*)

Stem the stroke at the backbone of a letter, supporting the ascender or descender

Stroke a mark made by the pen, without being lifted from the writing surface

Stuff the liquid mixture from which paper sheets are formed

Stylus a pointed object used as a writing instrument

Subscription the signature or signatures in a letter

Substratum the base material, usually parchment or paper, used as the surface for writing

Superscript a form of abbreviation, in which a letter is placed above another, to denote contraction or suspension, e.g., M^{rs} for mistress

Superscription the direction or address for a letter, usually on the outside

Supralinear literally, above the line; denoting the upper line of letters such as *d* and *h*

Suspension a form of abbreviation, in which a symbol or point denotes omitted letters, usually at the end

T

Text block the group of texts gathered together to be stitched as a single unit for binding

Textura a medieval hand, the basis of black letter; characterized by the use of individual strokes, lifting the pen from the writing surface, when forming the parts of a letter

Thorn a residual letterform from Old English, meaning the, and written in contemporary English as y^e

Tilde a form of punctuation, often used to mark missing letters in an abbreviated word

U

Upstroke a stroke of the pen upwards, often thin

Uterine vellum very fine, white parchment or vellum, previously believed to have been made from the hides of aborted calves or kids; recent DNA testing by the University of York has indicated that uterine vellum was made through the method of processing rather than the originating hide

V

Vatman the worker overseeing the dipping of the paper mold in a paper mill

Vellum another name for parchment

Verso the reverse side of a leaf of paper or parchment

Virgule a slash mark used to demarcate paragraph or verse breaks in manuscript

W

Wafer a thin dried paste of starch, used to seal letters or documents

Waste, manuscript pieces of disbound or otherwise destroyed manuscripts used as material in endpapers or bindings

Watermark a papermaker's mark, made with wire in the paper mold, and showing in relief in the finished sheet of paper

Wrapper a sheet, usually of paper or parchment, used as a soft binding around a text

X

Xylographic of or pertaining to a wood engraving (*OED*); a wood-carving or woodblock illustration

SELECTED BIBLIOGRAPHY

English Paleography

Hector, L.C. *The Handwriting of English Documents.* London: Edward Arnold, 1958; 1966.

Jenkinson, Hilary. *Palaeography and the Practical Study of Court Hand.* Cambridge: Cambridge University Press, 1915.

Leedham-Green, Elisabeth. "Early Modern Handwriting: An Introduction." In English Handwriting, 1500–1700: An Online Course. Ceres Online Publications Interactive [COPIA]. https://www.english.cam.ac.uk/ceres/ehoc/intro.html.

Petti, Anthony G. *English Literary Hands from Chaucer to Dryden.* Cambridge, Mass.: Harvard University Press, 1977.

Preston, Jean F., and Laetitia Yeandle. *English Handwriting, 1400–1650: An Introductory Manual.* Binghamton, N.Y.: Medieval & Renaissance Texts & Studies, 1992.

Wolfe, Heather. Early Modern Manuscripts Online. Washington, D.C.: Folger Shakespeare Library. https://emmo.folger.edu.

Manuscript Culture

Beal, Peter, ed. Catalogue of English Literary Manuscripts 1450–1700. CELM. http://www.celm-ms.org.uk.

Chartier, Roger. *The Author's Hand and the Printer's Mind.* Translated by Lydia G. Cochrane. Cambridge: Polity Press, 2014.

---. *The Order of Books: Readers, Authors, and Libraries in Europe between the Fourteenth and Eighteenth Centuries.* Translated by Lydia G. Cochrane. Cambridge: Polity Press, 1994.

---. "The Practical Impact of Writing." In *The Book History Reader,* edited by David Finkelstein and Alistair McCleery, 118–42. London: Routledge, 2002.

Clemens, Raymond, and Timothy Graham. *An Introduction to Manuscript Studies.* Ithaca: Cornell University Press, 2007.

Stallybrass, Peter, Roger Chartier, J. Franklin Mowery, and Heather Wolfe. "Hamlet's Tables and the Technologies of Writing in Renaissance England." *Shakespeare Quarterly* 55 (2004): 379–419.

Thomas, Keith. "The Meaning of Literacy in Early Modern England." In *The Written Word: Literacy in Transition,* edited by Gerd Baumann, 97–131. Oxford: Clarendon Press, 1986.

---. "Numeracy in Early Modern England." *Transactions of the Royal Historical Society* 37 (1987): 103–32.

Writing Materials

Paper

Baker, Cathleen A. *From the Hand to the Machine: Nineteenth-Century American Paper and Mediums: Technologies, Materials, and Conservation.* Ann Arbor: Legacy Press, 2010.

Barrett, Timothy D. *European Hand Papermaking: Traditions, Tools, and Techniques.* Ann Arbor: Legacy Press, 2018.

--- et al. *Paper through Time: Nondestructive Analysis of 14th- through 19th-Century Papers.* The University of Iowa. Last modified May 04, 2016. http://paper.lib.uiowa.edu/index.php.

Hunter, Dard. *Papermaking: The History and Technique of an Ancient Craft.* New York: Alfred Knopf, 1943.

Shorter, Alfred H. *Paper Mills and Paper Makers in England 1495–1800.* Hilversum, Holland: Paper Publications Society, 1957.

Wolfe, Heather. "'Neatly sealed, with silk, and Spanish wax or otherwise': The Practice of Letter-locking with Silk Floss in Early Modern England." In *In the Prayse of Writing: Early Modern Manuscript Studies. Essays in Honour of Peter Beal,* edited by S.P. Cerasano and Steven W. May, 169–89. London: The British Library, 2012.

---. "Was Early Modern Writing Paper Expensive?" *The Collation: Research and Exploration at the Folger.* February 13, 2018. https://collation.folger.edu/2018/02/writing-paper-expensive.

Parchment

Meyers, Jesse. Pergamena. https://www.pergamena.net.

Reed, Ronald. *The Nature and Making of Parchment.* Leeds: Elmete Press, 1975.

---. *Specimens of Parchment.* Los Angeles: Dawson's Book Shop, 1976.

Pens, Ink, & Other Materials

Finlay, Michael. *Western Writing Implements in the Age of the Quill Pen* (Wetheral, UK: Plains Books, 1990).

Johns, Adrian. "Ink." In *Materials and Expertise in Early Modern Europe: Between Market and Laboratory,* edited by Ursula Klein and E.C. Spary, 101–24. Chicago: University of Chicago Press, 2009.

Jutzi, Karen, Ainsley Joe, Marie-France Lemay, Christine McCarthy, Laura O'Brien-Miller, and Paula Zyats. *The Traveling Scriptorium.* Yale University Library. https://travelingscriptorium.library.yale.edu.

Lemay, Marie-France. "Inks and Pigments." *The Traveling Scriptorium.* Yale University Library. https://travelingscriptorium.library.yale.edu/inks-and-pigments.

Manuscript & Book Preparation & Binding

Avrin, Leila. *Scribes, Script and Books: The Book Arts from Antiquity to the Renaissance.* London: The British Library, 1991.

De Hamel, Christopher. *Scribes and Illuminators.* London: British Museum, 1992.

Foot, Mirjam M. *Bookbinders at Work: Their Roles and Methods.* London: British Library, 2006.

---, ed. *The Library on Bookbinding.* A virtual issue of *The Library.* https://academic.oup.com/library/pages/bookbinding_contents.

Mak, Bonnie. *How the Page Matters.* Toronto: University of Toronto Press, 2011.

Pearson, David. *Oxford Bookbinding 1500–1640.* Oxford: Oxford University Press, 2000.

Pickwood, Nicholas. "Cutting Corners: Some Deceptive Practices in Seventeenth-Century English Bookbinding." In *Roger Powell: The Compleat Binder,* edited by John L. Sharpe, 272–79. Turnhout: Brepols, 1996.

---. "The Interpretation of Binding Structure: An Examination of Sixteenth-Century Bindings in the Ramey Collection in the Pierpont Morgan Library." *The Library,* 6th ser., 17 (September 1995): 209–49.

---. "Onward and Downward: How Binders Coped with the Printing Press before 1800." In *A Millennium of the Book: Production, Design and Illustration in Manuscript and Print, 900–1900,* edited by Robin Myers and Michael Harris, 61–106. Delaware: Oak Knoll Press, 1994.

Pratt, Aaron T. "Stab-Stitching and the Status of Early English Playbooks as Literature." *The Library* 16 (September 2015): 304–28.

Zyats, Paula. "Binding Models." *The Traveling Scriptorium.* Yale University Library. https://travelingscriptorium.library.yale.edu/binding-models.

Housing, Shelving, Collections, & Readers as Owners

Keynes, Simon. "The Reconstruction of a Burnt Cottonian Manuscript: The Case of Cotton MS. Otho A. I." *The British Library Journal* 22 (1996): 113–60.

Knight, Jeffrey Todd. "'Furnished' for Action: Renaissance Books as Furniture." *Book History* 12 (2009): 37–73.

Leedham-Green, Elisabeth. *Books in Cambridge Inventories: Book-Lists from Vice-Chancellor's Court Probate Inventories in the Tudor and Stuart Periods,* 2 vols. Cambridge: Cambridge University Press, 1986.

Partington, Gill, and Adam Smyth, eds. *Book Destruction from the Medieval to the Contemporary.* New York: Palgrave Macmillan, 2014.

Scott-Warren, Jason. "Books in the Bedchamber: Religion, Accounting and the Library of Richard Stonley." In *Tudor Books and Readers: Materiality and the Construction of Meaning,* edited by John N. King, 232–62. Cambridge: Cambridge University Press, 2010.

Streeter, Burnett Hillman. *The Chained Library: A Survey of Four Centuries in the Evolution of the English Library* (1931; New York: Cambridge University Press, 2011).

Notes & Note-taking

Blair, Ann M. "Early Modern Attitudes toward the Delegation of Copying and Note-Taking." In *Forgetting Machines: Knowledge Management Evolution in Early Modern Europe,* edited by Alberto Cevolini, 265–85. Leiden: Brill, 2016.

---. *Too Much to Know: Managing Scholarly Information before the Modern Age.* New Haven: Yale University Press, 2010.

Fulton, Thomas. *Historical Milton: Manuscript, Print, and Political Culture in Revolutionary England.* Amherst: University of Massachusetts Press, 2010.

Moss, Ann. *Printed Commonplace-Books and the Structuring of Renaissance Thought.* Oxford: Clarendon Press, 1996.

Yeo, Richard R. *Notebooks, English Virtuosi, and Early Modern Science.* Chicago: University of Chicago Press, 2014.

Scribal Publication

King, Rachel Scarborough. "The Manuscript Newsletter and the Rise of the Newspaper, 1665–1715." *Huntington Library Quarterly* 79 (2016): 415–16.

Love, Harold. *Scribal Publication in Seventeenth-Century England.* Oxford: Clarendon Press, 1993.

Marotti, Arthur. *Manuscript, Print, and the English Renaissance Lyric.* Ithaca: Cornell University Press, 1995.

Millstone, Noah. *Manuscript Circulation and the Invention of Politics in Early Stuart England.* Cambridge: Cambridge University Press, 2016.

Woudhuysen, H.R. *Sir Philip Sidney and the Circulation of Manuscripts, 1558–1640.* Oxford: Clarendon Press, 1996.

Letters & Letter-writers

Dambrogio, Jana. "Historic Letterlocking: The Art and Security of Letter Writing." *Book Arts Arts du Livre Canada* 5 (2014): 21–23.

---. Letterlocking videos. https://www.youtube.com/channel/UCNPZ-f_IWDLz2S1hO027hRQ.

Daybell, James. *The Material Letter in Early Modern England: Manuscript Letters and the Culture and Practices of Letter-Writing, 1512–1635.* Basingstoke, UK: Palgrave Macmillan, 2012.

Starza Smith, Daniel. "The Material Features of Early Modern Letters: A Reader's Guide." April 2013. Bess of Hardwicke's Letters. https://www.bessofhardwick.org/background.jsp?id=143.

Stewart, Alan, and Heather Wolfe. *Letterwriting in Renaissance England.* Washington, D.C.: Folger Shakespeare Library, 2004.

Whyman, Susan E. *The Pen and the People: English Letter Writers 1660–1800.* Oxford: Oxford University Press, 2009.

Readers & Writers

Brayman Hackel, Heidi. *Reading Material in Early Modern England: Print, Gender, and Literacy.* Cambridge: Cambridge University Press, 2005.

Fleming, Juliet. *Graffiti and the Writing Arts of Early Modern England.* London: Reaktion Books, 2001.

Gibson, Jonathan. "The Queen's Two Hands." In *Representations of Elizabeth I in Early Modern Culture,* edited by Alessandra Petrina and Laura Tosi, 47–65. Basingstoke, UK: Palgrave Macmillan, 2011.

Goldberg, Jonathan. *Writing Matter: From the Hands of the English Renaissance.* Stanford: Stanford University Press, 1990.

Grafton, Anthony, and Lisa Jardine. "'Studied for Action': How Gabriel Harvey Read His Livy." *Past & Present* 129 (November 1990): 30–78.

James, Kathryn. "Reading Numbers in Early Modern England." *Journal of the British Society for the History of Mathematics* 26 (2011): 1–16.

Owens, Jessie Ann. *Composers at Work: The Craft of Musical Composition 1450–1600.* Oxford: Oxford University Press, 1997.

Sherman, William H. *Used Books: Marking Readers in Renaissance England.* Philadelphia: University of Pennsylvania Press, 2008.

Smyth, Adam. *Material Texts in Early Modern England.* Cambridge: Cambridge University Press, 2018.

Wrightson, Keith. *Ralph Tailor's Summer: A Scrivener, His City, and the Plague.* New Haven: Yale University Press, 2011.

Yale, Elizabeth. *Sociable Knowledge: Natural History and the Nation State in Early Modern Britain.* Baltimore, Md.: Johns Hopkins University Press, 2015.

INDEX

humanism, 16
    italic hand and, 100, 102
    note taking and, 141–42
humanist script (*littera antiqua*), 93, 100, 101 (fig. 122)
Hutchinson, Lucy, 178, 181 (figs. 228–229)
Huxley, James, 198 (fig. 254)
Huxley, John, 199 (fig. 255)

I

Idle, Peter, 58 (fig. 64), 163–64 (figs. 205–206)
illumination, 272
import (from Europe), 38–41
indentures, 85, 176
    of receipt, 69 (fig. 81), 225 (fig. 280)
indexes
    in commonplace books, 54, 142
    in notebooks, 159–62 (figs. 199–204)
information management
    catchwords for, 178
    indexing for, 159–60
    in transcription, 225
initial (letter position), 88, 272
ink(s), 26, 42
    carbon, 271, 272
    components of. *See* ink components
    for forgeries, 12, 254 n.2
    iron gall, 42, 95 (fig. 115), 194–95 (figs. 249–250), 272, 273
    printer's, 32, 42, 44 (fig. 46)
    recipes for, 42, 43 (figs. 43–44), 155 (fig. 193), 157 (fig. 196), 263 (fig. 311)
    sinking of, 274
ink components
    alcohol, 42
    gum arabic, 42, 272
    iron sulfate (coppresse), 42, 271
    oak gall, 42, 260 n.171, 273
    tannin, 42, 260 n.171, 273
inkhorn, 45 (fig. 48), 46, 171, 207, 272
inkwell (inkpot; standish), 45 (fig. 48), 46 (fig. 49), 272, 274
Inner Temple (London), 71
Inns of Chancery, 105
Inns of Court (London), 71–72, 178
    literary circle of, 152
An inquiry into the authenticity of certain miscellaneous papers and legal instruments (Malone), 15 (fig. 10)
inventories, 51 (fig. 56), 64, 65 (fig. 76)
    in account books, 196
    of booksellers' stock, 140
    by Crown (annual), 194
    at death, Parliament requires, 210, 212–13 (figs. 270–271), 261 n.201
    probate, 66, 68
    punctuation in, 119 (fig. 148)

Ireland, William Henry, 64, 204, 217 (fig. 275), 254 n.2
    Shakespeare forgeries by, 8–15 (figs. 2–7), 70, 131
iron gall ink, 42, 95 (fig. 115), 194–95 (figs. 249–250), 272, 273
italic (hand), 41, 82, 93, 96, 100, 102, 272
    examples, 100–103 (figs. 121–124)
    secretary hand and, 100, 102, 109

J

James VI & I, King of England, 63 (fig. 75), 102, 190, 200, 203
    account book of court of, 194–95 (figs. 249–250)
    petition to, 236–37 (figs. 293–294)
Jayne, Sears, 261 n.201
Jenkinson, Hilary, 18, 124
John, King of England, 204
"John Orde, His Wife, Anne, His Eldest Son, William, and a Servant" (Devis), 187 (fig. 238)
Johnson, Samuel, 50, 183 (fig. 231)
joke book(s), 108 (fig. 129), 141
Jonson, Ben, 25, 42 (fig. 42), 72 (fig. 85), 150, 238 (fig. 295)
"Judgment of wether by Diggs," 117 (fig. 141), 118 (figs. 142–145), 123 (fig. 154)
judicial system, English. *See* English judicial system
Julian calendar (old style dates), 120
Justices of the Peace, 72, 207

K

Kerr, Mrs. Christian, 246–47 (figs. 303–304)
The kings of England sithen William the Conqueror (Lydgate), 30–31 (figs. 22–23), 51 (fig. 55), 224 (fig. 279)
Knight, Jeff, 64, 66

L

The laboryouse iourney (Leland), 214
Lady Day, 120
Lambarde, William, 142, 143 (fig. 181)
language(s)
    for English administrative documents, 105
    study of, "substratum" in, 255 n.21
Latin (language), abbreviations in, 114
law terms
    Easter, 121, 199
    Hilary (winter), 121 (fig. 151), 199
    Michaelmas (fall), 121, 199
    Trinity (spring and early summer), 121, 199
leaf (sheet division), 50, 163, 272, 274
Leedham-Green, Elisabeth, 18, 66, 261 n.203

legal document(s), 66 (fig. 77), 70, 257 n.95. *See also* court hand(s); document(s)
    charters. *See* charter(s)
    contracts, 71, 85, 204
    court records as, 207–209
    indexes of, 162 (fig. 204)
    inventories. *See* inventories
    Latin and court hand banned for, 105
    manuscript collections of, 206 (fig. 265)
    receipts, 53, 199 (fig. 255)
    as template driven, 204
    wills, 53 (fig. 59), 68, 71, 85, 210–13 (figs. 268–269)
legal system, English. *See* English judicial system
Leland, John, 214
letter(s), 53, 270–71 (fig. 312)
    in binding, 58
    as central to early modern English relationships, 186
    collections of, 58, 188, 190–93 (figs. 243–248)
    dates on, 120
    financial transactions handled by, 196, 198–99
    folding methods for, 188, 260 n.190
    Fulwood's points to manage in, 186
    writing, instruction in, 186
letter books, 120 (fig. 149), 190–93 (figs. 243–248)
letterform(s), 272. *See also* alphabet(s)
    ascender, 88, 271, 274
    baseline in, 88, 95, 271, 272
    body, 88, 271, 272
    in calligraphic scripts, 83
    club, 88, 271
    compartment, 88
    cross-stroke, 88, 272
    descender, 88, 272
    downstroke in, 272
    ductus, 83, 88, 272
    finial (or curl), 88, 272
    foot, 88, 272
    head, 88, 272
    headline, 272
    hook, 88
    infralinear, 272
    initial, 88, 272
    of italic hand, 102
    ligatures in, 84, 272
    lobe, 88, 272
    majuscule (capital), 273
    medial, 272
    minim, 273
    minuscule (lower case), 273
    pen nib and, 83
    stem, 88, 272, 274
    stroke, 83, 84, 88, 102, 274
    supralinear, 88, 271, 274
    tail, 88, 272
    thorn, 114, 274
    upstroke in, 272, 274